RESEARCH IN ORGANIZATIONAL CHANGE AND DEVELOPMENT

Volume 2 • 1988

RESEARCH IN ORGANIZATIONAL CHANGE AND DEVELOPMENT

An Annual Series featuring Advances in Theory, Methodology and Research

Editors: WILLIAM A. PASMORE
Department of Organizational Behavior
Case Western Reserve University

RICHARD W. WOODMAN
Department of Management
Texas A & M University

VOLUME 2 • 1988

Ai JAI PRESS INC.

Greenwich, Connecticut

London, England

CONTENTS

LIST OF CONTRIBUTORS

Charleen Alderfer

Southern Connecticut State
University and the Bristol
Connecticut Hospital

Clayton P. Alderfer

School of Organization
and Management
Yale University

Achilles A. Armenakis

College of Business
Auburn University

Jean M. Bartunek

Department of Organizational Studies
Boston College

Dov Eden

Department of Management
Tel Aviv University

Mariann Jelinek

Weatherhead School of Management
Case Western Reserve University

Edward E. Lawler, III

Graduate School of Business
Administration
University of Southern California

Joseph A. Litterer

School of Business
University of Massachusetts

Meryl Reis Louis

School of Management
Boston University

Philip H. Mirvis

School of Management
Boston University

Peter Reason

Center for the Study of
   Organizational Change and
   Development
University of Bath

Leota M. Tucker

Connecticut Department of Mental
   Health

Robert C. Tucker

Southern New England
   Telecommunications

Marvin R. Weisbord

Block, Petrella, Weisbord

PREFACE

The second volume of *Research in Organizational Change and Development* continues what we hope will become a tradition of fine scholarship in this annual series. The nine chapters in Volume 2 treat a variety of issues pertaining to both the study and practice of organizational change. The first four chapters address the evolution of the field and its future directions; the next two chapters discuss current methodological controversies and offer advice to those scholars brave enough to inquire into the complexity of change processes; and the final three chapters deal with specific interventions that should prove of interest to practitioners of this art, now becoming a science.

The opening chapter by Phil Mirvis takes a nostalgic and sometimes irreverent look at Organization Development's evolution through the 1960s, 1970s, and 1980s. Using a case study which parallels the evolution of the field, Mirvis points out that OD adapted to its environment by changing its methods, values, and objectives. In this first part of a two-part series (Part II will appear in Volume 3) Mirvis concludes that OD is re-inventing itself in ways that are as fundamental as those which gave birth to the paradigm originally. The second part of Mirvis' series will examine some of the future directions the field may take.

Marv Weisbord, like Mirvis, sees changes occurring in the field of OD; but for Weisbord, some changes have been negative while others have not proceeded quickly enough. By comparing his thoughts today with those he wrote about just five years earlier, Weisbord sets out new guidelines for the practice of OD that include rethinking a wide range of issues pertaining to the purpose of OD activities, the processes by which those purposes are achieved, and the roles of clients and consultants in the change process.

Jean Bartunek and Meryl Louis provide answers to several questions about the relationship of OD to the relatively new field of Organizational Transformation. After defining each paradigm, Bartunek and Louis demonstrate how each perspective views organizational change, paying particular attention to their similarities and to opportunities for synergy in utilizing the perspectives simultaneously. The authors also point out differences in the way the two fields view the role of the consultant, how change is conceived, the types of change explored, the legitimacy of organizational decline, and approaches to the diagnosis of problems. Bartunek and Louis conclude with helpful suggestions concerning new opportunities for synthesis of the two paradigms.

Mariann Jelinek and Joseph Litterer challenge us to think about OD in strategic terms; they point out that organizational environments have changed since OD was invented, but that OD has not kept pace with these developments. Specifically, they argue that OD must address itself to issues that involve the globalization of markets, rapid scientific and technological advances, and short produce life cycles. This will require that we change our current assumptions about organizational design, the role of management, and the nature and scope of the field.

Achilles Armenakis, in the first of the two articles in this volume dealing with methodological concerns, reviews the research on the alpha, beta, gamma change typology. He discusses both statistical and experimental design approaches currently being used to tease out explanations for apparent shifts in attitudes that show up in evaluations of change efforts. These methods, when applied properly, can assist researchers in determining whether change has actually occurred or is an artifact of the methods used to gather data. Armenakis' treatment of this complex subject underscores both the progress we have made on this front and the controversy that continues to divide researchers in this area.

Peter Reason's contribution to this volume is very different from that of Armenakis; indeed, Reason might be mildly troubled by Armenakis' concern with precision in the evaluation of change efforts. Reason argues that research in the field has become too mechanized and non-participative. He calls for a new approach to inquiry which is cooperative, experiential, and even existential, yet rigorous. His thoughts here should stimulate healthy controversy and critical self-examination among scholars regarding both the process of inquiry and what we regard as knowledge in our field.

In the first of three articles touching on methods of intervention, Dov Eden demonstrates how the self-fulfilling prophecy effect can be applied to increase the success of change efforts. He argues that rather than avoiding creating expectancy effects in our work for fear that it will contaminate research findings, we should take greater advantage of the powerful changes self-fulfilling prophecies can produce. Eden goes on to outline specific guidelines for enhancing interventions, training, and management through the manipulation of expectations.

Clay Alderfer, Robert Tucker, Charleen Alderfer, and Leota Tucker tackle a topic which, in our opinion, has not received the attention it deserves by change agents: race relations in organizations. Through their thorough documentation of an eight-year project to improve race relations in an organization, the authors provide rich insights into the complexity and challenge of work in this area. Hopefully, their discussion will generate more serious attention to the study of this topic and continued application of methods the authors have developed.

Finally, Ed Lawler reviews theories and research on gainsharing, an increasingly popular technique for enhancing the commitment of organizational members to the success of their firm. Lawler makes it clear that despite the successes of gainsharing programs to date, there is still much that we need to learn about why they work, what types of plans work best, which processes are most effective in implementing them, what type of participation should accompany them, and whether gainsharing should lead or lag other organizational changes.

Together, these nine chapters represent the forefront of our field. They raise important questions concerning its identity, methods of inquiry, and modes of intervention. As is the case with most works of outstanding scholarship, they raise more questions than they answer. We hope that you will find yourself as moved as we are to continue the thoughtful dialogue these authors have begun.

William A. Pasmore
Richard W. Woodman
Series Editors

ORGANIZATION DEVELOPMENT:
PART I—AN EVOLUTIONARY PERSPECTIVE

Philip H. Mirvis

ABSTRACT

This chapter is Part I of a two-part essay on the evolution of organization development. It examines, first, definitions of the field in the 1960s, 1970s, and 1980s in
terms of its theory, interventions, and results. The focus is upon the content and
context of OD in the past three decades. The next section analyzes developments in
the field through several perspectives. These perspectives concern (1) the advance
of OD knowledge; (2) its development as a social movement; (3) its adaptation to
the demands of client organizations; and (4) its application by practitioners in the
marketplace. The final section contrasts originating and current conceptions of the
field.

This chapter reports on my experiences studying and consulting with an organization whose culture and use of OD have evolved during the past 30 years. This case
is intended to anchor the ideas reported here in concrete experience and, to a
degree, illustrate their source. Part II will take a future-oriented look at OD and
reconceptualize its history in a different fashion.

Research in Organizational Change and Development, Vol. 2, pages 1–57.
Copyright © 1988 by JAI Press Inc.
All rights of reproduction in any form reserved.
ISBN: 0-89232-772-3

INTRODUCTION

Finally, it was clear to me. I was dated, out of sync, perhaps an anachronism in my field. I am not talking about how Reaganomics, the material yearnings of yuppies, and the rise of global competition, nor about how strategy, cost consciousness, evangelism, and excellence are changing management today, though all are part of this. Rather, I am talking about matters of identity and what we call OD (organizational development). A company I have worked with for over 10 years has recently issued an *updated* statement of its beliefs and values. The old value statement, dating from the late 1960s, had been based in the CEO's abiding belief in people. It drew from the behavioral sciences and emphasized personal openness and teamwork as keys to the company culture. This new value statement, developed in the mid-1980s, addressed people, but also customers, innovation, products, strategy, the profit objectives of the company, and security of its workforce. It read, to my eyes, like so many other company philosophy statements in fashion today.

Back in the 1960s, the company's original values had been internalized by management in team building exercises and infused into the organization through participative management. These new values were developed in a series of position papers by top management and a new CEO. They were then communicated to the workforce in a glossy brochure.

Plainly the new CEO had a different outlook on managing people and the business. Through a series of management meetings and video tape presentations to employees, he criticized the time wasted by excessive amounts of participation and argued that a heavy reliance upon task forces blurred individual responsibility. Memos were issued stating that the company had to be "lean and mean" in the face of business challenges and staff reductions were undertaken in line with new strategic directions.

In the months that followed, top management meetings became more crisp and businesslike. There were fewer discussions of company philosophy and their own group process. It was left to division heads to develop their own management structures and to manage their people in the way they saw fit.

A subsequent diagnosis revealed there to be inconsistencies in management practices in the company: the data showed that some managers were now pressuring people, ignoring their inputs, and motivating them by fear while many others continued to use involvement, participation, and rewards to run their operations. Furthermore, interviews suggested that managers were adopting a divisional, rather than a company-wide perspective, and developing conflicts with other division heads.

When I presented these data on inconsistencies in management style and on rivalries between division heads to the new CEO, he saw no signs of trouble nor any needs for change. Instead, he estimated that the data reflected his emphasis on managerial autonomy and decentralization, and opined that a dose of healthy competition was needed in the firm. He also discounted survey data that current practices were in conflict with stated values and rejected the conclusion of many employees that the company was not practicing what it preached. In his view, I was "hung up" on the old company culture and employees were simply not attuned to new business realities and requirements.

When I subsequently expressed my frustrations to a professional colleague, he told me, simply, "Phil, you are into OD of the 1960s; you've got to get into OD of the 1980s; and get yourself ready for tomorrow."

This antediluvian sensation was not my first. In the 1970s I participated in a debate at the Academy of Management convention concerning the merits of OD versus QWL (quality of work life) as models of change. Michael Beer, formerly an OD man at Corning Glass, first made the case for OD. He reminded the audience of OD's humanistic values and emphasis on group problem solving. But, he added, OD had "grown up"; it was no longer limited to laboratory training; now it encompassed advanced forms of survey analysis and feedback, new organizational and work system designs, and a variety of employee and management involvement programs.

Theodore Mills, then at the American Center for Quality of Work Life, next made the case for QWL. He argued that OD's humanistic emphasis, while philosophically appealing, was not relevant to the bread-and-butter concerns of working people. It was not addressed to employee's rights, nor was it concerned with democracy in the workplace. In truth, he added, it was a management tool because OD efforts were led by management and practice was guided by business school theories. QWL programs, by contrast, were "co-directed" by management and workers, through joint labor-management committees; and QWL interventions were aimed at shop floor issues, not some psychologist's definition of what made people happy or some professor's productivity-raising scheme.

My role in this debate was to be a mediator. Thus I put a pox upon both debaters for drawing caricatures of OD and QWL. I noted, for example, that both fields of study drew from systems views of people and organizations and both forms of practice were concerned with improving human welfare and organizational effectiveness. I also spelled out common philosophical ground between the fields, argued that the processes and structures advancing change in each were compatible, and pointed out how both could advance the state of our knowledge (Mirvis, 1985a). The crowd seemed responsive when I urged scholars in the two fields to join together in the community.

Is it possible to reconcile the assumptions and philosophies, the knowledge and practices, and the goals and aspirations of OD of the 1980s with these earlier forms? The difficulty is not only to reconcile the early days of OD with the corporate "excellence" movement, but also with new emphases on entrepreneurship and new forms of technology, with megamergers and downsizing, and with a new set of cleavages in the economy and society. Is OD being developed, revised, or renewed in the model of "third wave" change called OT (organizational transformation) that is sweeping into practice today (Ackerman, 1986; Weisbord, 1987)? Or it is being abandoned? On the surface, anyway, 1960s values and 1970s directions for the field do not match the mood of practitioners and models of change in the 1980s.

Mike Beer, now at the Harvard Business School, was back at the Academy of Management convention in 1985 and again reported on the state of the field. However, he never addressed his remarks to OD; instead he put planned change into the rubric of human resource management. He, Ted Mills, and I had talked to 60 or so Academy members during the 1970s. Mike was talking to hundreds and had two big name executives on the panel with him. They never mentioned OD either.

To begin this analysis of OD in the last three decades, let me say, that it is always a problem to precisely define OD. To me it has meant a particular way of thinking about and relating to people and institutions, of understanding and promoting human growth and organization development, and even more so a mode of acting and being in helping clients and assisting firms. Definitions can trivialize the field. They can also be politicized, and twisted, and turned to make many "points" about what OD is, how it works, and what it can accomplish. I risk this in offering my definitions of OD in the 1960s, 1970s, and today.

This chapter is Part I of a two-part essay on the evolution of OD. It contains three sections. The first presents my definitions of the field in the past three decades. Admittedly, the definitions are idiosyncratic but are supported by references to each period's articles and books and are based upon the insights of many academicians and practitioners from whom I have learned. Needless to say, they are not responsible for my interpretations and judgments of the field.

The second section looks at the evolution of OD across the eras based upon (1) the advance of its knowledge; (2) its growth as a social movement; (3) its adaptation to organizational clients; and (4) its application by practitioners. The logic of this argument is that OD has followed, to a degree, a natural evolutionary path. This section also explores the influence of the larger societal development upon OD in each period.

The final section summarizes this evolutionary perspective. It highlights how definitions of OD have changed and points the way to Part II of the essay, to appear in the next volume in this series on organizational change and development.

DEFINITIONS OF OD: 1960s, 1970s, 1980s

Most definitions of OD focus upon what the field is, how it promotes change, and what it accomplishes. *What it is* is often defined in terms of theories about human nature and the processes of change. *How it works* is covered in descriptions of interventions and their application by practitioners. *What it accomplishes* shows how changes in individual and organizational behavior produced by OD can have a longer term impact upon human development and the effectiveness of organizations.

The definition of OD in the past three eras to be presented here also address what it is, how it works, and what it accomplishes. The first three points in each period's definition consider only these dimensions in terms of the *content* of OD. The last three points then lift OD's content into an historic *context*. These latter points in each definition serve to modify the former ones and produce a sentence description of OD in the 1960s, 1970s, and today.

OD in the 1960s

OD in the 1960s was defined fundamentally as a *philosophy*, a set of beliefs and values, about people and organizations. It celebrated the spirit and capacities of human beings and was part and parcel of the broader human potential movement. OD's core beliefs and values can be found in McGregor's (1960) Theory Y assumptions about human nature and in Maslow's (1954) conceptions of self-actualization. These humanistic perspectives stressed people's potential to learn and grow in their work and to contribute and express themselves more fully in humanly designed organizations. As OD drew on them, the assumptions were treated as ''givens'' and the theories were elevated to moral imperatives (Tannenbaum & Davis, 1969).

OD also embraced a new set of beliefs and values about management and organizational effectiveness. Warren Bennis (1966), for example, posited that bureaucratic modes of organization could not cope with the problems of coordination, innovation, and commitment posed by accelerating rates of social and economic change. OD, in turn, offered an approach to organizing that was more organic and adaptive. Rensis Likert (1961; 1967) devised a design for this organization in his linking pin model of management and presented a rationale for changing prevailing norms in his studies of the human organization and its value.

Table 1. Organization Development
in the 1960s

Content	OD as a . . .
what:	Philosophy & Process
how:	Facilitating
to what end:	Human Expression
Context	
for people and organizations:	Creating Cohesion
how:	Via Top-Down
	Human Association

What did OD have to offer? A *process*. OD of the 1960s featured two methods for achieving change. One involved laboratory training. In the "cultural island" of a training lab, small group exercises could "free up" people and "open" them to new ways of relating to others. Certainly, British Tavistock groups, American T-Groups, and the variety of Encounter groups differed in their methodologies. However, each was based in the assumption that people had, within themselves, the capacity to become more complete and expressive human beings. Feedback would help them identify factors inhibiting their potential, and support would help them to self-actualize. It was believed that by achieving self-awareness and gaining interpersonal competence, people could form more authentic and effective relationships with others back in their workplace.

The other OD technique, aimed more directly at improving the workplace, involved action research. This would have organization members, in small groups, identify problems in their work relationships, undertake a diagnosis of factors contributing to their problems, and then develop and implement needed solutions. The technique was derived from experiences in laboratory training and was supported by a series of experiments that showed how groups were more effective than individuals in identifying and solving problems (Lewin, 1948; Maier, 1952).

The founder of the group dynamics school of psychology, Kurt Lewin (1948), gave OD its first model of action research in his conception of change proceeding through phases of unfreezing, movement, and refreezing. One of Lewin's students, Alfred Marrow, first demonstrated the applicability of the model to organizations by undertaking an action research program in his factory where it yielded substantial improvements in morale and productivity (Coch & French, 1948). Among its many early proponents, Beckhard (1969) put the model to work most broadly to improve management capability, promote team management, address intergroup conflicts, and re-arrange the distribution of work in an organization.

The agents of change in OD were called facilitators and their role was to *facilitate* change in people and in organizations. Carl Rogers (1961) first defined the basic contours of this open, accepting, here-and-now facilitative posture in his descriptions of client-centered therapy. Gibb (1964) subsequently described its orientations and goals in laboratory training. As practice moved into organizations, however, the model of the facilitator as a process consultant emerged. Schein (1969) applied this model to organizational problems associated with managing authority, establishing group norms, improving communication, solving problems, and making decisions. This fit it into the action research emphasis of the field.

OD in the 1960s was aimed at facilitating *human expression* in organizations. Certainly this aim was consistent with its process orientation and consulting model. It was also consistent with the value base of OD. People were seen as basically good, eager to cooperate, and fundamentally able to address problems in their lives and work. Thus Chin and Benne (1969) described OD as a "normative—re-educative" approach to change. One of its aims was to release the energy and foster the growth of people making up a social system. The other, in turn, was to improve problem-solving capabilities within that system.

Certainly laboratory education was aimed at releasing human potential and promoting individual growth. As practice moved to the field, with McGregor at Union Carbide, Shepard at Esso, Beckhard at General Mills, and so many others venturing out into industry (see French, 1985), OD's problem-solving thrust became more prominent.

This brings us to the context of OD in the 1960s. In the organization setting of this era, the function of OD's aim was *creating cohesion*. Chris Argyris (1964) expressed this most clearly in his influential writings on the importance of integrating individual and organizational needs. His early research had shown how organizations, as traditionally structured and managed, subverted adult development (Argyris, 1957). OD provided a means for fostering adult development and creating work environments suited to mature human beings.

The aspiration of creating cohesion was also explicit in Likert's (1961) vision of the participatively managed organization. In turn, team building became a goal in "family" training groups, where supervisors and subordinates would come together, and soon become an OD intervention in its own right (Beckhard, 1972).

OD was targeted, as well, at reducing the impediments to cohesiveness in organizations. For example, Blake, Shephard, and Mouton (1964) applied it to intergroup conflicts, such as those between competing departments, headquarters and field offices, and line and staff managements. Walton (1969) put it to work to ameliorate interpersonal conflicts and later conflict between nation-states (1970). Always there was the belief that if only people would let go of the emotional barriers dividing them, then structural barriers could be surmounted, common problems could be addressed, and a common purpose could be achieved.

This belief sustained the notion that, in form, change should come *top down* through an organization. OD was seen, in some respects, as an extension of the human relations school of management. Indeed, many of its early proponents and clients saw no inherent conflict between hierarchy and collegiality in organizations (Perrow, 1972). There were also sound theoretical and pragmatic reasons for beginning OD at the top of organizations. For example, research was demonstrating that leaders could have a profound impact on the management style of their subordinates (Berlew & Hall, 1966). It was recognized that this "pygmalion effect" could prove a bane or boon to new management practices promoted by OD.

Thus, Dalton (1969), Bennis (1969), and many other early OD proponents, stressed that "support at the top" was essential to unfreezing an organization and to opening people up to try new ways of doing things. Top management would, in turn, "set the tone" for OD throughout the enterprise by modeling participative management and operating like a team.

Philosophically, this form of OD was all part of building more *human association* within enterprise. It was a culmination of Barnard's (1938) vision of the moral organization in that it bound people together in a web of human relationships and preserved legitimate authority in organizations. At the same time, it also fulfilled John Dewey's (1933) dream of a new society. It promoted individual growth and learning and provided people with more meaningful participation in the affairs of institutions.

1960s OD at Work: A Case Example

The organization that was studied turned to OD in the late 1960s. Its business was in a downturn and a new CEO was appointed in hopes of renewing the organization. He had been characterized as extremely tough, intellectually aggressive, and personally insensitive when head of the main operating division in the company. As he assumed the top leadership post, however, he saw a need to change his management style. Thus he read the books of Argyris, Bennis, Likert, and other OD pioneers, and, in consultation with them, undertook a personal development program.

First, he went to a T-Group. He described the lab as "hellish" but came away committed to changing his own behavior. Feedback from peers had helped him to "hear" the adverse consequences of his tough, dominating, and insensitive managerial manner. Next, he invited several behavioral scientists to meet with him and other top managers to educate them about OD's philosophy, processes, and models of change. Finally, he employed an external consultant, a clinical psychologist well versed in OD, to facilitate meetings between him and his direct reports.

A series of meetings served to build open relationships among them. They developed and shared personal "dreams" about their future and that of the corporation. They defined a common philosophy and management approach based in OD's values and practices. Subsequently, the top managers became a corporate management team, committed to examining their working processes and oriented to consensus-style decision making. Everyone was encouraged to critique and comment upon everyone else's function.

OD was spread into middle management through team building in the divisions in the early 1970s. A variety of task forces were formed to study organization-wide opportunities for change and improvement. To this point, however, OD was defined solely as a philosophy and process employed by management. Clerical and blue-collar workers were not yet involved in team building sessions and task forces were staffed only by managers and staff professionals. And they were addressing only those issues that management defined as most pressing.

In many respects, this epitomized the field. OD had not yet been applied widely in the nonmanagement ranks of organizations, nor were there yet forums for identifying and addressing problems from the "bottom up." The field had not yet grappled with applying OD to the conflicts between labor and management or faced the political impediments to moving change through an organization (Bennis, 1969; Strauss & Rosenstein, 1970). New approaches to organization and work system design, pioneered in Europe, were not yet a part of OD thinking. Concepts like self-management, profit sharing, and industrial democracy were simply not on OD's agenda. Enter the 1970s.

OD in the 1970s

OD was increasingly defined as a *technology* in the 1970s: its basic ideas and principles had become established; it was the time to formalize them and apply OD with technique (Burke & Hornstein, 1971; Beer, 1976). In a sense, this was a move from the "lab" to the "field." Basic conceptions of what OD is and could be were broadened during this period. The field kept its focus upon personal and group development but added more content to its intervention base with the introduction of life planning (Lippitt, 1970) and transactional analysis (Randall, 1973). OD also began to focus upon the building blocks of organization. Friedlander and Brown (1974) showed, for example, that OD's "human-processual" thrust was complemented by an emphasis on "techno-structural" forms of change in the 1970s. Early developments, in survey feedback (Mann, 1957) and socio-technical systems analysis (Trist & Bamforth, 1951), also yielded diagnostic protocols and interventions in this era (Bower & Franklin, 1972; Trist, Susman, & Brown, 1977).

Furthermore, basic research on organization design, reward systems, management practices, and the like entered the vocabulary and technology of the field. Academic texts reflected this new technological conception. Chapters delineated OD in terms of the content of specific interventions (French & Bell, 1973; Huse, 1975).

There were also countless refinements in technique in the 1970s. Diagnostic and planning models were introduced such that OD could be targeted to old,

Table 2.   Organization Development in the 1970s

Content	OD as a . . .
what:	Technology & Structure
how:	Promoting
to what end:	Human Identity
Context	
for people and organizations:	Creating Community
how:	Via Collateral
	Collective Involvement

established bureaucracies (Schein & Greiner, 1977) and to new, start up facilities (Walton, 1972). Attention turned, then, to picking and choosing amongst various strategies for undertaking OD.

Accordingly, theorists devised procedures for classifying OD in terms of the problems encountered in organizations, the range of intervention options, and the possible targets of change activities. These intervention "cubes" identified which interventions were suited to which problems encountered by individuals, groups, intergroups, and entire organizations (Schmuck & Miles, 1971; Blake & Mouton, 1976).

OD also took on the characteristics of a formal *structure* in the 1970s. Structure implies order: an arrangement to abstract concepts and material elements. OD became a formal discipline of study in this era and universities established graduate training programs for OD scholars and practitioners. OD also became a formal function in many corporations and practitioners were able to attain professional certification. Each of these developments, in turn, gave further structure to the field. As an example, seasoned practitioners began to talk about undertaking OD as a project, rather than as an experiment, and OD interventions came to be defined as "sets of structured activities" to effect planned change (French & Bell, 1973).

These developments legitimated OD as a field of scholarship in the academy. Likert (1967) introduced a model of systems development that showed how multiple OD interventions could be used to advance human welfare and organizational effectiveness as organizations moved from system stages 1 through 4. Argyris (1971), in turn, provided a philosophic and theoretical base for intervening at many levels in organizations in his formulation of the path from an XA to YB world.

These developments also legitimated OD as a form of professional practice. A celebrated article by Burke and Schmidt (1971) helped to make the case that OD was different than management development and required its own specialists. Standards of practices and codes of ethics began to circulate to guide this new profession (Walton, 1978; Mirvis & Seashore, 1979).

With formalization in technology, structure, and procedure, and with legitimation came a new conceptualization of how OD should be practiced and put to work. Process facilitation was downplayed. OD's knowledge was potent and its practitioners were skillful. Thus, OD agents came to be seen as advocates of change. OD, in turn, was defined as a means of *promoting* particular forms of individual and organizational behavior.

Certainly OD specialists had grounds for becoming advocates of their methods. The assumptions and aspirations of OD in the 1960s, while deeply appealing, had also been met with widespread skepticism by the pragmatic and financially oriented interests in organizations. In the next decade, the field could point to studies showing that investments in human development could produce both human and economic benefits in organizations (Likert, 1967; Mirvis & Macy, 1976).

Furthermore, whereas OD of the 1960s had emphasized the power of human potential in the workplace, a sobering set of failures highlighted how prevailing structures, technology, norms, and work arrangements could inhibit organizational change (Mirvis & Berg, 1977). The stage was set to bring more order and discipline to the problem-solving process in organizations. Argyris (1970) defined, in depth, the requirements of the interventionists's role in organizations and emphasized the "authority of knowledge" in problem solving alongside free choice and commitment as the key ingredients to effective intervention. Other scholars expanded upon the components of consultation in the 1970s (Michael & Mirvis, 1977).

Plainly this advocacy was aimed at promoting *human identity* in the workplace. Walton (1975a) and many others began to advance criteria of "quality of work life" in this era and OD was aimed at meeting these criteria in application. One of its aims, then, was to promote more human arrangements in the workplace. Thus the socio-technical school of work design was embraced by the field. Its aim, of jointly optimizing technical and social features of production, was consistent with OD's new mission. Socio-technical interventions elevated the role of people in the production process of the enterprise. New OD books on changing the physical environment (Steele, 1973) and work schedules (Cohen & Gadon, 1978) in organizations were also aimed at putting work back on a human scale.

Much as the content of OD in the 1970s changed, so did its context. Organizations could not simply renew their originating spirit and cohesion. They had to address employees' rights (Ewing, 1977) and confront structural barriers based upon race, sex, class, and organizational status and position. The function of OD in the 1970s was to tackle these barriers and create more pluralism in organizations.

Many OD practitioners began to work on this challenge of *creating community* in organizations in the 1970s. Laboratory training methods were adapted to this task. Barry Oshry, as an example, devised a lab to tackle the differences between haves and have-nots in organizations. Later he developed the "power and systems" lab to analyze and alter the roles of tops, middles, and bottoms in organizations. David Brown, in turn, formulated guidelines for intervening in disputes between groups having different cultures and unequal levels of power. Both saw their work as creating more egalitarian and communitarian forms of organization.

The QWL movement, involving organized labor and nonmanagement personnel, furthered the communitarian aspirations of OD. Early projects between General Motors and the United Auto Workers at Jamestown and at Tarrytown, New York had a broad community development emphasis. A project in Bolivar,

Tennessee involved the operation of a day care center and the creation of an educational curricula offering courses in English and in personal management.

OD had to take a different form to serve this communitarian function. The QWL projects provided one model. Plainly OD began to embrace what Chin and Benne (1969) call the use of "power based" forms of change. Conflict management was emphasized in QWL projects and change filtered through political institutions. To illustrate, labor-management projects were directed by a top-level steering committee composed of labor and management representatives and coordinated through tiers of lower level committees. QWL projects also had "shelter agreements" that outlined their charter and shielded them from contractual constraints.

More broadly, change would be guided by a variety of *collateral* structures in the 1970s. Zand (1974) applied this term to all types of multilevel and multifunction structures designed to manage the "ill-structured" problem in organizations. Alderfer (1977a), in turn, developed the model of managing change through a liaison system that would include representatives from all major positional and demographic groups in an enterprise. The aim was to have OD managed by all of the stakeholders in the organization.

This was all part of promoting *collective involvement* in the management of change in organizations. This would involve learning "on line" rather than in a lab. People would gain not only interpersonal competence, but also basic political and organizational skills (The O. M. Collective, 1971). Surely there was moral vision behind this model of organization, but it was not based in social exchange or paternalism. On the contrary, the norm was to be reciprocity and the form was to express our democratic ideals.

Many saw the expression of collective involvement evident in Europe with its work councils and forms of co-determination. Others saw it in Mao's China and Tito's Yugoslavia. There were, in the United States, hearings on worker alienation in the 1970s and proposals to legislate the quality of work life in organizations (Lawler, 1976). There were also monies to support projects based on these new forms of organization development and efforts to publicly account on the quality of work life in organizations (Lawler, 1982; Mirvis & Lawler, 1984). Plainly, the field was not only taking shape, it was also gathering momentum. This trend was evident in the company I began assisting as it sought to broaden the application of OD in the firm.

OD at Work in the 1970s: The Case Continued

OD continued to evolve in the firm with which I worked. The top management team developed to the point where process analysis and facilitation became an integral part of their operations. Divisional management group structures developed and members were trained in group process skills. OD became more formalized in the company as its management-by-objectives system measured OD activities and rewarded accomplishments. Furthermore, internal OD specialists were assigned to work in each of the company's divisions.

In the mid-1970s, the firm took a step forward in its efforts to move OD through its ranks. A task force of managers and hourly personnel was formed to study problems in the company's compensation system and recommend a new plan. The task force, working with a consultant, prepared a survey on employee's views of their pay and other aspects of work in the firm.

The survey results were used initially to develop a new compensation package. The data indicated, more broadly, that the company's OD emphases were not reaching the hourly workforce. Some basic needs concerning quality of work life were not being met. Accordingly, the firm began to undertake biennial surveys of QWL to identify employee's needs. Feedback meetings were then held with employees to discuss the data, define problems, and undertake interventions to address them.

This survey-feedback process helped to stimulate many innovations in the late 1970s in the company. Employees launched quality circles in several areas and the company increased its in-house training function. One plant converted its traditional work system into a socio-technical design. All of this was stimulated by data showing many employees lacked challenge in their jobs and involvement in decisions in their work areas.

QWL surveys also showed there to be misunderstanding and conflict between men and women in the company. Accordingly, an education and consciousness-raising program was developed to promote understanding and interchange between the sexes. Data on affirmative action was publicly reported in the organization.

To my mind, the emphasis on QWL shaped the orientation of OD in the company. It concentrated attention on the needs and concerns of nonmangerial personnel in the company. It also focused on work design, safety, and the physical shape of facilities as well as basic matters of pay, benefits and fair treatment. Previously, OD had been aimed at management, and its central focus had been on developing better human relations. Now, OD was company-wide and directed at people's bread-and-butter concerns.

Nevertheless, the OD effort in the company continued to be supported by the top of the organization and retained its emphasis on participative management. Interventions were more structured, but were still aimed at integrating individual and organizational objectives.

In the late 1970s, the firm was acquired by a larger conglomerate. The acquirer was characterized as more traditional in its management style and put a stronger emphasis on short-term return-on-investment. To my mind, there was a clash of cultures between the firms. As so often happens in such acquisitions, the company's CEO, with whom I had been working, retired some time after the sale. A new man, an insider, took the helm. This was a time of change in the company, as well as a time of change for the field.

OD in the 1980s

OD was conceptualized as an organizational *strategy* in the 1980s. By the end of the previous decade, OD applications were premised upon models showing that optimal work and organization structures were "contingent" upon characteristics of the firm's environment. Scholars had devised frameworks for diagnosing these contingencies and for planning interventions mindful of them (Nadler & Tushman, 1977; Beer & Driscoll, 1977). In the 1980s, these ideas and prescriptions were framed in the logic of strategic management.

Several developments in theory pushed OD in these directions. There was a new interest in organizational life cycles (Kimberly & Miles, 1980) which, in turn, suggested that OD should be tailored to the distinct needs of organizations at different points in their evolution. Analysis of environments, structures, and cultures of specific industries showed there to be distinct opportunities and applications for OD (Lawrence & Dyer, 1983). Finally, it was clear that the 1980s would bring wholesale changes in the ownership, structure, and technologies of industry. Thus, OD was recast as the strategic management of change (Tichy, 1983). Models of consultation and intervention were reframed in a strategic framework (Beer, 1980; Mirvis, 1985b).

Plainly, business environments have been more "turbulent" in the 1980s and the global economy has forced many companies to rethink their directions. Concepts concerning strategic and competitive analysis have gained currency in firms and guided their planning and priorities (Miles & Snow, 1978; Porter, 1980). Accordingly, OD practice and practitioners have kept pace. New techniques of environmental scanning, stakeholder analysis, and business planning (Mitroff & Emshoff, 1979; Mitroff, 1984) have been embraced by OD. Countless "Search Conferences" have been undertaken with executives to identify opportunities and map strategy.

Perhaps the clearest illustration of this changing conception of OD has been its linkage with the field of human resources management. Human resource man-

Table 3. Organization Development in the 1980s

Content	OD as a . . .
what:	Strategy & Vehicle
how:	Directing
to what end:	Human Achievement
Context	
for people and organizations:	Creating Coherence
how:	Via Networks of
	Cooperative Competition

agement texts devote chapters to OD and join it with what Chin and Benne (1969) regard as "rational-empirical" approaches to change. Human resource functions within organizations have been charged with staffing, training, and developing the organization to meet business requirements. No longer are OD people clamoring to be separated from the personnel function in the 1980s. Instead, OD has come to be aligned with human resource management in service of meeting strategic objectives.

As a result, OD has been defined as a *vehicle* for implementing the strategy of an enterprise. It has become a program of change in many organizations: specific projects can be defined, focused, and linked to broader objectives under a programmatic umbrella. Practitioners like this emblem. No longer is OD seen as a "technological fix." Rather it is integrated into the ongoing work of the enterprise.

Academic writing in the 1980s conveys this programmatic emphasis in OD. The diffusion of OD throughout companies was a key challenge in the last decade (Walton, 1975b). Today the emphasis is upon the institutionalization of change (Goodman & Dean, 1982). Furthermore, OD in the 1970s had focused upon the development of specific interventions. Today these are being fitted into the broader aspiration of restructuring work both in the United States and abroad (Walton, 1979; Cole, 1982).

Clearly, there are diverse forms of work restructuring underway in industry today. These include the formation of quality circles and semiautonomous work teams in production and service areas and the creation of strategic business units and skunkworks at the level of departments and divisions. However novel these interventions may seem, they are consistent with earlier precepts and, indeed, were anticipated by two of OD's seminal theorists. The concepts of self-managed work groups and loosely coupled organizational functions, for example, were centerpieces in Likert's model of a System 5 organization (Likert & Likert, 1976). In turn, the aspiration to create learning systems in organizations was central to Argyris's model of the truly effective human organization (Argyris & Schon, 1978).

Nonetheless, OD began to reformulate its emphasis on promoting individual and organizational change in the 1980s. Contemporary research has shown that visionary leaders and strong cultures can produce inspired and loyal followers (Bennis, 1983; Deal & Kennedy, 1982). Thus many interventions today are aimed at invigorating corporate leadership and strengthening company cultures. In essence, they work by *directing* people and channeling their energy.

OD's emphasis on facilitating human interaction and promoting human development was based in a person-centered model of consultation. Today, consultation is increasingly organization-centered. It has been recognized that rigid structures and inflexible systems get in the way of individual initiative and innovation. These barriers were not addressed directly by OD's original focus on human development. Thus interventions today involve aligning people, structures, and systems in results-oriented directions. Specifically, this entails "purposing" the organization (Vaill, 1982) with a strategic direction and "empowering" people with a vision of accomplishment (Nelson & Burns, 1984).

As a consequence, the aim of OD is now to direct *human achievement* in organizations. This has been behind the appeal of the Japanese management style and the range of Theory Z practices (Ouchi, 1981). They portend increased motivation, commitment, and a better economic payoff. The Americanized effort to direct achievement is best embodied in the "excellence" interventions. Peters and Waterman (1982) devised a set of organizing principles based upon their studies of excellent companies. OD has incorporated many of these principles and put them to work simplifying structures and systems in organizations. Emphasis is upon directing people to get close to the customer, to get their hands on the work, and to add value to products and services. All of this is aimed at "putting the 'work ethic' to work" (Yankelovich, 1981) and creating "high involvement management" (Lawler, 1986).

It can be debated as to whose ends are best served by this 1980 formulation of OD. Earlier conceptions of the field aimed it toward the integration of individual and organizational objectives. The 1980s strategic cast emphasizes integration of the individual and organization within the context of an organization's environment. Naturally, the content of interventions changes in a new context. In the same fashion, the thrust of OD changed in the context of the 1980s.

As it is now formulated, OD serves to *create coherence* in organizations. The 1960s and 1970s were a period of tumult in society. This was best represented by Toffler's (1971) book *Future Shock*. By the 1980s, however, a pattern was emerging. Toffler (1981) called it the *The Third Wave*. It should not be a surprise then, to see OD develop a set of "third wave" interventions (Weisbord, 1987) for this decade.

Basic organization research shows that people "make sense" of their organizations and that organizations "enact" their environments (Weick, 1969). The function of OD in the 1980s is likewise to capture and direct people's attentions and energies and to focus the organization on its strategic challenges and opportunities. It aligns people and their organization in purposeful direction and attunes organization members with meaning and common understanding (Harrison, 1983). This allows people to see how their efforts fit into the organization and allows the organization to gauge its relationship with the environment. This intellectual coherence, in turn, is complemented by emotional commitment— truly the search for excellence. Interestingly, Joiner (1984) has shown how the excellence principles promote a vision of order and harmony consistent with platonic ideals.

Within this order, based in strategic alignment and personal attunement, OD has become more chaotic in its form. OD increasingly takes place through *networks* in the 1980s. To be sure, the network form was anticipated in early formulations of ''temporary'' organizations (Bennis & Slater, 1968) and certainly characterizes collateral structures. The difference in the 1980s is that ''parallel'' structures have become institutionalized and operate alongside the formal organization as a mechanism for managing change (Stein & Kanter, 1980).

Clearly, organizations in our information age increasingly do their business through networks. Matrix structures within firms and inter-organizational networks have become established as effective forms for addressing complex problems. Indeed, such structures, with their fluidity, have been recommended as the American alternative to the clan-like structures of the Japanese (Ouchi, 1984). The network form in OD, however, implies that change no longer needs to flow from the top down or through formal structures such as labor-management committees. Instead, the management of change has become decentralized and it has become the provence of the ''change master'' (Kanter, 1983) whatever his or her formal title. Change can come top-down, but also bottom-up, side-to-side, and via electronic media in organizations in the 1980s.

As a result, the network form of OD has entered the milieu of *cooperative competition* in organizations. The organizations of today increasingly operate like a marketplace in which people compete for resources and visibility and also cooperate in producing innovation and change. In OD of the 1980s, cooperation is essential to the joining of interests, the directing of work, and the realization of achievement. Competition, it can be argued, is also needed to enlist people, expose misdirections, and distinguish accomplishment.

OD of earlier eras was premised upon the notion that change could be planned in light of organizational goals and that integration of individual and organizational objectives could be programmed into such a plan. Now goals are seen as emerging form the perceptions, choices, and behaviors of political interests and actors in organizations (March & Olsen, 1976) and satisfaction is seen as arising from people's interpretations of the meaning of their efforts (Staw, 1976). It is simply harder to plan in today's complex world. Thus, the form that OD has taken today fits its function of creating coherence.

Plainly, this form of OD is a departure from earlier conceptions. Early OD theorists envisioned OD operating through collegial mechanisms in organizations and those who advocated that OD fit into the political economy of enterprise saw it being governed by institutional interests, such as labor and management. This new form of OD operates through market mechanisms and lets exchange emerge through transaction and barter.

This new form is also a departure, to some extent, from earlier conceptions of adult development and learning. In OD of the 1960s, it was assumed that by developing people we could create healthier and more effective organizations. Today many advocate that we must develop organizations to create healthier and more effective people. In turn, learning in the 1960s took place in the security of the laboratory and was loosely connected to people's material circumstances. Today learning is done on-line and people are required to learn a living.

To my view, some of the new forms of OD have emphasized total cooperation to excess in the 1980s. Several practitioners have been accused of practicing "mind control" and sought to create totalitarian leaders and corporate cultures. Others have erred on the side of too much competition. They have directed achievement to the point where their people become jungle fighters and OD is employed as a weapon.

A new symbol has been circulating: A Chinese character that represents change. Many people in OD refer to it. The symbol incorporates two figures: One reflects opportunity and the other shows danger. In my opinion, this is a fitting symbol for OD in the 1980s.

OD at Work in the 1980s: The Case Evolves

The company that I have been working with continued to push OD down the organization in the 1980s. The semiautonomous work teams in one plant became fully autonomous as team members assumed all set up and quality assurance responsibilities and became self-supervising. Quality circles spread throughout the blue-collar ranks and a gainsharing system was devised to distribute the benefits of increased productivity.

Nonetheless, OD effort took some new directions in the company in the 1980s. These directions reflect those of the field. For example, as I have noted, the new CEO and top management team formulated a revised statement of the company's philosophy. They had two criticisms of the company's old precepts. First, they believed that management had become preoccupied with interpersonal relations and group process and that OD had been directed primarily at promoting employee participation and involvement. They wanted to focus more managerial energy on problems in the business and to direct employee's attention to matters concerning customers, service, productivity and product innovation. Second, they felt that the company had defined people's rights and diagnosed their needs, but had given less attention to defining people's responsibilities and demarking the needs of the organization.

Each member of the management group developed a position paper specifying his or her central values for running the company. Over the course of several months, these positions were refined to complete a roster of beliefs and values that top management regarded as central to the future success of the business and the welfare of its members.

The new value statement was part of an effort to reposition the company. Divisions were reorganized to move the company away from its product empha-

OD Practitioners

A final developmental perspective on OD considers the influence of its practitioners on the field. The definitions of OD presented here show the field advancing intellectually, professionally, and in the marketplace. This progress is also notable when considering OD as a service industry. There is a cycle to industrial development that begins with a period of "prospecting" when new products come into the market, moves into a period of "analyzing" when products and market niches are defined and refined, and culminates in a period of "defending" when niches are maintained until products become obsolete or a market is saturated or withers away (Miles & Snow, 1978).

As industries develop they must address problems of uncertainty in formulating their products and problems of competition in penetrating their market. The industrial development life cycle will be applied here to interpret how practitioners responded to these concerns through specialization and the achievement of functional identity within firms.

This perspective emphasizes the commercial development of OD. Lest this seem overly materialistic, a complementary perspective considers the development of OD as a religion. Bellah's (1964) analysis of the evolution of religion is used to show OD moving from a state of primitivism and idealism in its early days through periods of modernism to the point of establishing an institutional church.

The Role of History

In each of these developmental perspectives, broader developments, in society, politics, and the economy, have also had an influence on the field of OD. There have been broad analyses of the historical development of work system design (Trist, 1981), management and employment practices (Seashore, 1977; Handy, 1980) and trends in organization (Mirvis, 1984). Where appropriate, the influence of these broad forces upon the field is referenced. The references illustrate how the evolution of OD parallels other developments in society and in the applied sciences in the last three decades.

This type of analysis has been applied to other scientific fields to show how breakthroughs can be premature and command attention only when scientists and the public are ready to embrace them (Stent, 1972). It has also been applied to show how developments in science are seldom unique and often paralleled by complementary developments in related fields. What follows treats OD's development as a part of our social and intellectual history, within which OD knowledge and professionalism progressed and through which clients and practitioners also shaped the field.

The Development of OD—1960s

The definition of OD in the 1960s traces the field to an emerging philosophical and intellectual movement in that era and ascribes to its early proponents the highest of aspirations and ideals. The first aspect of its development to be considered concerns its intellectual foundations and forebears.

OD Knowledge in the 1960s: The Paradigm is Born

Three intellectual developments mark OD's paradigm as a revolution in thinking. First, general systems theory had a profound influence upon OD. Systems theory (von Bertalanffy, 1950) was initially applied to biological and physical phenomena, but was soon generalized to the analysis of any social system (Miller, 1955). In the mid-1960s, the principles were applied to the study of organizations (Katz & Kahn, 1966) and soon thereafter came to the field of OD (Lawrence & Lorsch, 1969). This gave OD a strong and generalizable foundation and a basis for conceptualizing individual, group, and organizational behavior in common social system terms.

Second, the development of dynamic models of the change process proved to be another seminal contribution to the field. Lewin's (1951) exposition of the stages of change and Lippitt's more extensive model of the change process (Lippitt, Watson, & Westley, 1958) established a framework for planning and undertaking OD interventions. Scholars subsequently defined the relationship between OD theory and practice (Benne, Chin, & Bennis, 1961), refined systems analysis concepts for diagnosis and intervention (Chin, 1961), and articulated principles for changing human and organizational behavior (Benne & Birnbaum, 1961).

The third contribution to OD's paradigm was the development of a model for laboratory training and organizational consultation. Core principles from existential philosophy and humanistic psychology were spreading throughout the social sciences in this period. They had a profound influence on the theories of Maslow and other forebears of the human potential movement. They also shaped the ideas of Martin Buber and Harry Stack-Sullivan who applied them to the practice of faith and healing. OD embraced existential and humanistic conceptions to establish its identity. It applied them in a Rogerian model of person-centered consultation in laboratory education and process facilitation. The aim of this mode of consultation was to release the energies and foster the growth of people making up a social system.

Kuhn treats the discovery of a paradigm as a revolution in science. No single discovery defined OD, but the joining of systems theory, action research, and the person-centered mode of consultation proved to be a revolutionary amalgam. It is important to note, moreover, that these revolutionary ideas informed many other disciplines during this period. Systems theory was applied to urban and environmental planning, to education and public health, and to the analysis and amelioration of problems addressed by social work, counseling psychology, and the other applied social sciences. Action research guided interventions in school systems, prisons, communities, and other social organizations. Person-centered therapy became a discipline unto itself. The point is that OD was part of a larger movement to solve societal problems with applied science theory and methods.

OD Movement in the 1960s: Utopian Ideals

The analysis of OD as a social movement sees it as evolving through several phases analogous to the stages of development for people, groups, and social systems. There are, for example, striking parallels between them in the first stages of development. In the first stage of Erikson's (1963) model of personality development, the child approaches the world with confidence and naivete, filled with hope and curiosity. Hartman and Gibbard (1974) characterize this initial stage of group development as involving fantasies of mystical fusion. Greiner (1972) and Sarason (1972) see this stage in organizations as characterized by creativity and zeal. More broadly, this initial stage of development is marked by utopian aspirations and ideals (Perkins, Nieva, & Lawler, 1983).

Certainly OD's core philosophy in the 1960s was based in a utopian view of people and of organizations. Its proponents have been recognized as visionaries. John Dewey, an intellectual forebear of OD, has been characterized as an optimist and man of great expectations (Sarason, 1977). McGregor, Maslow, Lewin, and Lippitt have all been portrayed as idealists and missionaries. Generally speaking, however, such optimism and idealism was prevalent in the early 1960s. It marked the outlook of the Kennedy's, Martin Luther King and of countless social reformers and do-gooders.

Changes in American lifestyles and values were very much in tune with OD in the 1960s. This was an era that emphasized personal growth and development. A great many free-thinking, growth-oriented adults gravitated toward a new consciousness and more personal potency through laboratory education and participation in social change activities. There seemed to be the possibility of righting past wrongs and the promise of fulfilling the values of democracy. Indeed, Bennis and Slater (1964) stated that democracy was "inevitable" in organizations and OD was a way for it to develop. Missionary zeal marked many utopian social movements in this era.

OD Clients in the 1960s: Early Adopters

Even though OD was part of a larger social movement sweeping society, it made few inroads into organizations during this era. The 1960s were economic boom years and organizations were not yet experiencing the "performance gaps" that stimulate the search for new ideas and innovations. In addition, OD had not yet demonstrated that it could provide an economic payoff to organizations.

Furthermore, many executives conformed to the values and aspirations of the proverbial "organization man" (Whyte, 1955) and had scant interest in OD's philosophy and aims. Upward mobility and material progress were still uppermost in the minds of supervisors, clerical, and blue-collar workers. The many social movements, including those of women, minorities, and the young, had not yet swept into the workplace. In essence, then, there was simply not much of a constituency for OD, nor was there yet a body of practitioners to deliver it.

Case Western Reserve started the first academic program to train OD professionals in 1960. Few other universities offered training and most management consultants still held to the expert consulting model. Frankly, the personnel department in many organizations was held in low esteem and, at best, personnel specialists offered management training but nothing approximating an organizational development service.

Conceptualizing OD as an innovation helps to explain the pace of its adoption in client organizations. The first years of OD were marked by invention. Laboratory education was developed and refined in universities and training centers. Action research was undertaken on an experimental basis. By the early 1960s, however, OD was introduced into the marketplace. Rogers' analysis of innovation adopters shows that the first users can be characterized as experimentalists; they are venturesome and bold. He finds them to be more "cosmopolitan" in outlook, well read, and risk takers at heart.

Many of the early adopters of OD in organizations fit this characterization. They were first exposed to it through "stranger" training labs. They then sought to bring this growth experience to peers in their own companies and undertook "family" labs. Other early adopters were in high-technology companies, in R&D functions, in more organic work situations. Their outlook and work situation was well suited to the action research orientation of the field. They also had sufficient slack in their companies to give an experimental technology a try.

By the late 1960s, however, a new generation of adopters was ready to make use of OD. This group has been characterized by Rogers as more "local" in outlook and more pragmatic in orientation. Second, adopters are especially interested in the theory behind new ideas and value the expertise of practitioners (Rogers & Shoemaker, 1971). At this point, OD began to draw from the organizational disciplines, codify its knowledge, and concentrate its technology on the specific problems encountered in organizations. Established companies, with sufficient resources and an innovative bent, began to sponsor OD projects and created OD functions. General Motors, as an example, commissioned Likert to spread OD through its management ranks and established a free-standing OD unit distinct from its personnel function.

As OD moved into organizations it was confronted by adopters concerned with its relevance and demanding expert applications. To succeed in this market, OD had to address a more complete roster of organizational problems. There arose a market for professionals credentialed in OD who could deliver pragmatic services. This market perspective treats OD not so much as a field of scholarship but rather as an industry. A last look at its development in the 1960s, therefore, focuses upon its practitioners.

OD Practitioners in the 1960s: Prospectors at Work

Certainly, market forces can be invoked to explain the development of a profession. Starr (1982), for example, uses them to interpret the evolution of modern medicine in his Pulitzer Prize winning analysis. There is some evidence, to be sure, that OD practitioners sought to carve out their own identities and turf in the academic and commercial marketplace in the 1960s. For example, their demarcation as facilitators served several functions for OD practitioners. First, it distinguished them from management consultants, most especially from those who favored an expert model of consultation. Second, it also differentiated them from clinical psychologists, particularly those practicing in the detached Freudian mode. Finally, it marked OD specialists as members of a new helping profession.

However, there are few signs that OD practitioners in the 1960s attempted to corner their markets by developing specialties or restricting access to the profession. Quite the opposite. In contrast to fields such as medicine, where there are strict rules over entry, defined training methods, well-developed socialization patterns, and institutional forms of governance, Alderfer and Berg (1977) find OD to be exceedingly under-organized as a profession.

In a sense, then, OD practitioners of the 1960s were prospectors and their field of practice was in a start up phase. The number of new entrants each year was small as a result of the lack of training and the absence of opportunity in the marketplace. By the 1970s, however, advances in technique would lead to the development of specialties and developments in the marketplace would lead some practitioners to specific niches.

More than economic forces shaped the practice of OD. Marvin Weisbord (1977) has called OD a secular religion and has likened its practitioners to priests. Religion follows a developmental path that begins with a stage of primitivism and idealism. While OD is a contemporary faith, there are appealing referent points to primitivism in its early applications. Woodworth and Nelson (1979), for example, compare OD practitioners with shamans, witch doctors, and messianics. Weisbord, too, talks about practitioners as wizards and their work as magic in a modern age. My own observations of the OD community indicate that a large number of ex-clergy and people with a spiritual orientation have gravitated to the field.

All of this means that early OD practitioners were both commercial prospectors and secular missionaries. Bethel, Maine, home of National Training Laboratories, was the mother church for many early OD proponents. More broadly speaking, however, society was full of missionaries during the 1960s. University students were tasting relevance in the curricula and being exposed to experiential learning methods. They were proselytizing about the new consciousness. Many adults were committed to social reform and socially relevant work.

John Kennedy's death, then King's, and then the death of Robert Kennedy showed the fragility of utopian ideals and messianic leadership. The ideal of many social movements in this era had been to develop and democratize our civilization. The Vietnam War showed the hubris of this calling and the moral bankruptcy of pacification campaigns. Here at home the community development movement spawned a helping bureaucracy and gave legitimacy to all sorts of cynical hustlers. The liberation movement, part of the spirit behind OD, led to excesses in personal consumption of sex, drugs, and freedom. The human association hoped for by OD and other ideologies in the era could be found in some communes, in some communities, and in a few organizations. Families, however, were torn by inter-generational conflicts and society was divided by a generation gap and the Vietnam War.

Such developments, while unique to the 1960s, inevitably influence popular social movements. Sarason (1972) notes that social systems develop myths about unlimited resources during their inception and develop unrealistic expectations about their future. For many who turned to OD, such myths were shattered and expectations gave way to disappointment and disillusion.

At the same time, many minds were opened to new possibilities in the 1960s; new modes of learning and developing were being devised; and OD was being readied to be put to work in a more pragmatic fashion. It was during the 1960s, moreover, that baby boomers, the next generation of OD scholars, practitioners, and clients, were coming of age. Many were learning organizational skills and self-management in their schools; and all were being infused with the dream that something more could be gained from life and from employment. Women and people of color were gaining the skills and legitimacy needed to move ahead toward a better future. The seeds were being planted that would flower in rising expectations about what the quality of work life could and should be. There would be increasing doubt about the vitality of traditional institutions and methods of managing change. There would also be increasing faith that a better way could be found to meet the challenges of the 1970s.

The Development of OD—1970s

This section considers the development of OD in the 1970s by focusing again, upon its knowledge base and advance as a social movement, and upon its client base and the changing character of its practitioners.

OD Knowledge in the 1970s: Normal Scientific Progress

Systems theory continued to inform the field and became the basis for organizational diagnosis (Levinson, 1972; Weisbord, 1978) and for intervention planning (Harrison, 1970; Alderfer, 1977b) in the 1970s. Chris Argryis (1970) made a summative statement about the processes of change in his volume *Intervention Theory and Method* and, with Donald Schon, refined the OD consultation model (Argryis & Schon, 1974). These contributions are not in any way demeaned by characterizing them as normal scientific progress in the Kuhnian framework. Through them OD reached the point where it would have a distinct identity in social science.

Nonetheless, the field also borrowed from developments in other disciplines and broadened its intervention base during this era. A volume entitled *Improving Life at Work* (Hackman & Suttle, 1977) traces the linkage between organizational behavior concepts and consequent OD interventions in the domains of work redesign, compensation, career development, and other aspects of managerial practice.

Much as OD drew ideas from many disciplines in the 1970s, so did other applied fields. Knowledge from marketing, the social sciences, and several organizational disciplines was integrated to refine the body of theory concerning the processes of innovation and factors predicting the adoption of innovations in organizations (Zaltman, Duncan, & Holbek, 1973). Multi-disciplinary scholars furthered understanding of the sources of poverty, urban and health problems, race and sex discrimination, and of the reasons behind increases in crime and declines in education. Countless social programs were launched to address these concerns. A field of study concerned with knowledge utilization grew to ensure that policies and programs directed toward these issues were guided by up-to-date theory and research data. Program evaluation methods were developed and implemented to monitor these interventions and keep them on track. OD, then, was only one of the applied sciences advancing in the 1970s through the path of normal scientific progress. It was also only one of many forms of social intervention taking shape during this era (Hornstein et al., 1971).

OD Movement in the 1970s: Conflict and Redirection

The social movement of OD also progressed in the 1970s through a period of conflict and redirection. Models of human, group, and system development indicate that the first stage of utopian and naive hope is followed by a period of challenge. At this stage, the child tests his or her will against the parents, and groups challenge authority figures. Social systems face a crisis of leadership. OD faced this challenge in confronting its forebear: the T-group. Robert Blake describes the conflict thusly: "It was learning to reject T-group, stranger-type labs that permitted OD to come into focus" (quoted in French & Bell, 1973).

Criticism of the T-group came from the mainstream organizational disciplines.

Alderfer and Berg (1977) report that many scholars were hostile to OD during this era, particularly to its "touchy-feely" aspects epitomized by the T-group. In a sense, then, this challenge to the T-group symbolized a "revolt" within the academic community. At the same time, it opened the door for incorporation of theories and interventions based in the organizational disciplines and gave mainstream scholars access to applied settings.

The next stage in developmental models is characterized as a time of resolution. Erikson calls it a period of initiative for the child, and group analysts refer to it as a period of catharsis. Certainly this matches the movement of OD of the 1970s. For one, scholarship in the field was recognized by academic journals and the academic community. Second, it gained currency in many more organizations. Greiner (1972) defines this stage of social system development as one of growth through direction. OD gained formal technique, structure, procedures, and legitimation during this period. Greiner notes that organizations gain order and control following a crisis in their leadership and redirect their energies.

OD scholarship gained great impetus in the 1970s. There was a dramatic increase in the number of universities offering training and credentialing in the field. Programs of research were undertaken to study the processes and outcomes of interventions. UCLA became a base for the application of socio-technical system design; a center at the University of Michigan focused on the application of survey feedback methods; and another center was begun there to study joint labor-management projects and knowledge about quality of work life.

Furthermore, emphasis was given to spreading knowledge about OD to more scholars, practitioners, and organizations. The Work in America Institute was established to diffuse knowledge about OD and the American Center for Quality of Work Life and American Center for Productivity were launched to educate the public about new work arrangements and to offer consulting services to organizations. The broader point is that OD, like many of the applied sciences, became established in the 1970s and reached out to the populace.

OD Clients in the 1970s: The Majority Buys In

The market for OD was readied by a broad range of social, political, and economic developments. The early 1970s were marked by dramatic signs of alienation in the workforce. There was a much publicized strike at Lordstown which hinged, in part, over what were termed dehumanizing work conditions. A study asking *Where Have All the Robots Gone?* (Sheppard & Herrick, 1972) showed that assembly line manufacturing was estranging large numbers of blue-collar workers. Plainly the blue-collar blues had arrived. *Work in America* (HEW, 1972) was published and showed growing national discontent in the workforce. Americans were, in large number, becoming overeducated for their jobs. Finally, national surveys showed precipitous declines in morale in the workforce (Quinn & Staines, 1979). The biggest declines were being registered by clerical, technical, and professional personnel. The white-collar woes had also come on the scene.

This decade also brought changes in the composition of the workforce. Baby boomers entered the workforce and many had what Daniel Yankelovich (1979) called a "new breed" work ethic. They sought meaningful work, resisted authoritarian leadership, and felt entitled to more on their jobs. In addition, growing numbers of women entered the workforce and, together with blacks, made claims for equal treatment, better wages, and more chances to advance. In a sense, the trends in the 1960s, found in pockets on campus and formed in the minds of those coming into the workforce, came full bloom into organizations in the 1970s.

There were, moreover, significant changes in society's views of organizations that came into play in the 1970s. This was the dawn of the consumer movement, the environmental movement, and the broader push toward corporate social responsibility. Finally, productivity slumped in the early 1970s and there came the first energy crisis. Japan Inc. arose as a global competitor and industrial strength in the third world loomed on the horizon. To many in industry, therefore, it was clear that "something" had to change.

Again the innovation adoption perspective helps to explain how the field developed in the 1970s. The literature notes that a performance gap stimulates the search for innovation. That so many firms needed to change led to the rapid diffusion of OD along the S curve. Leading journals in training (Sherwood, 1972), in personnel (French, 1971), and in management (Randall, 1971) described OD for their readers. National Training Laboratory developed a consultation skills laboratory and University Associates began to publish facilitator guides. Step-by-step manuals concerning the implementation of OD, survey feedback, and even socio-technical work design became available. This packaging of OD made it more accessible to lay practitioners. It also gave them products to market to clients and sell to their managers. The aim was to reach the third group of adopters whom Rogers calls the "deliberate."

OD of the 1960s had reached the "cosmopolitans" and those "locals" who were attracted to its theory and relevance. They had embraced it upon faith and upon credible experience. Studies of the third wave of innovation adopters show them to be more skeptical. This deliberate group was waiting for OD to prove itself. By the 1970s OD had attained "scientific status." Textbooks were devoted to the subject, its dissemination through management journals and seminars, and, most of all, its demonstrable social and economic payoff all convinced a majority of companies that OD was worth undertaking.

Parenthetically, it is worth noting that most American companies still insisted on evaluating their OD efforts and submitting them to cost-benefit analysis. Sociologist Robert Cole (1982) has found this to be a distinct concern among

American managers. Organizational leaders in Europe and Japan, by contrast, were willing to adopt new work designs and OD-like practices based upon their logic and sensibility.

In any case, OD was ready to deliver a payoff, as promised, to organizations. It had gone through an experimental phase and was now ready for more standardized applications. Researchers, too, were ready to document OD's selective effects. Porras and Roberts (1980) note that the bulk of OD research was directed at evaluating specific technologies and their impact.

Changes in industry gave further impetus to OD. Plainly many more executives were espousing values and outlooks, concerning participative management and social responsibility, that were compatible with the orientation and aims of OD (see Wardell, 1978). Several notable high-technology companies socialized their management in OD's philosophy and technologies and employed it to develop their business. Some smokestack enterprises came to see it as a tool for motivating personnel, introducing new technologies, addressing quality and productivity problems, and assisting in the turnaround of the organization.

Organized labor took an interest in OD in the form of quality of work life and employee involvement efforts. Over 100 Ford and General Motors projects involving the United Auto Workers were underway by the end of the 1970s. Political developments also played a role in the spread of OD. Congressional hearings were held on worker alienation and led to the creation of the National Commission on Productivity and Quality of Work Life. Many university research programs and some demonstration labor-management programs were supported by federal funds.

OD Practitioners in the 1970s: Analyzing the Marketplace

As demand for OD services grew, the practitioner industry took on a new shape. National management consulting firms moved into the market and offered their clients OD services alongside financial, operational, and planning assistance. Greater numbers of large- and medium-size companies established OD functions and smaller ones added OD responsibilities to personnel staffers. Competition grew and the industry moved out of its prospector phase. OD consultants developed specialties in team building, socio-technical systems design, and, especially, quality circles. They were becoming "analyzers" and finding the right product and market niche became a key factor in their survival.

University training programs mushroomed in this era and many were oriented toward part-time working students. National Training Laboratory and other training outfits began to offer special seminars in various facets of OD. To my view, OD scholarship was downplayed and education was directed to those with primarily a practitioner orientation.

It is fair to say that many OD professionals bemoaned this development. Clearly many university and training program graduates had neither the interest nor the talent to contribute to theory building. Furthermore, many moving into practice lacked both the credentials and socialization to be called full-fledged professionals. In effect, the practice market was becoming vertically differentiated with scholars defined as theory developers and knowledge disseminators and practitioners charged with intervention design and implementation.

Interestingly, the evolution of religion has parallels to the development of OD practice. Following periods of primitivism and idealism in the development of faiths comes a stage of modernism. Here dogma is disseminated, the church gains a formal structure, and priests are differentiated from the lay missionaries. OD's progress in the 1970s matches this point for point. Its principles were disseminated and tailored to more resistant and skeptical clients; it became structured in the academy and organizations; and the roles of OD scholar and practitioner were made distinct. This period in the evolution of religions often provokes splits between purists and pragmatists and between the mother church and parish houses. Competing faiths can gain credence in this tumult. The competition for OD came from the QWL movement.

To an extent, this was the conflict I encountered between Mike Beer and Ted Mills. Such conflicts are presaged in developmental models when children break away from their parents and groups divide into factions. The larger issue for social systems concerns identity and autonomy. The field struggled in the 1970s as to whether it should be linked with management or with labor, whether it should serve the needs of business or those of working people, and whether it should be tailored to the tastes of more conservative companies or continue to evolve in the service of innovators.

Internally, there was the question of whether OD and QWL were compatible, whether utopian ideals were sacrificed in pragmatic applications, and whether the field should have professional status or continue to be a social movement.

Furthermore, there were signs that developments in the 1980s were going to stretch the OD paradigm to its limits. The success of Japanese management models led to prescriptions that executives should become more inner-directed in style and "hold their cards closer to their chest" (Pascale & Athos, 1981). This dictum was surely at odds with OD's emphasis on other-directedness and interpersonal openness and candor. Calls for corporate excellence implied that executives should "lead" and that meritocracy would predominate in the corporate culture. This was at odds with QWL emphases on egalitarianism and communitarianism. In addition, there were efforts to link OD closely with the broader movement toward human resource management, perhaps because OD had a bad name for many academics and practitioners and in some companies in the 1970s.

The Development of OD—1980s

OD became more business-like in its conceptions and applications in the 1980s. To a degree, this relates to developments in its knowledge base and academic proponents. It also matches the mood of the period and the trends to be found in organizations and the practitioner community.

OD Knowledge in the 1980s: The Paradigm Fulfilled

Several developments mark the advance of OD knowledge during the late 1970s and into the 1980s. For one, existing theories and methods have been further codified and translated into standardized implementation guides. As an example, comprehensive checklists have been devised for undertaking an OD effort (French, 1978) and manuals concerning OD/QWL and socio-technical interventions have been made available to practitioners (Pasmore, 1980). Guides to consultation in labor-management situations (Nadler, 1979) and in non-commercial organizations (Schindler-Rainman & Lippitt, 1980) are becoming more sophisticated and elaborate. Such developments have helped to move the field from a project to programmatic orientation.

Second, the field has incorporated knowledge from disciplines related to organizational theory. Models of company life cycles and strategy have begun to inform intervention planning and implementation (Kimberly & Quinn, 1984) as have various formulations of industrial cooperation and democracy (Simmons & Mares, 1983). Organizational theory has also taken note of developments occurring across organizations, such as joint ventures, mergers, and industry-wide labor-management councils, in the 1980s. Accordingly, there have been advances in the theory and practice of trans-organizational development (Cummings, 1984).

All of this is to say that the OD paradigm has become even more robust and its applications have become more generalizable. OD knowledge is now taught in Schools of Public Health, Urban Affairs, and Social Work; it is being applied in broad scale in the industrialized world; and OD precepts and technologies are being adapted to development in the Third World (Brown & Tandon, 1983).

OD Movement in the 1980s: Equilibrium

Certainly there have been developments in the academic base of OD. To my view OD scholars have adopted a more managerial orientation in this period. More OD theorists can be located in Schools of Business and Management in the 1980s and business is funding more OD research. New research centers concerned with OD, such as the Center for Effective Organizations at Southern

California, are housed in business schools. All of this focus upon management, however, is part of a larger trend in American society in 1980s.

Plainly part of the Reagan agenda in this era has been to deregulate industry and privatize many social welfare functions. The larger message is that "business does it better" and that top-flight management is crucial to our economic success, and to a degree survival, in the rest of the century. Certainly, business and business management has captured the interest of many young people, witness the rise of MBA admissions, and recouped a measure of public confidence, witness the sale of books by corporate leaders Lee Iacocca and Harold Geenen.

The final stage of development for people, groups, and social systems involves the realization of a state of quiescence. In systems terminology this is called quasi-stationary equilibrium. There are signs that OD has reached such an equilibrium. Its knowledge has advanced the past decade along the path of normal scientific progress and conceptual advances have been incorporated readily into theory and practice. OD has become an established division of the Academy of Management and part of the curricula in the training of human resource specialists and, in some instances, managers. There is now a degree of uniformity in the training of university-credentialed OD specialists and the field has taken steps to come to agreement upon a common code of ethics. In short, the OD movement has become an established discipline and its proponents are, in effect, part of the "establishment."

This stage poses special challenges for individuals, groups, and social systems. According to Erikson, this is late adulthood and marked by the struggle between generativity versus stagnation. Groups move into a routine performance mode and social systems turn attention toward their maintenance. OD scholars have, to a degree, lost their unique identity: they have joined with colleagues from organizational behavior and theory and become members of the faculty in Schools of Management. It is simply harder today to see what unique contribution OD makes to theories of change, of human development, and of organizational effectiveness. OD scholarship has become mixed with analyses of human resource management and the implementation of corporate strategy. The question of OD's generativity versus stagnation is an issue for the rest of the 1980s and beyond. Many of the contemporary books on organizational change, such as Kanter's (1983) *The Change Masters,* focus upon the innovative actions of managers. Tracts describing the latest OD application, including Leavitt's (1986) *Corporate Pathfinders* and Block's (1987) *The Empowered Manager,* are addressed to executives.

This, of course, is part of a larger trend. The celebrated books, *In Search of Excellence* (Peters & Waterman, 1982) and *Megatrends* (Naisbitt, 1982), seem to divine principles and prescribe practices related to OD knowledge and intervention. Yet these volumes do not cite nor purport to represent OD research. On the contrary, they document managerially generated practices and trends reported in the popular press. It may be that, today, practice leads theory and that the OD movement is lagging developments in client organizations and the community of practice.

OD Clients in the 1980s: The Mass Market

The programming of OD, QWL, survey-feedback, and socio-technical system interventions in the 1980s reached the mass market. OD could be fitted into the portfolio of programs a human resource department might offer an organization. In a sense, its link with human resource management moved OD into the mainstream of business. It gave it more prowess as OD could address matters of business planning, product development, productivity and quality that had once been the sole province of line management.

Industry in the 1980s experienced changes and performance gaps only imagined in the 1970s. Foreign competitors continued to make inroads into domestic production and markets. Deregulation of industries and mega-mergers changed the economic structure and rules of the game. Massive technological changes swept into industry. Companies began to divest and to combine, to form internal skunkworks and to start joint ventures, to downsize and tool up. The strategic calculus made these developments coherent for organizations.

Organizations put OD to work on these agenda in the 1980s. The tasks of human resource management have been defined for companies facing distinct competitive and market conditions (Miles & Snow, 1984). Thus OD techniques have been employed in the integration of acquisitions (Blake & Mouton, 1985; Marks & Mirvis, 1986) and in the introduction of new technology (Ranney, 1982; Pava, 1983). They have been used to create new plants, to build management capability in new firms, and to downsize older firms and address problems of productivity and quality in the face of competition. Focal points of intervention, then, have been driven by strategy and defined by needs to align organizational systems and strengthen company cultures.

That OD has contributed to countless organizational developments has been well documented in the 1980s. It has also produced fallout. Studies show that middle managers and first-line supervisors can be threatened by new forms of work designs and overwhelmed by complex computerized control systems. Efforts to increase employee involvement, influence, and responsibility can take away from managers in the middle ranks (Schlesinger, 1982). Plainly OD efforts are more welcome and effective in cases where organizations are growing or mastering opportunities than where they are declining or going out of business (Mohrman & Mohrman, 1983). Finally, there have been many cases where OD efforts have been cosmetic in character and simply embraced as a fashion.

The broad point is that OD work is increasingly defined, managed, and controlled by client organizations in the 1980s. The life cycle model of innovation adoption helps to explain this. Early adopters, generally progressive companies, embraced OD knowledge in the 1960s and diffused it in the 1970s. Today OD principles have been institutionalized in these companies and OD problem-solving methods are now standard procedure. Companies who started labor-management projects in the 1970s today use them to oversee technological change and to assist in corporate restructing efforts. Certainly, many of these companies are downsizing, eliminating middle management and laying off employees, as well as computerizing, amping up job requirements, and adding to levels of stress and pressure. OD in the 1980s, now integral to enterprise, is part of the political economy of organizations. It is also caught in the cross fire between competing and often conflicting interests.

Surely OD has helped companies to downsize and computerize, and has assisted employees in relocation and retraining efforts. But in the corporate milieu of the 1980s it has also been seen as, at best, a palliative or as a bandaid on wounds inflicted by the new economic order and by powerful commercial interests. At worse, OD has been perceived as a potent weapon wielded by elite management.

In my view, many of whom Rogers' calls "late adopters" have grabbed on to OD to follow fashion or simply because no other management strategems have proven effective. OD applications have smacked of exploitation. Many quality circle programs, for example, have been poorly designed and badly supported. They have been directed at commercial gain without any orientation to people's needs. There have been participative change efforts undertaken where participation is mandated and manipulated in line with management fiat. Furthermore, some of the late adopters have cultures and values that are antithetical to OD. In such instances, as can be conceived as a "capitalist tool" that evokes a new form of "false consciousness" and that placates and exploits the working classes (Hecksher, 1980).

Through this innovation adoption perspective, OD in the 1980s can be seen most clearly as a product of the times. Its emphasis on directing human achievement in the context of cooperative competition fits the free market rhetoric popular today and all the push toward corporate excellence. It remains to consider where practitioners fit into all of this.

OD Practitioners in the 1980s: Mass Marketeers

It would not be accurate to say that OD practitioners became "defenders" of their industry in the same sense as other professional groups. Some practitioners have surely become identified with specialties and market niches, but within the field there are few barriers to entry and there remain few standards by which to judge the competence or professionalism of practitioners. There are no rigorous or uniform standards for training, socializing, certifying, or regulating practitioners. The profession, then, remains underorganized and professionals have not taken the steps necessary to ensure their security in the marketplace.

At the same time, practitioners have defended their niche by linking with the human resource movement and the human resource function in organizations. Furthermore, practice is defended by its focus on the central production functions and economic objectives of organizations.

It would also be unfair to say that OD has taken on the character of a modern religious institution. It has its high priests, of course, and various institutional centers, but no one dogma dominates the field and no ecclesiastic hierarchy governs practitioners. Indeed, by contrast, the OD faith continues to seek converts and has opened the way for the "laity" to put OD into practice.

There were countless seminars for human resource specialists and line managers in the 1980s that taught them how to do OD work. The *Ecology of Work* seminars were launched to bring together practitioners and managers to exchange case studies and experiences. For many of them, OD is neither conceived of nor practiced as a profession. Certainly, very few "do-it-yourselfers" have formal schooling in OD's philosophy and knowledge base. They have not been trained nor supervised in the use of many OD techniques. However, today, they have become the mass marketers of OD and its front line of practice.

This proliferation has been a bane for professionalism. Uniformed diagnoses, unproven technique, incapable consultation, and unethical practice are surely in more evidence today. This has given the field a bad name and shaken confidence in segments of the marketplace. Many of the highly trained in OD work view this with chagrin. Others are alarmed, and see it as the death of the field.

At the same time, growing numbers of converts could give the field new life. The analysis of OD as an intellectual and social movement suggested that the field had peaked in its growth: its paradigm has been fulfilled and its scholars are at a point of equilibrium. In other respects, the field has been captured by its client base and can develop no further or faster than the corporate agenda and what clients can afford to invest in it. To my view, however, there continues to be vitality in OD as a faith and creativity in the way OD is put to practice. A new generation of scholars has taken an interest in OD who may contribute a new perspective and fresh energy. A new generation of practitioners is coming into the field. Some come from a new sect, concerned with organizational transformation, and many approach their work with messianic fervor. Others simply are turning to OD to find more meaning and become more productive in their work lives. These are the managers, unionists, human resource representatives, work team leaders, and workers, and formerly clients, all of whom are now converts. What this means for the field will be taken up in Part II of this essay. Part I concludes with a summary of how OD has evolved from the 1960s to today and the challenge and dangers facing the field and the client with whom I have worked.

THE DEVELOPMENT OF OD: A SUMMARY

Table 4 lists the definitions of OD in the 1960s, 1970s, and 1980s. This section reviews their progression in light of the four developmental paths we have examined. The focus is upon change in the content and context of the definitions as represented by movement from initial conceptions of the field to current ones.

Table 4. Organization Development—1960s, 1970s, 1980s

Content	OD 1960s	OD 1970s	OD 1980s
what:	Philosphy & Process	Technology & Structure	Strategy & Vehicle
how:	Facilitating	Promoting	Directing
to what end:	Human Expression	Human Identity	Human Achievement
Context			
for people and organizations:	Creating Cohesion	Creating Community	Creating Coherence
how:	Via Top-Down Human Association	Via Collateral Collective Involvement	Via Networks of Cooperative Competition

Changes in OD's Content

What is OD?

Changes in our definitions of what OD is can be described as follows:

simple	→ complex
general	→ specific
idea	→ institution

The movement of OD from a simple to complex approach to managing change in organizations has been most evident in the development of its knowledge base. As the field incorporated knowledge from the many organizational disciplines, its base of theory enlarged and its range of applications increased. OD's core content now encompasses not only interventions focused on people, groups, structure and technology, it also includes interventions aimed at changing company's strategies, systems, and culture.

Complexity also marks the field today for practitioners and for organizations sponsoring OD efforts. To some extent this is due to wider acceptance of OD: change projects are now bigger and broader based because more companies are doing more OD and putting more demands upon practitioners to manage large-scale change efforts. In turn, our models of how to do OD have become more complex. Lewin's early three-stage model of change has given way to much more complicated formulations. Change-agents have identified countless micro-level steps in macro-level change programs (Carlson, 1980). And scholars have also shown there to be distinct phases of the change process within organizations (Walton, 1980).

How have we coped with this complexity? The field has moved from generic to more particular types of change; diagnosis has, in turn, become less global and more focused; and the profession has evolved from general practice to greater specialization.

This movement from a general to more specific mode of operations has been apparent in the formulation of OD interventions. To illustrate, the Addison-Wesley OD texts in the 1960s presented a general model of OD and showed its applicability to a broad range of personal and organizational situations. By contrast, texts in the 1980s are devoted to more specific interventions addressed to, for example, work design (Hackman & Oldham, 1980) and compensation (Lawler, 1981).

Such interventions are based on years of rigorous research in experimental laboratories and field settings. Their operating principles have been deduced by hard thinking, and tested with empirical scrutiny. What has this type of research yielded? Models of change now delineate which personal and organizational attributes are most amenable to what sort of interventions. Scholars can opine as to when to intervene and how and to what expected result. Needless to say, the underlying concepts, neatly arrayed in casual models, have been readily transformed into diagnostic and intervention packages for undertaking more surgical change efforts.

To an extent, comparable trends can be found in the progress of knowledge in any scholarly discipline. Professionalism generally evolves to specialties and specialists. Plainly many OD scholars have specialized in the study of one or another type of intervention. So, too, practitioners have specialized in applying one or another technique. Both earn their kudos and livelihoods based upon their distinctive competencies in the academic and commercial marketplace.

More broadly, OD has moved from being an idea to becoming an institution. This is evident in the way we talk about change efforts. OD efforts were first tried as experiments, were later called projects, and are now referred to as programs of change in organizations. OD's paradigm has been elaborated, translated into tested interventions, and generalized to specific situations to the point where it is an established body of thought and form of practice. OD theorists and researchers are now accepted in the community of scholars. Furthermore, it has gained acceptance in the marketplace. Many organizations regularly employ independent OD practitioners and some have made OD an internal function. In a sense, then, the field has "made it."

How Does OD Work?

A related set of movements have markedly changed our conceptions of how OD works:

loose	→ tight
organic	→ mechanical
helping	→ harnessing

The formalization of OD as a body of knowledge and professional undertaking moved the field from being "loose" to "tight" in its theoretical and practical formulations. Surely OD has always had a firm theoretical foundation. For example, basic studies of group dynamics, communication, and problem solving informed laboratory training methods. Later, experimental studies of job designs, compensation packages, and organizational structures guided techno-structural interventions. However, these discrete interventions were seldom conceptualized and tested as distinct components in organizational change programs. Emphasis was on the process rather than the content of OD efforts.

Today, by contrast, change-agents can draw tight connections between specific problem-solving activities and their effects (Kiedel, 1981). Studies have identified the discrete components of change programs (Porras, Harkness, & Kiebert, 1985) and specified their impact at each stage of a change effort (Mirvis, 1985c). On a larger scale, measures and methods can now be used to document, empirically, linkages between the components of change programs and their specific consequences for organizations and their members (Seashore et al., 1983).

The capacity to specify tight conceptual linkages between change and its outcomes has helped OD to gain greater scientific status in the academy. This status was achieved in organizations when these linkages were translated into diagnostic and intervention planning frameworks. Today diagnostic surveys purport to pinpoint specific organizational problems and prescribe interventions to ameliorate them (Bowers, Franklin, & Pecorella, 1975). Models also show how specific management practices can make an organization more strategically viable (Miles & Snow, 1984).

As a consequence, OD has moved from being organic and open-ended to a more mechanical and focused approach to change. To illustrate, T-groups were organic mediums for unfreezing people and moving them in self-defined directions. Team building efforts were more structured and were aimed at bringing groups to a common working purpose. Quality circles, the mechanized intervention of the 1980s, focus people on specific problems of productivity and quality in their areas of responsibility.

What accounts for this movement in the field? One explanation traces it to the increased emphasis on the scientific status and professionalism of OD. After all, a significant body of research in the 1960s showed that T-groups had limited transferability and were not effective at producing organization-wide change (Campbell & Dunnette, 1968). Furthermore, group trainers acquired a reputation as unreliable and, in some instances, irresponsible change-agents. Thus, a field searching for scientific status and professional credibility would necessarily move to more reliable and focused applications.

Quite another interpretation, however, traces this movement to the influence of practitioners and organizations. Many OD practitioners welcomed the development of discrete models and methods of change. They could instrument their diagnoses and, in effect, package their interventions. This, in turn, allowed them to specialize and differentiate themselves in the marketplace. Many organizations welcomed these developments in the field, too. Tight conceptions of change and mechanical methods of intervention fit our predilections to apply "fixes" to human and organizational problems (Michael & Mirvis, 1977). Frankly, this also made OD more saleable to managers and their firms.

Finally, there has been a change in our conceptions of OD consultation and the change process. OD has shifted from its initial emphasis upon helping people toward a new emphasis on harnessing their energies. In one respect, this attests to the maturation of OD. Interventions have become more potent and reliable in their capacity to produce predicted and desired change. Of course, gains in precision and reliability mark the progress of many applied sciences and professions.

In another respect, however, it reflects a shift in the academic base of the field. Early OD theorists were educated primarily in the behavioral and social sciences and were located in departments of psychology, counseling, and related disciplines. Many thought of themselves as members of a helping profession. Early OD theory and consultation was essentially person-centered and interventions were aimed at the development of people.

Today, by contrast, many OD scholars have been educated in either administrative science or some form of organizational studies. They can be found in Schools of Business or Management. Plainly the field has become more organization-centered and many academics direct their thinking and consultation toward improving the effectiveness of organizations. The organizational disciplines and Schools seem to emphasize pragmatism and the bottom line payoff more so than abstract ideals and the development of human beings.

Certainly client organizations and practitioners have influenced this direction in the field. The movement toward human resource management plainly has a pragmatic and financial bent. Furthermore, the problems posed by client organizations and the services offered by practitioners increasingly concern operational and financial matters. Human growth and development, then, becomes at best a byproduct of OD. To my view, this is one consequence of the field having "made it" in the marketplace.

This raises the important question of whether or not OD has "sold out." The answer, of course, depends upon who is selling and who is buying. And upon what OD purports to accomplish.

What Does OD Accomplish?

Changes in our conceptions of what OD accomplishes can be summarized as follows:

humanity	→ harmony
affiliation	→ empowerment
essence	→ excellence

The ends of OD in its early days were oriented to humanity. The ends today are toward harmony. This aspiration evolved as OD moved from its emphasis on personal and group development to system-wide organizational development. It follows from changes in our knowledge and conceptions of what OD is and how it works. In the 1960s, for example, theory postulated that by focusing on the development of people we would produce healthier and more effective organizations. Today a competing body of theory suggests that we should focus on developing companies because they provide the conditions that make people healthier and more effective.

Harmony marks the culture of the developed organization. It is achieved by the alignment of people, processes, and purposes with organizational forms, cultures, and goals. Many of the interventions of the 1980s strive to harmonize systemic elements in organizations. People in these systemic conceptions of organizations are but one of those elements.

OD's initial ideals and humanism have also been tempered by three decades of encounters with the "real world." OD was first practiced in the "cultural island" of the training lab. As it spread more broadly to society, however, it has become part and parcel of our culture. This process of acculturation influences any social movement as it evolves from its origins in utopian hopes, and then faces pragmatic challenges in the maelstrom of society. Certainly, religious movements of all sorts have been shaped by secular interests and the challenge of survival. Bellah notes that the institutional church is far different from its primitive origins.

So, too, by conceptualizing OD as an innovation, it is evident that it has been influenced by its client base. And, by treating practice as an industry, shaped by market factors, we have seen how commercial forces have influenced the directions of the field.

All of these forces have lessened OD's emphasis on human affiliation and community as ends unto themselves. Instead, OD is aimed today more at empowering people and stimulating them toward greater accomplishment. Certainly, these ends are to be valued. Motivations to achieve and exercise power are characteristic of high levels of human growth and maturity. They yield us material progress and contribute to our greatest civilizations (McClelland, 1961). However, unbridled achievement and unfettered drives for power can promote aggression and produce exploitation. These can undermine social progress and, in the end, destroy great civilizations (Gilligan, 1982).

The field is struggling today to reconcile competing ends and potentialities. Harrison (1983), for example, posits a need to counterbalance OD's focus upon systemic alignment with an equal emphasis upon interpersonal attunement. Alignment gives people direction and harmonizes them with their organization. Attunement, in turn, validate peoples and connects them to their colleagues.

It has been a group of managers and practitioners, untouched by the early days of OD and unschooled in OD training programs, who have sought to put these new theories into practice. They purport to have a new paradigm for developing people and organizations (Kiefer & Stroh, 1984) and interventions that deliver "high performance programming" (Nelson & Burns, 1984). This looks like "new age" OD or, as many refer to it, organizational transformation. Its proponents are part of the "third wave" (Toffler, 1981); are participating in a "megatrend" (Naisbitt, 1982); and aim to make companies excellent and infuse people with passion about OD (Peter & Austin, 1985).

However, all of this emphasis on excellence, rather than human essence, has changed the linkage between means and ends in OD. In the early days, process was the secret to OD's success. Practitioners worked to develop the right process for human expression under the assumption that the results would take care of themselves. Today, by contrast, they conduct "visioning" exercises to identify the right results and assume that human expression will follow. Once these results are envisioned, and people are aligned with and attuned to them, the process is expected to take care of itself.

Of course, many scholars rightly poke holes in this transformational logic and criticize its proponents as evangelists. Some go so far as to say that the whole movement is antithetical to science (Andre, 1985). It is not surprising to see scholars up in arms against this new "faith" and disparaging of its missionaries. It is not surprising, too, to see that some practitioners resent the market penetration of new-age OD people and that a few companies dismiss it all as gimmickry. I would suspect that there were comparable reactions to OD in the early 1960s.

What has been surprising, however, has been the ready acceptance of the excellence movement by many OD practitioners and practicing managers. They like its mix of pragmatism and spirituality. And they like the harmony they find with fellow travelers, the empowerment they experience directing human energy, and the excellent results they obtain with new-age forms of change.

Surely some valuable aspects of OD are lost in its new-age applications. Theory may be losing its connection to humanism, practice may be de-emphasizing affiliation, and new-age proponents may be advancing a misguided model of human essence in an effort to ''sell'' in today's marketplace. To begin to assess this requires an examination of the context in which OD is practiced today.

Changes in OD's Context

Shifts in the function of OD for persons and organizations and in the form it has taken can be summarized as follows:

$$\text{Gemeinschaft} \rightarrow \text{Gesellschaft}$$
$$\text{Renewal} \rightarrow \text{Re-invention}$$

The eminent scholars Tonnies (1887) first made the distinction between communities tied together by feeling (Gemeinschaft) and those tied by instrumental objectives (Gesellschaft). Certainly, our culture is maintained by both functions, and various forms of organization serve them. Looking over the various economic, political, social, and demographic developments in our society shows that there have been pendulum swings in each direction. To an extent, however, the context of the 1960s is diametrically opposite to that of the 1980s.

OD in its early days was borne of humanistic movements in the society and its early proponents had aspirations of making a better world. Lewin, the founder of the group dynamics movement, was a Jew who fled Nazi Germany. His first studies, comparing autocratic versus democratic leadership styles, was undertaken to prove the merits of American-style democracy as against Germanic autocracy. The first T-groups were undertaken to ease World War II veterans back into society and later to ease racial tensions in communities.

The philosophical foundations and consultation model of OD were matched by developments in other fields. Person-centered therapy came to counseling psychology and social work and Carl Roger's theories arose as an effective counterpoint to B. F. Skinner's pessimistic views of the nature of mankind. Buber undertook a re-definition of Christendom in this era and Stack-Sullivan's humanistic conceptions of man gained credence in the work of Timothy Leary and Hubert Coffey. These complementary developments put OD into the larger movement toward human expressiveness and community in the 1960s.

This era gave us the Peace Corps and the War on Poverty. It gave us a new consciousness of the natural environment and a richer appreciation of the interpersonal world (Reich, 1970). Surely this era spawned aggression, witness the Vietnam War, and empowerment was on society's agenda, in forms as varied as Black Power and Flower Power. But the larger emphasis was upon ties of feeling and community. OD was borne in this context. It aimed to free people from the emotional barriers that divided them and to allow them to join together.

Today Gesselschaft and individualism characterize society. In business and national politics, emphasis is upon Social Darwinism and self-interest. The welfare state is in retreat and poverty is on the rise. Our social problems are being privatized and wealth is being redistributed according to the "trickle down" theory. This national mood has necessarily affected people's outlooks and values. We have the "me" generation and new narcissists in the populace. College students have less interest in developing a meaningful philosophy of life, and more on making a good living for themselves. This context has, in turn, altered our conceptions of OD.

OD of the 1980s enables the heroic individual to achieve and gives the powerful more tools for gaining their sway Its self-help emphasis fits a society where people are looking out for #1. New-age OD fits the temperment of the new corporate personnae, whom Maccoby (1976) calls the "gamesman," and the outlook of young professionals, the so-called yuppies. Furthermore, its emphasis on visionary leadership and strong culture fits the values of many corporate chieftains and excellent companies that fund and support OD programs. Simply stated, OD's emphasis on harmony, empowerment, and excellence serves an important function in a society where people are regarded as instrumental and organizations are conceived of as instruments of purpose.

Surely this function is important and valuable. America is experiencing extraordinary competitive problems, a trade imbalance, a mounting national debt, and assorted economic ills today. That OD has become more pragmatic and can help organizations to compete more effectively is valuable in and of itself. However, there are risks that it will be used to manipulate by its savvier proponents and to exploit by self-aggrandizing corporate leaders. Studies find widespread cynicism in society today concerning the aims and motives of management (Kanter & Mirvis, 1986). To the extent that OD is seen as serving primarily the interests of the elite and self-interested, it risks rejection and repudiation by those it purports to harmonize, empower, and make excellent.

In its early day OD was cast as a form of renewal; it was a way to renew the potential of people and the promise of organization (Lippitt, 1969). The traditional management paradigm had emphasized personal independence, organizational control, and a mechanistic and grinding existence for plant and people. OD would emphasize interdependence, self-management, an organic form of organizing and even a joyful experience at work (Trist, 1970).

Warren Bennis (1970) noted, however, that "funny things" can happen on the way to the future. OD's form changed in the 1970s in keeping with the changing shape of society. It shed its exclusive connection to the human potential movement and was linked as well to societal aspirations for a higher quality of life. It reached many more blue-collar and clerical personnel in companies, as well as organized labor and the majority of companies. But it was still renewing people and organizations, albeit in a more communal form.

In the 1980s, however, OD, like corporations and the society, is in the midst of a form of re-invention (Naisbitt & Aburdene, 1985). Individualism is back, but re-invented in the form of intrapreneuring in organizations. Control is back, but re-invented in the form of gaining people's commitment. Ostensibly, mechanism and a grinding form of existence are gone in our information age. But some would say that we have re-invented the consequent distress with our emphasis upon the "survival of the fittest." Organizations are re-inventing themselves creating networks and letting change direct itself through the cooperative competition of the marketplace. Common visions and strong cultures create the coherence necessary for negotiating this form of organization.

OD's re-invention is taking many forms. The 1980s have brought the arrival of Theory Z forms of organization and the introduction of more zen-like approaches to management. Many of the Theory Z principles concerning the structure of organizations, the emphasis upon employee welfare, and the use of consensual decision making are quite compatible with OD tenets and QWL aims. At the same time, the Japanese style of decision making has been critized as "pseudo-participation" and Theory Z cultures have been characterized as totalitarian

At the other extreme, the "free market" orientation of OD today has been criticized as antithetical to community. In some respects, of course, this critique is a broader indictment in American society. Many see the Reagan agenda as dividing society into individual and organizational winners and losers at the expense of the common good (Bowles, Gordon, & Weisskopf, 1984). Plainly those who see OD re-inventing itself in this fashion believe that the upbeat rhetoric of new-age OD proponents masks the realities.

TOWARD PART II

In my judgment, OD is re-inventing itself today. It is, again, in an experimental period. Theorists are attempting again to define what organizational change really is: distinctions are being made between development, transitions, and transformations. This is yielding a new conception of how OD can and should contribute to human development (Tannenbaum & Hanna, 1985). Quinn and Cameron (1983) have, in turn, offered approaches for reconciling competing criteria of organizational effectiveness. They argue that companies can simultaneously meet the needs of their members and the demands of their marketplace.

The models of OD's advance as an intellectual and social movement presented here intimate that the field has peaked in its growth: its paradigm has been set and its professionalism has been established. The work of these scholars is a sign that movement is afoot to devise a new paradigm for the field and a new definition of its means and ends.

Today, for example, theorists and interventionists are beginning to apply "paradoxical" theory to organizational, group, and individual behavior and to develop paradoxical forms of intervention (see review by Smith & Berg, 1987).

This movement from an "either/or" to "both/and" conceptualization of social systems has been well documented and paradoxical modes of intervention have a strong foundation in family therapy. It may well be that parodoxical theory will have an impact upon the re-invention of OD akin to that of early systems theory.

Furthermore, notions of what OD can accomplish are being reconsidered. Generalizations to new problems and different settings have raised fresh questions about both its content and its application in other contexts. For example, early OD interventions stressed the potential of "pushing" people and groups through stages to reach higher levels of development. Transformational interventions, by contrast, propose to "pull" them to higher spiritual and performance planes. Early OD interventions emphasized overcoming inter-personal barriers to change whereas later interventions focused on surmounting structural barriers. A new generation of theories emphasize the problems of overcoming structural barriers embedded in interpersonal relations. This line of thinking, along with transformational approaches to intervention, promises to turn assumptions about the content of change upside down.

In turn, the application of OD to new contexts raises fresh questions about its pedagogical and participative aspects. Early OD emphasized education of both the head and the heart through action research and laboratory training. Many have turned toward a more "wholistic" model of education emphasizing development of the body and spirit when working with people in outdoor training labs or in creative mind-expanding activities. In turn, emphasis upon participation has been challenged by factions as diverse as those who believe a strong dose of authoritarianism is essential to "freeing" people up and those who believe that a far more conflictual and political approach is needed for those seeking freedom from oppression.

The point is that OD is in the midst of revolutionary change today. Part II will look at the components of today's revolution and revisit some of OD's earlier history to determine to what extent revolution—rather than evolution—best explains its progress over the past three decades. To complete Part I, let me present a postscript on how my client organization is handling OD today.

Post-Script: OD At Work in the Client Company

The 1980s have shaped OD efforts in my client organization. Efforts to push OD down to the blue-collar workforce have been successful. Hourly workers in autonomous work teams and quality circles have more favorable view of their jobs and have registered gains in productivity. Also, their ratings of participation and involvement are higher. Interestingly, survey results for clerical workers show that they are thirsting for more involvement. They have been targeted for attention in the next months. Already task forces are being formed to follow up on survey data and address clerical concerns.

The company continues to do well on the basic bread-and-butter factors. Personnel were also queried, in the past survey, as to the company's success in putting its newly articulated values into practice. The great majority said the firm was manufacturing high-quality products, delivering good customer service, doing business ethically, and treating people with dignity and respect. Nevertheless, strategic changes in the company and 1980s-style OD brought some new conflicts to the firm. For example, the new emphasis on divisionalization has created rivalries and promoted conflicts between the marketing-oriented divisions. The growing business gripe about the equality of effort in the company and the declining ones complain about the equality of sacrifice. Downsizing has led many to the perception that there is deadwood in the company and the belief that management should be tougher on those that do not do their fair share. To an extent, these cleavages are common to firms in the strategic positions of my client organization. The way my client responded to these conflicts, however, has changed.

In earlier years, the top management would have wrestled with the issues and gathered more company-wide data to clarify the problems and their import. A task group, composed of people from different divisions, might have been put to work on divisional equity and a company-wide initiative to emphasize the importance of people's contributions might have been launched. This year the CEO sent a video tape to all departments reviewing the state of the business, the role of each division, and the need for each employee to work hard and deliver. Top management met to affirm the rationale for divisional budget allocations and for stronger performance management. Cost control, performance evaluation, and merit pay systems are being tailored to reinforce this strategic direction. It has been left to the divisions to undertake any further OD-type work needed.

Proponents of the new regiment see this as crisp and business-like. Interestingly, detractors do too. They fault it, however, for being too impersonal and directive. They question whether it will truly stimulate commitment and common purpose. They also question whether the marketplace approach and competitive stimulus might fracture community and negate cooperation.

Surely there are signs that the community is fracturing. There is no sense of exploitation or unrelenting pressure. Indeed, most continue to see it as a fine place to work. However, the majority now feels that the company puts more emphasis on profits than on people. There is also a growing sense that the company is less committed to participative management and that any management style is appropriate, so long as it produces results.

What explains these findings? Competition has forced the company to contain costs. Its parent company has demanded higher profits. Strategy has thus dictated a divisional emphasis and a strategic management emphasis has put systems to work in service of strategy. The new CEO wants results and is more laissez-faire in his approach and orientation. He is business minded and less inclined than his predecessor toward participative management.

In my opinion, these results also relate to the changing shape of OD in the company, which is now driven by strategy and positioned to serve the firm's business needs. Some welcome this re-invention of the function, while others worry that OD is losing its people orientation and focus on personal development.

There is opportunity in the company today. OD initiatives are making a difference in the quality of the worklife of people, and action research continues in the survey-feedback program. Management remains committed to integrating the needs of people with those of the organization. But there is also danger that while the organization adapts to its environment, it may alienate its people. Whatever cooperative competition adds to profits, it could, in turn, tear the fabric of the organizational community.

Initially, the new CEO "pooh poohed" these dangers and resisted further analysis and follow up to concerns expressed about the company's leadership and culture. The OD officer and some key members of the top management group persisted, however, and an off-site meeting of the top officers was scheduled. The top management group worked on alignment, of people, not just systems, with company directions. They also wrestled with attunement and undertook a team-building session amongst themselves.

They left the meeting ready to "re-invent" the company. Some months later they made a leveraged buyout from the acquirer and now have the firm's destiny in their own hands. It remains to be seen, however, whether or not they can re-invent a people orientation as strong as the one that marked the company back in the 1960s. More broadly, the question may be whether or not they can re-invent themselves.

REFERENCES

Ackerman, L. (1986). Development, transition, or transformation: The question of change in organizations. *OD Practitioner,* December, 1–8.
Alderfer, C. (1977a). Organization development. *Annual Review of Psychology, 28,* 197–223.
Alderfer, C. (1977b). Improving organizational communication through long term intergroup intervention. *Journal of Applied Behavioral Science, 13,* 193–210.
Alderfer, C. & Berg, D. (1977). Organization development: The profession and the practitioner. In P. Mirvis & D. Berg (Eds.), *Failures in organization development and change.* New York: Wiley Interscience.

Andre. R. (1985). The scientist, the artist, and the evangelist. *New Management, 2,* 16–21.

Argyris, C. (1957). *Personality and organization.* New York: Harper.

Argyris, C. (1964). *Integrating the individual and the organization.* New York: Wiley.

Argryis, C. (1970). *Intervention theory and method: A behavioral science view.* Reading, MA: Addison-Wesley.

Argryis, C. (1971). *Management and organizational development: The path from XA to YB.* New York: McGraw-Hill.

Argyris, C. & Schön, D. (1974). *Theory in practice.* San Francisco: Jossey-Bass.

Argyris, C. & Schön, D. (1978). *Organizational learning: A theory of action perspective.* Reading, MA: Addison-Wesley.

Barnard, C. (1938). *The functions of the executive.* Cambridge, MA: Harvard University Press.

Beckhard, R. (1969). *Organization development: Strategies and models.* Reading, MA: Addison-Wesley.

Beckhard, R. (1972). Optimizing team-building efforts. *Journal of Contemporary Business, 1,* Summer, 23–32.

Beer, M. (1976). The social technology of organization development. In M. Dunnette (Ed.), *Handbook of industrial and organizational psychology.* Chicago: Rand McNally.

Beer, M. (1980). *Organization change and development: A systems view.* Santa Monica, CA: Goodyear.

Beer, M. & Driscoll, J. (1977). Strategies for change. In J. Hackman & J. Suttle (Eds.), *Improving life at work.* Santa Monica, CA: Goodyear.

Bellah, R. (1964). Religious evolution. *American Sociological Review, 29,* 358–374.

Benne, K. & Birnbaum, M. (1961). Principles of changing. In W. G. Bennis, K. Benne, & R. Chin (Eds.), *The planning of change.* New York: Holt, Rinehart and Winston.

Benne, K., Chin, R., & Bennis, W. (1961). Science and practice. In W. Bennis, K. Benne, & R. Chin (Eds.), *The planning of change.* New York: Holt, Rinehart and Winston.

Bennis, W. (1966). *Changing organizations: Essays on the development and evolution of human organizations.* New York: McGraw-Hill.

Bennis, W. (1969). *Organization development: Its nature, origins, and prospects.* Reading, MA: Addison-Wesley.

Bennis, W. (1970). A funny thing happened on the way to the future. *American Psychologist, 25,* 595–608.

Bennis, W. (1983). The artform of leadership. In S. Srivastva (Ed.), *The executive mind: New insights on managerial thought and action.* San Francisco: Jossey-Bass.

Bennis, W. & Slater, P. (1964). Democracy is inevitable. *Harvard Business Review,* March–April.

Bennis, W. & Slater, P. (1968). *The temporary society.* New York: Harper & Row.

Berlew, D. & Hall, D. (1966). The socialization of managers: Effects of expectations on performance. *Administrative Science Quarterly, 11,* 207–223.

Blake, R., Shepard, H., & Mouton, J. (1964). *Managing intergroup conflict in industry.* Houston: Gulf.

Blake, R. & Mouton, J. (1976). *Consultation.* Reading, MA: Addison-Wesley.

Blake, R. & Mouton, J. (1985). How to achieve integration of the human side of a merger. *Organizational Dynamics, 13,* 41–56.

Block, P. (1987). *The empowered manager.* San Francisco: Jossey-Bass.

Bowers, D. & Franklin, J. (1972). Survey guided development: Using human resources measurement in organizational change. *Journal of Contemporary Business, 1,* Summer, 43–55.

Bowers, D., Franklin, J., & Pecorella, P. (1975). Matching problems, precursors, and interventions in OD: A systemic approach. *Journal of Applied Behavioral Science, 11,* 391–409.

Bowles, S., Gordon, D., & Weisskopf, T. (1984). *Beyond the waste land*. Garden City, NY: Anchor Press.

Brown, L. & Tandon, R. (1983). Ideology and political economy in inquiry: Action research and participatory research. *The Journal of Applied Behavioral Science, 19,* 277–294.

Burke, W. & Schmidt, W. (1971). Primary target for change: The manager or the organization? In H. Hornstein, B. Bunker, W. Burke, M. Gindes, & R. Lewicki (Eds.), *Social intervention*. New York: Free Press.

Burke, W. & Hornstein, H. (1971). *The social technology of organization development*. Wash, DC: NTL Learning Resources Corporation.

Campbell, J. & Dunnette, M. (1968). Effectiveness of T-group experiences in managerial training and development. *Psychological Bulletin, 70,* 73–104.

Carlson, H. (1980). A model of quality of work life as a developmental process. In W. Burke & L. Goodstein (Eds.), *Trends and issues in OD: Current theory and practice*. San Diego, CA: University Associates.

Chin, R. (1961). The utility of system models and developmental models for practitioners. In W. Bennis, K. Benne, & R. Chin (Eds.), *The planning of change*. New York: Holt, Rinehart and Winston.

Chin, R. & Benne, K. (1969). General strategies for effecting changes in human systems. In W. Bennis, K. Benne, & R. Chin (Eds.), *The planning of change, 2d edition*. New York: Holt, Rinehart and Winston.

Coch, L. & French, J., Jr. (1948). Overcoming resistance to change. *Human Relations, 1,* 512–532.

Cole, R. (1982). Diffusion of participatory work structures in Japan, Sweden, and the United States. In P. S. Goodman (Ed.), *Change in organizations*. San Francisco: Jossey Bass.

Cohen, A. & Gadon, J. (1978). *Alternative work schedules*. Reading, MA: Addison-Wesley.

Cummings, T. (1984). Transorganizational development. In B. Staw & L. Cummings, (Eds.), *Research in Organizational Behavior, Vol. 6*. Greenwich, CT: JAI Press.

Dalton, W. (1969). *Influence and organizational change*. Paper presented to Conference on Organizational Behavior, Kent State University.

Deal, T. & Kennedy, A. (1982). *Corporate cultures*. Reading, MA: Addison-Wesley.

Dewey, J. (1933). *How we think*. New York: Heath.

Erikson, E. (1963). *Childhood and society*. New York: Norton.

Ewing, D. (1978). *Freedom inside the organization*. New York: Dutton.

French, W. (1971). Organizational development: What it is and is not. *Personnel Administrator, 16,* 1971, 2–8, 46.

French, W. (1978). A checklist for organizing and implementing an OD effort. In W. French, C. Bell, & R. Zawacki (Eds.), *Organization development*. Dallas, TX: Business Publications, Inc.

French, W. (1985). The emergence and early history of organization development with reference to influences upon and interactions among some of the key actors. In D. Warwick (Ed.), *Contemporary organization development*. Glenview, IL: Scott, Foresman and Company.

French, W. & Bell, C. (1973). *Organization development*. Englewood Cliffs, NJ: Prentice-Hall.

Friedlander, F. & Brown, L. (1974). Organizational development. *Annual Review of Psychology, 25,* 313–341.

Gibb, J. (1964). Climate for trust formation. In L. Bradford, J. Gibb, & K. Benne (Eds.), *T-group theory and the laboratory method*. New York: John Wiley & Sons.

Gilligan, C. (1982). *In a different voice*. Cambridge, MA: Harvard University Press.

Goodman, P. & Dean, J. (1982). Creating long-term organizational change. In P. S. Goodman (Ed.), *Change in organizations*. San Francisco: Jossey-Bass.

Greiner, L. (1972). Evolution and revolution as organizations grow. *Harvard Business Review, 50,* 37–46.

Hackman, J. & Oldham, G. (1980). *Work redesign*. Reading, MA: Addison-Wesley.

Hackman, J. & Suttle, J. (1977). *Improving life at work*. Santa Monica, CA: Goodyear.

Handy, C. (1980). The changing shape of work. *Organizational dynamics*, Autumn, 26–34.

Harrison, R. (1970). Choosing the depth of organizational intervention. *Journal of Applied Behavioral Science, 6*, 181–202.

Harrison, R. (1983). Strategies for a new age. *Human Resource Management, 22*, 209–235.

Hartman, J. & Gibbard, G. (1974). A note on fantasy themes in the evolution of group culture. In G. Gibbard, J. Harman, & R. Mann (Eds.), *Analysis of groups*. San Francisco: Jossey-Bass.

Heckscher, C. (1980). Worker participation and management control. *Journal of Social Reconstruction, 1*, 77–101.

Hornstein, H., Bunker, B., Burke, W., Gindes, R., & Lewicki, R. (1971). *Social intervention*. New York: Free Press.

Huse, E. (1975). *Organization development and change*. St. Paul, MN: West.

Joiner, W. (1984). Waking up in Plato's cave: An ancient vision for transforming contemporary management. *ReVision, 7*, 89–100.

Kanter, R. (1983). *The change masters*. New York: Simon and Schuster.

Kanter, D. & Mirvis, P. (1986). Managing the jaundiced worker. *New Management, 3*, 50–54.

Katz, D. & Kahn, R. (1966). *The social psychology of organizations*. New York: John Wiley & Sons.

Kiedel, R. (1981). Theme appreciation as a construct for organizational change. *Management Science, 27*, 1261–1278.

Kiefer, C. & Stroh, P. (1984). A new paradigm for developing organizations. In J. Adams (Ed.), *Transforming work*. Alexandria, VA: Miles River Press.

Kimberly, J. & Miles, R. (1980). *The organizational life cycle*. San Francisco: Jossey-Bass.

Kimberly, J. & Quinn, R. (1984). *New futures: The challenge of managing corporate transitions*. Homewood, IL: Dow Jones-Irwin.

Kuhn, T. (1970). *The structure of scientific revolutions*. Chicago: University of Chicago Press.

Lawler, E. (1976). Should the quality of work life be legislated? *Personnel Administrator, 21*, 17–21.

Lawler, E. (1981). *Pay and organization development*. Reading, MA: Addison-Wesley.

Lawler, E. (1982). Strategies for improving the quality of work life. *American Psychologist, 37*, 486–493.

Lawler, E. (1986). *High involvement management*. San Francisco: Jossey-Bass

Lawrence, P. & Lorsch, J. (1969). *Developing organizations: Diagnosis and action*. Reading, MA: Addison-Wesley.

Lawrence, P. & Dyer, D. (1983). *Renewing American industry*. New York: Free Press.

Leavitt, H. (1986). *Corporate pathfinders*. Homewood, IL: Dow Jones-Irwin.

Levinson, H. (1972). *Organizational diagnosis*. Cambridge: Harvard University Press.

Lewin, K. (1948). *Resolving social conflicts*. New York: Harper & Row.

Lewin, K. (1951). *Field theory in social science*. New York: Harper & Row.

Likert, R. (1961). *New patterns of management*. New York: McGraw-Hill.

Likert, R. (1967). *The human organization: Its management and value*. New York: McGraw-Hill.

Likert, R. & Likert, J. (1976). *New ways of managing conflict*. New York: McGraw-Hill.

Lippit, R., Watson, J., & Westley, B. (1958). *The dynamics of planned change*. New York: Harcourt, Brace and World.

Lippitt, G. (1969). *Organizational renewal*. Englewood Cliffs, NJ: Prentice Hall.

Lippitt, G. (1970). Developing life plans: A new concept and design for training and development. *Training and Development Journal, May*, 2–7.

Maccoby, M. (1976). *The gamesman: The new corporate leaders*. New York: Simon & Schuster.

Maier, R. (1952). *Principles of human relations*. New York: Wiley.

Mann, F. (1957). Studying and creating change: A means to understanding social organization.

Research in Industrial Human Relations. Industrial Relations Research Association. Publication No. 17.

March, J. & Olsen, J. (1976). *Ambiguity and choice in organizations.* Bergen, Norway: Universitets-forlaget.

Marks, M. & Mirvis, P. (1986). The merger syndrome: When corporate cultures collide. *Psychology Today, October,* 36–42.

Maslow, A. (1954). *Motivation and personality.* New York: Harper.

McClelland, D. (1961). *The achieving society.* New York: Van Nostrand Reinhold.

McGregor, D. (1960). *The human side of enterprise.* New York: McGraw-Hill.

Michael, D. & Mirvis, P. (1977). Changing, erring, and learning. In P. Mirvis & D. Berg (Eds.), *Failures in organization development and change.* New York: Wiley Interscience.

Miles, R. & Snow, C. (1978). *Organizational strategy, structure, and process.* New York: McGraw-Hill.

Miles, R. & Snow, C. (1984). Designing strategic human resource systems. *Organizational Dynamics, Summer,* 36–52.

Miller, J. (1955). Toward a general theory for the behavioral sciences. *American Psychologist, 10,* 513–531.

Mirvis, P. (1984). *Work in the 20th century: America's trends & tracts, visions & values, economic & human developments.* Cambridge, MA: Revision/Rudi Press.

Mirvis, P. (1985a). OD vs. QWL. In D. Warwick (Ed.) *Contemporary organization development.* Glenview, IL: Scott, Foresman and Company.

Mirvis, P. (1985b). Formulating and implementing human resource strategy. *Human Resource Management, 24,* 385–412.

Mirvis, P. (1985c). Measuring program implementation, adoption, and intermediate goal attainment: Missing links in OD program evaluations. In D. D. Warwick (Ed.), *Contemporary organization development.* Glenview, IL: Scott, Foresman and Company.

Mirvis, P. & Macy, B. (1976). Accounting for the costs and benefits of human resource development programs. *Organizations, Accounting & Society, 1,* 179–194.

Mirvis, P. & Lawler, E. (1977). Measuring the financial impact of employee attitudes. *Journal of Applied Psychology, 62,* 1–8.

Mirvis, P. & Berg, D. (1977). *Failures in organization development and change.* New York: Wiley Interscience.

Mirvis, P. & Seashore, S. (1979). Being ethical in organizational research. *American Psychologist, 34,* 766–780.

Mirvis, P. & Lawler, E. (1984). Accounting for the quality of work life. *Journal of Occupational Behavior, 5,* 197–212.

Mitroff, I. & Emshoff, J. (1979). On strategic assumption making: A dialectical approach to policy and planning. *Academy of Management Review, 4,* 1–12.

Mitroff, I. (1984). *Stakeholders of the organization mind.* San Francisco: Jossey-Bass.

Mohrman, S. & Mohrman, A. (1983). Employee involvement in declining organizations. *Human Resource Management, 22,* 445–467.

Nadler, D. (1979). Consulting with labor and management: Some learning from quality of work life projects. In W. Burke (Ed.), *The cutting edge.* La Jolla, CA: University Associates.

Nadler, D. & Tushman, M. (1977). A diagnostic model for organization behavior. In J. Hackman, E. Lawler, & L. Porter (Eds.), *Perspectives on behavior in organizations.* New York: McGraw-Hill.

Naisbitt, J. (1982). *Megatrends.* New York: Warner Books.

Naisbitt, J. & Aburdene, P. (1985). *Re-Inventing the corporation.* New York: Warner Books.

Nelson, L. & Burns, F. (1984). High performance programming: A framework for transforming organizations. In J. Adams (Ed.), *Transforming work.* Alexandria, VA: Miles River Press.

Ouchi, W. (1981). *Theory Z.* Reading, MA: Addison-Wesley.

Ouchi, W. (1984). *The M-Form society*. Reading, MA: Addison-Wesley.

Pascale, R. & Athos, A. (1981). *The art of Japanese management*. New York: Simon and Schuster.

Pasmore, W. & Associates. (1980). *Model for sociotechnical intervention*. Cleveland, Ohio: Case Western Reserve University.

Pasmore, W. (1985). A comprehensive approach to planning an OD/QWL strategy. In D. Warwick (Ed.), *Contemporary organization development*. Glenview, IL: Scott, Foresman and Company.

Pava, C. (1983). *Managing new office technology*. New York: Free Press.

Perkins, D., Nieva, V. & Lawler, E. (1983). *Managing creation*. New York: Wiley Interscience.

Perrow, C. (1972). *Complex organizations*. Glenview, IL: Scott, Foresman and Company.

Peters, T. & Waterman, R. (1982). *In search of excellence*. New York: Harper & Row.

Peters, T. & Zenger/Miller. (1984). *Toward excellence*. Zenger/Miller Associates.

Peters, T. & Austin, N. (1985). *A passion for excellence*. New York: Random House.

Porras, J. & Roberts, N. (1980). Toward a typology of organization development research. *Journal of Occupational Behavior, 1,* 163–179.

Porras, J., Harkness, J., & Kiebert, C. (1985). Stream analysis: A method for decomposing organization development interventions. In D. Warwick (Ed.), *Contemporary organization development*. Glenview, IL: Scott, Foresman and Company.

Porter, M. (1980). *Competitive strategy: Techniques for analyzing industries and competitors*. New York: Free Press.

Quinn, R. & Staines, G. (1979). *The 1977 quality of employment survey*. Ann Arbor, MI: Survey Research Center, Institute for Social Research.

Quinn, R. & Cameron, K. (1983). Organizational life cycles and the criteria of effectiveness. *Management Science, 29,* 33–51.

Randall, L. (1971). Common questions and tentative answers regarding organization development. *California Management Review, 13,* 45–52.

Randall, L. (1973). Red, white, and blue TA at 600 MPH. In D. Jongeward (Ed.), *Everybody wins: Transactional analysis applied to organizations*. Reading, MA: Addison-Wesley.

Ranney, J. (1982). Quality of work life in the office: The distributed payroll project. *Training and Development, 34,* 74–84.

Reich, C. (1970). *The greening of America*. New York: Random House.

Rogers, C. (1961). *On becoming a person*. Boston: Houghton Mifflin Co.

Rogers, E. (1962). *Diffusion of innovations*. New York: Free Press of Glencoe.

Rogers, E. & Shoemaker, F. (1971). *Communication of innovations*. New York: The Free Press.

Sarason, S. (1972). *The creation of settings and future societies*. San Francisco: Jossey-Bass.

Sarason, S. (1977). *Work, aging, and social change*. New York: Free Press.

Schein, E. (1969). *Process consultation: Its role in organization development*. Reading, MA: Addison-Wesley.

Schein, V. & Griener, L. (1977). Can organization development be fine tuned to bureaucracies? *Organizational Dynamics, Winter,* 48–61.

Schindler-Rainman, E. & Lippitt, R. (1980). *Building the collaborative community: Mobilizing citizens for action*. University of California Extension.

Schlesinger, L. (1982). *Quality of work life and the supervisor*. New York: Praeger.

Schmuck, R. & Miles, M. (1971). *OD in schools*. La Jolla, CA: University Associates.

Seashore, S. (1977). Monitoring the quality of working life. In Hymans, S. & Shapiro, H. (Eds.), *The economic outlook for 1977*. Ann Arbor, MI: The University of Michigan, Department of Economics.

Seashore, S., Lawler, E., Mirvis, P., & Camman, C. (1983). *Assessing organizational change*. New York: Wiley Interscience.

Sheppard, H. & Herrick, N. (1972). *Where have all the robots gone?* New York: Free Press.

Sherwood, J. (1972). An introduction to organization development. In *The 1972 Annual Handbook for Group Facilitators*. La Jolla, CA: University Associates.

Simmons, J. & Mares, W. (1983). *Working together*. New York: Alfred A. Knopf.

Slater, P. (1966). *Microcosm*. New York: Wiley Interscience.

Smith, K. & Berg, D. (1987). *Paradoxes of group life*. San Francisco: Jossey-Bass.

Starr, P. (1982). *The social transformation of American medicine*. New York: Basic Books.

Staw, B. (1976). *Intrinsic and extrinsic motivation*. Morristown, NJ: General Learning Press.

Steele, F. (1973). *Physical settings and organization development*. Reading, MA: Addison-Wesley.

Stein, B. & Kanter, R. (1980). Building the parallel organization: Creating mechanisms for permanent quality of work life. *The Journal of Applied Behavioral Science, 16*, 371–388.

Stent, G. (1972). Prematurity and uniqueness in scientific discovery. *Scientific American, 227*, 84–93.

Strauss, G. & Rosenstein, E. (1970). Worker participation: A critical review. *Industrial Relations, 9*, 197–214.

Tannenbaum, R. & Davis, S. (1969). Values, man, and organizations. *Industrial Management Review, 10*, 67–83.

Tannenbaum, R. & Hanna, R. (1985). Holding on, letting go, and moving on: Understanding a neglected perspective on change. In R. Tannenbaum, N. Marguiles, F. Massarik, & Associates (Eds.), *Human systems development*. San Francisco: Jossey-Bass.

The O.M. Collective. (1971). *The organizer's manual*. New York: Bantam Books.

Tichy, N. (1983). *Managing strategic change*. New York: Wiley Interscience.

Toffler, A. (1971). *Future shock*. New York: Bantam.

Toffler, A. (1981). *The third wave*. New York: Bantam.

Tonnies, F. (1887). *Gemeinschaft and gesellschaft*. Translated and edited by Loomis, C., 1957. East Lansing: Michigan State University Press.

Trist, E. (1970). Between cultures: The current crisis in transition. In W. Schmidt (Ed.), *Organizational frontiers and human values*. Belmont, CA: Wadsworth Publishing.

Trist, E. (1981). *The evolution of socio-technical systems*. Ontario Quality of Working Life Centre.

Trist, E. & Bamforth, K. (1951). Some social and psychological consequences of the longwall method of coal getting. *Human Relations, 4*, 3–38.

Trist, E., Susman, G., & Brown, G. (1977). An experiment in autonomous working in an American underground coal mine. *Human Relations, 30*, 201–236.

U. S. Department of Health, Education, and Welfare. (1972). *Work in America*. Cambridge: MIT Press.

Vaill, P. (1982). The purposing of high-performing systems. *Organizational Dynamics*, Autumn, 23–39.

Von Bertalanffy, L. (1950). The theory of open systems in physics and biology, *Science, 3*, 23–29.

Walton, R. (1969). *Interpersonal peacemaking: Confrontations and third party consultation*. Reading, MA: Addison-Wesley.

Walton, R. (1970). A problem-solving workshop on border conflicts in East Africa. *The Journal of Applied Behavioral Science, 6*, 453–489.

Walton, R. (1972). How to counter alienation in the plant. *Harvard Business Review, November–December, 70–81*.

Walton, R. (1975a). *Criteria for quality of work life*. In L. Davis & A. Cherns (Eds.), *The quality of working life*. New York: Free Press.

Walton, R. (1975b). The diffusion of new work structures: Explaining why the success didn't take. *Organizational Dynamics*, Winter, 3–22.

Walton, R. (1978). The ethics of organization development. In G. Bermant, H. Kelman, & D. Warwick (Eds.), *The ethics of social intervention*. Washington: Hemisphere.

Walton, R. (1979). Work innovations in the United States. *Harvard Business Review*, July–August, 88–98.

Walton. R. (1980). Establishing and maintaining high commitment work systems. In J. Kimberly & R. Miles (Eds.), *The organizational life cycle*. San Francisco: Jossey-Bass.

Wardell, N. (1978). The corporation. *Daedalus,* Winter, 97–110.

Weick, K. (1969). *The social psychology of organizing.* Reading. MA: Addison-Wesley.

Weisbord, M. (1977). How do you know it works if you don't know what it is? *OD Practitioner, 9,* 1–8.

Weisbord, M. (1978). *Organizational diagnosis.* Reading, MA: Addison-Wesley.

Weisbord, M. (1987). Toward third wave managing and consulting. *Organizational Dynamics,* Spring, 5–24.

Whyte, W. (1956). *The organization man.* New York: Simon and Schuster.

Woodworth, W. & Nelson, R. (1979). Witch doctors, messianics, sorcerers, and OD consultants: Parallels and paradigms. *Organizational Dynamics,* Autumn, 17–33.

Yankelovich, D. (1979). Work, values, and the new breed. In C. Kerr & J. Rosow (Eds.), *Work in America: The decade ahead.* New York: Van Nostrams.

Yankelovich, D. (1982). *The new rules: Searching for self-fulfillment in a world turned upside down.* New York: Random House.

Zaltman, G., Duncan, R., & Holbek, J. (1973). *Innovations and organizations.* New York: Wiley Interscience.

Zand, D. (1974). Collateral organization: A new change strategy. *The Journal of Applied Behavioral Science, 10,* 63–89.

TOWARDS A NEW PRACTICE THEORY OF OD:

NOTES ON SNAPSHOOTING AND MOVIEMAKING

Marvin R. Weisbord

ABSTRACT

This article was written in two sections, one part in 1982, expressing my growing dissatisfaction with how fragmented OD had become, the second in 1987, reflecting my ideas after writing *Productive Workplaces* (1987a) in an effort to provide a more unified theory of practice that would cover diverse disciplines and whole systems thinking. The two parts are presented as a dialogue with myself, then and now, showing my efforts to honor Kurt Lewin's monumental contributions by building on his work in a new way. In particular, I address the dilemma of "unfreezing," "moving," and "refreezing" systems that never stop changing, and question whether it is possible to "unfreeze," in any rational, deliberate way, those few systems that are stuck.

Research in Organizational Change and Development, Vol. 2, pages 59–96.
Copyright © 1988 by JAI Press Inc.
All rights of reproduction in any form reserved.
ISBN: 0-89232-772-3

If you want to understand what a science is, you should look in the first instance not at its theories or its findings, and certainly not at what its apologists say about it; you should look at what the practitioners of it do.

Clifford Geertz

INTRODUCTION

For some years I have been concerned about the fragmentation of OD into subspecialties—the same dilemma that drives client organizations to hire consultants. In the late 1970s I tried to use this concern as a jumping off point to write a book on OD. I could not do it. Instead, in speeches and articles (Weisbord, 1977, 1978, 1981,) I expressed my growing awareness that OD practitioners are driven by "a search for social meaning in a technological junkyard." In 1981 I began a long essay on what I thought needed to be taken into account in a more coherent theory of practice. I never published it.

Consulting to Bethlehem Steel in 1980, I discovered that Frederick W. Taylor (1915), the "father of scientific management," who gave Bethlehem the world's most efficient machine shop 80 years earlier, had as his central purpose "cooperative relations between employers and men." I began to see OD in a historical perspective beyond behavioral science knowledge applied to organizations. We were attempting to do with psychology what Taylor had attempted through engineering—to remove authoritarianism from management, enhance cooperation, find the keys to motivation in the workplace.

In 1986 my friend, William Schmidt, recommended an extraordinary sociology book, *Habits of the Heart* by Robert S. Bellah and colleagues (1985), who wrote of the tensions between individualism and commitment in the United States. As I read it, I recognized that for me OD represented a search for what Tolstoy in *Anna Karenina* called the "necessary connection existing between personal and general interests." This ancient philosophical issue metamorphosed— thanks to the industrial revolution—into a business school version, the "better fit between the individual and the organization." New nineteenth-century technologies created in industrial societies more widespread wealth than the world had ever known. On their heels came twentieth-century psychologists showing how profoundly *threatening* to self-esteem, dignity, and community was technology married to bureaucracy.

That understanding enabled me to continue with my book. I was now writing a personal statement integrating my own history with that of some exemplary figures who shaped my practice—Frederick Taylor, Kurt Lewin, Douglas McGregor, Eric Trist, Fred Emery, and others. I was now writing about personal and general interests, about my own large systems change projects from the 1970s, about the origins of OD and socio-technical thinking, about how many of us have shaped a new practice in recent years. I began to articulate a theory of practice based on values of community, meaning, and dignity in the workplace as core aspirations of people in democratic societies. That theme was hardly new. Yet, somewhere during the years I had been in OD, it had blurred into obscurity as I—we—sought to integrate all of human knowledge into more comprehensive and rational strategies and models.

As a contribution to these volumes, I want to revisit my old essay, and to discuss what I did with it in the course of writing my book. Those sections marked "1982" represent ideas formulated in the 1970s. Those marked "1987" represent my changing perspectives on practice, captured by the metaphor "productive workplaces."

TOWARDS NEW OD GUIDELINES

1982: What Must Be Accounted For

This paper concerns my changing perspectives on OD practice. I find myself increasingly questioning some tenets of practice and more confidently asserting others. I would like to build a more accurate theory about what OD consultants do—a theory based on experience, not wishes or fantasies. I believe enough experience exists now to begin to conceive one. I intend this paper as a start—an outline of some of the dimensions of such a theory.

A well-rounded practice theory of OD must account for:

- The central tasks, or "core mission" of the organization to be developed.
- Core values, which influential people want to act out.
- Ways of mapping/conceptualizing how well the organization carries out its mission and lives the core values.
- Client leadership required to initiate and sustain new activities.
- Effective consulting behavior.

The theory must link these aspects to existing theories of diagnosis and action upon which OD practice is built.

1987: Four Guidelines for Practice

In a "third wave practice theory" (Weisbord, 1987b) I seek to integrate these four issues. By "third wave" I mean Alvin Toffler's (1980) idea that the change from machine to knowledge work constitutes a shift in human consciousness equal to the agricultural and industrial revolutions. I build this theory in my book through successive iterations of the work of Taylor, Lewin, McGregor, Emery, and Trist, seeking to show how similar values were embodied in engineering, in psychology, and now in whole systems thinking. I especially demonstrate the need for this way of thinking by presenting a series of cases from my own practice in the 1970s.

Having done all that I now can summarize succinctly what I learned from my long journey. In 1900 Taylor had experts solve problems for people—"scientific management." Circa 1950 Lewin's inheritors started everybody solving their own problems—participative management. In 1965 experts discovered the power of systems thinking, most notably in socio-technical projects, and began improving whole systems *for* other people. Now, we are learning how to get everybody improving whole systems. That, in a nutshell, is the evolution and challenge to organizational development. We are moving simultaneously along two continuums from experts doing the job towards everybody doing the job, and from solving discrete problems toward improving whole systems. Working these movements requires *acting out* the open systems model, and not simply (or even actually) presenting it to groups on a flip chart. When five levels of management from Bethlehem Steel's Sparrows Point plate mill, for example, spent two weeks in 1983 working on identifying and solving mill problems, and improving relations with their bosses and each other, and visiting customers and suppliers, and interacting with the sales force, and improving decision-making skills, and examining their own leader behavior, they were engaged in an "everybody im-

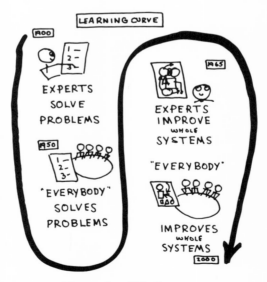

Figure 1.   OD Curve

proves the whole system exercise.'' There must be a hundred additional examples. Involving large numbers in whole systems improvement tasks is the challenge for OD now and for the indefinite future (see Figure 1).

On consultant behavior, my main observation is that the consultant always arrives in the middle of somebody else's movie and leaves before the end. We are stage managers at best, not directors. I also believe that we can consult only under relatively narrow circumstances. Where a client leader is willing to stick his or her neck out, where there is a pressing organizational dilemma, where some people are already searching for a way out. As for core values, I believe now that the search for community in the workplace, joining with others to do worthy tasks which lead to organizational survival and personal growth—is the source of dignity and meaning.

In my book I argue that dignity and meaning are the ''bottom line'' of bottom lines. Without them, technology can't be fully utilized, or organizations run economically. Thus I reconceptualize OD practice: We help people take charge of core business processes—economics and technology—through the collaborative organization and design of their own work. This leads to (a) greater customer focus, (b) higher quality and output, (c) lower costs, (d) better jobs, (e) fewer layers of management and less authoritarian behavior. Above all, it satisfies the hunger everywhere for cooperation and community in a world of (potentially) hostile technologies. These aspirations are nearly identical to Frederick Taylor's. If you doubt this, read the parallels between Taylor's ideas on scientific management and a contemporary view of quality of work life.

Here are my guidelines for a ''third wave practice theory'' of managing and consulting. Notice that they embody the directions in which many practitioners are moving—regardless of what or how they name what they do. As we make more conscious choices we will stop entirely mixing old (paradigm) practices in with the new.

- ASSESS THE POTENTIAL FOR ACTION (instead of diagnosing problems)
- GET THE WHOLE SYSTEM IN THE ROOM (work towards 100 percent participation, even when it's impossible)
- FOCUS ON THE FUTURE (downplay problem solving, engage more of the right brain in devising attractive future scenarios)
- STRUCTURE SYSTEMS TASKS PEOPLE CAN DO FOR THEM- SELVES (reduce consultant and facilitator dependency)

SNAPSHOTS AND MOVIES

1982: OD Needs Two Theories That Really Are One

Two qualitatively different kinds of theories underlie OD practice, theories of diagnosis and theories of action. Consulting can be seen as an interplay between

What SCIENTIFIC MANAGEMENT is NOT . . . (1912)

". . . not an efficiency device . . . not a device of any kind for securing efficiency . . . nor any bunch or group of efficiency devices . . . not a system of figuring costs . . . not a new scheme of paying men . . . not a piecework system . . . not a bonus system . . . not a premium system . . . no stopwatch on a man and writing things down about him . . . not time study . . . not motion study or an analysis of the movements of men . . . not divided foremanship or functional foremanship . . . not any of the devices which the average man calls to mind when scientific management is spoken of."

"In essence, scientific management involves a complete mental revolution on the part of the working men—and on the part of those on the management side, the foreman, the superintendent, the owner of the business, the Board of Directors—as to their duties towards their fellow workers in the management, towards their workmen and toward all of their problems."

—-Frederick W. Taylor, Testimony to a Special Committee, U.S. House of Representatives, January 25–30, 1912, Washington, D.C.

What QUALITY OF WORK LIFE is NOT . . . (1978)

". . . not a single, specific notion . . . not a soft, touchy feely approach to working . . . not a vague, imprecise kind of notion . . . not a threat to power—management's or union's . . . not quick . . . not easy . . . not a panacea . . . not a closed system, not an end . . . not job enrichment, not a productivity gimmick . . . not imposable . . . not manipulative . . . not an ideology . . . not a passing fad . . . not elitist . . ."

". . . the cluster of notions it sucks into itself combine to suggest something simple, operationally feasible, intensely human and even more intensely cost-effective . . . that something is to provide people at work (managers, supervisors, rank and file workers) with structured opportunities to become actively involved in a new interpersonal process of problem-solving toward both a better way of working and a more effective work organization, the payoff from which includes the best interests of employees and employers in equal measure."

—Ted Mills, Director, American Center for the Quality of Work Life, Speech entitled "The Name that Isn't There," to Centre International de Recherches et d'Etudes en Management, June 8, 1978, Montreal, Canada.

Figure 2. The Every-New-Idea-Has-Nomenclature-Problems Department.

Note: From *Productive Workplaces:* Organizing and Managing for Dignity, Meaning and Community. Copyright © 1987 by Jossey-Bass, Inc. and Marvin R. Weisbord. Reprinted with permission.

the two. Diagnosis is analogous to snapshooting. We freeze the action at a moment in time, arrange key factors in a conceptual framework, and observe—with our clients—the relationships highlighted by the conceptual frame. Diagnosis has two purposes: to produce valid guidelines to action and to stir up more people than the person we first contacted to want to do something. This stirring up can be thought of as a moviemaking problem. With the client we craft a script we hope will have a happy ending.

Two "laws" govern my behavior in this activity. There are no exemptions from either, not in labs, textbooks, or science.

First Law of OD—Snapshooting: WHAT YOU LOOK FOR IS WHAT YOU FIND

Corollary: What theory you use determines what you look for.

Our theories determine what we consider important. We may, for example, have a theory of organizational functioning that says manager behavior influences subordinates' motivation which in turn determines unit performance (Likert, 1960). If that is the case, we will attempt to classify manager behavior into motivating and demotivating actions, to find examples of each, and to match each set of examples to a set of outcomes. We might build a model of manager behavior, say a Grid (after Blake & Mouton), which identifies the key dimensions as concern for people versus concern for output. We might analyze manager behavior in terms of various "styles" questionnaires to probe more deeply into the orientations which explain why we do what we do. In every case, the model we use determines what we look for and how we talk about it.

If, on the other hand, we have a theory of culture—that the symbols, legends, myths, and rituals determine what members of a unit will do, we then attempt to observe and build on these phenomena. Inevitably, we will look at "manager behavior," but through a very different lens. Now, instead of "seeing" a style of behavior, we may observe a mythic replay of an ancient Greek tragedy, the relationship between the gods and mortals. More prosaically, we may focus on the primal struggle between parent and child. We may have a theory about the importance of the "right brain" and seek to validate it by sorting organizational activity bilaterally, based on which half of the brain is presumed to control it.

Each of these snapshots may be equally valid and interesting. I have no idea how many snapshooting theories there are. The number must run into the hundreds. There's no reason why you couldn't construct a diagnostic theory of organizational functioning around biorhythms, correlating "critical days" with output. You probably could make something out of position in family. Are you a sister or brother, with older or younger siblings? That will predict how you interact with people of various ages.

Perhaps you really want to account for "all" the data. In that case you need a "grand design" theory—one that takes into account in the same picture frame goals, values, technologies, people, problems, planning, rewards, structure, innovation, levels of supervision, control, decision making, human needs, motives, rates of change, turbulence, old and new paradigms, transformational forces . . . and many more. I have seen some of these models and admire them, like pictures in a museum, for their completeness, complexity, technical virtuosity. However, I would not know what to do with one.

No snapshooting tool, however sharp, accurate, and well-cared for, encompasses the whole of reality. What we look for is what we find. and no matter how much we find, we always leave a lot out. How, then, to select the "right" diagnostic theory for the job? Suppose our theory leaves out something important? Ah, but it does. The better the theory the more it will leave out important things, but, it will also include some important things. Which brings me to moviemaking.

Second Law of OD—The Law of Moviemaking: HOW YOU LOOK DETERMINES WHETHER ANYBODY ELSE WILL SEE IT CLEARLY ENOUGH TO WANT TO DO SOMETHING ABOUT IT.

First Corollary: There is no direct connection between the accuracy of a diagnosis and people's willingness to act on it. Second Corollary: People only improve what they want to improve. Therefore, a good theory highlights things people want to improve.

I have worked with dozens of concepts, theories, and models in countless places. I'm convinced that any conceptual model can be used if the consultant understands it and believes it. However, a good, practical theory has four features:

1. It's simple.
2. It fits the client's values, highlighting things considered important.
3. It validates the client's experience, putting recognizable things in a new light.
4. It suggests practical next steps.

Good moviemaking is wholly dependent on what people are interested in doing. Snapshooting is the surest way to find out. Thus, diagnosis must focus equally on conditions to be changed *and* the potential for changing them. The snapshot is part of the movie.

Thus, the "right" theory in a given situation is the one that:

1. the consultant believes in;
2. fits the four criteria;
3. seems appropriate to the client in the context of the request for help.

That means the theory specifically sheds light on the reorganization, or the quality improvement project, or the merger, or the office automation program. Notice, that each of these "business opportunities" has within it the seeds of practically any theory we could imagine using. However, we can only work with theories we know. And we are wise to stick to theories that excite us. Therefore, choosing the right theory is not so complicated: OD consultants succeed only with theories *they* know (not what the other person knows) when they are excited and able to communicate the relevance of their theory to the request at hand. This is a necessary, but not sufficient, condition for success. Much of the fantasy and disappointment surrounding OD comes from imagining that if we know lots of snapshooting theories we can make a movie.

1987: Rethinking Diagnosis

Hardly had I written a book on *Organizational Diagnosis* (1978) when I found myself increasingly talking "snapshots" and "movies" rather than diagnosis and intervention. Now I'm ready to give up diagnostic language entirely. It's an "old paradigm" medical concept, which reinforces an outmoded search for prescriptions. Instead we need to go whole hog for systemic improvement. That can't be done by picking three priorities off a problem diagnosis list and writing down action steps. People have to be helped to make sense of their own experiences in their own way. Not that this behavior is irrelevant, it's just that the "problem solving" is five percent of the action, rather than the heart of the matter. OD practice has tended to focus on fancier and fancier ways to diagnose "issues" rather than engaging people in what Russell Ackoff calls the whole "mess."

The consultant is not a doctor, clients are not patients, and organizations, in my opinion, are beset by perpetual change anyway, whether or not the consultant intervenes. Confusion in the face of ongoing change is as natural as breathing. It is not "sick" behavior. To the extent consultants keep using lingo with that implication, we reinforce a stereotype of our own omniscience—one we claim to be against. I would rather talk about "assessing the potential for action" as a first step. Is there a leader, are there business matters of serious concern, are there people already full of energy and acting? How can all three be put together? What tasks can people do together that will help them know and control their system more ably? We must become aware that to the extent consultants collect and feed back "data" and "work through" resistance we may inadvertently create a self-fulfilling prophecy and slow people down.

That statement may surprise some fans of my widely used "six box model" (Weisbord, 1978b). Yet that model, as many people have found, has many uses besides diagnosing problems. For example, it can advance organizational learning, it encourages people to think about how the everything fits together. It is

general enough—purposes, structure, relationships, leadership, helpful mechanisms—to be a projection screen for whatever content its users want to put into
the boxes. If I used it today, though, I'd steer away from zeroing in on problems
with it. I would rather encourage people to make their own connections among
whole sets of problems to the values, beliefs, and assumptions that support them.
The model's "expert" function is to make better open systems analysts of each
of us. Its best "everybody" function (for those who can own it) is as a future
planning tool. What sort of system do we want to see five or ten years from now?
In terms of the six categories (or any local categories that help make sense of a
whole system), does our work design or reorganization plan account for each
category in a way that's consistent with our values?

A model may reduce anxiety and frustration, but it cannot take them away. I
think we are in the business of helping people convert anxiety into energy. It is
somewhat analogous to what the practitioners of traditional Chinese medicine
do. They "listen" to your pulses, all of them, for a long time, and then insert
needles designed to unblock the flow of energy through the body and allow the
system to heal itself. Rarely do they put the needles where the symptoms are.
Nor do they punish you for not having already fixed yourself.

TOWARD ASSESSMENT RATHER THAN DIAGNOSIS

1982: The "Crunch Point"

I want to discuss in no special order some speculations on what must be
thought through to produce a coherent integration of snapshooting and moviemaking.

Here is one example. About a third of the way into any long group activity—
training, team building, planning meetings—groups lock up, skilled people have
two left feet. A consultant who misinterprets this phenomenon may panic,
scratching frantically on the flip chart, feeling out-of-control and incompetent.
("I should have used Exercise A instead of Task B!" says he or she privately.)
Group development theories predict this blockage. It is unrelated to technology
or group goals.

What can a consultant do? My practice theory is that this "resistance" connects to the decision each person must make about how deeply to become
involved. Some come in having made up their minds to participate. Many have
not. As it dawns on people that they are being asked to *do* something, not simply
react, in effect to take control of their own future, they become anxious, with-

holding, and watchful. One by one they decide to involve themselves. The "resistance" ends when more than half the group decides to become part of the action. What applies to a workshop also applies to any long, programmatic activity. It happens at every stage of each cycle in every human life. (In mid-life we call it a "crisis.") It is as natural as eating, as inevitable as breathing.

There is very little a consultant can do during this process, except live through it. Allan Drexler and I once did a team-building workshop with a medical school psychiatry department. At the "crunch" point the psychiatrists were faced with a choice: go more deeply into their own relationships with each other, or go more deeply into the overlaps and redundancies of the department's committee structure.

As the anxiety grew, the chairman became more defensive, people began clearing their throats and shifting their chairs, the consultants, not knowing what else to do, called for a break. In the hallway my partner said, "It's enough to make you climb the walls." I looked at the wall that had protruding stones every few feet, and, much to my own surprise, started climbing.

After coffee, a lively discussion began on the relative merits of working interpersonal or organizational problems. Finally, the chairman turned to us: "What would you guys do?" Allan and I looked at each other. "We can go either way. You asked us to help you build an administrative group to run the department more effectively than you can do alone. Which is the more important blockage now, the committee structure or your relations with each other? We'll help you with either. What do you want to do?" After long debate, the group chose the committee structure. During the afternoon and next morning they analyzed goals, membership, results, eliminated some groups, and streamlined others. Later, several reported it had been their most productive two-and-a-half days together.

This incident happened more than a decade ago. I have never figured out a better technique than wall-climbing for getting through an emotionally charged session. That's too bad, because most hotel walls are not climbable. Not that I haven't learned anything since. I understand better now the connections between brain and body—that physical exertion restores emotional balance. (I might have known this when I climbed the wall—but I didn't know that I knew it.) These days I might suggest to people they stand and stretch, take some deep breaths, go for a walk. My security blanket is the knowledge, born of many repetitions, that if the contract was sensible to begin with, if there is an important task to be done, if the person in charge really wants to do it, hopeless feeling will turn into energy. There is no high point without a low point to measure it against.

Now, a practice theory of OD must account for this phenomenon. People come to consultation skills workshops looking for an exemption, a *technique* that will prevent "crunch" points. With luck, they learn that it's okay not to know what to do, that, indeed, in the midst of any arduous work, everybody, even "experts," eventually reach the limit of their techniques. (In one way, our whole society has reached the outer limits of technology—nuclear power, for example, which threatens us with extinction even as it provides a cheap source of energy.)

A practice theory of OD would include a guideline that in every group activity comes a point where living through it, not "doing" anything, is the expert's solution.

1987: Redefining the Crunch

The phenomenon I was talking about is best illuminated by the "four-room apartment" of Swedish social psychologist Claes Janssen (1975) shown in Figure 3. I have found it more useful as an assessment tool in deciding what can be done. Janssen's concept, illustrated below, is that each of us lives sometimes in each room. Changes—in our work, home life, companies, society—trigger movement from one room to another. Organizations move in roughly the same way.

In Contentment we like things the way they are. If somebody "helps" us we may start with good-natured acceptance and soon turn our backs on the helper if pushed to do something new. We may even be thrown by the helper into denying that the offer of help is a problem. In Denial we repress feelings of anger, fear, anxiety brought on by change, pretending everything's okay. If we become aware of and own our feelings, then we move into Confusion. In that room we admit openly up that we don't know what to do, are worried, upset, unsure. We are helpable. In Renewal we become aware of more opportunities than we can actualize. Working through that (good) dilemma puts us back in Contentment.

Janssen's concept struck me as a useful diagnostic tool, the simple way of assessing "readiness." We can't consult to people in Contentment or Denial. We should not even try. The best we can do is validate people's right to be there. The room hospitable to flip charts, models, and rational problem solving is Confusion. And we might be helpful in Renewal if we're fast enough with new ideas and can keep up with the clients. In my book I made this theory part of the first useful guideline—"assess the potential for action." If you think of an OD project, or potential project, we cycle through the rooms many times in the course of intervening. However, I still believe you should join the game in Confusion or Renewal.

I also speculated—a challenge to my academic colleagues—that if OD case studies were to be revisited from this perspective, we might find that "failures" happen more when action research or experiential workshops are inserted into organizations deeply in Contentment or Denial.

So I conclude that "assessment," not diagnosis, is the starting place, the key questions being not what is wrong and what will fix it, but what is happening out

Figure 3.

there, and who cares. Who would support me if I offered to help? Consultants must learn to say "not now" more often—the rock bottom "consulting skill." That's a key point in a book by my partner, Peter Block, *Flawless Consulting* (1981).

FROM DEMOCRATIC VALUES TO MINDLESS TECHNIQUES AND BACK AGAIN

1982

The main theoretical and value bases for OD were established more than 20 years ago. Between 1958 and 1969 such pioneers as Argyris (1970), Beckhard (1969), Bennis, Benne, and Chin (1961), Lippitt, Watson, and Westley (1958), Douglas McGregor (1960), Rensis Likert (1961, 1967), set out the visions, principles, and practices which shaped the field's development.

Two strong values emerge from this literature: the importance of personal fulfillment in work, and the essentiality of democratic processes for organizing the workplace. The subtle tension between these values has become a focal tension for the field ever since. Much of the confusion about what OD does, means, is, can be, and should be derives from its identification with personal growth workshops. For some time organizational change was equated with personal change. Practitioners early on attempted to prescribe T-group activity—giving and receiving interpersonal feedback—as a means for carrying out planned, total systems change.

The literature of recent years has dealt more with theoretical and technical elaboration—fancier how-to-do-its, more comprehensive diagnostic models—than assessment of where we are, and what unique perspectives we have to add to the world of organized endeavor. Many textbooks now summarize the diverse trends in the field. They cover such a variety of perspectives while I get vertigo each time I pick one up. I pity the poor graduate students trying to memorize and apply all the stuff in an excellent OD textbook like Warner Burke's (1982).

Values, in current OD practice, tend to be reduced to a technique—"values clarification," helping clients figure out what they believe, or confront the gaps between belief and action, rather than a set of principles that govern practitioner behavior. Are there a set of core values that govern the field? Warner Burke (1982, p. 92) has listed values from his courses and from Noel Tichy's work—to influence decisions that affect us, to be assertive about personal needs, to have more interesting work, to participate in setting goals, and more. Neither list includes democratic workplaces, or the connections between satisfaction and productivity, or the need for organizations to survive.

What interests me most now is what actually happens when practitioners attempt to actualize the field's core values. I want to understand the conditions under which this is possible, the connection between conditions and methods used, and the kinds of (predictable) actions that determine success or failure of a particular course of action.

OD once seemed to me to be a value-directed and fairly coherent practice. We struggled to make organizations more open, to provide greater opportunities for people to grow and to participate more fully in problems and decisions affecting their lives. That is a pretty straightforward mission. It has been enormously compromised, I think, by attempts to incorporate into the practice, piecemeal, all of human knowledge. This has led to both a growth spurt and an identity crisis. A practice that agglomerates everything stands for nothing.

One popular exercise is to ask practitioners where they think the organizational world is heading, and what they must do to be "ready" when the world arrives. Thus, ASTD Journal (April 1981) listed 83 "Ideal 'Core Skills' and Advanced Skills for the Future OD Practitioner." This Bionic Superperson will need such "skills" as management policy and strategy, transorganization theory, job measurement, operations research, marketing, accounting, systems engineering, cultural anthropology, finance, and hypnosis. Lest you begin to feel obsolete, there are also old standbys like power, conflict, leadership, motivation, and active listening.

Recently, I reviewed a manuscript analyzing the impact of survey data feedback on faculty skills and morale in 11 colleges. The authors admit sheepishly that some negative results may have happened because they, not the dean or president, cooked up the research scheme, hoping that survey feedback, useful tool that it is, might help the faculty uncover and solve some problems. All of this is symptomatic of a field in search of itself. Those of us who contribute to these lists, typologies, and research designs collude unwittingly, while perpetuating the disease that makes organizations sick—fragmentation, alienation, impotence at being lost in a forest where there are so many species we can no longer remember their names. Until I had struggled some hours with this essay, I did not realize how much tension I feel reconciling what for me have been inviolable tenets of OD with what I (and many others) actually do when we practice.

It is a tension, I believe, between science and democracy in the workplace. You can say it other ways: between freedom and constraint; between technology and participation; between task and process; between self-governance and authoritarianism. There is a kind of ''Gresham's Law'' in our society—that technological values tend to drive out social values. Nowhere is this more evident than in the workplace. And OD practitioners, children of the times, are just as susceptible as anybody else.

My practice is built on the shoulders of some extraordinary people with remarkable ideas—about democracy, science, the human condition, the meaning of work, the place of technology in society. Increasingly, I find our formal theories inadequate statements of what I should do and how. Larry Porter (1978) likens it to pitching a tent in your living room using printed instructions, versus doing it at night in the woods with the rain falling ''and somewhere out there in the dark are low growling sounds.'' It's my hypothesis that this tension in practitioners, teachers, and researchers between the field's popular wisdom and actual practice leads us straight to a misplaced focus on technologies, quick fixes, new models, arguments over whether we should be contingent or normative, and whether team building works better than TA.

My practice seems a great deal more heuristic than the written descriptions of it. This means, roughly translated, that far from planning cultural change, we mostly muddle through, chasing good ideas, clining to certain values, enlarging our horizons by adding to our knowledge of the ''whole system,'' advocating a certain way of acting and being as co-equal to ''outcomes'' like higher output, lower costs, better quality. For that reason I think action research—in the various senses that term was used by Kurt Lewin (Marrow, 1969)—makes a sensible description for what we should be doing.

However, you can action research anything from stress to production to equal opportunity to the relationship between position in family to management style to transorganizational, intergalactic synergistic transformations! One serious problem for every OD practitioner is the choice of *content* to accompany more democratic, participative processes. Clearly, expert management consultants have the edge here. They get into the central processes of organizations—with their strategic and marketing studies, production scheduling systems, office automation, compensation schemes, cost-cutting exercises, engineering proposals, and financial analysis models.

Any of these specialties can be worked in an action research mode, using more socially viable processes than simply writing a report and delivering a presentation, complete with overheads and (lately) color computer graphics. It is terribly tempting for an OD consultant to want to be an expert too on something besides "people problems."

While this was happening in the States, the Tavistock people in England took a whole different tack. They observed that how people behave at work is linked closely to the structure of jobs and the distribution of authority. Rather than teach managers and supervisors new behavior, the socio-technical approach to organizational improvement became to reduce the number of managers and supervisors needed, pushing downward decisions, expertise, and freedom to act, providing people access to a broader range of skills at all levels (Emery & Trist, 1960).

Thus, the NTL approach was to work directly on behavior, the Tavistock to work on structure. OD, of course, involves a subtle interplay of both. In this regard, socio-technical systems design has a great deal to recommend it over traditional OD approaches based on interpersonal and group processes and more recently, political and power dynamics. For one thing, it has a "content" more firmly grounded in the day-to-day work processes of an organization. For another, socio-technical practitioners can articulate a set of principles about the design of work and their linkage to larger issues like community, personal growth and philosophies of life and work. Finally, socio-technical approaches are grounded solidly in action research—getting involved with the client in working out more compatible relationships among people, machines, and systems.

"Quality of Working Life," a term coined by Louis Davis at an international conference in 1972 (Trist, 1981), could provide the umbrella for a merger of socio-technical and OD techniques. From the socio-technical perspective, we have a number of diagnostic and analytical tools linking social and technological systems. From the OD side we have a sophisticated understanding of the connections among task and process. Blending the perspectives can enlarge any practice. But we need a set of principles that embraces both viewpoints.

1987: Merging OD and Sociotech

In *Productive Workplaces* (Weisbord, 1987a) I suggest the way to get OD and socio-technical viewpoints together is to help people work on systemic tasks— reorganizations, the redesign of work, strategic reorientation. I am convinced that there can be no behavioral change without structural change—and vice versa. So long, for example, as work at the bottom is narrowly specialized and traditional supervisory roles remain intact, we can do supervisory training until the moon becomes an earth colony without making fundamental cultural, social, or other changes—like broader skills and responsibility, lower costs, or more opportunities to grow. We can talk empowerment, myths, heroes, and war stories. Unless we are also ready to stand up and speak for involving people in the redesign of their own work—from the ground up—our aspirations will always exceed our practice. We are engaged in a massive rethink of both authority and expertise. In a world gone bonkers on technology, we can't afford to leave our fate up to experts and bosses, nor can we hope to make things happen all alone. It's a profound paradox of personal and general interests.

I think socio-technical practice needs some fine tuning, too. It can be made so complex and mysterious that it takes three years of training and a Ph.D. just to get your arms around the analytical tools. It is worth remembering that the practice derived from a spontaneous invention by some uneducated coal miners in Great Britain in 1949 in response to a new technology of roof control. They created self-managing work teams without 40 hours of process skill training. And still output and work satisfaction went up, accidents and turnover and absenteeism down. One reason I feel so much passion about this is that I started self-managing teams in the 1960s without any training and saw major social and economic improvements happen as people felt free to work together in new ways (Weisbord, 1985b). So I *know* that learning can be simple and self-managed too. Just because we have sophisticated processes for doing something does not mean they are required to make our values live—or to achieve the hoped for results. The first socio-technical principle—antidote to Taylor's "one best way" to do everything, is "equifinality." That means there are a lot of ways to skin a cat. I think simple is better, not easier by any means, but more accessible to the presumed beneficiaries.

THE ITCH TO DO OD

1982: Matching Client and Consultant Itches

OD consulting seems to me very much a matter of the internal organs. It begins deep inside each consultant, planted there long before any of us chose this marginal way of earning a living. It means an impulse, a "hook," an urgent sense that work, the workplace, people who work, the design of work, the connectedness of co-workers, some combination of these matters very much in human affairs. It seems to me terribly significant that the practice of OD—at its best the collaborative improvement of the workplace—is done mainly by lone wolves who experience little ongoing collaboration in their lives. It's as if we're both looking for and running away at the same time.

OD starts when a consultant with an itch to scratch and a client in the same condition find each other. I am convinced that OD's founders and their clients of the 1950s and 60s had complementary itches that wanted scratching. Whatever their other motives, they sought to place science at the service of democratic values, to make a humane marriage between technology and worklife. "I do believe," wrote Warren Bennis, one of the pioneers, in *Changing Organizations* (1966), "that the values and moral imperatives of science and democracy are appropriate and necessary everywhere today."

Elsewhere, I've written about some core values of OD—science, democracy, learning, work (Weisbord, 1978a). Some version of these values must reside deeply in a consultant who aspires to success in OD. Without such itches to scratch the consultant becomes largely a technician, a posturer, a sham—like the Wizard of Oz—who created an elaborate set of illusions to maintain his fakery and convince people he had a lot more power than he really did (Baum, 1900).

The itch drives the consultant. Techniques are simply alternative ways of scratching. Itches come in all shapes, sizes, forms, styles. Beware of the potential client who has no itch to scratch, who does not feel passion about a particular process, belief, deeply desired outcome. It hardly matters whether the problem is "the right one." In time, we will find it. Initially, we take whatever problem the client presents.

I have worked with people who wanted to scratch the turnover itch, the low morale itch, the production itch, the medical school management itch, the hospital cost itch, the low product quality itch, the labor-management cooperation itch. In each case I asked myself, Is this an itch I want to scratch too? Could I do it? Is there a chance here to enhance *both* the viability of this organization and the quality of people's work experience? Can I work on this in a way that people feel enhanced, more influential, more supported, and more productive? A practice theory of OD must take account of the importance of mutual itches.

1987: Values, Vision, and Productive Workplaces

The itch—call it "values" in last year's formulation or "vision" in this year's—is the passion, the authentic feeling, the self in action. It determines whether we see consulting as a calling, a vocation, or just a way to turn a dollar. My itch, I know now, has always been a struggle to make not just a living but a contribution. I think that's what the people who hire me want too. Seeing my own purpose as working towards productive communities—workplaces where each person can find dignity and meaning—makes it easier for me to say yes or no to client requests. I am unlikely to contract with people who put my work in the same category as a carpet-cleaning service—shop around until you get the best, then turn the job over to them. I'm looking for temporary partners—people who want whatever they want so passionately they will put their own tails on the line and ask others to do likewise.

There's another dimension, too. In studying the commonalities between Frederick Taylor and Douglas McGregor, I came to look at Theories X and Y another way. I once thought they represented two contradictory sets of assumptions, embodied in contrasting management styles. From Claes Janssen's work, from identifying with my own clients' dilemmas and owning up to my own, I reach a different perception. X and Y are an internal dialogue in each of us. For McGregor, they embodied an ongoing correspondence he really had with his father, an evangelical preacher, who ran a mission for homeless laborers. The elder McGregor, surrounded by human dregs, concluded people were at bottom lazy, irresponsible, and sinful. The son, more optimistic, a disciple of Kurt Lewin's psychology, saw human potential as the key, supportive behavior and policies as the necessary conditions.

If you see both sets of assumptions at work in each of us, our constructive and "shadow" selves, a tug of war between our hidden and public sides (to paraphrase the Johari Window), you are much less likely to label people "change resisters," or "Theory X types." Such labeling is the kiss of death for change efforts.

DIAGNOSIS AS INTERVENTION

1982: The First Contract is Always Diagnostic

Although I fantasize about techniques as much as the next person, when I have my wits about me I always propose as a first step a joint diagnosis, a snapshooting session, to freeze the action momentarily and study its main features. It is a central tenet of practice that the first contract always be diagnostic. What is not so well understood is that frequently that is the *only* contract desired or needed by the client.

Every carpenter wants to build houses. Many homeowners only want bookshelves. Consultants want to do "total systems change." Many clients have more modest passions, more modest itches. They may develop a grand itch along the way. But the function of a large systems change model, a model of comprehensive organization design, a model of organizational diagnosis and functioning, is to help the consultant take a snapshot, to help the client decide where to scratch first. Having received such help, many clients say, "Thank you very much, I can take it from here." This is not very satisfying to a consultant who believes people need training, new policies, new systems, and a long course in futurizing, values analysis, and leadership styles. However, a diagnosis responsive to the core values of OD—and respectful of those values—is an important contribution to the stream of constructive social change.

Diagnoses must be contracted so that clients help define the problems, participate in the data collection and analysis, and make up their own minds what to do next. I find Chris Argyris' (1970) formulations about valid data, free choice, and commitment to act the best guidelines I know for consultant behavior. However, a full practice theory of OD must recognize that "total systems change" is a myth, an artifact, a form of benevolent, though frustrating, megalomania. What we do is practice the best way we know how. Systems change takes care of itself.

1987: Why "Unfreezing" Is Irrelevant

My old stuff still sounds seductively plausible. I have revised it, though, in writing my book. I do not want to do conventional diagnoses anymore. That's easier to say than act upon. In the 1970s I found myself mixing modes—old paradigm and new—all in the same work. I was diagnosing systems, defining problems, and developing strategies all at once. In parallel I kept changing my approach, either finding ways to include more of the system in the diagnostic map (whole systems thinking) or more of the system in the room (whole systems participation). The rate of change and uncertainty now requires us to do both. I want to stop thinking about diagnosing problems and learn to assess the potential for whole systems improvement. In my book I trace OD diagnostic thinking to Kurt Lewin's field theory—the idea that the person can only be understood in a particular here-and-now situation, and vice versa (Lewin, 1947). More, in the Lewinian modification of cause-effect thinking, organizations needed to be "unfrozen" in order to be deliberately altered. The "diagnosis" was intended as an unfreezing step. By collecting data and framing hypotheses, we would confront people with gaps between what they say and what they do. This "cognitive dissonance" would provide motivation to want to change—to make their words and actions more congruent.

But—a major point of my book—suppose organizations move more like bullet trains than melting icebergs? If markets, technologies, and aspirations are in a state of perpetual meltdown, it may be that "unfreezing" is no longer a central consulting service. In that case, why diagnose *for* people? If the consultant is called in because change is already going too fast to handle, why not get "the whole system in the room" and have people look at how it works together? Why borrow their watch and tell them the time? Why not help others experience their dilemmas as a totality—in terms of the work they perform as a whole system, the pressures on it, and how it fits each person. Then help them redo it in more satisfying ways. This does not require a rehashing of problems, people or any other kind, by consultants. It requires focusing on aspirations, and coalescing in one room various strands of activity already underway, so that new things can happen. That, after all, is a whole systems change strategy, but of a different sort from the more rational planned change strategies I cut my teeth (and stubbed my toes) on.

To do whole systems change consistent with my values, I need to get everybody involved, not just represented. I know that is not always practical. Yet it's the right objective. If we can go to the moon, we can figure out how to involve everybody—in assessing what needs to be done, in doing it. If not this year, then next, by the year 2010 at the latest. In this way of thinking "diagnosis" metamorphoses into an assessment of possibilities. What's the potential for action here, and who cares? (Not, what's the problem and which technique will fix it?) How can I get "everybody" to do a systems improvement task together?

Indeed, I now believe many clients only want a *report,* not change. That's why large expert consulting firms have a thousand consultants and the average OD firm has three. The report serves many purposes—including the avoidance of change, an intention conveniently blamed on the difficulty in implementing (excellent) suggestions not invented here. Indeed, the first law of reports says: implementation varies inversely with comprehensiveness. To the extent I supply a diagnosis I reinforce a form of action I don't believe in. I also set myself up to fail.

In my book I retell the story of the Wright brothers momentous achievement in inventing the airplane. How did two bicycle mechanics from Ohio succeed at a task that had eluded the best engineering brains of the nineteenth century? Alone among their contemporaries, they were systems thinkers. They flew a wing successfully under its own power because they conceptualized the problem right. They had to (1) get it in the air, (2) keep it in the air, and (3) make it go where they wanted, said Orville and Wilbur. Unless they solved all three problems they hadn't solved any of them.

The OD analogy goes something like, (1) involve everybody, (2) focus on the future, (3) get people working on technical and economic tasks together. And there is a fourth dimension, essential to the concept of productive workplaces. We need to make employment secure. We cannot expect people to OD (or sociotech) themselves out of work. There's a paradox here. In every work design project I have been associated with, people figure out how to do more with less, especially less management and supervision. Yet everybody needs dignified and meaningful work. How to employ everybody? If you say it is not "practical," I can only tell you that neither was flying before 1903.

TASK AND PROCESS—THE CHICKEN AND EGG OF OD

1982: Everything Counts

OD is largely a matter of connections. We should focus on task and process both, and never exclude either for long. Events go sour from both forms of excess. Consultants may chase processes which, like fairies on the lawn, only they can see (let's check up on your decision making, or control, never asking what's to be decided or controlled). Then there are the macho tough-talkers (not all men) who use "bottom line" in every other sentence. "These guys," said

one industrial engineer I used to work with, jerking a thumb towards me and
Tony Petrella, "play kissy-face. I play hardball!"

It's our obligation, I think, to make the linkage between kissy-face and hardball. We need to assert that processes unconnected to outcomes and outcomes at
the expense of self-esteem, support, or influence *both* erode what Lewin called
the "life value" of work. What to do/how to do it, for an OD consultant,
become inseparable. It's essential I attend in equal measure to task and process.
That is the surest thing I know about how to practice organization development.
We should not prefer ends over means, techniques over results, freedom over
constraint. We always risk toppling too far one way or the other. OD can be
thought of as a balancing act—tapping the healthy impulse towards wholeness
that resides in each person.

My most dependable practice theory is that means and ends always become
tangled, that any deeply desired result will *always* be thwarted by unconscious,
unobserved processes. Some we can control, others we cannot. My responsibility as consultant is to continually help people remove blocks when they can and
walk around or live with them when they cannot.

A practice theory of OD should incorporate the reciprocal link between ends
and means and the consultant's responsibility for asserting it.

1987: The Tension between Experts and Users

In *Productive Workplaces* I show how "Taylorism" evolved as the finest
example of cause-effect thinking in the workplace. Taylor really believed he had
a foolproof system for finding the one best way to anything—from machining
tools to hitting golfballs. (He was not always wrong. In 1887 he won—with his
brother-in-law—the U.S. Lawn Tennis Association doubles championship,
using a racket of his own design.) This thinking did not end with the evolution of
open systems thinking in the 1950s. Those who saw or read Tom Wolfe's *The
Right Stuff* (1980) may remember that a central theme of the story was the
struggle between astronauts and engineers over how much control the pilots
would have of their spacecraft.

This tension between technical experts and users continues. It has brought us
Three Mile Island, Chernobyl, and many other social disasters, which can only
be avoided through a different way of thinking about the link between technical
knowledge and controlling the devices it creates. Wherever systems have been
designed by engineers *for* others—even when "input" was solicited—they have
had major design flaws discovered only in use. This has been documented in
many socio-technical projects. The only way safely to operate a technical system
is to have operators, engineers, and staff people design the whole contraption
together—and continue to work that way forever, learning constantly from each
other as they go.

That is wholly contradictory to the American interpretation of the industrial revolution. The Japanese have known it longer than we have. In the 1970s the Japanese Union of Engineers and Scientists made a policy decision to give their expertise to workers and managers, not to hold it close and mysterious. That is the real secret of quality circle success and the world marketing miracle. I have heard Eric Trist talk about that, but it still is not widely understood among manufacturing managers who tried and gave up on quality circles and are now "gung ho" for just-in-time inventory systems.

LIGHTNING RODS

1982: Every Intervention Attracts Every Issue

Every organization has its central "process issue." This is the dilemma everybody experiences and nobody can talk about, or the frustration everybody talks about and nobody manages. This theme—it could be a product, a market, a leader's behavior, an unresolved conflict, a dysfunctional structure, a goal—intrudes at every step. Every event becomes a lightning rod, on every agenda the central process issue is the hidden item. No matter what we appear to be doing, the central theme walks silently into the room, sits down in the corner, and takes over the meeting. When all efforts to get things on track fail, we know that an organizational process issue has got people feeling out of control.

I remember a medical task force that took a day to discover a dirty secret: physicians did not like having a Ph.D. for their dean. Until they owned it, they couldn't work. I think of the paralyzing connection between marketing and production that colors every event in one factory where I work. The marketing person opposes change, the producfion manager insists on it, and the common boss refuses to become involved. Such themes mock our theories of practice and defy our technologies. Despite them, we plug away, seeking to preserve our core values with those who value what we do, struggling to keep what we cannot control from aborting the good that might still be done.

An OD practice theory won't be of much practical value if it doesn't account for the lightning rod effect of every intervention.

1987: Using the Phenomenon

Getting whole systems in the room to flow chart themselves (work design), or to look at past, present, and future (search conference) takes advantage of the lightning rod effect. Everything of consequence is attracted by the setting and the tasks. Because people are present across functions and levels, they have a chance both to learn and redo. The task itself—not the diagnosis and action plan—takes care of the symptoms. (Notice, even here I can't yet give up medical lingo!) The most extraordinary offshoots of work redesign frequently are neither planned nor anticipated. They happen in "real time" *during* the design process, as people start redoing their work based on what they have learned in meetings. I have seen dramatic changes take place in systems long before the design team has a new plan. (Try selling that service to clients!)

DIFFERENT STROKES FOR DIFFERENT FOLKS

1982: Input and Output

For years I've been bemused by the fact that most OD success stories come from factories. Elsewhere I've discussed the differences between "input-focused" organizations—hospitals, law firms, personnel departments—and "output-focused" industry with concrete goals and measureable results (Weisbord, 1978a). I have never doubted these differences have profound implications for a practice based on participative and collaborative processes. By now every practitioner knows that not every task calls for mutual work, and professionals in particular resist accountability. Every organization, however, has a core process which matters vey much to its members, and on which its survival depends. Invariably this is linked to the "customer." In R&D labs, for instance, two competing processes are the heart of the matter—fire-fighting, and innovation. In hospitals, quality patient care and lower costs are key driving forces; in factories, product quality at low cost; in sales organizations, product knowledge and selling skills.

A new practice theory of OD would put these core organizational issues front and center in *every* intervention. No matter what the "presenting problem" is, we would seek to diagnose and reinterpret in light of what we know about that organization's raison d'être. The client, in the most profound sense, moves to center stage, not the consultant, not the technique, and not process-focused solutions like conflict management. Our technology would be placed at the service of linking the core issue, individual needs and concerns, and various techniques for enhancing support, self-esteem, influence, problem solving and output.

I believe the shortest road to valid data, free choice, and commitment lies in the direction of an organization's survival issue. This is not obvious to clients. Yet, if we are to make a more whole profession of OD, we must learn how to articulate this phenomenon in our practice theory.

1987: Working on Economics and Technology

In my book I make a case for improving relationships faster through structural change—giving people broader responsibility for economics and technology—than with the "talking cure." Hence my notion of assessing the potential for change, and not revisiting the problem list. OD, in my view, ought not be done as a "health checkup," nor as a trip through past problems with an eye to solving them. Instead, we need a unifying purpose—adapting to new markets, or new technologies, or new leadership, or saving jobs—that affects everybody. OD needs to be task-focused and system-focused to succeed. That requires leadership and some energized people. Without them, nothing works. With them, a problem "diagnosis" is not needed, only a plausible rationale for bringing people together, and systems improvement tasks for them to do. These are best figured out in collaboration with members of the organization.

IS IT OD OR TRAINING?

1982: An Increasingly Useless Distinction

For years I saw a clear distinction between OD and "just" training. The distinction is reinforced in numerous training departments where education has been disconnected from the core purposes of the organization, and relegated to a technical specialty which builds individual competence. OD's development is largely the story of our struggle to transfer workshop learning to the workplace.

Team building supplanted T-groups as a preferred way for learning and applying task/process knowledge because it short-circuits this problem. The boss supplies impetus; the consultant a procedure and a theory; the team data, energy, and ideas. People learn and do in tandem. Is it training? Or consulting? Does the distinction matter?

Increasingly, I see all forms of training as consultation—learners supplying data, consultants "contracting" with the learners for content and process, learning and doing. The more I consult the more obvious it becomes to me that every consulting intervention has a potential educational component. It's impossible to change a policy, procedure, system, start a new organization, reorganize an old one, bring in a new technology, without identifying some important things people need to know how to do. Each change points towards training. Each training event points towards policies, procedures, systems, or practices which should be changed to support the skills and attitudes being learned.

Finally, both training and policy/procedural change usually surface "ill-structured" problems, the ones not subject to solution in the formal system. These require group problem solving and decision making. This in turn requires training, which in turn raises policy questions. A practice theory of OD will incorporate this developmental cycle linking individual learning with organizational processes, rather than reinforce artificial distinctions between learning and doing.

1987

The trouble with "training" is that it smacks of perpetuating authority-dependency relationships. That's obviously so when people are ordered into it, no matter how "good" the content is. It's paradoxical that people have been ordered into workshops purporting to teach openness, free choice, and commitment. In my book I discuss my own ambivalence with training. I've usually been either too soon or too late. The "wrong people" often turn out to be in the room. Partly my ambivalence comes from experience. In the 1960s I started self-managing work teams in a company where I was executive vice president, a story I have written about elsewhere (Weisbord, 1985) and in the prologue to my book. Every hoped for result—economic, social, and technical—flowed from that restructuring of work. People's relationships improved without interpersonal skills training. Conflict was reduced without conflict management workshops. Meetings became productive without meeting management workshops. People began finishing work at 3:00 p.m. and prowled the office looking for useful work—without training in time management. So I know that eliminating traditional supervision, building in self-control, and broadening everybody's skills goes a long way towards realizing "OD values" without any process training at all. Yet, I value what I have learned about the task-process relationship, and how this understanding contributes to my knowledge of work. It leads me to be much more judicious about prescribing training for whatever ails people.

I'm skeptical that people can't embark on "change" projects until they've been trained how to do it. That's one way to go, but not the only way. We must be very clear that our need to train others—before we let them into our ball game—perpetuates and reinforces dependency, which we claim to be against. This can only be obviated when the learners really can make an informed choice about whether and when to have workshops. Hence my "useful guildine" that we should seek to structure tasks that people can do for themselves, rather than train facilitators or become de facto group leaders for long stretches.

This understanding has been greatly reinforced for me in the work of Merrelyn (1982) and Fred Emergy. As a result of it, my firm has been able to manage unusual work reorganization conferences of 30–80 people looking together at their own organization and redesigning it with minimal "training" input. A notable example is Great Lakes Steel Co., where five labor-management teams in 1986 were redesigning all the operations, working under the guidance of union and management people who had studied what was possible and some simple ways to make it happen.

CULTURAL CHANGE

1982: Cultures Persist

Much OD rhetoric holds out "cultural change" as the purpose of organization development. I find this a hard proposition to accept anymore for three reasons. First, the predominant characteristics of cultures are their durability, persistence, functionality, and consistency of features. When a whole culture changes itself, it's in response to intolerable outside pressures over time—an irresistable new technology, like automobiles or computers—rather than through rational planning of its members. Secondly, what we call "cultural change"—towards a more open, supportive place, where people have influence, responsibility, a chance to grow and achieve and succeed in the world—can be as ephemeral as an early morning fog.

A new boss can dismantle in weeks or months a "culture" that took years to develop. Can a quality so fragile truly be called "cultural change?" Just as democracy is never secure in society, so open systems cannot be secured once and for all at work through planned OD techniques. Finally, there is another way to think entirely about the link between organizations and culture. The democratic values underlying OD derive squarely from a larger culture. They are values widely supported and institutionalized in our society. The "change" we advocate is to bring American values into the workplace—to make work more congruent with our beliefs about social and political organizations in general. This can be seen as cultural affirmation as much as change—the creation of more open systems in the workplace.

What I see myself doing, rhetoric aside, is to invite, help, push, cajole, entice, facilitate this person, these people—the ones sitting here with me now, today, this minute, in this room—to compare notes they've never compared before, to say what means most to them, to understand their situation in a new way, to find the better parts of themselves, the constructive impulses for wholeness and community. If a culture is under enough pressure to change, the culture will change itself, whether we intervene or not. I am at once awed and humbled by this realization. We can nudge an organization down a path its leaders have chosen or help dampen the wild careening when it's caught in the rapids of change. No "OD tricks" will help an organization whose members have not chosen their own path, or chosen to influence the path they have been forced to travel.

A theory of OD based on how we actually practice ought to include the observation that change has already occurred when somebody chooses to contract with us. We are the result as much as the cause. It's as easy to say change plans us rather than the other way around. The nature of the desired change is "process" as much as outcome. Thus, there is no one point in time when we say, "Aha, the culture has now changed."

Rather, the process of change continues in the right direction depending largely on how each of us behaves right now. We are honest or we lie. We include others or we cut them out. We find links between our techniques and people's needs or run a game on somebody until they balk. We advocate grand schemes or modest ones. Each intervention represents a change. Each must portray our beliefs and values as accurately as possible, and our practice theory must highlight the essentiality of this.

1987: OD as Cultural Preservation

I see work restructuring as cultural preservation—preserving the most cherished values of American democracy. It is a profoundly conservative practice this way, radical only in its assertion that the traditional boss/subordinate relationship with its expectations, performance appraisals and all the rest is the best way to achieve output. Self-managing teams achieve greater output than the world has ever known before, greater than Frederick Taylor imagined was possible, and greater than the limits imposed by engineers who design machinery today. These teams operate with norms closer to American ideals of individual dignity and collective security than the average bureaucracy will permit.

One more thing, Edward Lawler (1986) makes a point I have not seen in print before. His research shows that places that have operated a long time under participative principles are just as hard to "regress" to more authoritarian modes as they were to change in the first place. That is a new development in my experience, and very encouraging.

RESISTANCE TO CHANGE

1982: Who Shall Overcome?

For years I've been bemused by the tendency of true believers, including client converts, to label co-workers "change resisters," or "Theory X types" or "authoritarians." This is done in the name of behavioral science. Yet, among the few things we know for sure in this work are (1) labeling people puts them further behind the eight-ball. "Behind the resistance," writes Peter Block (1981), "are certain feelings. You cannot talk people out of how they are feeling. Feelings pass and change when they get expressed directly."

Tony Petrella has a structure he calls "skeptics corner." Those opposed to a course of action are invited to talk it over alone, then make their case, to which others are asked to give a serious hearing. This nearly always results in better mutual understanding. The advocates of change find merit in the skeptics' arguments. The skeptics find their worst fears may be less scary in daylight than hidden in dark corners, and expressed only through the restroom door.

The implications for an OD practice theory are at once simple and profound. If we wish to help a system become more open, better balanced, more fit to survive, a better place to work, we must seek out, encourage, support and get a legitimate hearing for "resistance," especially when our own pet ideas are at stake. We should encourage the possibility that what we represent has drawbacks that need to be taken seriously. We should seek to internalize this so thoroughly it is not a technique but a core value. We should require that people demonstrate competence in it before receiving an MBA.

Finally, I think we should use more descriptive, less pejorative words for the "holding on" phenomenon: legitimate concerns, reservations, other points of view. The energy represented by people with legitimate concerns is an enormous force for good. We should welcome it when we find it, trust that it can't be wished away, and work diligently to harness its constructive potential.

1987

Amen.

FREEZING AND UNFREEZING—THE THEORY OF (SEMI) STEADY STATES

1982: Updating Lewin

While I strongly advocate action research, I can't practice any longer to another of the late Kurt Lewin's concepts—that organizations are altered by "unfreezing," "moving," and "refreezing." This theory contends that when a system experiences enough trauma it comes apart at the seams, disrupting the status quo. This forces new practices that in turn become the norm.

My recent practice has been in two kinds of industries—those in decline, such as steel and autos, and those on the rise, like computers and software. Steel companies are in constant turmoil—reduced work forces, closed plants, reduced executive compensation, fewer levels of management, labor/management participation teams, a rethinking of production, maintenance, quality, and capital equipment. People feel demoralized, insecure, out-of-control, and overstressed. This trend is likely to go on indefinitely. It's hard to imagine a new "steady state," for steel, but only a state of rapid and ongoing transition.

In the computer world, I see the same phenomenon on the up side—a growth curve so rapid that each new organizational form, policy, procedure, or system seems to have a half-life of approximately three months. The new "generations" of products tumble out so fast that the machine you buy today is obsolete before you open the box. If you wait six months, you jump three generations. Computer people are drowning in a sea of opportunity. A software house I know will go from 400 to 1,600 people in a few years. None of its managers ever ran a business before this one. People feel upbeat, optimistic, on the one hand, and insecure, out-of-control, and overstressed, on the other. What's the competition doing? Who will get "there" first? In short, I see a state of permanent change, transition, movement, with things put "in place" this week and rearranged next.

I can't practice an "unfreezing-refreezing" model in these places. But what *do* I do? It would be dandy if the computer folk would sit still for some in-depth management training. And if ever a place needed a thorough socio-technical redesign it's an American steel mill. But what do I do while looking for somebody who wishes to implement my grand prescriptions? People wracked this way and that by the winds of change tend to spend all their time wiring things together.

So I consult to as much of the system as will have me and I look for openings. I listen. I watch for who wants to scratch which itches. I draw graphs and charts, and conceptualize how Group A and Group B relate to Customer C. I do not do any unfreezing—people are already awash in hot water. I ride along in a state of permanent, ongoing transition, looking for ways to carve out projects, programs, and activities that will enhance people's sense of competence, enlarge their influence and mutual support, teach them something about problem solving, increase productivity.

1987: Who Needs Unfreezing?

The action research model evolved as a way of unfreezing systems. The purpose of a diagnosis is to confront people with discrepancies—between the way things are and the way they should be, between what they say and what they do. The assumption is that this data collection and feedback creates "cognitive dissonance," that out of the discussion the "ownership" of the diagnosis is transferred from consultant to client, and that only when this happens does the real work begin. But under conditions of what my friend Peter Vaill calls "permanent white water," why should the consultant "own" the data, even temporarily, if there is no need to unfreeze a system? That leads me into rethinking what the consultant's stance should be toward data and diagnosis. I have already expressed why I do not like the medical lingo. Perhaps "assessment" is a better term for the initial consultant activity. And what should be assessed is the potential for action—the locus of leadership, the fact of a business opportunity, the existence of some energized people already doing things responsive to the organization's dilemmas. The action proposal should be a structure for weaving all that into a way for people to take firmer charge of their futures. In my book I make the point that to honor Lewin today, we must go beyond him. We are not dealing with "quasi-stationery" equilibriums any more (if we ever were). If we are to take the cause-effect thinking out of it, eliminate the medical jargon, reaffirm the centrality of community, dignity, and meaning, then we have to look critically at traditional action research. It was a half-way house between Taylorism and "new paradigm" thinking. But we have a long way to go to make new paradigms live in OD practice. We will not do it so long as consultants believe it is their role to collect the data, organize it, feed it back, and lead people by the hand to figure out what it means and what to do about it. That's last decade's model.

GRAND STRATEGIES, TOTAL SYSTEMS CHANGE

1982: Few Stay the Course

Blake and Mouton's (1964) "Grid OD" involves six phases of increasing complexity involving an entire system. Few organizations have gone beyond the second phase. Likert's (1967) survey methodology—moving from System 1 towards System 4, has been used by a number of organizations. Only a tiny handful have ever taken the whole course—annual resurveys, feedback and problem solving at all levels. Socio-technical redesign—the rethinking of an entire system—has been done in several factories. In many ways it is the most practical of the whole system change strategies. Yet, only 13 percent of the United States workforce can be found in factories, and the number is shrinking. While the concept can be modified to fit office work, hospitals, or schools, many problems attend its widespread application in these places.

There are a number of new total systems change models under the general heading of quality-of-working-life. Only a tiny handful of organizations have sought to apply them. I have been involved in perhaps 6 or 8 of these "total system" efforts in 15 years. I've been unusually lucky, many OD consultants, especially internal, never get to work on a large systems effort, using grand designs, multiple techniques, and long-range strategies.

Yet, this "whole culture" approach to change, contracted up front by all parties, is what many textbooks say defines our field. By extension that means if you're doing anything less, you aren't doing "it." This perpetuates the OD analogue to the business school mystique, in which every graduate of certain elite places comes out expecting to be president. Every budding OD consultant emerges from the cocoon expecting to change corporate, academic, governmental cultures—to contract with people who are thinking of nothing else. Of course, such fantasies lead to disappointment.

Just as all physicians cannot be neurosurgeons, all OD consultants cannot work on grand strategies. Relatively few people are prepared to contract for the service. For that reason, a general theory of OD practice must come to grips with the myriad of other things OD consultants do besides move whole systems all at once.

For every success story there are hundreds of workaday OD projects, consultants and clients slogging through the mud together, working to make things better. Our models, strategies and rhetoric do not account for this, although clearly the thousand-mile journey is always made one step at a time.

When I was a manager I had a recurring fantasy: Somebody comes in one day and says, "We're sharpening too many pencils around here." I investigate and find myself involved with every nook and cranny of the business—from customer service, purchasing, production, shipping, receiving, billing, and bad debts. I find loopholes in order processing, disconnects in the factory, coordination gaps between sales and manufacturing, glaring inequities among young and old, black and white, men and women, labor and management, Italians, Jews, Poles, and Wasps, a leaky faucet dripping on machine no. 3, a lost inventory of products abandoned years before in a remote corner of the factory, and, probably, a stowaway living in the washroom.

I have no doubt everything is hooked up to everything else, mind, body, technology, people, cultures, societies, continents, and the cosmos. I am equally certain that nobody, but nobody, works on all of it at the same time, or is even capable of conceiving the connections. *Measuring and Assessing Organizations* (Van de Ven & Ferry, 1980) lists 42 variables a consultant might work on and hundreds of questions for checking them out. New variables are being added all the time.

What we need are simple concepts that cover a lot of ground—always diagnosing a system in terms of the one it's a part of, for example. The important thing, I think, is to be mindful that an organization is a system. Let us not confuse our ability to conceptualize the system with the power to change it.

1987: Whole-Brain Thinking

I'm more convinced than ever that the answer to the dilemma I raised above is in "whole-brain" thinking (Buzan, 1974). One "old paradigm" notion dressed up in new paradigm clothes is the concept of "planned changed," a super-rational exercise of steps, phases, strategies, models, explicit philosophies and value statements, and conscious choices at every turn. This has resurfaced as transformation in some quarters—new content, old processes, What constitutes "systems change" and how is it achieved?

In search conferences and work redesign projects I have been involved with the past five years, I have noticed a recurring phenomenon. People will do a technical analysis—a flow chart of the whole system and what's not working where. This is one early step in a redesign, which may be months away. Yet, the very next day people start using what they have learned to alter the system. They are able to do this because (a) the analytical task focuses on how the whole contraption works, rather than discrete problems, (b) all the relevant actors are present in the room and arrive together at new understandings of how things work. They cannot help using what they have learned, they would be irresponsible if they did not. I've never seen an analogous result from normative diagnoses. People can list the "unwritten rules of behavior" until it's apple blossom time in Anarctica. They can make pious declarations—we are now going to permit and learn from mistakes—but I have never seen them go out next day and change anything of consequence as a result. A workplace is a system glued together by its work, not its norms. Unless we change the structure and processes of the work, we stand not a prayer of altering its norms. The structure and processes cannot be altered by solving piecemeal undifferentiated problems listed and prioritized on a flip chart. Each person has to see how the whole contraption functions, from what comes in to what goes out, and what the customer experiences—for it to be called "systems change."

LEADERSHIP

1982: Not Genetic

Social science has never been able to find a "leadership gene," a set of innate traits shared by successful leaders. At the same time, the research on successful organizations has largely been empirical—watching what the high performers do that the low performers don't do. That's what Lawrence and Lorsch (1967) did, comparing factories in the same industry to figure out why one was so much more productive than another. That's what the late Rensis Likert (1960) did when he compared high- and low-producing managers and concluded that the secret of success was high standards, supportive behavior, and group methods of supervision.

Peter Vaill (1982) has observed that leaders of high-performing systems care passionately, work their tails off, and have an intuitive feel for the (few) right variables to manage. In short, what we know about leadership behavior comes from watching successful people do it. Management development evolved as a practice in the belief that what high performers do already can be bottled and imbibed by the rest of us. This is a hypothesis, not a fact. Our models purport to help managers zero in on the right variables, but we have no training technologies to help them learn to work their tails off or to care very much. I don't know how to instill Likert's high standards into somebody who has low standards, sloppy standards, or no standards. I think supportive behavior can be learned, and so can group methods. But a certain orientation towards goals and purposes, I think, is either there or it isn't. It may be latent, in which case we help somebody awaken that side of themselves. But if it isn't there, we cannot put it there.

Theory X, I am convinced, is rooted deeply in Western religious concepts of original sin and eternal punishment. Parents who act on it undermine latent self-esteem in babies, and supervisors inadvertently reinforce low self-esteem in grown-ups. It is very difficult for somebody with a lousy self-concept to successfully lead an organization down paths of risk taking, experimentation, open dialogue, and a problem-solving approach to interpersonal and task conflict.

I think successful OD clients are those whose values already tend towards Theory Y, whose self-image is strong enough to risk failure, whose beliefs are strong enough to risk having them translated into action. Curiously, the best clients turn out to be those with the least "need." Because they are good users of resources, they know how to ask for help.

My complete practice theory must incorporate the centrality of a *person* as driving force—some visionary in the client organization willing and able to mobilize energy.

1987: The X/Y Dialogue in Each of Us

I now see X and Y as two sides of each of us, each with a positive valence *and* a negative one. The "shadow"—unconscious, avoided impulses—dogs all of us, pushing us towards and away from this or that idea, value, or practice. The projection—parts of me I admire or reject—leads me to like and join or separate from others. Theory X can be reinterpreted constructively as a need for structure, stability, and certainty, and Theory Y negatively as ambivalence, anarchy, and purposelessness. In my book I show why this might be so. Suffice to say here that connecting with a person—a leader who wants to make certain values live— is the core dimension of OD practice. Our techniques are not willy-nilly useable because they're such good techniques. They "work" only for people who have compatible values that can be hooked by the activities proposed by the consultant.

I think my 1982 formulation of the client is too idealistic and dogmatic. Part of the consultant's responsibility is to see how much of the hidden dimension can be evoked and put in service of organizational tasks. I'll settle for somebody with an itch to scratch who is willing to include others and is open to trying on for size unfamiliar behavior. I can't help somebody who insists they already know the answer, or have figured out in detail what they want me to do—unless I can move them off it.

OPEN SYSTEMS

1982: A Key Concept

I am thinking of the concept, not the planning technique. Open systems is more than a concept—it is for me the quintessential linkage between democracy and science. I believe that the core process of OD, its central value, is in fostering greater openess, between people, groups, organizations. Closed systems strangle, open systems balance themselves. Paradoxically, the proliferation of small computers may have a greater impact on opening systems than all the combined OD interventions of the past 30 years.

"When computers are installed," writes business editor Tom Richman (1982), "the men at the top can no longer control information. They can't parcel it out when they want, to whom they want. The computer is smashing the Soviet pyramid, and the same thing is happening in the U.S. corporation."

A practice theory of OD ought to account for the human advantages of more open systems.

1987: Look What's Happening

I think that the core behavioral value of OD—openness—is both a scientific and political reality in Western democracies. And the Russian move towards *glasnost* validates Richman's observation. In researching my book I found that Fred Emery had brought systems thinking to Tavistock in the early 1950s—starting a stream of work that continues to evolve to this day. The most obvious manifestation is in "search conferences," meetings of 50–60 or more people to look together at the past, present, and future of a system they care about. This is open systems thinking in action.

EVALUATION

1982: Proving That "It Works"

Burke (1982) lists 10 major studies proving that OD "works." Dunn and Swierzek's (1976) studies of successful major change efforts showed weak correlations of success with participation and collaboration, and no correlations with anything else. Since all versions of OD incorporate some combination of process and outcome, obviously success means desirable outcomes achieved by desirable processes.

Nothing less will do. So I think it's asking the wrong question to ask whether survey feedback or team building "work"—or socio-technical redesign, or open systems planning. Everything works. Nothing works. In OD there are no cause-effect relationships, and everybody knows this. It is hardly necessary to research the technologies anymore—they have all worked brilliantly, and they have all failed. To paraphrase Shakespeare, the fault is not in our models, it's in ourselves. Bad contracts make for bad interventions.

What's a bad contract? It's one in which the core values of OD are somehow compromised. If I were building an evaluation model of OD, I'd include these questions:

1. Was the self-esteem and competence of the people I worked with enhanced, or at least not reduced?
2. Was there evidence of increased mutual support and mutual influence among co-workers?
3. Did people move towards making decisions and solving problems considered important and not acted on before?
4. Did output, results, performance—as an organization—improve?

Bad contracts invariably result from:

1. A weak rationale for doing anything (e.g., the consultant's need for research, the boss's wish to "fix" somebody else's department).

2. A diagnosis in which the consultant did not participate. Somebody else wrote the prescription and hired a consultant as a sort of pharmacist/nurse, to mix and administer it.
3. Cutting out of the original decision one or more people whose influence and support are important.
4. Acting in such a way that others feel less competent, more helpless—threatening workshop exercises, for example, where only the consultant knows the intent and acts very mysterious.
5. Failure to link the contract, whatever it happens to be, to central purposes and requirements of the organization.
6. Failure to build into the contract a chance for diverse views to be heard and taken seriously.
7. Failure to contract with a person in authority who has energy, vision, commitment and a willingness to take some personal risk in order to learn something new.
8. Failure to choose and apply a theory of change to the situation which fits client experience, values, and desire to act.

These are all failures of consultant behavior, not technologies. Techniques in my opinion, are all contingent—what you do, use, recommend, depends on the situation. Snapshooting is largely a contingency matter. There are as many ways to diagnose a system as there are consultants, problems, and clients multiplied by each other. There is, in my opinion, only one way to make a movie. Acting out the process of change is normative, as indicated by the rules implied by my eight failure scripts.

Sometimes we facilitate, sometimes we prescribe. Always, we keep our eyes on others' self-esteem, influence, support, energy, and output, as well as our own. It's not good enough to hit two or three. We need all of them. We need them now, in this meeting. We need not wait to figure out what we've got.

When I join in listing 83 skills for future practitioners, it seems to me, I collude with and perpetuate the very diseases consultants ought to be fighting: fragmentation, alienation from knowledge, feelings of hopelessness in the face of complexity, a sense that I'll never know enough to be able to cope. The more complicated and diverse the models, technologies, and typologies of OD become, the more fragmented, uneven, and confusing is the practice.

To talk about these matters, we need a much simpler common language—one rooted in everyday experience and corresponding more closely to the way practitioners experience what they do. This is no small task. If it were easy, we wouldn't all be groping and there would be a great deal more clarity about the connections between theory and practice. I would like to know—in more than an experiential way—the power and limits of this new variation on an old theme called OD. Of course, I am, in the jargon of the trade, speaking only for myself. However, I'm very curious to know how other members of the group feel.

1987: OD as Directionality

After writing for five years, I was able, one week before my publisher's deadline, to put the story of *Productive Workplaces* on one sheet of paper. The chart labeled "Learning Curve" sums up my story. If you believe in community, dignity, and meaning as critical for viable organizations, if you believe that whole-brain thinking and whole systems improvement go hand in hand, if you believe all people have a right and a responsibility to participate in deciding their own workplace's future, if you believe the world is changing too fast for experts, if you believe that bringing people together across lines of status, hierarchy, function, specialty, culture, race, gender, and national borders is the only way to save our planet, you cannot escape the learning curve. We must learn the right moves along both dimensions at once, from problem solving to whole systems improvement, from experts doing it to everybody doing it. That's what OD's past tells me, what our present behavior suggests, and what our future requires.

REFERENCES

Argyris, C. (1970). *Intervention theory and method.* Reading, MA: Addison-Wesley.

Baum, L. (1900). *The wizard of Oz.* New York: Grosset and Dunlap.

Bellah, R., Madsen, R., Sullivan, W., Swidler, A., & Tipton, S. (1985). *Habits of the heart: Individualism and commitment in American life.* Berkeley: University of California Press.

Beckhard, R. (1969). *Organization development: Strategies and models.* Reading, MA: Addison-Wesley.

Bennis, W. (1966). *Changing organizations.* New York: McGraw-Hill.

Bennis, W., Benne, K., & Chin, R. (1969). *The planning of change,* (2d Ed.), New York: Holt, Rinehart and Winston.

Blake, R. & Mouton, J. (1964). *The managerial grid.* Houston, Texas: Gulf Publishing.

Block, P. (1981). *Flawless consulting.* Austin, Texas: Learning Concepts.

Burke, W. (1982). *Organization development; principles and practices.* Boston: Little, Brown and Company.

Buzan, T. (1974). *Use both sides of your brain.* New York: E. P. Dutton, Publishers.

Dunn, W. & Swierzek, F. (1977). Planned organizational change: Toward grounded theory. *Journal of Applied Behavioral Science, 13,* Vol. 2, 135–157.

Emery, F. & Trist, E. (1960). Sociotechnical systems. In F. E. Emery (Ed.), *Systems thinking.* Harmondsworth, Penguin.

Emery, M. (1982). Searching: For new directions, in new ways for new times. Canberra, Australia. Centre for Continuing Education, Australian National University. GPO Box 4, Canberra 2601.

Geertz, C. (1973). *The interpretation of cultures.* New York: Basic Books.

Janssen, C. (1975). *Personlig dialektik.* Stockholm: Liber, 2d Ed., 1982.

Lawler, E., III (1968). *High-involvement management.* San Francisco: Jossey-Bass.

Lawrence, P. & Lorsch, J. (1967). *Organization and environment.* Boston, MA: Harvard University Press.

Lewin, K. (1947). Frontiers in group dynamics: Concept, method and reality in social science: Social equilibria and social change. Human Relations, 1, 5–41.

Likert, R. (1960). *New patterns of management.* New York: McGraw-Hill.

Lippitt, R., Watson, J., & Westley, B. (1958). *Planned change.* New York: Harcourt, Brace & World.

Marrow, A. (1969). *The practical theorist*. New York: Basic Books.

Richman, T. (1982). Peering into tomorrow. *INC., October*, 45–48.

Shepard, K. D., and Raia, A. P. (1981). "The OD Training Challenge," *Training & Development Journal*, April, 90–96.

Taylor, F. (1915). *The principles of scientific management*. New York: Harper & Brothers.

Toffler, A. (1980). *The Third Wave*. New York: McGraw-Hill.

Tolstoy, L. (1978). *Anna Karenina*. Indianapolis: Bobbs-Merrill.

Trist, E. (1981). *The evolution of sociotechnical systems: A conceptual framework and an action research program*. Occasional paper No. 2, June. Ontario Quality of Working Life Centre, Ontario, Canada.

Trist, E. & Emery F. (1960). Report on the Barford conference for Bristol/Siddeley, Areo-Engine Corp. July 10–16, Tavistock TIHR, Document No. 598, London.

Van De Ven, A. & Ferry, D. (1980). *Measuring and assessing organizations*. New York: John Wiley & Sons.

Vaill, B. (1982). The purposing of high-performance systems. *Organizational Dynamics*, Autumn. New York: American Management Associations.

Weisbord, M. (1977). How do you know it works if you don't know what it is? *OD Practitioner, 9(3), October.*

Weisbord, M. (1978a). Input versus output-focused organizations: Notes on a contingency theory of practice. In W. W. Burke (Ed.), *The cutting edge: Current theory and practice in organization development*. La Jolla, CA: University Associates.

Weisbord, M. (1978b). *Organizational diagnosis: A workbook of theory and practice*. New York: Addison-Wesley.

Weisbord, M. (1978c). The wizard of OD: Or, what have magic slippers to do with burnout, evaluation, resistance, planned change, and action research? *OD Practitioner, 10(2), July.*

Weisbord, M. (1981). Some reflections on OD's identity crisis. *Group & Organization Studies, 6(2), June,* 161–175.

Weisbord, M. (1985a). The cat in the hat breaks through: Reflections on OD's past, present, and future. In D. D. Warrick (Ed.), *Contemporary organization development: Current thinking & applications*. Glenview, IL: Scott Foreman & Co., 2–11.

Weisbord, M. (1985b). Participative work design: A personal odyssey. *Organizational Dynamics, 13(4),* Spring.

Weisbord, M. (1987a). *Productive workplaces: Organizing and managing for dignity, meaning and community*. San Francisco, Jossey-Bass.

Weisbord, M. (1987b). Toward third-wave managing and consulting. *Organizational dynamics, 15(3),* Winter.

Wolfe, T. (1980). *The right stuff*. New York: Bantam.

THE INTERPLAY OF
ORGANIZATION DEVELOPMENT
AND ORGANIZATIONAL
TRANSFORMATION

Jean M. Bartunek and Meryl Reis Louis

ABSTRACT

Organization Development and organizational transformation represent two different approaches to the understanding of organizational change. Each approach has
its own integrity. However, they also overlap in several ways. This chapter has two
purposes: to enable OD and organizational transformation to inform the other and
to enable the two approaches, considered jointly, to inform the larger understanding of change. We first situate OD and organizational transformation within the
larger context of change and explore similarities and differences between them.
Then we describe the contributions each approach can make to the other. Finally,
on the basis of the joint consideration of the two approaches, we pose several

Research in Organizational Change and Development, Vol. 2, pages 97–134.
Copyright © 1988 by JAI Press Inc.
All rights of reproduction in any form reserved.
ISBN: 0-89232-772-3

questions that should be addressed for a more adequate understanding of organizational change. Issues considered in the chapter include the implications of particular transformations and life cycle stages for OD interventions, ways in which learnings from OD practice can foster a more complete understanding of the dynamics of transformations, the meanings of the consultant role, directions of organizational change, the labeling of problems, and, finally, appropriate questions to be asked in the assessment of change.

INTRODUCTION

What do Organization Development and organizational transformation have to say to each other? How can each approach foster the development of the other? How can their joint consideration foster an increased understanding of larger issues regarding organizational change? These questions introduce the central concerns addressed in this chapter.

Since its early years, Organization Development has included several core components, such as an emphasis on humanistic, democratic values, the use of action research, a focus on changing an organization's culture, and the use of consultants to facilitate change (e.g., Burke, 1982, 1987; French & Bell, 1984; Huse & Cummings, 1985; Margulies & Raia, 1978). Several successful diagnostic and intervention techniques that derive from these core components have been developed and widely disseminated. They have enabled a "high involvement" paradigm for OD/QWL practice to emerge (e.g., Lawler, 1986; Mohrman & Lawler, 1985). They have also enabled evaluations of change which assess whether particular pre-specified outcomes of OD efforts such as increased participation in decision making and improved conflict management skills are achieved (e.g., Woodman & Wayne, 1985). Finally, they have enabled the beginnings of a theory of organizational change formulated from an OD perspective (e.g., Porras & Robertson, 1987).

Organization development is not the only approach to organizational change. In the past few years a different approach, variously labeled as organizational transformation (e.g., Quinn & Cameron, in press), or as an organizational life cycle perspective (e.g., Kimberly & Miles, 1980), has been developing. In general, this alternative perspective has had as its primary focus large-scale changes in organizational form that occur throughout an organization's life cycle. Examples of such transformations include the YMCA's change from a Christian reading club in London to a "gym with social services attached" (March, 1981), AT&T's transformations from an R&D organization to a telephone system to a high-technology company (Tunstall, 1985; Tushman & Romanelli, 1985), Triangle Industries' change from a juke box and vending machine manufacturer to a can maker and food packager, and American Can's shift from a can maker to a financial services and specialty retail business (Schmitt,

1986). More narrow changes in the understanding of how to carry out some specific organizational function are also considered by the transformational perspective. Chao, Moch, and Malik (1986), for example, have described how shifts in performance appraisal systems from those based on traditional management approaches to those based on the high involvement paradigm are analogous, on a smaller level, to more large-scale changes in organizational form.

The types of phenomena explored by investigators who focus on OD and organizational transformation are in some respects quite similar. For example, both groups are concerned about the culture of an organization, its shared meanings, beliefs, and values. Both groups have a special interest in how culture may change. Moreover, OD interventions sometimes require organizational transformation to be successful (Bartunek & Moch, 1987). However, while the two groups deal with some of the same phenomena, they frequently address different questions regarding change. Three illustrations follow. The primary focus of OD is on processes through which to facilitate (often) pre-specified changes (such as, for example, improved conflict management skills). In contrast, the primary focus of organizational transformation is on a mapping of patterns of change in organizational form (such as, for example, changes in the organization's mission, values, and structure). The ways the two approaches link a consultant role with change attempts are quite different, with this role considered central to OD but not crucial for organizational transformation. Finally, the types of research methods considered integral for studying change vary considerably, with direct researcher involvement in change part of the action research tradition of OD, but not part of the organizational transformation approach.

Both OD and organizational transformation offer well developed perspectives on organizational change, perspectives which have their own integrity. In this chapter, we attempt neither to combine or collapse them into a single perspective, nor to synthesize a new perspective out of the differing "old" ones. Rather, we treat OD and organizational transformation as two distinct points of view concerning overlapping phenomenal domains. We attempt to enrich each approach by examining it simultaneously with the other, suggesting ways each can inform the other, and moving toward a more comprehensive approach to organizational change by working with both views in mind. Contrary to some other discussions (e.g., Beer & Walton, 1987), we are not attempting to develop a new vision or orientation for either OD or organizational transformation that corresponds directly to the other approach. Instead, our aim has more of a process orientation. We hope to set in motion processes by which dialogue between the two approaches can foster the ongoing development of understandings of organizational change.

To achieve our purposes for this chapter, we first indicate some basic distinctions that can be made about types of organizational change and describe both approaches within the context of these distinctions. We then identify similarities and differences between OD and organizational transformation approaches.

From there we outline implications for the theory, practice, and assessment of the two approaches to change and organizational change in general.

TYPES OF ORGANIZATIONAL CHANGE

What types of change occur in organizations, and what are the perspectives of OD and organizational transformation on them? We introduce below two issues regarding change that will be pertinent to our future discussion.

First- and Second-order Change

On a regular basis throughout their life cycles, organizations experience events that signal and/or provoke a need to change in some way. Many of these changes represent incremental modifications in ways of acting, improvements that take place within already accepted frameworks. These types of change have been labeled first order (cf. Argyris & Schön, 1978; Bartunek, 1984; Bartunek & Moch, 1987; Golembiewski, 1986; Hedberg, 1981; Watzlawick, Weakland, & Fisch, 1974). One example of first-order change is an increase in employee participation in decision making when the definition of participation remains constant. A second is increased commitment to the organization's mission.

In contrast, other changes represent discontinuous shifts in frameworks, in which organizational members come to understand constructs in new ways. These have been labeled second-order changes (cf. Argyris & Schön, 1978; Bartunek, 1984; Bartunek & Moch, 1987; Golembiewski, 1986; Hedberg, 1981; Levy, 1986; Watzlawick, Weakland, & Fisch, 1974). One example might be a qualitative change in the understanding of participation in decision making. Employees might no longer think of consultation in decisions as illustrative of participation, but might, instead, view employee ownership as necessary for real participation to be taking place. Another example might be a qualitative shift in the understanding of the organization's mission and identity such as that described earlier for AT&T, in which organizational members come to think of their primary purpose in new ways.

As indicated in these two examples, the scope of second-order change may be comparatively narrow or comparatively wide. Changes in the understanding of an organizational function such as participation are relatively narrow. Overall changes in the organization's mission and identity are quite wide, implying changes in several other organizational functions as well (cf. Tushman, Newman, & Romanelli, 1986).

The major difference between first- and second-order organizational change is in whether or not a particular framework for understanding is altered. In first-order change the framework remains the same, but in second-order change it shifts in some way. The alterations of framework in second-order change have an effect on the assessment of change. In first-order change some particular content is affected in a specifiable direction that can be thought of as better or worse in itself: commitment to the mission becomes greater or less, while participation increases or declines. Because the primary shift in second-order change is in the framework itself, it is more difficult when this type of change occurs to determine whether the change results in better or worse outcomes than before. For example, consultative decision making and employee ownership are not as directly comparable as differing amounts of consultation are. To determine the effectiveness of second-order change it is necessary to add some additional criterion. Thus, assessment of the value of shifting from consultation to employee ownership demands assessment of whether this new form of participation meets additional criteria such as higher quality and acceptance of decisions.

The issue of first- versus second-order change in OD has been raised, sometimes implicitly, by several commentators. Morgan (1984) and Ross (1971), for example, suggest that OD practice frequently takes a management-determined status quo interpretation of the organization for granted and works to make incremental changes within that framework. Golembiewski (1986; Golembiewski, Billingsley, & Yeager, 1976) asserts that the primary aim of OD is second-order change, but that, on the whole, adequate ways of assessing whether second-order change occurs have not been developed. Most studies of OD assess whether measurable first-order changes have occurred. For example, the Woodman and Wayne (1985) review described several specific content outcomes such as organizational climate and team effectiveness, and noted whether these had increased or decreased as a result of organizational interventions.

Organizational transformations, by definition, entail second-order change. Most discussions of transformation focus on overall changes in organizational form, but they implicitly include the more narrow changes in particular functions as well. These discussions also consider whether an organization's members are capable of second-order change in their understanding of some phenomenon (e.g., Nystrom & Starbuck, 1984). They also focus more explicitly than OD does on the difficulties of discontinuous shifts in frameworks (e.g., Greiner, 1972; Starbuck, 1982, 1983).

Time of Organizational Transformation

When do organizational transformations occur? How predictable are they?

There are differences of opinion on this topic among proponents of the transformation perspective. Some authors, for example, assert that organizations pass through relatively clearly defined stages during their entire life cycle, that these stages can be predicted in advance, and that transformations occur in conjunction with each stage (e.g., Quinn & Cameron, 1983; Torbert, 1976, 1987). Others disagree with this approach. They state that, although periods of transformation may alternate with periods of relative stability in mature organizations, these periods are relatively unpredictable and are not best understood as fully discrete stages (e.g., Miller & Friesen, 1984; Tushman & Romanelli, 1985).

While there is not a unanimous opinion about the nature of all transformations in organizations, there are some points on which there is substantial agreement. First, there is agreement that the early development of organizations is characterized by several stages, and that predictable transformations link the conclusion of one stage with the beginning of another. These are sometimes described as transformations of emergence (cf. Lundberg, 1984). In addition, regardless of whether mature organizations are considered to pass through stages, there is agreement that crises that signal or provoke transformations from one relatively stable period to another always occur sooner or later. During particular stages or stable periods both first-order changes and second-order changes in certain functions may occur. That is, incremental modifications aimed at improving performance within the already defined context of the stage or stable period may take place. In addition, the need may arise to achieve qualitatively new understandings of a particular organizational feature.

While the focus of theorizing on organizational transformation has included the entire life cycle, the focus of OD has been almost exclusively on mature organizations. On the other hand, discussions of OD have paid much more attention than discussions of transformation have to the dynamics associated with particular changes. These are two of the areas in which OD and organizational transformation can potentially inform each other.

We assume that readers of this volume are likely to be more familiar with one of the perspectives on change than the other. We also assume that more readers are familiar with the OD perspective than with the transformational perspective. If OD and organizational transformation are to contribute to each other, proponents of each perspective need to understand the other's point of view. Consequently, we introduce both approaches in the following section, summarizing representative descriptions of each. First we introduce the transformational perspective in some detail by presenting an overview of transformations throughout the organizational life cycle. Then we summarize the OD perspective by indicating phases typically associated with OD interventions and hypothesized processes through which OD-based changes occur.

ORGANIZATIONAL TRANSFORMATION

There are several models of the specific stages and transformations that occur during the organization's life cycle (e.g., Bartunek & Betters-Reed, 1987; Greiner, 1972; Kimberly, 1979; Quinn & Cameron, 1983; Torbert, 1976; 1987; Van de Ven, 1980; Van de Ven, Hudson, & Schroeder, 1984). We will summarize two models of the stages that occur during organizational emergence. We will also summarize a model of the process through which transformations occur in mature organizations. These transformations may be initiators of either decline or renewal.

Transformation of Emergence

The transformational perspective suggests that organizations pass through different stages both prior to and after their actual birth as organizations. Bartunek and Betters-Reed (1987) have developed a model of the stages that occur prior to birth and Quinn and Cameron (1983; see also, Cameron & Whetten, 1983) have developed a model of stages that occur after birth. Bartunek and Betters-Reed (1987) label the three pre-birth stages as ''First Ideas,'' ''Commitment and Early Planning,'' and ''Implementation.'' Quinn and Cameron (1983) label the three post-birth stages as ''entrepreneurial,'' ''collectivity,'' and ''formalization.''

These models include descriptions of the characteristic events that take place during the stages and crises or problems that occur following on successful completion of a stage. The crises represent the beginnings of transformations between stages. They are the signals that the types of action that were adequate during a previous stage are no longer sufficient, in part because the problems of the previous stage have been solved, giving way to new problems.

Finally, the descriptions also include material on critical issues (Bartunek & Betters-Reed, 1987) or criteria for effective organizational behavior during each stage (Quinn & Cameron, 1983). The critical issues are the types of issues or dilemmas whose resolution is crucial to the organization's success in dealing with a particular stage, while the effectiveness criteria refer, in essence, to the kind of behavior the organization must engage in to deal effectively with the critical issues.

A summary of these crises and of the characteristic events and critical issues of the three pre-birth stages is presented in Table 1. The stages are described briefly below.

First Ideas

Bartunek and Betters-Reed (1987) suggest that the crisis that leads to the first ideas for an organization is a perception of a problem (or opportunity) by an originator (the person who has the initial ideas for an organization) and a sense that previous attempts to solve the problem have not succeeded. The stage itself includes first ideas, or fantasies, about how the problem may be addressed and is characterized by strong feelings of discomfort about the problem and excitement and hope about the first ideas for the solution. Critical issues include the creativity and thoroughness of the development of the first idea and the originator's relationship with the idea, whether he or she cares about the problem on its own terms or primarily for extrinsic reasons.

Table 1.   Transformational Problems/Crises, Characteristic Experiences,
and Critical Issues of the Pre-birth Stages of Organizational Emergence
(Adapted from Bartunek & Betters-Reed, 1987)

Transformation	*Stage*	
First Ideas Crises/Problems	Characteristic Experiences	Critical Issues
•Originator perception of a problem not being adequately addressed	•Initial ideas of organizational arrangements that might address the problem •conception of a mission •tentative informal testing and revision of the ideas	•creativity and thoroughness of formulation of the first ideas •originator's relationship with the ideas
Commitment and Early Planning Crises/Problems	Characteristic Experiences	Critical Issues
•need to incorporate planners and members of the surrounding community into the planning process	•originator makes a commitment to develop first ideas into an organization •development of plan for the organization •establishment of relationships among originator, planners, and environmental groups	•creativity and thoroughness of the planning process •depth of commitment of originator and planners to the organization •internal dynamics among originator and planners •quality of planners' relationship with the environment
Implementation Crises/Problems	Characteristic Experiences	Critical Issues
•need to give concrete expression to the plan	•translation of ideas into concrete organizational features such as selecting new members (including a new leader) and choosing and preparing the physical setting	•adequacy of resources •mechanisms to ensure correspondence between use of resources and mission •manner in which the first ideas and plan are transmitted to new members, especially the new leader •relationship between leader and new members

Commitment and Early Planning

The commitment and early planning stage begins with a commitment by the originator to create a new organization. This commitment initiates a crisis. To develop the first idea into a viable organizational plan, it is usually necessary for the originator to work with others—both other planners and members of a surrounding ''community'' who will be affected by the organization being conceived. These people are likely to disagree with the originator about planning issues. The dilemmas to be addressed at this stage include issues such as how much the original idea should be protected by the originator, how authority will be exercised during planning, how conflicts will be addressed, and how the planners should negotiate their relationships with external groups who feel threatened by the organization. Critical issues include the creativity and thoroughness of planning, and the relationships among the planners and between the planners and external groups.

Implementation

The next crisis arises once there is some viable organizational plan. This crisis derives from the need to implement the plan and to obtain the resources necessary for its implementation. In this stage the plan begins to be formalized in specific organizational arrangements such as obtaining and planning the use of financial and physical resources and choosing the leader (if the originator does not assume that role) and other new members. This stage is more satisfying than the previous one, because abstract plans are finally being formalized. However, this formalization has a flip side as well; it is often discovered at this point that available resources are not adequate for the translation of the original plan into practice.

A typical problem encountered during implementation is the need to transmit the original idea and plan to new organizational members and to a new leader. New organizational members other than the leader are more likely to ask ''what'' to do rather than ''why,'' so be less likely than the planners to understand the basic principles of the organization. New leaders are likely to assume that the organization is *really* starting with them (otherwise, why were they chosen?), and thus tempted not to implement the already developed plans. Critical issues of the implementation stage include the ways resources are used, and the relationships between the planners, new leaders, and new organizational members.

Birth

These stages culminate in the birth of the organization, its formal opening, which in turn initiates several post-birth transformations and stages. A summary description of the problems or crises, characteristic events, and effectiveness criteria that Quinn and Cameron (1983) propose as associated with the post-birth stages is presented in Table 2.

Transformations and Stages following Organizational Birth

Entrepreneurial Stage

The major problems that initiate this stage are the needs to deal with the organization's liabilities of newness (Stinchcombe, 1965) and to find the right

Table 2. Transformational Problems/Crises, Characteristic Tasks, and
Effectiveness Criteria of the Post-birth Stages of Organizational Emergence
(Adapted from Quinn & Cameron, 1983 and Cameron & Whetten, 1983)

Transformation	*Stage*	
Entrepreneurial Stage		
Crises/Problems	Characteristic Experiences	Effectiveness Criteria
•need to find the right niche	•leader is center of attention	•flexibility of the organization
•need to deal with the ''liabilities of newness''	•little planning and coordination	•acquisition of necessary resources
	•little differentiation by position	•development of external support
	•crude information processing and decision making	
	•considerable risk taking	
Collectivity		
Crises/Problems	Characteristic Experiences	Effectiveness Criteria
•lack of coordination and cohesion	•informal communication	•extent to which human resources development, morale, and cohesion develop
	•development of a sense of collectivity	
	•innovation and commitment	
	•slight formalization of structure	
	•broadening of product-market scope	
Formalization		
Crises/Problems	Characteristic Experiences	Effectiveness Criteria
•disorganization	•formalization of rules	•goal setting and achievement
•lack of effectiveness of informal communication	•emergence of bureaucratic structure	•efficiency of information management
•desire of members to settle down	•emphasis on efficiency and maintenance	•stability and control
•pressure towards formalization	•institutionalization of procedures	
	•consolidation of strategy and slower growth	

niche. During this stage the first leader, or entrepreneur, is the center of organizational attention. There tends to be relatively little planning and coordination. Rather, power is highly centralized in the hands of the entrepreneur. The structure is more informal than formal, the organization is relatively undifferentiated by function, there is very crude information processing and decision making, and considerable innovation and risk taking. Given the primary concerns and characteristics of this stage, the criteria for effectiveness are whether the organization is sufficiently flexible, acquires the resources it needs, and develops the necessary external support.

Collectivity Stage

Certain crises result from the focus of the entrepreneurial stage. In particular, there is a lack of coordination and cohesion; organizational members tend to work primarily for their own goals rather than the organization's (Cameron & Whetten, 1983). The characteristic events of the collectivity stage represent responses to these problems.

During this stage a strong sense of collectivity develops among the organizational members. That is, organizational members spend long hours at work and in the process develop a collective organizational mission. The stage is characterized by continued innovation and high commitment. The structure becomes slightly formalized, although there is still considerable informal communication. Moreover, there is some tentative development of formal information-processing and decision-making methods, as well as some broadening of the product-market scope into related areas. The leader, or entrepreneur, is less the center of attention than was the case before.

Because of the focus on relationships, Quinn and Cameron (1983) suggest that human relations issues are critical during this stage. The primary criteria for effectiveness are the extent to which human resources development, morale, cohesion, and need satisfaction are achieved.

Formalization Stage

The emphases of the collectivity stage also result in problems. The organization is disorganized, especially if it is growing and the types of work it is involved in are expanding. Informal communication structures no longer work adequately, and there are likely to be both external and internal pressures towards formalization. In addition, individuals often burn out because of their high involvement during collectivity. Consequently, organizational members are likely to have a desire to settle down, and to get into a routine (Quinn & Anderson, 1984; Quinn & Cameron, 1983).

The characteristics of the formalization stage are in part a response to these problems. They include the formalization of rules, creation of a stable structure, emphasis on efficiency and maintenance, conservatism, and institutionalization of procedures. During this stage a formal bureaucratic structure tends to emerge, along with a consolidation of strategy and slower growth. These characteristics tend to be accompanied by other phenomena as well. Torbert (1976) notes, for example, that organizations in this stage tend to measure their success almost exclusively by the success of their product; they often ignore other criteria such as the effectiveness of their work processes.

Quinn and Cameron (1983) suggest that the primary criteria for effectiveness during the formalization stage relate to production and efficiency. They describe effective organizational behavior at this stage as including goal setting and achievement, productivity, efficiency of information management, and stability and control.

Up to this point in its development, the organization will have experienced relatively frequent transformations. From this point, however, when the organization reaches a point where members feel they know what they are doing and formalize the organization's approach, major changes are more rare and problematic. It is much more likely from now on that the organization will be inclined towards first-order changes, improvements within the already defined mode of operation, than second-order re-orientations (cf. Miller & Friesen, 1984; Torbert, 1987; Tushman & Romanelli, 1985). Sometimes, especially if environmental conditions remain relatively constant, the organization may stay in the same formalization stage for years.

Transformations in Mature Organizations

Periods of transformation in mature organizations have sometimes been labeled as stages in themselves (e.g., Quinn and Cameron's [1983] "elaboration of structure" stage). They have also been labeled as times of renewal, when an organization's overall understanding of itself or its general interpretive schemes changes (e.g., Gioia, 1986).

As noted above, these types of transformations may be more wide or narrow in scope, encompassing the organization's total identity or its understanding of how to carry out some particular function, such as job design, problem solving, or performance appraisal. Actually, second-order change in one of these functions probably requires eventual wider transformation if it is to endure. This is so because organizations tend to develop mutually reinforcing and convergent strategies, structures, and norms (Miller & Friesen, 1984; Tushman, Newman, & Romanelli, 1986; Tushman & Romanelli, 1985). For example, Lawler (1986) indicates that changes towards more enriched jobs typically require changes in the supervisory structure and reward systems of companies as well.

There has been considerable discussion of the dynamics of transformation in mature organizations. In the following pages we discuss these transformation processes.

Several different types of crises may occur. For example, performance may be poor, a managerial succession may occur, some powerful subgroups' interests may not be served by present modes of operation, particular management practices may not be successful, or there may be a major environmental shift (e.g., Bartunek, 1984, in press; Gray, Bougon, & Donnellon, 1985; Hedberg, 1981; Tushman, Newman, & Romanelli, 1986). Such shifts might make formerly successful practices or products obsolete.

The mere existence of a crisis does not ensure that a transformation will take place. Many organizations' systems become so routinized during periods of formalization that they are unable to respond to crises (Nystrom & Starbuck, 1984; Starbuck, 1982, 1983). Rather, the crisis may initiate a decline accompanied by dynamics such as increased centralization of decision making, tighter control by managers, and both psychological and physical withdrawal by organizational members (Whetten, 1980; Zammuto, 1982). Such periods often include positive feedback loops; once the decline process is started, its processes may reinforce each other. For a transformation to commence, it is necessary that the destructive positive feedback loops be broken and that organizational members present understandings and frames become unfrozen. The primary aim of the transformation will be to develop a more appropriate understanding of issues pertinent to the crisis—of how, for example, to respond to the changing environment.

Recently, Bartunek (in press) has proposed a model that suggests that the transformation process proceeds through several steps which parallel steps of creative processes (cf. Amabile, 1983). This model is presented in Figure 1.

The model suggests that the development of new frameworks that characterize transformations in mature organizations proceeds as follows. First, there must be an unfreezing of current frames through a crisis strong enough to convince organizational members that present ways of operating in some particular domain are no longer adequate. If this crisis succeeds in unsettling current understandings, there begins to occur a development of information pertinent to the problem that caused the crisis and potential new ways of understanding the issues involved. Different information about the problem is likely to be developed in the various subgroups. For example, management might be likely to attribute perfor-

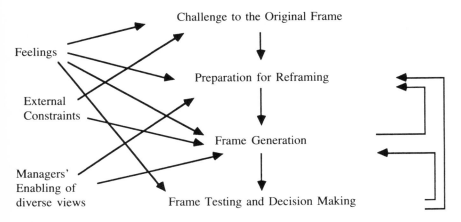

Figure 1.   Stages of Organizational Reframing
(adapted from Bartunek, in press).

mance problems to the environment or poor labor practices, while other organizational members are more likely to attribute it to managerial deficiencies.

New possible understandings, or frames, are then generated from the information developed earlier. This period is also affected by subgroups. During it the various subgroups are likely to develop different frames and to interact with each other in one of several ways: particular perspectives may dominate or the potential value of several perspectives may be acknowledged.

Eventually a new understanding will be developed that incorporates conflicting frames to some extent. When such an understanding feels comfortable to powerful organizational members it will be adopted and refrozen, or formalized, in the organization.

The process through which this change occurs is not free of affect. Rather, it is accompanied by considerable feeling. Organizational members are likely to experience anxiety, shock, and defensiveness at the beginning and ambiguity and possible hopelessness in the middle of the process when it is clear that the old way of operating is no longer effective, but nothing adequate has arisen to replace it. There is likely to be considerable conflict between groups holding conflicting views and information. Eventually, groups whose perspectives have been incorporated in the new understanding should experience a sense of comfort and "rightness" with the new framework developed. Because the process includes so much ambiguity and tension, there may be considerable turnover during the period of change.

Factors Affecting Transformation

The consistent presence of factors supporting change, managers' abilities to stimulate and encourage new understandings on the part of organizational members, and external constraints all affect the organizational reframing process. Bartunek and Moch (1987) suggest that if a strong stimulus for change is not present throughout the reframing process, it will often be difficult to sustain the change, even when such change is appropriate. One obvious stimulus comes from a manager's own development of new frameworks and understandings (e.g., Bass, 1985; Tichy & Devanna, 1986). A second stimulus which may usefully accompany this one is the presence of decentralized structural features such as collateral or parallel groups or matrix structures (e.g., Kilmann, 1985; Rubinstein & Woodman, 1984; Zand, 1974). These structures are more likely than traditional ones to foster the development of alternative viewpoints in an organization. If new viewpoints and structures that support them are not present at the beginning of change or do not emerge, the organization is more likely to enter into decline than a renewing transformation.

Managers' own new insights and the presence of decentralized structures are not enough in themselves. The extent to which managers can allow contrasting viewpoints to be developed and taken into consideration is also important. Recent work (e.g., Bass, 1985; Louis, 1986) has suggested that leaders who are successful in achieving transformations in organizational members' understandings not only present their own views, but also encourage the development of organizational members' own understandings. The more managers can allow the alternative perspectives held by different groups to be heard, the more adequate and expressive of a new overall organizational perspective the understanding that eventually develops should be.

Finally, external constraints play a large role in the development of new understandings. Organizations sometimes develop "faddish" characteristics whose primary purpose is not to reflect deep-seated convictions, but to signal to an external environment that the organization is acceptable (e.g., "Business Fads . . . ," 1986; Meyer & Rowan, 1977). The more a transformation in understanding evolves in response to experienced needs on the part of the organization rather than simply in compliance with external constraints, the more the organization will develop new understandings that are appropriate for itself.

ORGANIZATION DEVELOPMENT

Organization development includes less of an explicit theory of change than organizational transformation approaches do (Beer & Walton, 1987; Porras & Hoffer, 1986), although several mid-range theories derived from specific interventions have been developed. Recently, attempts have been made to cull out from existing literature the underlying models of OD-based change processes. Two types of models have been identified: an implementation theory that focuses on the sequence of activities during planned change (Bullock & Batten, 1985; Porras & Robertson, 1987) and a change process theory that focuses on the dynamics of change (Porras & Hoffer, 1986; Porras & Robertson, 1987). These two types of models are summarized below.

Implementation Theories

Several types of implementation theories have been developed. Some deal with strategies of change, some with procedures for change, and some with techniques by which to implement one of the steps of a procedure. Most attention is currently being paid to procedures: the various stages or phases throughout an OD intervention. Implementation theories that include at least some phases of interventions have been developed by Lippitt, Watson and Westley (1958), Frohman, Sashkin, and Kavanaugh (1976), Beckhard and Harris (1977), Cummings and Srivastva (1977), Beer (1980), and Burke (1982, 1987), among others.

Bullock and Batten (1985) suggest that there are several underlying assumptions of implementation theories: they have a broad time horizon, conceive of change as gradual and continuous, include fluidity in phase definition (i.e., allow some overlap in phases), and assume an irreversible sequential ordering of phases. Finally, they are based on the activities of OD practitioners, rather than the organization in which the intervention is occurring.

On the basis of their review, Bullock and Batten (1985) suggest that OD interventions include four separate phases: exploration (including need awareness, search, and contracting), planning (including diagnosis, design, and decision), action (including implementation and evaluation), and, finally, integration (including stabilization, diffusion, and renewal).

These phases can be summarized as follows. The exploration phase typically begins with an organization's awareness of some need it has. This awareness leads organizational members to search for consulting assistance. They develop contacts with various consultants and eventually establish a contract with a consultant.

Once key resources have been committed to consultation, a planning phase begins. This phase is conducted by the consultant in collaboration with organizational members. It first includes data collection about the problems, typically through interviews, questionnaires, or workshops. It then includes a joint consultant-organization diagnosis of organizational goals and problems. On the basis of the diagnosis, organizational members set goals for action and develop action strategies for meeting these goals.

In the action phase the action strategies are implemented by organizational members, sometimes through a series of steps, and their effects are evaluated. If these effects are seen as beneficial, a new phase begins: the organization will attempt to integrate the change program into its ongoing system. This integration might occur in a number of ways, perhaps by developing a self-supporting change system or by shifting from external to internal consultants.

Change Process Theories

Models of change processes have different emphases than implementation theories do. These models attempt to explain the dynamics of change processes by specifying intended outcomes of change attempts, manipulable variables (organizational elements a consultant can directly influence), mediator variables (which comprise the middle of the causal chain between manipulable variables and intended outcomes), and moderator variables (factors that affect the causal relationships between the variables). Models of change processes have been proposed by Goodman and Dean (1982), Lawler (1982), and Nadler (1977), among others.

Porras and Robertson (1987) note that the number of change process theories is relatively small. Moreover, the theories that do exist do not build on each other very much; they have a particular intervention strategy, rather than an overarching theory of change, as a guiding framework. These theories do have some characteristics in common. For example, the primary manipulable variable most of the theories discuss is some type of increased information among organizational members.

Because of the lack of generalizability of the change process theories, we will not present an overall summary of the mechanisms through which OD-based changes occur; an initial attempt to create such a summary is available in Porras and Robertson (1987). Rather, we will describe one of the theories, that of Nadler (1977), in terms of the various change process components. Nadler's model provides a good illustration of this type of approach.

Nadler's (1977) theory concerns the means through which one particular intervention, survey feedback, leads individual organizational members to change their behavior. Such change represents the intended outcome, the target variable of survey feedback attempts. Nadler's primary manipulable variable is increased information about the organization, as obtained from the collection, feedback, and joint diagnosis of data.

Nadler suggests that there are two types of mediating variables of the information-behavior change link: what he calls motivational and directing functions. First, feedback that leads to behavior change has a motivational component, in that it implies both internal and external reward expectancies. Thus, feedback may serve as a reward or sanction in itself by signaling how effective some particular behavior is. Feedback may also lead to perceptions that behavioral changes that occur due to the data fed back will lead to rewards or sanctions provided by others. Feedback also directs behavior, both by giving cues about appropriate changes and indicating needs for learning. By giving people information about whether behavior is proceeding well or poorly according to some standard, feedback may give a cue about the types of behavior that are appropriate. On the other hand, in complex situations where problems do not have obvious solutions, feedback may direct organizational members to conduct further diagnoses or learn more about what the underlying problem really is.

These motivating and directing functions are not always successful. Several moderators, what Nadler calls necessary conditions, limit the extent to which the motivating and directing functions will take place. For example, for the motivating functions to work, the level of behavior necessary for successful change must be attainable. For the directing function to work, feedback must be specific and must imply clear correction or search routines. Nadler describes several other moderating variables as well.

Nadler's model, as we noted, is simply one of a number of change process models. It shows the difference in approach between implementation and change process models in that it focuses much less on sequences of events and much more on underlying mechanisms that affect whether manipulated variables will have the intended effect on the target of change.

COMPARISON OF OD AND ORGANIZATIONAL TRANSFORMATION APPROACHES

Links between Organizational Transformation and OD

In our discussion of transformation, we have focused on two types of transformations that organizations might experience. Emergence transformations are likely to be experienced by all organizations and to be quite difficult, a fact attested to by the high death rate of young organizations (e.g., Singh, Tucker, & House, 1986). Emergence transformations probably occur only once during the organizational life cycle. This differentiates them from transformations in mature organizations, which may occur several times.

We have also alluded to other dimensions of transformations, especially the fact that they include powerful affective components and that multiple characteristics affect how successfully they are carried out. These components and characteristics, some of which have been part of the purview of OD for years, suggest links between OD and organizational transformation. For example, suggestions that effective transformations in mature organizations depend partly on decentralization and participation, at least in frame generation, are consistent with approaches dating back to Lewin (1947) regarding the importance of participation in decision making for significant organizational change.

We have also described two different types of OD-based approaches to change. The first is an implementation theory, a description of the sequential phases of OD interventions. The second is a change process approach, which includes descriptions of the manipulable and mediating variables by which intervention outcomes are achieved.

These components also suggest links between OD and transformation. For example, there is at least a superficial correspondence between descriptions or implementation phases and descriptions of transformations of emergence in that both deal with sequential and irreversible patterns of change. In addition, both OD change process theories and transformations in mature organizations include mediating variables as essential.

As noted earlier, our ultimate aim is to indicate how the two approaches can inform each other and the overall understanding of change. Because of the particular overlaps that exist between OD and transformation approaches, achievement of this aim requires that we first highlight similarities and differences between the two approaches. Even in ways in which the approaches are similar, there tend to be differences in many of their specific emphases.

Similarities between OD and Organizational Transformation

Focus on Cultural Change

Most definitions of OD focus on changes in the organization's culture, its shared beliefs and values (e.g., Burke, 1987; French & Bell, 1984). A premise in

much of the OD literature is that appropriate cultural changes are usually necessary for more effective organizational functioning as shown in other indices
(such as improved performance).

Attention to cultural change also characterizes the organizational transformation literature. In particular, the literature on transformations in mature organizations focuses on changes in the organization's or subgroups' shared meanings,
beliefs, and values (e.g., Bartunek & Moch, 1987; Beer & Walton, 1987). The
transformation literature, and the materials on organizational social cognition
that often accompany it (e.g., Sims & Gioia, 1986), go considerably beyond
OD's approach on this point, describing an organization's shared meanings and
values and various ways they may be transformed in much more detail.

Appreciation of the Reciprocal Effects of Behavior and Culture

The action research focus of OD has emphasized the cyclical process of
action, evaluation, and feedback leading to another round of action. Thus, this
approach makes explicit links between an organization's culture and the appropriateness of a particular change strategy, showing how each affects the other.
Action research seems consistent with the approach taken in much of the organizational transformation literature. That literature assumes, for example, that
transformations do not happen once and for all; the results of one sequence of
major change have the potential for precipitating another one. The transformation literature is also concerned with how organizational structure, behavior, and
culture affect each other (e.g., Ranson, Hinings, & Greenwood, 1980).

Assumption that Some Ways of Organizing are More Effective than Others

As indicated in its high-involvement paradigm (e.g., Lawler, 1986) OD practitioners have developed a relatively clear sense of appropriate ways of organizing (i.e., of outcomes of change attempts). These include such components as
enriched jobs, more organic organizational structures, and diffuse participation
in decision making. The components are often drawn from the organizational
behavior literature, and OD has become, in recent years, a means of application
of some of that literature.

The transformation literature also focuses on appropriate ways of organizing,
as shown in discussions of critical issues and effectiveness criteria. However, the
transformation approach adopts a more contingent perspective than OD does. In
the transformation approach appropriateness is stage specific, rather than uniform throughout the organizational life cycle. Thus, a collectively based, relatively informal and undifferentiated organizational structure is considered appropriate for the collectivity stage, but not for the formalization stage, in which the
development of more centralized and formalized modes is considered apt. Organization development practitioners tend not to distinguish between stages when
they define appropriate outcomes of change attempts.

Advance Specification of Appropriate Directions of Change

The assumption of much of the transformation literature is that it is possible in emergence transformations to specify the direction in which change will occur. An implementation stage will necessarily follow a commitment and early planning stage, and formalization will not happen before there is an experience of collectivity. This approach is, on a superficial level, consistent with implementation theories of OD which assert that, for example, action always follows planning (Bullock & Batten, 1985). In addition, OD-based change process theories assume that setting particular processes in motion will result in predictable outcomes. For example, participation in decision making should typically result both in perceptions of increased participation and a more equalized distribution of power between superiors and subordinates (Bartunek & Keys, 1982). The specific types of effects presumed to be specifiable in advance differ somewhat in discussions of OD and organizational transformation. The focus in discussions of emergence transformations is on how dealing successfully with one crisis will result ultimately in the emergence of another one, while the focus in OD is more on how the manipulation of specific variables can achieve a particular effect on a target variable.

Characterizing the Starting Point of Change

Organization development assumes that planned change is difficult to commence: for such change to take place something needs to happen to unfreeze current modes of understanding and operation. Similarly, the organizational transformation literature focuses on the necessity of some type of crisis for change to begin, and assumes that this crisis must be experienced fairly strongly.

Differences between OD and Organizational Transformations

Different Understandings of the Role of the Consultant

The literatures on organizational transformation and OD differ in at least three respects in their approach to the role of the consultant. First, the focus of OD is that consultants are an integral part of an intervention (cf. the definition of OD by French & Bell, 1984). In the organizational transformation literature, there is comparatively little discussion of any role of consultants in change, although there is an awareness that consultants can sometimes play a useful role in facilitating specific processes (e.g., Beer & Walton, 1987).

Further, there is an implication in OD that, while consultants are an integral part of change, they are also external to it. They are somewhat marginal to the change taking place (Argyris, 1970, Ch. 6; Burke, 1987, Ch. 8; Margulies, 1978). The implicit focus in the organizational transformation literature is that when consultants are present they are a part of the system in which the change is occurring rather than separate from it. Obtaining consultation is simply one component of the overall transformation process.

Finally, OD treats the major role of consultants in change as facilitative. They work primarily, although not exclusively, with the organization's processes, and their purpose is to help facilitate the organization's growth and development. In contrast, an implicit focus of the transformational approach, at least for the more narrow second-order changes, is that when consultants are involved a major role they can play is to advocate a particular perspective that differs from the organization's current one (e.g., Bartunek & Moch, in press). According to this approach, when consultants act simply in a facilitative role they neither force unfreezing of particular perspectives nor sustain change processes set in motion. Consequently, they reduce the chances that the organization will be able to achieve major changes in perspective. For the transformational approach, strong advocacy of a particular perspective both fosters a crisis and supports second-order change processes.

Focus on Different Perspectives for Viewing Change

Consistent with the different types of attention they pay to the role of the consultant, the OD and transformational approaches explore the experience of change from very different perspectives. The attention of OD is to the proactive behavior of the change-agent. Both the implementation and change process theories summarized by Porras and Robertson (1987) focus on the consultant's activities during change, on conducting the diagnosis, for example, or manipulating particular variables. The transformational approach, in contrast, focuses on the organization undergoing the change. This approach deals very little with ways organizational members other than the manager cause change to happen, although it does emphasize the importance of the manager's role in the change process.

Different Perspectives on the "Meaning" of Changes Taking Place

The focus of OD practice tends to be on addressing particular problems such as communication or conflict (e.g., Keys, in press; Woodman & Wayne, 1985) or particular types of relationships in organizations. In QWL interventions, for example, attention is paid to improving ways management and labor work together over the long term. Transformational approaches dealing with large-scale change focus less on particular contents of change and more on different periods, types of crises, or stages for which particular content issues are somewhat of a surface manifestation (e.g., Quinn & Cameron, 1983).

Different Types of Change Explored

As noted above, OD tends to assume that the appropriate sequences and directions of particular change attempts can often be specified in advance. This assumption allows for pre-post tests of the effectiveness of particular interventions. Discussions of emergence transformations agree that some particular types of change are likely to follow others in prespecified sequences. However, discussions of transformations in mature organizations suggest that it is not possible to prespecify the particular outcomes of the initiation of these types of changes. Rather, once a transformational change begins, its own dialectical or paradoxical dynamics will, almost of necessity, take the change to a new place (Bartunek, in press; Bartunek & Moch, 1987; Beer & Walton, 1987). Although a consultant can have some effect on the process of change, the effect is more through supporting particular directions of change while being open to others than through facilitating totally open group processes.

Different Views of Decline

Writers on OD do not discuss the topic of decline and death very much. The focus of OD, as is suggested in its title, is on continued development, which implicitly suggests a growth. Some organizational transformation literature, on the other hand, does discuss decline and death, making it clear that these are common features in organizational life (e.g., Singh, Tucker, & House, 1986; Whetten, 1980; Zammuto, 1982).

Different Approaches to the Diagnosis of Problems

Much of the OD literature focuses on how to diagnose problems. Two issues are fairly explicit in this literature. First, it is expected that organizational members should have a role in diagnosing particular problems, perhaps through means such as survey feedback interventions. Second, diagnostic models of types of underlying problems that are likely to occur (such as intra or intergroup problems, or organization-wide problems, [cf. French & Bell, 1984, Ch. 6; Nielsen, 1984, Ch. 6; Porras and Hoffer, 1986]) are being established.

The diagnostic categories used in OD differ from the categories used in organizational transformation. There is more in the transformation literature that focuses on organizations passing through a particular transformation, and on whether they are dealing effectively with that transformation (e.g., Quinn & Anderson, 1984). One consequence of the transformation approach, illustrated by Quinn and Anderson (1984), is that some issues that OD practitioners treat as particular content problems can also be understood as a component of a particular stage of development.

CONTRIBUTIONS OF THE APPROACHES
TO EACH OTHER

Having highlighted similarities and differences between the OD and organizational transformation approaches, we describe contributions each approach can make to the other. Then we discuss the questions their joint consideration raises about the understanding, practice, and assessment of change.

Contributions of Organizational Transformation to OD

Increased Awareness of Impacts of the Life Cycle

One major contribution organizational transformation can make to OD is to increase OD practitioners' awareness that interventions occur during particular stages or transformations in the life cycle. OD practitioners have, on the whole, treated problems as though they were in a temporal vacuum. With a few notable exceptions (e.g., Lavoie & Culbert, 1978; Lippitt, 1982), they have operated without a very great historical or developmental sense. In studies of organizational transformation, in contrast, a developmental perspective aids considerably in understanding a particular problem.

Other contributions of transformation to OD follow directly on this one. They deal with the occasions in which interventions may be appropriate, the effects of life cycle stage on problem diagnosis, and the larger meaning of helping an organization deal with a particular problem.

Occasions in which Interventions are Appropriate

First, OD interventions are appropriate throughout an organization's life cycle. Notwithstanding Quinn and Anderson's (1984) paper on how to help organizations move into the formalization stage, relatively little has been written about how OD practitioners might intervene at particular stages.

We have suggested that one aspect of an organization's effectiveness derives from how the organization deals with the critical issues of a particular stage. OD consultants could have roles throughout the life cycle in helping organizations deal effectively with the critical issues they experience. As an illustration of such interventions, we explore what OD consultants might do during the commitment and early planning stage.

As noted above, the critical issues at this stage center around the creativity and thoroughness of the planning process, the depth of the planners' commitment, and relationships among the originator, planners, and the larger community (Bartunek & Betters-Reed, 1987). Given these critical issues, the broad goals of OD consultation might be to help the originator and planners (a) use competent planning, problem-solving, and interpersonal processes, (b) explore their commitment to the developing organization, and (c) achieve necessary support from the external environment. Some of the ways OD practitioners might achieve these broad goals are through acting as process consultants (Schein, 1969) and working with planning groups to address such issues as the norms they are establishing, the ways they are sharing decision-making power, and the ways they are managing conflict. Consultants might also help the planners use appropriate problem-solving processes for the ambiguous, ill-defined tasks they are facing. Finally, they can also help foster relationships between planning groups and their external environments. One way they can do this is by helping the planners provide opportunities in which people likely to be affected by the new organization have the opportunity to voice their feelings and concerns and to be heard in a way that fosters, rather than impedes development. Van de Ven (1980), for example, describes how the nominal group technique can be adapted to gain the input of various community groups about their concerns.

In addition to helping organizations carry out the work associated with particular stages, there is a role for OD consultants to play in transformations that occur during maturity. One primary role is in helping the organization to determine whether a particular problem really signals the need for second-order transformation; some problems are much more easily (and appropriately) solved through first-order changes. When second-order change is appropriate, Bartunek and Moch (in press) suggest several specific roles for the consultant to play. The first role is applicable in a situation in which an organization should experience and attend to a crisis, but for some reason is not doing so. Some organizational members, for example, might be oblivious to problems. Based on methods developed for family therapy (e.g., Weakland, Fisch, & Segal, 1982; Woodruff & Engle, 1985), consultants might relabel current behavior or symbols as a way of fostering attention to problems. For example, Tunstall (1985) described how during AT&T's divestiture process Charles Brown (the chairman of AT&T) retired the "Ma Bell" symbol, calling it inadequate for a high-technology company. OD consultants can also make use of the fact that, in organizational settings, only some members' interests are typically served by particular frameworks (Giddens, 1979), and they can increase other members' awareness that their interests are not being served. This type of intervention should increase the likelihood of organizational members initiating change themselves.

A consultant can also help to sustain the second-order change process, in part, as indicated above, by advocating a new perspective (Bartunek & Moch, 1987). The consultant's aim here is *not* to have the alternative perspective adopted as stated, but to maintain a strong enough impetus for change in understanding to take place (Bartunek, in press).

Finally, OD practitioners have a role to play during decline. There are two issues involved here. One is that the beginnings of decline are really the same as the beginnings of a transformation; the fact that an organization is declining does not mean that it must necessarily continue along that route. When there is a realistic chance because of environmental conditions that the organization can survive, OD consultants can help the organization reverse cyclical patterns of decline and begin transformation processes instead.

Sometimes, perhaps because of environmental conditions beyond the organization's control, decline and eventual death are inevitable. Organizations have developed several rites aimed at enabling them to die well (e.g., Harris & Sutton, 1986). One role a practitioner might play is to facilitate this process in a way that leaves organizational members with a sense of hope for future ventures.

Clearly there are roles for OD consultants from prior to the organization's "cradle" to its "grave." We have merely begun the process of suggesting what the roles might be.

Effects of the Life Cycle on Diagnosis

A second implication of organizational transformation is that diagnosis should include understanding the effects of a particular stage on the ways a problem is experienced. While relatively little work has been done on how OD practitioners might intervene at various stages of the life cycle, even less has been done on what the problems mean to organizational members at these different stages. It is a reasonable guess that, for example, team problems mean something very different at the collectivity stage than at the formalization stage or during a transformation in a mature organization. Team problems during a collectivity stage might signal that the organization's fundamental ability to serve as a collective group is in question. At a formalization stage, they may signal that the organization's structure needs alignment. Perhaps because of increased size, the organization's coordination needs have changed and adequate structures have not been designed to meet them. Consequently, organizational members inappropriately attribute structural problems to interpersonal relationships.

During transformations in mature organizations, there are likely to be team problems of another sort. As described above, these transformations are typically characterized by conflict between organizational members and ambiguity about directions the organization should take (Bartunek, 1984; in press). It is necessary for the organization to foster means for such conflict and ambiguity to occur productively if a qualitatively new resolution of the problems being faced is to take place. Conflict management strategies employed at this stage should focus more on maintaining differences between people in a way that enables the evolution of new understandings than on determining ways to resolve conflict prematurely, before the new perspective has emerged of its own accord.

Expanded Meaning of Addressing Particular Problems

A third contribution is the awareness that when OD practitioners work with an organization to address some particular problem, they may have a much greater impact than simply on resolution of the focal problem. Working with the specific problems of an organization undergoing a particular transformation may affect how the organization will pass through the stage associated with that transformation regardless of whether the focus of the intervention is the transformation per se. If OD practitioners help resolve particular critical issues of the commitment and early planning stage, for example, they will not only be helping to solve these particular problems, but also strengthening the organization for its later functioning. When OD practitioners help an organization initiate and sustain second-order change well, they may not only be helping to accomplish particular shifts in perspective, but also affecting the organization's capacity to continue such perspective shifts later.

Contributions of OD to Organizational Transformation

While OD can benefit from the theoretical perspective of the transformation approach, it can also contribute to that approach. The fact that OD practitioners are typically marginal to client organizations—"in but not of" the organizations—means they may be able to gain more valid information about organizations than external researchers (including most of those who focus on organizational transformation) or organizational members who view their experiences solely within the organization's framework for understanding (cf. Argyris, 1970; Bartunek, 1983; Evered & Louis, 1981; Heron, 1981). Based on their action research approach, OD practitioners can contribute to the transformational perspective by describing the dynamics of transformations and surfacing problems that occur during transformations that the transformational perspective has not addressed. Each of these contributions is discussed below.

Describing the Dynamics of Transformation

While the transformational perspective presents a broad overview of types of events that occur during second-order change, it also tends to take a somewhat static approach to the description of these events. It presents a somewhat abstract description of characteristics—such as, for example, formalization or decentralization—that are present during a particular stage. OD practitioners who work with organizational members undergoing a particular transformation have a greater appreciation of the nuances of the different components and processes of change. They have a greater understanding, for example, of the several meanings a concept like formalization might have in an organization, or of the variety of ways formalization might be experienced.

Research on organizational transformation is in its infancy (Torbert, 1987). The conceptual models described in the transformational literature are not based on voluminous amounts of data. OD practitioners who can describe experiences and understandings of their clients during transformations (or potential transformations) can thus add considerably to the conceptual understanding of this phenomenon.

As one example of this type of contribution, Pasmore and Friedlander (1982) described an action research intervention in a company experiencing an abnormal number of physical injuries. The company had spent several years conducting traditional technical and medical studies to determine the causes of the injuries, but these studies had not been successful. The company had not elicited employee input in any of the studies, and at the time the intervention began had very little tradition of employee input or participation in decision making.

The action research approach the consultants used involved much more employee participation than before. It implied a qualitatively different type of relationship between employees and management, one in which they would work together on a more equal basis. This type of shift can be described as a second-order change in the understanding of employee-management relationships.

A task force of managers and employees worked to diagnose and address the injury problem, establishing a climate of openness and co-inquiry in their group. However, when task force members reported their initial findings to top managers, the managers reacted very defensively, and gave the impression that they were concerned about losing control. The conflict that emerged between the managers and the task force was never totally resolved, although management did eventually listen to the task force and make certain changes based on their suggestions. The changes had the eventual impact of substantially reducing the injury problem.

This description suggests some of the dynamics that may occur during second-order change. It suggests, for example, the kind of crisis managers who are used to a high level of control are likely to experience when a centralized approach to decision making is challenged by a more participative one. It suggests some of the ways this crisis is likely to be acted out, such as in defensive reactions to employee suggestions. It suggests that resentments created early in the process of change due to the introduction of a new perspective may endure, even if the new approach leads to valuable ways of dealing with a problem. If OD practitioners consciously contribute information such as this to discussions of the transformational perspective, they can greatly enrich it.

Surfacing New Problems During Transformation

OD practitioners can do more than simply describe the dynamics of transformation. They can also make use of these dynamics to surface types of organizational problems that have not been addressed by current theory and research. Their problem descriptions can thus stimulate research aimed at more thorough understanding. For instance, consider OD research evaluating the effectiveness of QWL programs in a hospital (Hanlon, Nadler, & Gladstein, 1985) and a food processing plant (Bartunek & Moch, 1987). In both cases, the programs were less than fully successful, due in part to top management's lack of encouragement of meaningful participation.

Bartunek and Moch (1987) raised the question of why the managers in these two programs had failed to encourage participation. They wondered, for example, whether particular organizational frameworks for understanding had impeded the managers' ability to foster participative approaches. Their analysis suggested that this was indeed the case. For example, Hanlon, Nadler, & Gladstein (1985) learned that at the time of the intervention in the hospital, the hospital president's primary aim (because of mounting operational deficits and the physician dominated culture) was to increase managerial control, which he viewed as necessary for effective functioning. Bartunek and Moch (1987) suggested that the food processing plant was operating out of a parental schema, shared by management and employees, in which, in essence, management played the role of parents and other employees played the role of children. This schema implied that managers took care of the employees. The schemata operating in both organizations—the managerial control schema in the hospital and the parental schema in the food processing plant—were incompatible with the equal responsibility notions implied by QWL programs. Thus, it was reasonable that participation approaches, especially as introduced in these programs, would have great difficulty succeeding.

The learnings about the relationship between organizational frames and participation illustrated in these two studies suggest ways OD practitioners can contribute by suggesting new problem areas. In particular, they suggest that when an organization formalizes a particular way of operating, part of what is formalized will be a framework or schema—perhaps a managerial control schema or a paternalistic schema—for relationships. These schemata will be an integral part of the culture of the organization. There are undoubtedly a large number of schemata for relationships that organizations or subgroups in them might hold, just as there are a large number of cultures that might characterize a particular organization (e.g., Louis, 1985). The presence of multiple schemata means, for example, that a description of a transformation such as, say, "organizations move from a formalization stage to a renewal stage accompanied by decentralization" is far too simple. To understand what the transformation means, and why it is sometimes resisted, it is necessary to develop a broader understanding of the various components—such as schemata describing superior-subordinate relationships—that characterize the different stages. By reflecting on the dynamics of interventions in which they are involved, OD practitioners are in a position to contribute to the understanding of what such schemata mean.

Comparative Status of the Types of Contributions

In the above analysis, the contributions of the transformational perspective to OD have been stated in a format that suggests that the contribution has already been made, and needs only to be assimilated. The contributions of OD to organizational transformation have been presented in a different fashion. For those contributions the potential for increased understanding has been emphasized more than the contribution already made. This is the case for two reasons. One is that OD tends to focus more on practice than on conceptual contributions (cf. Beer & Walton, 1987; Cooperrider & Srivastva, 1987). The other is that, on the whole, there is comparatively little discussion in the OD literature that is explicitly pertinent to the transformational perspective. There is much more existing material in the transformational perspective that can obviously inform OD. The potential is present for OD practitioners to make a much greater conceptual contribution than they have to this point.

INFORMING THE UNDERSTANDING OF ORGANIZATIONAL CHANGE

We have seen ways OD and transformation approaches can contribute to each other. Taken together they can also facilitate a broader appreciation of organizational change. In particular, their joint consideration calls attention to new perspectives and raises questions concerning the understanding of change from both consultant and organizational perspectives, the understanding of the consultant role itself, directions of change, social systems unfreezing, and the assessment of change. These questions are discussed below.

What are the Comparative Experiences of Consultants and the Organization During Change?

As we noted above, the organizational transformation literature has focused on the experience of organizations undergoing change, while attributing proactive intent primarily to managers. The OD literature has focused more on the actions consultants take and their effects in the organization. However, relatively little literature has explored in depth the reactions of consultants and the actions of organizational members other than managers during an intervention. The joint consideration of OD and organizational transformation suggests that it would be useful to explore these different types of experiences and actions. For example, we described an intervention by Pasmore and Friedlander (1982) in which managers responded very negatively to task force suggestions. The Pasmore and Friedlander paper described a consultant learning from that experience that consultants often need to work with managers to help them accept difficult feedback. But what was the consultants' emotional experience when the negative reactions occurred? How did the event color their later intervention activities?

Similarly, both the transformation and OD literature contain comparatively passive descriptions of the experiences of organizational members other than managers (e.g., Beer & Walton, 1987). What actions do other organizational members take that contribute to transformation? When particular problems emerge, what are various organizational members' strategies for addressing them, and how do these different strategies affect the outcomes of managerial strategies or OD interventions? In general, the juncture of the two approaches suggests that it is possible to explore the dynamics of change processes from more perspectives than is typically done.

What are the Impacts of the Marginality of the Consultant Role?

We have noted above that both the transformation and OD literature raise issues of the ways OD consultants are ''in'' or ''out'' of client systems. By definition, a person who is not totally a part of any one system is marginal to it (e.g., Margulies, 1978; Ziller, 1973). Argyris (1970), Browne, Cotton, and Golembiewski, (1977), and Burke (1987) indicate that many OD consultants experience themselves as marginal. However, since Margulies' (1978) work there has been very little explicit consideration of what the marginal nature of the consultant role might mean.

The juxtaposition of the OD and organizational transformation approaches suggests particular questions that might be more fully raised in considerations of the role of the consultant or others who initiate change, are consultants' primary experiences ones of marginality? How much of the experience is due to consultants' roles, and how much is due to underlying personality characteristics? Are managers who initiate second-order change more likely than other managers to experience themselves as marginal? To what degree is the experience positive or negative (perhaps leading to early burnout)? Ziller (1973) suggests that some people are more effective and comfortable in marginal roles than nonmarginal roles. Is this true for OD consultants and for managers of transforming organizations?

What Does it Mean to Specify the Direction(s) of Change?

Specifying the direction of change in OD typically means that particular expected outcomes can be stated in advance. Specifying the direction of change in emergence transformations typically means that crises that will lead to one particular stage and issues that will be critical there can be specified, and that when one transformation is more or less successfully completed it will lead almost automatically into the set of crises associated with the next one. The direction of change of transformations in mature organizations is not considered specifiable in advance; the resulting outcome will depend on the interaction of perspectives.

The different approaches suggest several questions. How can directions of change be understood in more encompassing ways? Are there some content outcomes of a change attempt which, although good in themselves, have negative effects on the organization's overall development? What are specific ''good'' outcomes of transformations in mature organizations (cf. Torbert, 1987)? If new crises are sometimes appropriate outcomes of change, how should the effectiveness of a particular change be determined?

What do Particular Problems Signify?

As we have suggested above, particular problems OD practitioners deal with (such as conflict or team problems) can also be seen as signifying a particular stage the organization is in or a transformation it is facing. The fact that problems can be understood as simultaneously having two different meanings is potentially important. It is possible for organizational members to perceive themselves as experiencing a transformation (e.g., to a collectivity stage) that is expressed as a communication problem or to consider communication itself as the focal concern. The different understandings should affect the actions organizational members take to resolve the dilemmas. They should also affect the criteria by which organizational members determine the effectiveness of change.

The different meanings implied by the transformation and OD perspectives raise several questions. For example: what is the variety of meanings particular organizational problems can take? How do these meanings affect how organizational members deal with the problems they encounter? What roles, in general, do problems play in an organization or intervention? How does participating in an OD intervention or believing themselves to be undergoing transformation affect organizational members' understandings of problems they are encountering?

How can Social Systems Unfreezing be Better Understood?

A fundamental tenet of change theory in both organizational transformation and OD is that the beginnings of change are crucial. For OD, there must be some unfreezing event that initiates change; for organizational transformation there must be some major problem or crisis. In both perspectives, the unfreezing event or crisis is emotionally difficult for organizational members.

The conjunction of the two approaches suggests the value of increased attention to organizational members' reactions to the initiation of change. What does resistance mean in the context of a transformation? Is it a reaction to be overcome (Coch & French, 1948) or a part of a normal process of holding on to a formerly successful mode of operating (Tannenbaum & Hanna, 1985)? Can resistance sometimes be proactive, rather than reactive (Weisbord, 1987)? In general, what are the most effective reactions to crises that organizational members can take?

How Should Organizational Change be Assessed?

Finally, the issues we have raised call into question traditional methods for assessing organizational change. In particular, they suggest that it is often not enough simply to ask if there are differences in mean scores on some predetermined criterion as the result of a particular transformation, regardless of whether OD consultants were involved in the transformation or not. As Golembiewski (1986; Golembiewski, Billingsley, & Yeager, 1976) has pointed out, transformations are likely not to be reflected in changes in mean scores, simply because the types of changes that have occurred make the original measurement categories obsolete. The more important question is what type of change occurred, if any. The type of change might be one in which the issues previously viewed as the central problems are now seen as peripheral. It might be one in which some new resolution of a problem is achieved through a creative juxtaposition of opposing viewpoints on some issue. In other words, as we have noted above, the definition of an outcome of an intervention needs to be expanded. Given the larger understanding of outcome variables, it is also necessary to expand the understanding of the instigators to and processes through which change occurs. In particular, it is useful to trace both the social and historical processes of change.

When transformations occur, one of their major effects is likely to be in the organization's culture. Thus, it is essential that the researcher be able to assess organizational cultures, as well as to determine ways they change. One major method for studying culture is through careful attention to and analyses of linguistic symbols, such as stories, legends, rites, and, especially, metaphors (Louis, 1985; Martin et al., 1983; Moch & Fields, 1985; Moch & Huff, 1983; Trice & Beyer, 1984). In addition, Golembiewski, Billingsley, and Yeager (1976) have designed a way of assessing shared meanings and first- and second-order change in them through a sophisticated use of factor analysis, in which questionnaire items that form common factors are studied. Golembiewski's approach has been expanded by Schmitt (1982) and is discussed in detail by Armenakis (1988).

These methods represent important beginnings for the assessment of organizational change, but could fruitfully be developed much further in two directions: the types of questions they ask and the basis of their inquiry. First, as noted at the beginning of this paper, measures of second-order change are not yet easily capable of determining whether a particular change is better or worse. It would be useful to develop methods of measuring transformations that make answering this question much more straightforward.

In addition measurement methods developed are, almost exclusively, "inquiries from the outside" (Evered & Louis, 1981); that is, methods designed for the external evaluation of change. Although action research was originally designed to serve as an inside assessment of change that could also contribute to outside knowledge, it has not often been used for that purpose. How can action research methods that are integral to an intervention and methodologically sound be developed (cf. Cooperrider & Srivastva, 1987)? How can consultants learn to use them in a way that will enable more sophisticated consultant contributions to the general understanding of change?

CONCLUSION

We have examined the relationship between organizational transformation and organization development, tracing similarities and differences between the two approaches as well as contributions they can make to each other. We have also raised questions the conjunction of the two approaches suggests about larger issues of organizational change.

By taking this approach we are also taking a particular position about the most appropriate ways of discussing OD and organizational transformation. In particular, we are suggesting that synthesizing the two approaches (e.g., Beer & Walton, 1987) is inappropriate at this point. Organizational transformation and OD are not referring to identical phenomena, even though they include overlapping components. For example, first-order change is sometimes the appropriate target of an OD intervention, and organizational transformations are not always planned.

While the approaches should continue to be treated separately, we have also suggested that they are not complete as they are presently formulated. In our discussion of similarities and differences between the approaches, as well as their potential contributions to each other, we have indicated ways organizational transformation and OD can inform and confront each other, thus contributing to each other's development. This discussion of similarities and differences, the superimposition of the approaches on each other as it were, also raises other questions about organizational change that the individual perspectives, considered alone, are much less likely to surface.

The approach we are taking in this paper—that OD and organizational transformation have their own integrity but that each can help develop the other—is based in part on the model of transformation in mature organizations we described above. We are proposing, in essence, that OD and organizational transformation offer particular frames for understanding change. If each frame interacts with other approaches the potential is present for it to undergo second-order change towards a more adequate formulation. The particular outcome of the development of each approach cannot be known in advance; it will be created out of the interaction of different perspectives.

By taking a transformational approach, this chapter not only serves as a description of the approaches to change, but also as an intervention aimed at fostering it. We believe this approach has the potential for initiating creative and new understandings of OD, organizational transformation, and the larger understanding of change, not only incremental improvements in already accepted understandings.

ACKNOWLEDGMENTS

We are grateful to Christopher Keys, William Pasmore, Robin Reid, and Richard Woodman for their helpful comments on an earlier version of this chapter.

REFERENCES

Amabile, T. (1983). *The social psychology of creativity.* New York: Springer-Verlag.

Argyris, C. (1970). *Intervention theory and method.* Reading, MA: Addison-Wesley.

Argyris, C. & Schön, D. (1978). *Organizational learning.* Reading, MA: Addison-Wesley.

Armenakis, A. (1988). A review of research on the change typology. In R. W. Woodman & W. A. Pasmore (Eds.), *Research in organizational change and development, Vol. 2* (pp. 163–194). Greenwich, CT: JAI Press.

Bartunek, J. (1983). How organization development can develop organizational theory. *Group and Organization Studies, 8,* 303–318.

Bartunek, J. (1984). Changing interpretive schemes and organizational restructuring: The example of a religious order. *Administrative Science Quarterly, 29,* 355–372.

Bartunek, J. (in press). The dynamics of personal and organizational reframing. In R. Quinn & K. Cameron (Eds.), *Paradox and Transformation: Towards a theory of change in organization and management.* Cambridge, MA: Ballinger.

Bartunek, J. & Betters-Reed, B. (1987). The stages of organizational creation. *American Journal of Community Psychology, 15,* 287–303.

Bartunek, J. & Keys, C. (1982). Power equalization in schools through organization development. *Journal of Applied Behavioral Science, 18,* 171–183.

Bartunek, J. & Moch, M. (1987). First, second, and third order change and organization development interventions: A cognitive approach. *Journal of Applied Behavioral Science, 23,* 483–500.

Bass, B. (1985). *Leadership and performance beyond expectations.* New York: Free Press.

Beckhard, R. & Harris, R. (1977). *Organizational transitions: Managing complex change.* Reading, MA: Addison-Wesley.

Beer, M. (1980). *Organization change and development.* Santa Monica, CA: Goodyear.

Beer, M. & Walton, R. (1987). Organization change and development. *Annual Review of Psychology, 38,* 339–367.

Browne, P., Cotton, C., & Golembiewski, R. (1977). Marginality and the OD practitioner. *Journal of Applied Behavioral Science, 13,* 493–506.

Bullock, R. & Batten, D. (1985). It's just a phase we're going through: A review and synthesis of OD phase analysis. *Group and Organization Studies, 10,* 383–412.

Burke, W. (1982). *Organization development: Principles and practices.* Boston: Little Brown.

Burke, W. (1987). *Organization development: A normative view.* Reading, MA: Addison-Wesley.

''Business fads: What's in—and out.'' (1986, Jan. 20). *Business Week:* 52–61.

Cameron, K. & Whetten, D. (1983). Models of the organizational life cycle: Applications to higher education. *Review of Higher Education, 6,* 269–299.

Chao, G., Moch, M., & Malik, S. (1986, August). QWL, career paths, and performance appraisal: A cognitive perspective. Paper presented at the Academy of Management meetings, Chicago.

Coch, L. & French, J. (1948). Overcoming resistance to change. *Human Relations, 1,* 512–532.

Cooperrider, D. & Srivastva, S. (1987). Appreciative inquiry in organizational life. In R. Woodman & W. Pasmore (Eds.), *Research in organizational change and development, Vol. 1* (pp. 129–169). Greenwich, CT: JAI Press.

Cummings, T. & Srivastva, S. (1977). *Management of work: A socio-technical systems approach.* San Diego: University Associates.

Evered, R. & Louis, M. (1981). Alternative perspectives in the organizational sciences: "Inquiry from the inside" and "inquiry from the outside." *Academy of Management Review, 6,* 385–395.

Fiol, C. & Lyles, M. (1985). Organizational learning. *Academy of Management Review, 10,* 803–813.

French, W. & Bell, C. (1984). *Organization development: Behavioral science principles for organizational improvement* (3rd ed.). Englewood Cliffs: Prentice-Hall.

Frohman, M., Sashkin, M., & Kavanaugh, M. (1976). Action research as applied to organization development. *Organization and Administrative Sciences, 7,* 129–161.

Gemmill, G. & Smith, C. (1985). A dissipative structure model of organization transformation. *Human Relations, 38,* 751–766.

Giddens, A. (1979). *Central problems in social theory.* Berkeley, CA: University of California Press.

Gioia, D. (1986). Symbols, scripts, and sensemaking. In H. Sims & D. Gioia (Eds.), *The thinking organization* (pp. 49–74). San Francisco: Jossey-Bass.

Golembiewski, R. (1986). Contours in social change: Elemental graphics and a surrogate variable for gamma change. *Academy of Management Review, 11,* 550–566.

Golembiewski, R., Billingsley, K., & Yeager, S. (1976). Measuring change and persistence in human affairs: Types of change generated by OD designs. *Journal of Applied Behavioral Science, 12,* 133–157.

Goodman, P. & Dean, J. (1982). Creating long-term organizational change. In P. S. Goodman and Associates, *Change in organizations* (pp. 226–279). San Francisco: Jossey-Bass.

Gray, B., Bougon, M., & Donnellon, A. (1985). Organizations as constructions and destructions of meaning. *Journal of Management, 11,* 83–95.

Greiner, L. (1972). Evolution and revolution as organizations grow. *Harvard Business Review, 50*(4), 37–46.

Halon, M., Nadler, D., & Gladstein, D. (1985). *Attempting work reform: The case of "Parkside" hospital.* New York: Wiley.

Harris, S. & Sutton, R. (1986). Functions of parting ceremonies in dying organizations. *Academy of Management Journal, 29,* 5–31.

Hedberg, B. (1981). How organizations learn and unlearn. In P. C. Nystrom & W. Starbuck (Eds.), *Handbook of organizational design, Vol. 1* (pp. 3–27). Oxford: Oxford University Press.

Heron, J. (1981). Experiential research methodology. In P. Reason & J. Rowan (Eds.), *Human Inquiry* (pp. 153–166). Chichester, England: Wiley.

Huse, E. & Cummings, T. (1985). *Organization development and change* (3rd ed.). St. Paul: West.

Keys, C. (in press). Organization development: An approach to mental health consultation. In V. Mannino, M. Shore, E. Trickett, & M. Grady (Eds.), *Handbook of mental health consultation.* Washington: Government Printing Office.

Kilmann, R. (1985). Understanding matrix organization: Keeping the dialectic alive and well. In D. Warrick (Ed.), *Contemporary organization development: Current thinking and application* (pp. 152–165). Glenview, IL: Scott Foresman.

Kimberly, J. (1979). Issues in the creation of organizations: Initiation, innovation, and institutionalization. *Academy of Management Journal, 22,* 437–457.

Kimberly, J. & Miles, R. (1980). *The organizational life cycle.* San Francisco: Jossey-Bass.

Lavoie, D. & Culbert, S. (1978). Stages of organization and development. *Human Relations, 31,* 417–438.

Lawler, E. III (1982). Increasing worker involvement to enhance organizational effectiveness. In P. S. Goodman and Associates, *Change in organizations* (pp. 280–315). San Francisco: Jossey-Bass.

Lawler, E. III (1986). *High-involvement management.* San Francisco: Jossey-Bass.

Levy, A. (1986). Second order planned change: Definition and conceptualization. *Organizational Dynamics, 15*(1), 4–20.

Lewin, K. (1947). Frontiers in group dynamics. *Human Relations, 1,* 1–41.

Lippitt, G. (1982). *Organization renewal* (2nd ed.). Englewood Cliffs, NJ: Prentice-Hall.

Lippitt, R., Watson, J., & Westley, B. (1958). *Dynamics of planned change.* New York: Harcourt Brace.

Louis, M. (1985). An investigator's guide to workplace culture. In P. Frost, L. Moore, M. Louis, C. Lundberg, & J. Martin (Eds.), *Organizational culture* (pp. 73–93). Beverly Hills: Sage.

Louis, M. (1986). Putting executive action in context: An alternative view of power. In S. Srivastva (Ed.), *Executive Power* (pp. 111–131). San Francisco: Jossey-Bass.

Lundberg, C. (1984). Strategies for organizational transitioning. In J. Kimberly & R. Quinn (Eds.), *Managing organizational transitions* (pp. 60–84). Homewood, IL: Irwin.

March, J. (1981). Footnotes to organizational change. *Administrative Science Quarterly, 26,* 563–577.

Margulies, N. (1978). Perspectives on the marginality of the consultant's role. In W. Burke (Ed.), *The cutting edge: Current theory and practice in organization development* (pp. 60–69). La Jolla, CA: University Associates.

Margulies, N. & Raia, A. (1978). *Conceptual foundations of organizational development.* New York: McGraw-Hill.

Martin, J., Feldman, M., Hatch, M., & Simkin, S. (1983). The uniqueness paradox in organizational stories. *Administrative Science Quarterly, 28,* 438–453.

Meyer, J. & Rowan, B. (1977). Institutionalized organizations: Formal structure as myth and ceremony. *American Journal of Sociology, 83,* 340–363.

Miller, D. & Friesen, P. (1984). *Organizations: A quantum view.* Englewood Cliffs, NJ: Prentice-Hall.

Moch, M. & Fields, W. (1985). Developing a content analysis of language use for facilitating understanding in organizations. In S. Mitchell & S. Bacharach (Eds.), *Perspectives in organizational sociology: Theory and research, Vol. 5* (pp. 81–126). Greenwich, CT: JAI Press.

Moch, M. & Huff, A. (1983). Power enactment through language and ritual. *Journal of Business Research, 11,* 293–316.

Mohrman, A. & Lawler, E. III (1985). The diffusion of QWL as a paradigm shift. In W. Bennis, K. Benne, & R. Chin (Eds.), *The planning of change* (4th ed., pp. 149–159). New York: Holt, Rinehart, and Winston.

Morgan, G. (1984). Opportunities arising from paradigm diversity. *Administration and Society, 16,* 306–327.

Nadler, D. (1977). *Feedback and organization development: Using data-based methods.* Reading, MA: Addison-Wesley.

Nielsen, E. (1984). *Becoming an OD practitioner.* Englewood Cliffs, NJ: Prentice-Hall.

Nystrom, P. & Starbuck, W. (1984). To avoid organizational crises, unlearn. *Organizational Dynamics, 12,*(4), 53–65.

Pasmore, W. & Friedlander, F. (1982). An action-research program for increasing employee involvement in problem-solving. *Administrative Science Quarterly, 27,* 343–362.

Porras, J. & Hoffer, S. (1986). Common behavior changes in successful organization development efforts. *Journal of Applied Behavioral Science, 22,* 477–494.

Porras, J. & Robertson, P. (1987). Organization development theory: A typology and evaluation. In R. Woodman & W. Pasmore (Eds.), *Research in organizational change and development, Vol. 1* (pp. 1–57). Greenwich, CT: JAI Press.

Quinn, R. & Anderson, D. (1984). Formalization as crisis: Transition planning for a young organization. In J. Kimberly & R. Quinn (Eds.), *Managing organizational transitions* (pp. 11–28). Homewood, IL: Irwin.

Quinn, R. & Cameron, K. (1983). Organizational life cycles and the criteria of effectiveness. *Management Science, 29,* 33–51.

Quinn, R. & Cameron, K. (Eds.) (in press). *Paradox and transformation: Towards a theory of change in organization and management.* Cambridge, MA: Ballinger.

Ranson, S., Hinings, B., & Greenwood, R. (1980). The structuring of organizational structures. *Administrative Science Quarterly, 25,* 1–17.

Ross, R. (1971). OD for whom? *Journal of Applied Behavioral Science, 7,* 580–585.

Rubinstein, D. & Woodman, R. (1984). Spiderman and the Burma raiders: Collateral organization theory in action. *Journal of Applied Behavioral Science, 20,* 1–16.

Schein, E. (1969). *Process consultation.* Reading, MA: Addison-Wesley.

Schmitt, E. (1986, July 18). American can to sell its packaging business. *The New York Times,* pp. D1, D3.

Schmitt, N. (1982). The use of analysis of covariance structures to assess beta and gamma change. *Multivariate Behavioral Research, 8,* 343–358.

Sims, H. & Gioia, D. (Eds.) (1986). *The thinking organization.* San Francisco: Jossey-Bass.

Singh, J., Tucker, D., & House, R. (1986). Organizational legitimacy and the liability of newness. *Administrative Science Quarterly, 31,* 171–193.

Starbuck, W. (1982). Congealing oil: Inventing ideologies to justify acting ideologies out. *Journal of Management Studies, 19,* 3–27.

Starbuck, W. (1983). Organizations as action generators. *American Sociological Review, 48,* 91–102.

Stinchcombe, A. (1965). Social structure and organizations. In J. March (Ed.), *Handbook of organizations* (pp. 142–193). Chicago, IL: Rand McNally.

Tannenbaum, R. & Hanna, R. (1985). Holding on, letting go, and moving on: Understanding a neglected perspective on change. In R. Tannenbaum, N. Margulies, & F. Massarik (Eds.), *Human systems development* (pp. 95–121). San Francisco: Jossey-Bass.

Tichy, N. & Devanna, M. (1986). *The transformational leader.* New York: Wiley.

Torbert, W. (1976). *Creating a community of inquiry.* London: Wiley.

Torbert, W. (1987). *Managing the corporate dream.* Homewood, IL: Dow Jones-Irwin.

Trice, H. & Beyer, J. (1984). Studying organizational cultures through rites and ceremonials. *Academy of Management Review, 9,* 653–669.

Tunstall, W. (1985). Break up of the Bell System: A case study in cultural transformation. In R. Kilmann, M. Saxton, & R. Serpa (Eds.), *Gaining control of the corporate culture* (pp. 44–65). San Francisco: Jossey-Bass.

Tushman, M., Newman, W., & Romanelli, E. (1986). Convergence and upheaval: Managing the unsteady pace of organizational evolution. *California Management Review, 29*(1), 29–44.

Tushman, M. & Romanelli, E. (1985). Organizational evolution: A metamorphosis model of convergence and reorientation. In L. Cummings & B. Staw (Eds.), *Research in organizational behavior, Vol. 7* (pp. 171–222). Greenwich, CT: JAI Press.

Van de Ven, A. (1980). Early planning, implementation, and performance in new organizations. In J. Kimberly & R. Miles (Eds.), *The organizational life cycle* (pp. 83–133). San Francisco: Jossey-Bass.

Van de Ven, A., Hudson, R., & Schroeder, D. (1984). Designing new business startups: Entrepreneurial, organizational and ecological considerations. *Journal of Management, 10,* 87–107.

Watzlawick, P., Weakland, J., & Fisch, R. (1974). *Change: Principles of problem formation and problem resolution.* New York: Norton.

Weakland, J., Fisch, R., & Segal, L. (1982). *The tactics of change.* San Francisco: Jossey-Bass.

Weisbord, M. (1987). Toward third wave management and consulting. *Organizational Dynamics, 15*(3), 5–24.

Whetten, D. (1980). Sources, responses, and effects of organizational decline. In J. Kimberly & R. Miles (Eds.), *The organizational life cycle* (pp. 342–375). San Francisco: Jossey-Bass.

Woodman, R. & Wayne, S. (1985). An investigation of positive findings bias in evaluation of organization development interventions. *Academy of Management Journal, 28,* 889–913.

Woodruff, A. & Engle, T. (1985). Strategic therapy and agency development: Using circular thinking to turn the corner. *Journal of Strategic and Systemic Therapies, 4*(4), 25–29.

Zammuto, R. (1982). Organizational decline and management education. *Exchange: The organizational behavior teaching journal, 7*(3), 5–12.

Zand, D. (1974). Collateral organizations: A new change strategy. *Journal of Applied Behavioral Science, 10,* 63–89.

Ziller, R. (1973). *The social self.* New York: Pergamon.

WHY OD MUST BECOME
STRATEGIC

Mariann Jelinek and Joseph A. Litterer

ABSTRACT

In the face of overwhelming technological and economic changes, and unprece-
dented strategic challenges, managers have never needed OD skills more. Yet
OD's traditional focus on discrete small groups and its traditional indifference to
organizational goals has often alienated those who need OD most. In the context of
survival struggles and urgent needs for integration across organizational units,
OD's focuses and limitations damage its legitimacy.

Change is increasingly important for all organizations, both now and in the future.
Survival in a global economic marketplace characterized by rapid technological
change, short product life cycles, and complex environmental changes depends on
effective change management. Even the hoped-for "technological fix" of advanced manufacturing technology depends firmly upon facilitation skills and
change management—expertise at the heart of OD.

If OD is to reach the managers who need it, OD practitioners must expand their
horizons to emphasize integration of groups within the organization and in service

Research in Organizational Change and Development, Vol. 2, pages 135–162.
ISBN: 0-89232-772-3

of larger organizational goals. They must recognize real and urgent pressures for performance, and take into account changing strategic goals. Without key OD skills and perspectives, managerial efforts to change culture, shift strategy or organizational mission, or implement complex new technologies will falter. Without important shifts in perspectives, OD will be unable to communicate with managers who need these skills.

The required new perspective constitutes a strategic OD, well versed in the external realities that create change within organizations and sensitive to the pervasive impact of changes in technology, competitive environment, and organizational demands. Such a strategic OD will not abandon traditional counseling and small group roles, but will vastly expand its horizons to include a whole gamut of new responsibilities.

INTRODUCTION

Consider two perspectives:

Organizational Development really doesn't work. It is often considered an illegitimate exercise of either altruism or personal intrusion, and certainly of no legitimacy or relevance to the operation of a business. Its lack of credibility is underlined in the heightened competitive situation of today, when economic efficiency and even survival are at issue.

Change is at the heart of business survival today and in the future. Successful innovation, the effective management of change, and high responsiveness to a complex and changing environment are vital for organizational survival. The skills that facilitate change are OD skills, and never have they been needed more urgently or more broadly than today.

Both of these opposing statements are true. The paradox this entails is the focus of our discussion. Without substantive change, Organizational Development may emulate the dinosaur, failing to adapt as the world changes around it. The dinosaur was well fitted to the conditions into which it was born, but it was unable to cope with a colder climate. The situation of business organizations, and thus of OD, has altered—drastically, basically, and structurally—to a far more competitive and demanding climate. If OD is to survive, it must change substantially and change now. To "wait and see" in hopes that the world will return to the old ways, is an invitation to extinction.

Organizations today face an unexpected, complex interaction of multiple changes in environment, technology, and society. These are not ordinary times. Managers who are skilled at recognizing typical organizational problems and dealing with them find that their old solutions, and even their old diagnoses, are somehow awry. The changes are so profound that they affect the unexamined underpinnings of our world. Old assumptions and beliefs, now obsolete, may seriously mislead. This makes effective response doubly difficult.

Such changes offer sweeping opportunities for a fundamental revitalization of OD. Managers need new paradigms that take into account the changing realities that face them. They need ways of understanding and making sense of newly risen crucial issues that did not exist, or could be simply ignored, not long ago. Organizations too must change, to respond effectively to new conditions. That shift has already begun. Tentatively sometimes, inefficiently and by trial and error, managers have already begun to restructure their organizations and management practices. They have found little help from traditional OD, focused as it is on interpersonal conflict or group relations. This OD seems simply irrelevant to the central concerns of today because it has little to say of organizational goals, economic survival, technological change as a strategic issue with organization-wide consequences, or the integration of specialists across groups, especially where hierarchy and expertise do not align. Yet changing managers' mental models and providing effective heuristics for operating amid complex realities should be right up OD's alley. So, too, should the team building, goal communication, and consensus-building skills that managers need so urgently today. None of this will be perceived by clients desperately in need of these skills, however, unless OD can recast its practice into the context of real organizational needs—in language that managers can understand.

We will begin by describing the interactive factors creating the new environment of business organizations. OD practitioners must be conversant with this reality, or be dismissed as irrelevant. Next, we will briefly describe the new organizations emerging to function in this world. Because they must operate in new conditions and serve changed purposes, these organizations differ from those of the past. As a result, their members and managers must create and fill new roles. These changes in turn imply new roles and tasks for OD. Our discussion will conclude with a strategy for OD. Indeed, we suggest, OD is in need of a new statement of its professional mission, a new understanding of how that mission is to be served, and appropriate vocabulary for communicating with clients through their concerns.

INTERACTIVE TRENDS CREATING THE NEW WORLD

Many basic features of the world of organizations and business are changing simultaneously. Change in any feature would require significant adaptation, but the combined effect is overwhelming. The changes are by no means completed, nor is it possible to predict all the details of their outcome. Nevertheless, the impact of several key dimensions is already taking visible shape, creating a vastly different strategic arena for business. OD must understand this new ocean to navigate in it. Three factors are central to the changes. Competition is increasingly global, and there are essentially no protected "domestic" markets. Manufacturing (and much of service as well) is being revolutionized by an increasing science base, available to competitors around the world. And computers are being broadly utilized. The result is accelerating competition, with intense pressure on firms' abilities to respond to change and provide both quality and low cost.

Success cannot be had as a "technological fix," despite the importance of technical mastery (see, for example, Abernathy, 1978; Graham & Rosenthal, 1985; Kolodny & Stjernberg, 1985). Indeed, the technology itself cannot be made to work without much higher interpersonal management skills than are typical in traditional organizations. Rather than a technological fix, new models of organization and new visions of strategy and management practice are required. If OD is to serve these needs, OD practitioners must understand the impact of new technology on management tasks and roles. Most especially, OD practitioners must comprehend the changed world of management and the multiple, interactive factors that create it.

The Globalization of Business

The shift from international business to global business signals more than a fashionable figure of speech. Formerly, substantial emphasis on foreign markets was the exception rather than the norm, a luxury typically isolated from the "real" action of the domestic marketplace. While some industries have been more international than others, truly global perspectives are a recent phenomenon. For many U.S. firms, until recently, foreign sales were an opportunity for dumping surplus output, or for smoothing onshore activities—if demand increased at home, exports could easily be curtailed; if domestic demand slumped, exports might ease the crunch. Firms somewhat more serious about foreign activities might go so far as to identify a separate department or unit, or perhaps even a foreign subsidiary. Foreign markets were clearly an ancillary activity (Fouraker & Stopford, 1968; Merryfield, 1983). When foreign firms expanded into U.S. markets, until recently, it was often in a limited way through price competition or in specialty areas such as couturier clothing and high-performance autos. They did not compete across all our markets nor with a wide variety of marketing approaches. International business—both ours and theirs—was for the most part limited and partial.

Today, this picture is radically changed. Virtually every industry faces increasingly global competition. The Department of Commerce estimates that 70 percent of U.S. business faces significant foreign competition in home markets (Merryfield, 1983). Massive trade deficits in recent years, especially with Japan, compel a growing recognition that we are part of a global economy, and must compete in a global marketplace. Steel, electronics, and automobiles highlight the nature of the changed competition. In each of these industries, the U.S. dominated world markets for decades; in each, strenuous competition now exists both at home and abroad. Leaving aside for the moment the complexities of dumping allegations, foreign government subsidies to favored industries, and very real differences in wage rates, the underlying data suggest that some fundamentally new ways of organizing have evolved (Jelinek & Goldhar, 1986; Kolodny & Stjernberg, 1985; Ouchi, 1981; Thurow, 1985; Vogel, 1979). Offshore manufacturers can out-produce U.S. manufacturers by a healthy margin, to deliver lower cost products despite shipping and tariff charges (Abegglen & Stalk, 1985; Walleck, 1985).

In steel, foreign competition seems highly successful: Far Eastern producers seem to have a firm grasp on perhaps 25 percent of the U.S. market for commodity steel. Their success is founded on highly efficient production and lower cost for comparable quality. There are exceptions; specialty steel markers in the United States, and the so-called "minimills" have retained market share despite competition. Moreover, the best U.S. mills produce with fewer man-hours per ton than anyone in the world. On average, however, U.S. steelmakers have lost out, and employment in this basic industry is down by over 50 percent from the peak in 1952, with the trends in employment most sharply down recently (Abegglen & Stalk, 1985; Eckstein et al., 1984).

In automobiles, the story is still more striking. Several reliable sources concur on a cost advantage of $1600 to $2400 per *landed* Japanese compact car (including shipping and duty) over small cars of U.S. manufacture (Abernathy et al., 1983; Walleck, 1985). Nor is price the only appeal. For the 1985 model year, Japanese cars average about half the problems per hundred cars as major U.S. makers (Jensen, 1985). Until quite recently, Japanese cars were under voluntary quota restrictions limiting the number that might be imported, and U.S. consumers either paid a premium, waited, or both. Imports now hold about one-third of the U.S. market. GM has been surpassed as the largest manufacturer of motor vehicles in the world, and U.S. car makers have suffered substantial market share losses abroad as well.

Vast improvements in communications and physical distribution have lessened the isolation of distant countries. Industrial development has spread as well. The rapid build-up of plant capacity and business skills in many countries which have very small internal markets and therefore must export has led many of them to think of the world as their market. Firms in more developed nations also often see themselves more dependent upon exports than has been typical in the United States, and they, too, have developed a global view of their business. The world is their market, and also the setting of their factories and research laboratories. For example, VW locates its factories around the world with parts coming from plants in several countries to assembly factories located near population centers.

Direct Labor: Not the Main Issue. Global rather than a national thinking is increasing among U.S. firms, but it has been slower to emerge here than abroad—often to our cost. Many firms have more or less backed into operations abroad in search of lower labor costs. Often, however, lower wage rates are the least important consequence of foreign operations, as numerous Japanese operations in the high-cost labor market of the United States will perhaps suggest. Market entry, establishing a base of operations within a sphere of tariffs, a desire to spread risk, satisfying local requirements for domestic value added, proximity to markets, and other, larger considerations of truly global operations are of greater concern, and greater long-term benefit.

Markets abroad are important, and foreign competitors see our domestic markets as legitimate and important targets. U.S. markets both here and abroad are under attack with a variety of approaches—not merely low cost or luxury items, but often technologically superior goods as well (Abegglen & Stalk, 1985; Kottler, Fahey, & Jatusripitak, 1985; Walleck, 1985). The impact for all firms, whether they have adopted a global perspective or not, is that they are now competing in a global economy. It is difficult to find a U.S. industry that is not being buffeted by foreign competitors who have a wide variety of competing products or offer substitute products with attractive new features, often at lower prices or with better quality. Foreign firms' operating strategies, highly successful and very different from the normal U.S. practice, seem new and confusing.

A brief return to the auto industry will underline the nature of the problem. In 1980, Ford Europe was arguably the most efficient of the Western automakers. Ford Europe made 1,500,000 cars and trucks that year, with a total census of 140,000 employees at all levels. In 1980, Mazda manufactured 1,100,000 vehicles—with 22,000 employees (Miles & Rosenberg, 1982). These figures testify not to incremental improvements, nor even simply to eliminating direct labor by automation. Indeed, it is rare that more than 20 percent of total cost is due to direct labor in any manufacturing operation, and for cars the percentage is only about 8½ percent in the United States today. The figures testify to a radically different approach to organizing work. In a global economy, such advances come quickly to bear upon organizations around the world: a new and higher standard of competition is set. As a result, firms who previously had functioned in relatively ordered and well understood markets now find themselves in fragmented, poorly understood and swiftly changing markets, beset by competitive strategies they do not understand.

What this Means for OD.   The globalization of business means, as we noted earlier, not just thinking of a world-wide market but of conducting business on a world scale, where not only the market is thought of in global scope but also manufacturing, the conduct of research, and in fact all business functions. For OD, it means helping business executives ask the most basic questions: "What is our business?" "What is the domain in which we carry out this business?" "What is our charter?" These core questions are not easy to pose, let alone to answer. Managers are unlikely to undertake the search for answers unless they understand a real need to do so. Here the OD practitioner can help managers recognize the need to address such fundamental identity issues. Simply because OD can focus on paradigms and frames of reference, OD can help to properly frame the discussion, pointing to paradigm issues and larger realities which managers themselves may find especially difficult to articulate.

Global business also means managing across diverse cultures, whether brought together through mergers, joint ventures or subsidiaries, or as customers and firm employees. Corporate culture is far broader, more various, and more important in a global enterprise than the current buzz words and stereotypes imply (Adler & Jelinek, 1986). Here, too, OD has a role to play, in fostering understanding and tolerance, as well as effective collaboration.

Increased Science Base for Business

Technology has also changed radically, rendering the unexamined underpinnings of managers' thinking dangerously obsolete. Technological change per se is not new: the first industrial revolution started with new technology in business, and science and engineering have fed the growth of business since. For much of this time, however, knowledge was produced by small numbers of technically trained people, themselves educated and aggregated in a few key locations. These places became the driving centers of business. Today, that picture has changed. At least 90 percent of all scientists who ever lived are alive today (Merryfield, 1983) and they are no longer concentrated in a few locations. The pool of technical talent has grown large enough to bring about a qualitative change. Not only are more engineers and scientists developing new products and processes, but they are being used directly in manufacturing, marketing, and management activities in numbers and in ways that are altering the basic ways firms operate. Firms that do not employ sufficient numbers of technical personnel throughout their organization are in danger of falling behind better staffed competitors.

The Japanese advantage in manufacturing and their ability to move products from laboratory to marketplace swiftly are but two examples of how the science base affects business. Japanese managers more typically have science or engineering backgrounds than do U.S. managers. Their technical expertise leads to a widespread emphasis on production. All Japanese employees (not just managers) pay fanatical attention to production details. Their mastery was achieved for the most part before the application of robotics or computer controls to production and assembly processes by virtue of attention, statistical process control, and top-level commitment to quality in manufacturing (Schoenberger, 1982; Hayes & Garvin, 1982). German organizations are similar. What is visible in both is a different way of managing people and technology, one in which technology is everyone's concern, not just the concern of specialists or technical management.

The level of expertise required has grown rapidly over a relatively short time. Often new techniques and materials together offer physical characteristics, performance, and economies that were inconceivable not long ago. To garner these benefits, however, highly complex production processes with excruciatingly exact standards have become routine. Semiconductor manufacture, with parts-per-million materials control and sub-micron circuit architecture under clean-room conditions (10,000 times cleaner in particle counts per volume of air than a good hospital operating room), suggests the complexity. Managing this complexity is different from managing the over-simplified tasks of highly divided work. Increasingly, meticulous precision must be achieved by a vast array of highly trained technical specialists—whose technical expertise often has a very short obsolescence "half-life," requiring virtually constant training. The tasks are more demanding, the diversity greater, and the requirement that everything "come together" even more imperative than in the past. This cannot be managed in the old way.

The integration of technical specialists in research and engineering and manufacturing, marketing and other personnel has been pursued for years by line-staff organizations and matrix organizations. Their efforts have sought to integrate specialized knowledge or efforts into a common product or service; no common or shared perspective was needed beyond this. The infusion of scientific knowledge into manufacturing has made it necessary to not only integrate specialized pools of knowledge but to create common, shared technical knowledge of a high order, knowledge based in the organization and its needs, not in a specialist discipline. Organic organizations of a new, truly integrated kind are needed.

What this Means for the OD Practitioner. Besides helping managers to explore and understand the implications of new technology for their assumptions about organizing, people, and business, OD can help to articulate and respond to motivation, training, succession, and obsolescence issues. Human Resource Management is moving in this direction, but the need is far more pervasive than is usually recognized. Massive retraining efforts—including training for managers—is only a portion of what is needed. Major organizational changes and new structures are implied by technology change. Managers must determine the dimensions of the technical knowledge that organization members must share to be technically literate in their business. They will have to design and bring into being newer, more organic forms of organizations. Professionals and technicians will have to continuously maintain very high performance standards amidst constant change. Truly integrated working teams must be created that nevertheless readily accept change after change—in products, processes, and personnel—all the while achieving extraordinary precision and performance without burnout. Within these stresses OD's traditional strengths in motivation, team building, and values clarification can offer important assistance, but only if they are linked to a pervasively strategic view.

Computer Applications

Under these conditions, computers offer important gains in precision, quality, and replicability, as well as speed. The third key trend, the application of computers across the whole array of organizational activities, intensifies both the pace of change and the science base of manufacturing. Computers can also be applied to design, engineering, manufacturing support, accounting, inventory, and other indirect cost activities. There, too, meticulous attention to details, highly accurate and timely information, and instantaneous change and update make for enormous productivity and quality improvements. Getting computers and automatic manufacturing to work properly is difficult. When they work, computers permit production efficiencies orders of magnitude better than those of the past. Similar gains are available in service businesses.

Perhaps more importantly, however, computers carry new assumptions for the economics of production, the management of people within organizations and indeed for organization structure. Product designers can avoid the waste and drudgery of constantly reinventing the wheel, while tailoring new designs to customer need. Using simulation, costly errors can be eliminated before committing to expensive prototyping or tooling. From product concept to actual operation of tools, computers can assist manufacturing in managing change. These benefits require effective integration, however.

In a fundamental way, computers permit organizations to embrace change where once they shunned it: programmable automation makes manufacture of variety inexpensive. This "economy of scope" concept (Goldhar & Jelinek, 1983) is radically different from familiar economy of scale notions. While technology makes this possible, people must make it work. None of this occurs successfully without meticulous attention to details, thoroughgoing commitment to making all the details work together, and wide cooperation. A different way of working must evolve to insure success, emphasizing integration and change rather than the separate boundaries and stability of the past. Neither management nor workers can approach the task in the adversarial, hierarchical mode of the past.

What this Means for the OD Practitioner.   For computers to be used fully in this way requires new practices and assumptions about information and communication. All too commonly today individuals and units within organizations maintain private stocks of data to get their work done or to protect themselves from criticism. Protected information is often an important source of power. Full computer utilization means data will be shared far more widely than ever before. Information about materials, the stage of work, schedules, and capabilities throughout an entire factory have to be available to many decision makers at need. Participation in so open a system, without private files, requires a level of trust considerably higher than often exists today.

Flexible manufacturing, which computers make possible, also means flexible organizations, flexible roles, and flexible people (Graham & Rosenthal, 1985). Change is no longer an intermittent event, but continuous. Commitment to a product, a skill or discipline, long a source of pride and satisfaction, can become a source of rigidity and friction in a flexible manufacturing setting. Commitment to the organization and its success becomes the preferred organizing focus. In such a context conflict and adversarial relationships have a very high potential for destructive disruption, and effective change management is essential. Technical literacy, and willingness to acquire new technical skills, will be important, too. Throughout these changes, people must find support and satisfaction in (and from) their organizations.

These are issues the OD practitioner has long addressed: handling change, building trust and commitment, devising effective structures, reducing conflict and adversarial behavior. The difference is that in the new manufacturing organization the scope and intensity of organizational coupling has greatly increased. People, their decisions and their actions are more widely connected with others and the connections are tighter. One person's mistake, misunderstanding, or shortfall in performance is more widely and intensely felt than in organizations in the past. Equally, one person's insight or achievement can be multiplied and reproduced by others almost instantly, if it is communicated through a computer system. The ramifications of individual action, for good and for ill, are greatly increased. As a result, OD's traditional emphasis on the value of the individual gains added importance. The focus, however, is upon shared participation in a community of goals and effort, rather than the individual as an abstraction or ideal.

The Impact on Organizations

The impact on organizations can be summarized neatly: all members of the organization must be more technologically literate, and more attuned to change than ever before. In an environment far more complex than in the past, a mere tolerance for change is insufficient. To exploit the capabilities that technology makes possible, organizations must develop a passion for successful change. Because change is more rapid and competition far more fierce, organization members must be more aware of goals, more integrated in their activities, and more autonomous in their work. At the same time, because human values and the quality of life at work are more central than ever before in our society, individuals' needs to be involved and committed are also salient. In short, organizations need their members more—and must find better ways to blend individuals' needs and goals with those of the organization. Both opportunity and threat reside here: managed humanely, organizations today offer greater possibilities for individual development and satisfaction than ever before, because organizations truly need their members' best.

Badly run organizations will fail to meet this challenge. Poorly managed organizations offer extraordinary potentials for dehumanizing, demoralizing, and degrading people—and for more economic ruin, social disaster, and enduring poverty than before. Technological developments and new economic changes offer greater potential for failure, and more pervasive consequences. First, success requires greater mastery of more details. Next, interpersonal expertise to insure effective collaboration and communication, despite differences in ethnic background, nationality, culture, or specialist expertise, is vastly more important. Finally, the psychological consequences of failure where individuals have become so deeply committed is more serious. Yet commitment is central to success.

To achieve such commitment, OD can help both managers and others to understand the nature of the new technology and its needs—if OD practitioners understand it. This is a significant challenge in itself, as many mature industries face the need to adopt computers and other advanced technology. "Technological phobia" and unthinking technological acceptance alike can undermine success. Even in older industries, the pace of technological change will be swift, and change far more prevalent than before. OD expertise can help design successful, flexible, change-tolerant organizations that do truly integrate varied specialist perspectives. Firms, and even whole economies not prepared to join these developments will be left hopelessly behind.

SPECIFICATIONS FOR A NEW ORGANIZATION

Traditional formal organizational methods will be inadequate in the environment we have been describing. Deliberately derived procedures, codified in written form to be learned and monitored, require too much time to develop. They change with difficulty, and far too slowly. They require too much monitoring and surveillance to permit the widely distributed decision making, flexibility, and responsiveness needed in a complex, fragmented environment. Informality and distributed decision making, integrated around shared goals and values, will be characteristic of the future.

Warren Bennis argued for such changes in 1964—perhaps a bit ahead of the times, for he admitted in 1970 that such changes were unlikely (Bennis, 1964, 1966, 1970). Significant changes in environment and technology—most notably a truly global economy, an increasing science base to virtually all industry, and the proliferation of computers that we have been discussing—have occured since. While we are no closer to utopia than was Bennis in 1970, the force of economic rationality validates and legitimates these changes, as do the widely appreciated example of Japanese successes, high-tech firms, innovators and entrepreneurs (e.g., Drucker, 1985; Kanter, 1983; Ouchi, 1981; Peters & Austin, 1985; Peters & Waterman, 1982). Bennis' proposed agenda for OD has acquired a new legitimacy, because we can see organizations of this sort addressing the changed environment, often among high-technology firms.

The changes we have been describing require a new form of organization, a new form of management stressing responsiveness to a complex, changing, fragmented environment. Plant and capital assets are needed of a sort and scale that will permit rapid redeployment. Personnel, too, must be change-tolerant and multi-skilled. These requirements for organizations will not be met with traditional approaches to organization design; traditional management practices; or traditionally circumscribed practices in organization development.

Decentralization

Older organizations had begun to move from wholly centralized decision making toward some decentralization long ago. However, most important decisions remain centralized. North American management, often emphasizing formal strategic planning, still typically rests on top-down guidance and decision making (Hayes, 1985). Such organization may be suitable for a stable, unchanging environment, but it is proving inadequate in today's turbulent environment of technological change and intensified competition. Organizations today require more speed and capability for decision making than this approach is capable of providing. Instead of partial decentralization on small matters, a thoroughgoing decentralization that encourages widespread entrepreneurship in service of the organization and its members is required. Too many decisions, too many details of strategy and implementation must be managed for these key tasks to be centralized.

Computers and computer-assisted management offer the needed information processing capability. Increasing technical knowledge and rising levels of business sophistication among organization members provide many more people throughout organizations potentially capable of using the data that can be made available. The capabilities are there. Whether they will be used is another question. New perspectives and the changed organizational forms and processes required must be developed. What will they look like and how will they differ from present day organizations?

More fully decentralized operations require a massive change in thinking about organizations, the people in them and how they are managed. The very sort of control to be exercised must change. For a complexly interactive environment, management cannot specify the behaviors employees are to follow, nor the procedures to attain results. Individuals and groups must do more on their own. But to be autonomous within the requirements of highly complex, technical and precise work, individuals and groups must be thoroughly familiar with the organization's goals and strategies. Often, the organization's strategic goals themselves must be proposed or at least fundamentally shaped from the bottom up—especially where high orders of technically based or customer-based change are involved. Only grass-roots insight can guide organization members effectively through such changes. Yet simultaneously, management must stimulate overall perspectives that facilitate individuals' integration of their diverse efforts in the service both of organizational goals and individual needs. Without organizational goals understood in their essence (not merely espoused), diverse efforts cannot be integrated.

Reintegrating the Planning and Execution of Work

The topsy-turvy situation of mis-match between organizational hierarchy and required expertise hints at another dilemma emerging out of technological change. Ever since Frederick Taylor, management theory has operated on the premise that planning should be separated from execution. It has been presumed that knowledge of how to coordinate and plan was scarcer (and thus more valuable) than the knowledge of how to carry out the plan. Therefore it seemed rational to separate planning and coordinating from executing, and to specialize people according to their abilities to do these different types of work. The limits of this assumption have long been recognized. Work denuded of planning and responsibility for coordination becomes demoralizing and alienating. Form rather than the substance of goals become central, people "maliciously comply" by doing only and exactly what they are told, and personal responsibility for results disappears (March & Simon, 1958; Roethlisberger & Dickson, 1939; Walker & Guest, 1952).

People often feel alienated and distant from work that is planned for them, and which they only execute. For intended objectives and complex, sophisticated tasks, such alienation is untenable. As contrasted to being motivated to follow orders or carry out previously specified tasks, the new technologies require the intelligent involvement of people in development of objectives they are to attain. Similarly, in many kinds of work, such as complex craft work, much engineering, art, and design, and professional work in general (among other sorts), separation of planning from doing is simply not possible. Planning the work is integral with doing it.

The underlying philosophy of Taylor's time is concisely captured by Reinhard Bendix (1956), who describes how the common term "factory *hands*" encapsules more than a slightly archaic phrase. Indeed, management at the time would have been just as happy to hire the "hands" and leave the head and heart at home. A persistent separation of planning from doing, and of execution from involvement and ownership, has had major impact on the practice of OD, as we shall later discuss. A traditional strength of OD has been its emphasis on the need to unite planning with doing. Today the separation is breaking down, driven both by technology and values. The social values of today emphasize humans as unique and valuable resources (e.g., Miles, 1965; Miles & Rosenberg, 1982). Management practice too has moved increasingly to break down Taylor's distinction. These issues have, of course, been a central feature of OD practice. In this area the OD practitioner will not add new work, but will do much more of the old work, with greater legitimacy. But here, too, the old emphasis on individuals and small groups will be cast into the larger context of the organization and its changing environment and strategy.

Decentralized Scheduling and Decisions

While individuals and small groups have been brought into planning local work methods in contemporary organizations, they have rarely been involved in the scheduling of work beyond their immediate task assignment. As noted earlier, the need to assemble widely scattered information to make scheduling decisions leads to a centralized decision structure. The advent of computers offers a powerful alternative which has been largely unutilized. Because information needed for scheduling can be readily available at any workstation, local control by individuals becomes practical. Decisions other than scheduling are similarly susceptible to decentralization through computer-supported decisions. Firms that exploit this possibility will have an advantage. The classic OD issues of trust and responsibility, autonomy and shared goals reappear in a strategic context. Such scheduling is made feasible by information systems, and it is demanded by increasingly fragmented markets and flexible technology. Equally, such scheduling can occur only if the key OD skills are brought to bear.

REVISING OUR ORGANIZATIONAL ASSUMPTIONS

Traditional organization design has called for dividing the environment and specializing individuals to deal with explicit sectors (Weber, 1946); deliberately buffering and isolating core technical units from the environment (Thompson, 1967); having clear job description and assignments, assigning an individual only one superior (Fayol, 1930; Urwick, 1943). All represent time honored precepts of "good organization design." Unfortunately, some of these precepts are actively dysfunctional in current organizational situations, and all are predictably inadequate for future organizations, because they presume a stable environment.

If all members of the organization are to be involved to some degree in setting goals and planning, then all will need far more diverse information about the environment. If more decisions must be made more frequently in the future, then more organization members must be competent and entitled to commit the organization. If new production facilities are to be effectively utilized in the future, then people using those facilities will have to be better connected with that complex, changing environment.

All of the honored prescriptions center on the underlying assumption of bounded rationality (March, 1948; March & Simon, 1958) built into our organizations. People are wonderful problem solvers and decision makers, but limited in how much information thay can process at one time and in their ability to relate diverse data, to calculate, to problem solve, to sort. Organizations are created to remedy these limitations. But are these assumptions of human abilities too modest and too pessimistic? "One boss" seems natural and "right," yet we learned decades ago with matrix organization (Davis & Lawrence, 1977; Galbraith, 1971; Litterer, 1963) if not in traditional families, that people can adapt to having two superiors and function very well. In more organic organizations (Burns & Stalker, 1961) it was discovered that individuals can follow the lead of many others, or lead at one time and be led at another. Flexible advanced technologies and computer-based information systems seem to blur unit boundaries.

It is true that people can be overloaded with information, particularly when they process items serially (Miller, 1964). But people can quickly see patterns in masses of data and it is often the pattern and not specific facts that are needed. Contemporary organizations cope with human information processing limitations by restricting data flow, rather than providing help to recognize patterns and take action on them. Computers offer an alternativee.

A related set of limiting assumptions involve the importance of rational, logical (and often quantitative) thought. Rational thinking is valuable, but it is an error to assume that the mind moves only in a rational way, that only the quantitative is valuable. Problem formulation may be more useful than problem solving, pattern recognition may be more useful than linear thought, seeing "fit" may be more valuable than calculating the highest return (Watzlawick, Weakland, & Fisch, 1974). The non-linear, non-rational right brain activities acquire more value as organizations become more like open systems, as the environment becomes more turbulent, and as problems become more unstructured. All this suggests that we need to revise our assumptions, not only about how to manage people as organization members, but also about what sorts of organizations can be built.

New Design Concepts

We need to move from defining jobs and assignments small enough to not overload individuals with too much information, to developing people's capacity to handle larger amounts of information in new, useful ways. Rather than training people to do specified jobs already designed for them, we must develop people's skills at defining (and redefining) their own jobs and finding means to carry out objectives they share with others. From training people to be expert in a single, narrowly focused job specialty, we must move to developing people to be experts on a class of problems. This expertise must encompass recognizing when the class of problems occurs, and even how to redefine it. We must reemphasize continuous training and knowledge acquisition. Instead of teaching people to carry out a specified job exactly, regardless of consequences, so long as they follow orders, we must train people to treasure adaptation—accomplishing an organizational objective in changing circumstances, or even calling the objective into question, where appropriate. We must build for flexibility and change, rather than stability.

Redefining the Management Role

These changes constitute a shift from management as leading, directing, and controlling to management as facilitating. Managers no longer know better than others, particularly in technical areas; instead, the necessary expertise is widely spread throughout the organization. A complex, rapidly changing, technologically rich environment will not tolerate a long cycle of data aggregation, data analysis, decision making, and directing action centrally managed through a long loop of many levels and organizational positions. Data must be acted upon in real time throughout the organization for effective coordination and control.

As a result, managers have had to relinquish much direct control—first of immediate job activities, then of basic boundary transactions. Now, the setting of organization objectives and developing strategy must also become widely shared. Direct control is simply becoming less and less practical for such activities. Nevertheless, managers' traditional responsibility for assuring successful execution remains. Increasingly, to achieve it, managers must craft an organization to support members' performance of these former managerial tasks. The manager's role at all levels is changing from getting work done through people (by directing or managing) to getting work done through organizations (creating the context to facilitate others' achievement). Managers will do less commanding and more leading, less directing and more facilitating, less organizing and more organization building. As always, organization goals will be central. Now, however, creating the means to meld individuals' goals with those of the organization will become increasingly important, since individuals will often have to define how to achieve organizational goals.

As these changes occur, it becomes less possible for managers to be "in command," the central actors in the drama. Instead, managers must become facilitators of a collective effort. Managers must craft a true partnership of shared vision, such that organizational objectives can be reformulated repeatedly over time.

High-technology firms offer the exemplar: only the technically proficient organization member—in close contact with customer needs—can formulate new objectives; top management's expertise may simply be inadequate, or obsolete. At the same time, the technical specialist whose expertise is so essential most typically resides at lower organizational levels—and may well lack the business perspectives and organizational credibility needed to make strategy effective. The managerial task is to unite these divergent resources repeatedly. Because this cannot be done personally and directly, an organizational context is created that permits and facilitates such unions (Jelinek & Schoonhoven, 1984).

But while high-technology firms offer a readily visible instance of such developments, they are by no means the only place where management roles must change. Because the shaping forces of electronics and the science base change, and the global economy affect mature industries too, we surmise that virtually all organizations will face similar needs for innovation through the repeated regrouping of people and resources. The skills visible in high-technology firms today are needed for all firms for the future.

Growing Integration Capabilities

In the organization of the future, initiative and self-defined responsibility, rather than pre-set job-descriptions, will be the norm. Commitment, rather than rules or structure will be the source of control. Structure in these organizations will not be a permanent arrangement of positions or jobs, units, or departments, but a network of individuals possessing different needed skills, which also shift and change over time. A key ability will be the skill of uniting people quickly and effectively into productive, task-based temporary groups and short-term teams, as the example of high-technology firms corroborates.

In such organizations, individuals' independence will be less cherished than their ability to multiply their impact by joining with others. Managers' abilities to join the resources of their people, expertise, or area with others in service of goals will be required for success—not the individualistic pursuit or sub-optimized departmental aims. To attain integration, managers will seek to foster cooperation within the organization, rather than competition among its departments—whose boundaries seem ever more arbitrary. Integration will be especially important because groups will so frequently dissolve and reform around changing organizational needs and goals. Assessing needs, setting goals and strategies, uniting people into effective, sustaining temporary teams will be common and recurrent management tasks. Each requires traditional OD skills— but each requires the application of those skills within a broad, highly strategic perspective of organizational goals and resources.

Developing Self-Control

Centralized control through prior specification and external monitoring, we argue, is becoming less and less adequate. Yet the need for control and coordination is, if anything, increased by the highly complex aims and means of contemporary organizations. That control can come only from sources within each individual. Self-control is needed, where organization members choose appropriate behaviors, tasks, and methods; monitor their own behaviors; and correct their actions or even their goals to insure desireable results. We have examined how the skill to plan work cannot be separated from the ability to carry out complex work in a changing environment. The issue still remains whether these skills will be used to advance organization objectives, and whether individuals will apply themselves to organization goals. This in turn rests on two issues. Do organization members know what they are to accomplish? Are they motivated to use their skills to accomplish these ends? These questions, far more than ordering, controlling, or planning, are at the heart of management's new responsibilities.

To know what they are to accomplish, organization members need a vision of organizational ends and a sense of how their individual achievement fits into the overall effort. Barnard (1938) defined this organizational objective as an understanding of how individual effort and its output fits with the collective effort and output. All three elements—the collective aim, the individual work objective, and the relationship between them—are necessary for an organizational objective. To know the collective objective without knowing how one's own behavior fits in creates a feeling of purposelessness. To know one's own objective without relating it to a larger purpose creates a feeling of meaninglessness. This connection between the individual and the "something larger" of organizational goals is an important motivator, especially among technical professionals (see, for example, Jelinek, 1979).

Organizational objectives and personal objectives may not coincide, however. A person may get satisfaction from a particular task, such as designing an elegant computer program, but have little interest in how that program will serve users or support a new computer. If the organization wants elegance in state-of-the-art software, there is no gap between the collective objective and the individual's. If the organization's goal is to have a workable but relatively inexpensive program, the company may need a "quick and dirty" solution to the software problem—not the ultimate in software engineering excellence.

If the individual is unaware of any difference between personal goals and organizational objectives, skills may be applied to an inappropriate purpose. If the individual knows the two are different and does not accept or commit to the organizational objective, it will not be accomplished. If the organizational objective is accepted, the individual can work successfully in the organization despite different personal goals. Gaining acceptance of organizational objectives and commitment to them becomes a critical part of a self-control system. While mentioned less often, creating a goal structure that serves individuals well enough to gain their acceptance and commitment is also essential for self-control.

The new organizational form will have individuals who are committed to organizational objectives, and feel responsible not just for their own performance but for the collective effort and their contribution to it as well. Individuals will decide on work methods and schedules, in light of the present state of both their own work and the organization as a whole. The primary control system will be that of self-control in a network of individuals and groups characterized by their relevant skills and abilities, rather than their hierarchical positions or formally delineated responsibilities. The more complex and unpredictable the working environment of organizations becomes, the greater the need for such self-direction and open organizational goals.

CHANGES IN MANAGERIAL FUNCTIONS

From these arguments, it would seem that managers' new skill needs can be identified. Managers need to facilitate the definition of organizational objectives, as contrasted to personally deciding them. They must develop commitment, as contrasted to insuring compliance. It will be important to facilitate the development and maintenance of networks of people possessing requisite skills, as contrasted to creating a stable formal structure and systems. Managers will pay special attention to the fit of their unit with the rest of the organization, and the fit of the organization in its environment, as contrasted to focusing on intra-unit matters alone. Finally, managers will need to insure that "subordinates" also know what is going on, in some detail. Subordinates, too, must be aware of the state of their unit as well as how it should fit with the rest of the organization, and how the organization is to fit with its environment. By contrast with older managerial norms, such "new managers" will have to simultaneously stress high performance demands and genuine facilitation—both task- and people-oriented leadership roles.

The Skills of Ideas

To manage effectively in this new environment, managers will need new skills and concepts. Many present skills and concepts will become obsolete, or even counterproductive. The contemporary vision of the manager as "one in charge" will have to be replaced with an image of "one who brings together all those with necessary expertise to decide what to do and to make it happen." Perhaps the best term for such a manger is facilitator. Replacing many old, previously valuable skills with new and often poorly understood skills is difficult and frightening, both for managers themselves and others. In short, managers will have far greater need of OD skills.

Advanced technologies for information handling—computers—are central to these changes, and to the sharing of decisions and information that were formerly exclusively managerial. As the computer more fully takes on the task of organizing and disseminating quantitative information, the need for managers to be involved in this aspect will diminish. Even some decisions will be delegated to computers. For example, GE's Large Steam Turbine Generator Works schedules production automatically, by computer. What was formerly a source of great power for the manager in charge is now gone, replaced by an algorithm. But while managers may be less involved with information which can be quantified or computed, they will be more involved with other sorts of information. As more members of the organization become involved with developing organizational goals, information for that task will have to be more widely disseminated. Here, too, managerial power from control of information will decline. However, interpretive expertise will become more important. This involves the transmission of ideas, insights, priorities, consequences, speculations, hopes and fears; all things that cannot be easily captured in numerical form. Often, such information is difficult even to capture in words (Mintzberg, 1980). The need for skillful interpersonal communication to gather and convey this information increases. Managers will have to become masters at facilitating communication for understanding, using a variety of symbol forms and interpersonal processes that transcend the limitations of numbers or even written words. Nuances and "seed ideas" that spark fruitful insights in others will be far more important than "the right answer."

The Social Skills

The new organizational form requires its members to move comfortably and repeatedly among a variety of groupings and socio-technical arrangements. Multiple, shifting leader-follower relations, not stable and unitary relations, will be the norm. The indeterminate context, shifting relationships, and complex responsibilities will doubtless cause tensions and confusion. People will have to live in a work context unlike anything they have experienced before, in which familiar roles and interpretations will be missing. Moreover, familiar ways of stabilizing a personal identity—often, in our culture, defined by "what we do at work" and formal positions or titles—will also be absent or uncertain. Despite these ambiguities managers must become involved with developing others' skills and their own at networking, communication, forming productive temporary working relationships, communicating changing concepts and visions, dealing with tensions and frustrations, and working out issues of revised identity and power which all members of the new organization will experience. Much time will be devoted to interpersonal issues, and much to creating a productive, supportive organizational context.

The Pressures for Performance

One factor for future organizations will change very little, except perhaps to intensify. It is the pressure to perform. Both for managers and for organization members, a stringent competitive environment will translate into intense pressure to perform. Indeed, because members will be more aware of their organization's status vis-à-vis its environment, they may experience significantly more pressure for performance. This pressure is not of management's creation, nor is it the result of top management's "driving" or autocratic style. It is the inescapable consequence of a highly interconnected world we described earlier. Regardless of management's preferences or those of members, organizations must perform on a higher level than in the past—or lose out to others who outpace them.

It is especially important to underline here that the choice is not "advanced methods and pressure" versus "older methods and no pressure." The choice is "advanced methods to meet pressure" or "failure." Nor is the tradeoff between "pressure to perform" and "attention to people." Along with the increased pressure to perform come revolutionary opportunities to shift organizations toward more democratic, inclusive, and organic norms, justified and legitimated on the basis of performance. Indeed, only through advanced leadership and management skills of the sort we have been describing can organizations get complex new technologies to work, or achieve the new and sharply higher performance standards now required for survival in a global economy.

NEW TASKS, ROLES, AND SKILLS FOR THE OD PRACTITIONER

Since the roles and functions of the manager and other organization members will be different, OD practitioners will encounter a new context within which to work. What the OD practitioner does with clients must shift to support these new needs. Above all, OD professionals need a sense of what has changed, and what their mission must be.

Recognizing and Facilitating Paradigm Shifts

OD practitioners need a new paradigm of management. To help develop the new organization forms, structures, and assumptions needed, OD must first see the changes. The new organization is not simply an extension or an adaption of what has existed until now, but a new form based upon new requirements and different basic assumptions than those held previously. Such changes require organization members, particularly those involved with developing the organization, to look at the organization and the process of organizing from a different perspective. Indeed, so much is changed that organizations need a different paradigm or underlying framework for thought. Paradigm shift has been described as revolutionary (Kuhn, 1962) to indicate how disruptive the process is. It does not occur without substantial chaos, much conflict, and protracted uncertainty.

The OD dilemma is like that of a physician who is going frantically from one ill patient to another, doing her best to heal, then suddenly becoming aware that it might be better to correct people's unsanitary living conditions than to attempt to cure the diseases they contract from living that way. To do this, the physician might get involved with surveying population densities, assessing existing sanitary facilities, drawing up plans for new facilities, raising funds to build them, instructing people in their use and in other matters of sanitation. These are all very different activities, requiring different skills than previously used. The physician may well ask, "What am I doing? What does all this have to do with curing disease? Am I a statistician, an engineer, a fund-raiser, or am I a person who works directly with people to cure their illness?" There is a new perspective here of preventing rather than curing disease. The new activities and new understandings of what has to be done and why ultimately create a new self-concept. Such complex shifts, involving so many factors, do not come easily.

For OD, the traditional counseling role, the small group emphasis and even socio-technical approaches blending group needs with technology demands are limited in their effectiveness. The changes facing organizations today are so systemic that a systemic diagnosis and systemic remedies are needed. The parallel to the physician's shift to broader needs is the OD specialist's shift to organization-wide, strategically based perspectives.

Developing a Strategic Perspective

The shift in paradigm for organization members opens the prospect for a new OD paradigm as well. OD practitioners must first recognize that a paradigm shift is occurring (rather than an organization change); an effective response to a paradigm shift is different from that for an organizational change (Litterer & Young, 1981, 1984; Young & Litterer, 1981). Unless the problem is properly defined as paradigmatic, rather than incremental, it is impossible to resolve. Then practitioners must be able to facilitate the traumatic process of moving to a new paradigm, both for themselves and for their clients.

To begin, we must separate the paradigm problem from operational problems. Operational problems are those which can be solved within an existing paradigm and a limited focus. If, for example, there is a conflict between two departments over which is responsible for an agreed-upon class of activities, this is solvable using previous paradigms defining the existence of positions and groups of positions, of boundaries between jobs and between departments. A paradigmatic problem is one that cannot be solved with the present paradigm, which has neither categories nor relations within it to define the difficulty. Without a new paradigm, conflict in such a case persists between groups of individuals after exhausting all solutions possible—none seems to address the underlying dilemma. In such an instance, we need to abandon the present paradigm and turn to another, more appropriate one. Chronic conflict in organizations indicates either that the wrong paradigm is being used or that the parties do not share the same paradigm. In light of the pervasive changes facing organizations and managers today, there is an urgent need for reexamination of older paradigms and their limits. Because change is so extensive, the very underpinnings of organizational assumptions and managerial roles are called into question.

OD can help client managers develop a new paradigm, given an understanding of the new environment and its demands on organizations, managers, and members. A useful parallel to the shift in organizational paradigm is the change accompanying organizational socialization (Schein, 1968) or change (Lewin, 1965). We can anticipate a period of upending or unfreezing, in which the presently held set of beliefs and behaviors are called into question because they fail to deal with changed conditions. A period of reeducation follows, when new behaviors, values, understandings and outlooks are introduced. Then, through reinforcement, the individual is encouraged and supported when trying new behaviors or living with new values, and rewards "fix" the new behaviors and values as permanent features.

In Schein's model, the "new" behaviors, norms, and values already exist, so the major issue is to inculcate them into the new organization member. In the case of paradigmatic shift, the new vision, goals, behavior patterns, and values are yet to be created. Guidelines clearly exist, such as those we have outlined above, but the specifics must be evolved for every individual organization. In facilitating this process, the OD specialist cannot simply take what exists and work on helping individuals or groups adapt more easily to them. Instead, the client must be helped to create the new vision, norms, and behaviors as the shift occurs. The OD specialist will have to take a more proactive role.

Developing OD's Strategy—and Strategic OD

Because the changes are so central, organizational survival is involved. To intervene effectively, OD must "come to the client," framing the issues in the vocabulary and with the context meaningful to managers and organization members in their situation. This means that OD must adopt a more strategic framework to help the client move into the uncharted and very confusing future.

To begin with, OD's all-too-frequently circumscribed perspective, emphasizing individual, interpersonal, and group process without content, must change. Instead, OD must encompass the key concerns of managers facing the changed conditions noted here, yet responsible for organizational performance despite the difficulties. OD fails to serve managers, members, or organizations if performance is not addressed. Performance necessarily demands attention to organizational goals, group and unit goals—not merely the goals of the individuals involved, or the group as a discrete entity. A group's internal processes can be marvelous, yet that group can fail for want of "performance" as defined in organizational terms, or because the group simply fails to effectively manage its relations within the larger organizational context around it (McCormick, 1985).

This by no means denigrates the value of good group dynamics, effective communication, or humane management practices. It does argue that the perceptions of the clients—in this case, organization members and managers—are quintessentially focused on organizationally defined performance.

To achieve improved performance, organization members, managers, and OD practitioners must address the larger issues of strategy we have described. Because managers and members must integrate their efforts across specialty areas and departmental lines, OD personnel must think more broadly, across those very lines. Because organizational groups and members must rethink how their efforts contribute to larger organizational goals, OD professionals too must consider such goals and how to usefully assess performance against them. Further, because organizational goals themselves are being called into question, OD must expand its view to assist in the process of recasting goals and reconfiguring organizations.

In contrast with the earlier passive practices, waiting for the client to annunciate needs, we suggest that the future needs an active, broadly focused OD approach, with much attention to strategy and its consequences. Organizational strategy and its links with groups' and individuals' performance is one strategic focus; the other is the strategy of intervention for OD itself—its mission and identity in a world where organizational survival is at stake.

To communicate effectively, OD's traditional insights must be linked to members' purposes, managers' needs, and organizations' ends. As change-agents, OD practitioners must practice what they preach, finding effective vocabulary to address organizational concerns and forge the linkages between organizational survival needs and what OD offers. OD must acquire the language of strategic change, and connect strategic dimensions to the individual, group, and intergroup issues that flow from strategic change. Technology, too, must be a part of OD's repertoire, and OD dimensions of the changes that it imposes or requires must be a key focus.

In the present circumstances, crucial needs for integration of specialists, for the broad involvement of organizational members in governance and strategy issues, and for openly participative rethinking of strategies offer a golden opportunity to truly revise organizations. There is substantial overlap between the needs of organizations, in the emerging environment of change, and the espoused humanistic values of traditional OD. OD techniques for improved communication, team building, productive confrontation of differences, consensus establishment, and change management are all of critical importance. In essence, OD is in the position of saying, "We always told you these skills were crucial." Now, because the environment has caught up with the compromises and limitations of the past, OD is right, if only OD can communicate with its clients effectively. Table 1 summarizes some of the needed additions, to move from OD and strategy to strategic OD.

Table 1.   From OD and Strategy to Strategic OD

OD	Strategy	Strategic OD
Group process	Developing product and market strategies	Using group processes to develop robust designs for products reflecting not only manufacturing and marketing, but changing strategic needs
Designing jobs for individuals participatively	Creating organization designs appropriate to technology and market demands	Creating a climate to foster information sharing and new definitions of managerial roles and power
Team building, socialization	Analysis of merger potential	Making cultural adaptation among merged units effective
Group decision making	Strategic planning	Facilitating coalitions to envision and create new strategic potential
Managing organizational change	Identifying new product or market opportunities	Helping managers craft new strategic organizational paradigms
Helping teams cope with stress	Setting achieveable goals	Recognizing performance pressure and facilitating new technology and structure to achieve vast improvements humanely
Socio-technical focus on work teams	Technology selection	Broad organizational and systems designs to link activities and teams across the organization

SUMMARY

The interlinked changes in technology, the global economy, an increasing science base for organizational activities, the broad application of computers and intensified competition have created a new world for organizations. This changed world requires new organizational forms and new managerial processes, often precisely counter to the assumptions underlying much management practice from the past. Because existing managerial and organizational paradigms are subverted, diagnosis and understanding are difficult. Managers and organization members need OD skills to help to navigate these difficult shoals. OD must create the bridges, through thoughtful analysis and careful articulation, to join strategic management needs with OD skills.

Comprehensive organizational change, change in culture or strategic mission are by definition "strategic," and inseparably intertwined with classic OD skills. This situation presents a major opportunity to OD practitioners. To seize the opportunity, they will have to abandon the insularity of their traditional reactive posture, responding to needs and problems as clients request assistance and focusing on interpersonal and internal group difficulties. Instead, OD must look ahead to actively forecast and diagnose client needs in light of the changing environment. Both the proactive stance and the strategic perspective—seeking to link many new and varied interpersonal competences and group skills to organizational performance in the long term—require important changes in viewpoint and approach for OD. OD's skills have never been more important, but to intervene effectively, they must be related to the changing competitive context of organizations and their members.

REFERENCES

Abegglen, J., & Stalk, G., Jr. (1985). *Kaisha*. New York: Basic Books.

Abernathy, W. (1978). *The productivity dilemma*. Baltimore: Johns Hopkins University Press.

Abernathy, W., Clark, K., & Kantrow, A. (1983). *Industrial renaissance: Producing a competitive future for America*. New York: Basic Books.

Adler, N., & Jelinek, M. (1986). Why organization culture is culture bound. *Human Resource Management, 25*(1), 73–90.

Barnard, C. (1939). *The functions of the executive*. Cambridge, MA: Harvard University Press.

Bendix, R. (1956). *Work and authority in industry*. New York: Wiley.

Bennis, W. (1966). Organizational developments and the fate of bureaucracy. *Industrial Management Review, 7*, 41–55. (Presented at the annual meeting of the American Psychological Association, Los Angeles, 4 September 1964.)

Bennis, W. G. (1964). Organizational Developments and the Fate of Bureaucracy. Invited address delivered before the American Psychological Association, September 5, 1964.

Bennis, W. (1970). A funny thing happened on the way to the future. *American Psychologist, 25*, 595–608.

Burns, T. & Stalker, G. (1961). *The management of innovation*. London: Tavistock.

Davis, L. (1979). Optimizing organization-plant design: A complementary structure for technical and social systems. *Organization Dynamics*, Autumn, 2–15.

Davis, S., & Lawrence, P. (1977). *Matrix*. Reading, MA: Addison-Wesley.

Drucker, P. (1985). *Innovation and entrepreneurship*. New York: Harper and Row.

Eckstein, O., Caton, C., Brinner, R., & Duprey, P. (1984). *The DRI report on U.S. manufacturing industries*. New York: McGraw-Hill.

Fayol, H. (1930). *Industrial and general administration*. London: Pitman.

Ford, R. (1969). *Motivation through work itself*. New York: American Management Association.

Fouraker, L. & Stopford, J. (1968). Organizational structure and the multinational strategy. *Administrative Science Quarterly, 13*, 47–64.

Galbraith, J. (1971, February). Matrix organization designs. *Business Horizons*, 29–40.

Goldhar, J. & Jelinek, M. (1983). Plan for economies of scope. *Harvard Business Review, 61*, 141–148.

Graham, M. & Rosenthal, S. (1985, November). Flexible manufacturing systems require flexible people. Presented at the TIMS/ORSA national meeting in Atlanta, Georgia.

Hackman, J., Oldham, G., Janson, R., & Purdy, K. (1975). A new strategy for job enrichment. *California Management Review,* Summer, 57–71.

Hayes, R. (1985). Strategic planning—forward in reverse? *Harvard Business Review, 85*(6), 111–119.

Jelinek, M. (1979). *Institutionalizing innovation.* New York: Praeger.

Jelinek, M. & Goldhar, J. (1985, November). A new world of manufacturing: Strategic and organizational implications of advanced manufacturing techniques. Presented at the national TIMS/ORSA meeting in Atlanta, Georgia.

Jelinek, M. & Schoonhoven, C. (1984, October). The management of change: Lessons from the high technology firms. Presented at the annual Strategic Management Society meeting, Philadelphia.

Jensen, C. (1985, November 3). Japanese best on list of problem cars. *Cleveland Plain Dealer,* p. 6D.

Kanter, R. (1983). *The change masters.* New York: Simon and Schuster.

Kolb, D. & Boyatzis, R. (1974). Goal-setting and self-directed behavior change. In Kolb, Rubin & McIntyre, (Eds.), *Organizational psychology: A book of readings,* 2nd ed. Englewood Cliffs, NJ: Prentice-Hall.

Kolodny, H. & Stjernberg, T. (1985, November). The change process in innovative work designs: New design and redesign in Sweden, Canada and the U.S.A. Presented at the TIMS/ORSA national meeting in Atlanta, Georgia.

Kotter, J. (1973). The psychological contract: Managing the joining-up process. *California Management Review, 15*(4), 91–99.

Kottler, P., Fahey, L. & Jatusripitak, S. (1985). *The new competition.* Englewood Cliffs, NJ: Prentice-Hall.

Kuhn, T. (1962). *The structure of scientific revolutions.* Chicago: University of Chicago Press.

Lawrence, P. & Lorsch, J. (1967). Differentiation and integration in complex organizations. *Administrative Science Quarterly, 12,* 1–47.

Lewin, K. (1965). Group decision and social change. In H. Proshansky & B. Seidenberg (Eds.), *Basic studies in social psychology.* New York: Holt, Rinehart and Winston.

Litterer, J. (1963). Program management: Organizing for stability and flexibility. *Personnel, 40,* 24–34.

Litterer, J. & Young, S. (1984, August). Organizational paradigms as a tool in analyzing organizations and their problems. Paper presented at the national meeting of the Academy of Management, Boston.

Litterer, J. & Young, S. (1981). Non-conscious elements of cognitive structures: A theoretical exploration of managerial paradigms. *Proceedings,* O.D. Network, Seattle.

March, J. & Simon, H. (1958). *Organizations.* New York: Wiley.

McCormick, D. (1985). A developmental model of an effective relationship between a planned change group and its environment. Unpublished Ph.D. dissertation, Department of Organizational Behavior, Case Western Reserve University, Cleveland, OH.

McGregor, D. (1960). *The human side of enterprise.* New York: McGraw-Hill.

Merryfield, D. (1983, January 29). Forces of change affecting high technology industries. *National Journal,* p. 255.

Miles, R. (1965). Human relations or human resources. *Harvard Business Review,* July-August. 148–152, 154, 156, 158, 162–163.

Miles, R. & Rosenberg, H. (1982). The human resources approach to management: Second-generation issues. *Organizational Dynamics,* Winter. 26–41.

Miller, J. (1964). Disorders of communication. *Research Publications, A.R.N.M.D.,* Vol. XLII. The Association for Research in Nervous and Mental Disease.

Mintzberg, H. (1980). *The nature of Managerial Work.* Englewood Cliffs, NJ: Prentice-Hall.

Ouchi, W. (1981). *Theory Z.* Reading, MA: Addison-Wesley.

Peters, T. & Austin, N. (1985). *A passion for excellence.* New York: Random House.

Peters, T. & Waterman, R., Jr. (1982). *In search of excellence.* New York: Harper and Row.
Reif, W. & Luthans, F. (1972). Does job enrichment really pay off? *California Management Review,* Fall. 30–37.
Roethlisberger, F. & Dickson, W. (1939). *Management and the worker.* Cambridge, MA: Harvard University Press.
Schein, E. (1968). Organizational socialization and the profession of management. *Industrial Management Review,* Winter, 1–16.
Taylor, F. (1911). *The principles of scientific management.* New York: Harper and Row.
Thompson, J. (1967). *Organizations in action.* New York: Wiley.
Thurow, L. (1985). *The zero-sum solution.* New York: Simon and Schuster.
Urwick, L. (1943). *The elements of administration.* New York: Harper & Row.
Vogel, E. (1979). *Japan as number one.* Cambridge, MA: Harvard University Press.
Walker, C. & Guest, R. (1952). *Man on the assembly line.* Cambridge, MA: Harvard University Press.
Walleck, S. (1985, April 1). Strategic manufacturing provides the competitive edge. *Electronic Business,* pp. 93–97.
Walton, R. (1978). Teaching an old dog food new tricks. *The Warton Magazine,* Winter, 26–37.
Watzlawick, P., Weakland, J., & Fisch, R. (1974). *Change: Principles of problem formation and problem resolution.* New York: W. W. Norton & Co.
Weber, M. (1946). *From Max Weber: Essays in sociology.* (edited and translated by H. Gerth and C. Wright Mills). New York: Oxford University Press.
Young, S. & Litterer, J. (1981). Development of management reflective skills. *Proceedings,* Northeast Division of the American Institute for Decision Sciences, Boston: 71–73.

A REVIEW OF RESEARCH ON THE CHANGE TYPOLOGY

Achilles A. Armenakis

ABSTRACT

Methods for detecting alpha change (behavioral change), beta change (scale recalibration), and gamma change (concept redefinition) are categorized into statistical and design approaches. Statistical approaches include the Transformation Method, Coefficients of Congruence Method, and Analysis of Covariance Structures. Design Approaches include the Ideal Scale Approach, Retrospective Procedure, and Criterion Approach. A summary and an example of each method is provided. Furthermore, an assessment is offered regarding the convergence of the findings between, as well as, within approaches. Directions for future research are advanced.

INTRODUCTION

Researchers' interest in evaluating organizational change dates to the early 1960s (cf. Blake et al., 1964; Harrison, 1962). Bennis (1965), stressed that equal effort

Research in Organizational Change and Development, Vol. 2, pages 163–194.
Copyright © 1988 by JAI Press Inc.
ISBN: 0-89232-772-3

should be expended in evaluating change as in implementing it. Since those early published efforts, research on organizational change has progressed through three distinct but overlapping phases: Phase One: Identification of General Evaluation Problems and Development of Evaluation Guidelines; Phase Two: Demonstrations of Methods to Deal with Commonly Encountered Evaluation Problems; and Phase Three: Resolution of Specific Methodological Problems (Armenakis, Bedeian, & Pond, 1983).

The purpose of this chapter is to review the origins of the current phase (Resolution of Specific Methodological Problems) and to explore the likely direction of the next developmental phase. Because undeveloped fields of research are a pastiche of guidelines and methodologies any review of developmental phases will generate more questions than answers. The chapter presents background information on the development of soft criteria for assessing organizational performance as well as an introduction to the change typology (i.e., gamma change—concept redefinition, beta change—scale recalibration, and alpha change—behavioral change). In addition, the procedures used in the detection of the types of change are grouped into statistical and design approaches. The statistical approaches presented are the Transformation Method, Coefficients of Congruence Method, and Analysis of Covariance Structures. The design approaches explained are the Retrospective Procedure, Ideal Scale Approach, and Criterion Approach. For each approach an example is presented and an assessment is included.

CRITERIA FOR EVALUATING CHANGE

Change interventions are typically aimed at improving organizational performance. Available interventions range from standard development programs to modifications in job and organization design to laboratory training. The impact of these efforts is purportedly reflected in increased sales, decreased costs, and higher productivity. Using hard criteria to assess change, however, is frequently impractical, if not impossible. Hard criteria, such as sales, may be subject to uncontrollable external influences. Managerial productivity, for instance, can seldom be measured quantitatively, so causal links between changes in behavior and changes in outcome criteria are at best questionable (especially across time). And management information systems often lack the sensitivity required to gauge variations in outcome criteria at lower levels of analysis (i.e., group or individual performance levels).

These limitations stimulated research on the concept of organizational effectiveness. Georgopoulos and Tannenbaum (1957), for example, attempted early on to determine what factors relate to hard criteria. They concluded that intraorganizational strain and organizational flexibility are associated with effectiveness. Likert (1961, 1967) demonstrated that measurements of factors like communication, decision-making processes, and control processes are related to effectiveness and efficiency. Therefore, the lack of suitable criteria has contributed to use of behavioral criteria as surrogates for hard criteria in evaluating organizational interventions.

Criteria should be defined prior to any intervention so that baseline measures can be compared with criteria after the intervention has been implemented. Changes in criteria are noted and the effectiveness of the change program assessed. Defining evaluation criteria contributes to diagnosis since these criteria are used in diagnosing the need for change.

During diagnosis and evaluation, organizational members provide primary data, although some information may be available from organizational archives (cf. Jick, 1979). An evaluator typically collects data from organizational members by observing their behavior and practices, conducting personal interviews, and administering survey questionnaires. A review of research on evaluating organizational change reveals that the Specific Methodological Problem Phase is concerned exclusively with survey research methodology.

CHANGE TYPOLOGY

The Specific Methodological Problem Phase began with the operationalization of the change typology by Golembiewski, Billingsley, and Yeager (1976). The three types of change described are alpha, or behavioral change, beta change, or scale recalibration, and gamma change, or concept redefinition.

Concept redefinition is the reconceptualization of a referent variable: a subject's understanding of the criterion being measured changes from one testing period to another. Thus, peer leadership may mean something quite different to a subject at time-1 than it does at time-2, especially if a planned treatment, or intervention, was directed at enhancing that subject's understanding of leadership or related concepts.

Scale recalibration occurs when the standard of measurement used by a subject to assess a stimulus changes from one testing period to another. Such change indicates that a subject has reassessed an internalized measurement scale. Thus, a subject may rate a certain leader behavior a 2 (on a Likert scale) at time-1 and the identical behavior a 3 at time-2.

When concept redefinition and scale recalibration cannot account for a change on a measurement scale, behavioral change must be considered. If, after determining that neither concept redefinition nor scale recalibration has occurred, a researcher observes a difference in subject responses from time-1 to time-2, behavioral change can be said to have been detected.

Whether concept redefinition, scale recalibration, and behavioral change are legitimate goals depends on the objectives of a change intervention. Scale recalibration, for instance, is a common objective of programs that train administrators to use performance evaluation systems. Such training teaches evaluators not only to recognize and evaluate specific behaviors but to use those evaluations as a basis for making equitable salary adjustments. Unintentional concept redefinition or scale recalibration, however, can be especially problematic.

STATISTICAL AND DESIGN APPROACHES IN IDENTIFYING TYPES OF CHANGE

Methodology for identifying the change typology can be grouped into (1) statistical approaches and (2) design approaches. Statistical approaches mathematically manipulate responses to a survey research questionnaire. Analyzing the resulting transformation permits the researcher to conclude whether a specific type of change has been detected. Three statistical approaches have been used: (1) the Transformation Method (Ahmavaara, 1954) used by Golembiewski, Billingsley, and Yeager (1976); (2) the Coefficients of Congruence Method (Burt, 1948; Tucker, 1951; Wrigley & Neuhaus, 1955) used by Armenakis and colleagues (cf. Armenakis & Smith, 1978); and Covariance Analysis (Jöreskog & Sörbom, 1981) used by Schmitt (1982).

Design approaches, unlike statistical approaches, are based on detecting types of change by analyzing data acquired from respondents through special adaptations of research design. That is, a specific research design is implemented that purportedly permits the researcher to draw conclusions about a specific type of change. The logic supporting each design approach is the same: a *standard of measurement* is sought which will indicate whether respondents have redefined concepts or recalibrated measurement scales. Three design approaches are currently proposed: (1) the Ideal Scale Approach (Zmud & Armenakis, 1978), (2) the Retrospective Procedure (Terborg, Howard, & Maxwell, 1980), and (3) the Criterion Approach (van de Vliert, Huismans, & Stok, 1985).

The following explanation of the statistical and design approaches deals first with concept redefinition. The statistical approaches are assessed in terms of the extent to which each can replicate the results of the other (within-approach convergent validity). The design approaches are likewise assessed in terms of replicating the results of statistical approaches (between-approach convergent validity). Empirical research pertinent to each approach is used to provide additional information for assessment. Directions for future research are offered.

DETECTING CONCEPT REDEFINITION

The statistical approaches to detecting concept redefinition deal only with the group level of analysis. The design approach to detecting concept redefinition, however, deals with both the group and the individual levels of analysis.

Statistical Approaches: Group Level of Analysis

The statistical approaches used for assessing concept redefinition incorporate the Transformation Method (Golembiewski, Billingsley, & Yeager, 1976), the Co-efficients of Congruence Method (Armenakis, Feild, & Wilmoth, 1977), and Analysis of Covariance Structures (Schmitt, 1982). The three approaches are similar in that each deals with the group level of analysis, however, the mathematical steps necessary to execute each test differ.

Transformation Method. The original paper by Golembiewski, Billingsley, and Yeager (1976) defined concept redefinition (gamma change) in terms of changes in factor structures. A factor analysis of responses to a self-report instrument at time-1 compared to an analysis of responses at time-2 can be used to determine the absence or presence of concept redefinition. Similar factor structures are representative of no concept redefinition while factor structures that are not similar represent concept redefinition.

The Transformation Method is included in the OSIRIS III computer package (Barge & Marks, 1974). The inputs to this method are the factor solutions of the responses to a self-report instrument at time-1 and time-2 (referred to as the *problem* and *target* matrices). The method provides a matrix of test-vector co-efficients (referred to as the *comparison* matrix) ranging from a $+1.00$ (perfect similarity) to a -1.00 (perfect dissimilarity) with a zero value for no similarity. These coefficients should be interpreted in the same fashion as correlation coefficients. That is, the researcher is concerned with whether the test-vector coefficients are weak (values close to zero) or strong (values close to $+1$ or -1). The output of the Transformation Method thus allows a researcher to perform a factor-by-factor comparison to determine the degree of similarity between the factor solutions of two samples. One drawback of the Transformation Method is that an appropriate statistical test has not been developed for assessing the significance of the values that comprise the comparison matrix.

As an additional feature, the OSIRIS III program also produces a product-moment correlation coefficient (to determine pattern similarity) and an intraclass correlation coefficient (to determine pattern and magnitude similarity) of the two matrices. Although not part of the Transformation Method as originally developed, these measures are useful for summarizing the overall similarity between two factor analytic solutions.

An Example. Armenakis, Randolph, and Bedeian (1982) provided an application of the Transformation Method. The Comparison Matrix, reproduced in Table 1, is from data collected as part of an OD project with a student service organization (Randolph, 1982).

The information derived from the Transformation Method and the supplemen-

Table 1.   Results of the Transformation
Method in Detecting Concept Redefinition

		Time-2 Factors				
		1	2	3	4	5
	1	.99	−.09	.04	.04	.03
Time-1	5	.12	.92	−.17	−.15	.30
Factors	2	.05	.23	.76	−.60	−.10
	4	.31	.18	−.60	−.69	−.19
	3	.21	.87	−.15	.33	.27

Supplementary Information:
Intraclass Coefficient (IC) = .86
Product Moment Coefficient (PMC) = .86
Common Variance (CV = PMC^2) = 74%

tary statistics supplied by the OSIRIS III package indicate that the factor structures at time-1 and time-2 do not directly correspond. The intraclass coefficient
(IC) equals .86, and the percentage of common variance (CV) equals .74.

A factor-by-factor evaluation of the Comparison Matrix provides further
grounds for assessing the time-1 and time-2 factor structures. Such an evaluation
requires matching the factors identified in the Comparison Matrix based on the
computed test-vector coefficients. The most commonly accepted procedure is to
match the factors on the basis of the strength of their similarity beginning with
the strongest test-vector coefficient and proceeding until all factors have been
matched (Gorsuch, 1974; Harman, 1976).

For the Comparison Matrix provided as Table 1, Factor One at time-1 corresponds highly to Factor One at time-2 ($T_{11} = .99$). Factor Five at time-1 aligns
closely with Factor Two at time-2 ($T_{52} = .92$). The remaining test-vector coefficients, however, do not reflect a clear pattern. For instance, Factor Two at time-1
appears to be only somewhat similar to Factor Three at time-2 ($T_{23} = .76$); Factor
Four at time-1 is highly dissimilar to Factor Four at time-2 ($T_{44} = −.69$). Likewise, Factor Three at time-1 reflects greater similarity with Factor Two at time-2
($T_{32} = .87$) than to Factor Five at time-2 ($T_{35} = .27$). It should, however, be
stressed that these assessments were not tested for statistical significance.

As pointed out above the IC and CV statistics may be used to evaluate the
overall matrix; that is, a general statement may be made about the concepts that
were redefined in an intervention. These overall conclusions may, however,
mask some specific findings relating to the concepts that were redefined, whereas a factor by factor comparison may reveal whether a specific concept has been
redefined. However, with the overall and the specific statistics the conclusions
cannot be drawn with the guidance of inferential statistics.

Coefficients of Congruence Method. Another similarity measure of two factor analytic solutions can be obtained through the Coefficients of Congruence Method (cf. Harman, 1976). Output from this method consists of a coefficients of congruence matrix summarizing interrelationships among factors in one factor structure (e.g., at time-1) with those in another (e.g., at time-2). The algorithm for computing the coefficients is provided in Armenakis, Feild, and Wilmoth (1977). Like the inputs to the Transformation Method, the inputs to the Coefficients of Congruence Method are the factor solutions of the responses to a questionnaire administered at time-1 and time-2.

A procedure for calculating the significance of congruence coefficients has been developed by Korth and Tucker (1975).

Step 1: Determine the appropriate number of degrees of freedom and obtain the critical *t*-value to achieve statistical significance. The degrees of freedom are equal to the difference between number of items factored in an analysis and number of factors in a factor solution for time-1. After degrees of freedom are computed, the critical value of *t* can be ascertained by referring to a standard *t*-table.

Step 2: Compute the minimum value (MINVAL) the first coefficient of congruence (φ_{11}) must attain to be significant at the desired level of statistical significance (e.g., p < .05). MINVAL is defined by the formula:

$$\text{MINVAL} = \text{hyperbolic tangent of } x = \frac{e^x - e^{-x}}{e^x + e^{-x}} \tag{1}$$

where, $x = [(\text{critical value of } t) * (\sigma_z)] + \bar{X}_z$
$e = 2.7183$ (base of the natural system of logarithms).

Values of σ_z (the standard deviation of the congruence coefficients converted to Fisher Z's) and $\bar{X}_z$ (the mean of the congruence coefficients converted to Fisher Z's) are given in Korth and Tucker (1975; Table 4).

Step 3: Determine if the computed φ (coefficient of congruence) equals or exceeds the required MINVAL (Equation 1). If so, the content or "meaning" of the factors extracted from two samples may be considered similar.

One limitation of the coefficients of congruence method is that the factor structures being compared must contain an equal number of factors. Thus, unless an equal number of factors occurs naturally, a researcher will have to manipulate the underlying factor analyses. Like the Transformation Method, this technique requires that the items in each sample be the same and be arranged in the same order.

An Example. Results of computations from the Coefficients of Congruence Method (from the same database as that used for Table 1) are presented in Table

Table 2. Results of the Coefficients
of Congruence Method in Detecting
Concept Redefinition

		Time-2 Factors				
		1	*2*	*3*	*4*	*5*
	1	.89	.52	.52	.32	.39
Time-1	2	.69	.86	.23	.28	.34
Factors	4	.38	.39	.85	.22	.31
	5	.22	.06	.08	.81	.37
	3	.44	.71	.41	.14	.62

Supplementary Information:
Minimum Values[a] (MINVALS) for the coefficients
of congruence are as follows:

1. $MINVAL_1 = .94$ 2. $MINVAL_2 = .78$
3. $MINVAL_3 = .60$ 4. $MINVAL_4 = .39$
5. $MINVAL_5 = .26$

[a]Computed using the procedure described in Korth and
Tucker (1975) and in this chapter. If ϕ term $\geq$ MINVAL,
the similarity of the two factors is not attributed to chance
($p \leq .05$).

2. Also included are the MINVALs required for the coefficients to reach statistical significance. This information suggests a mixed-pattern of alignment between time-1 and time-2 factor structures.

As indicated, the initial coefficient ($\varphi_{11} = .89$) fails to reach the required minimum value (MINVAL $= .94$) that is considered statistically meaningful. In contrast, Factor Two at time-1 was found to be statistically similar to Factor Two at time-2 ($\varphi_{22} = .86 >$ MINVAL$_2 = .78$). Likewise, Factor Four at time-1 was statistically similar to Factor Three at time-2 ($\varphi_{43} = .85 >$ MINVAL$_3 = .60$) and Factor Five at time-1 was statistically similar to Factor Four at time-2 ($\varphi_{54} = .81 >$ MINVAL$_4 = .39$). Finally, Factor Three at time-1 was statistically similar to Factor Five at time-2 ($\varphi_{35} = .62 >$ MINVAL$_5 = .26$).

Analysis of Covariance Structures. A third statistical procedure for detecting concept redefinition, proposed by Schmitt (1982), is an analysis of covariance structures through LISREL V (Jöreskog & Sörbom, 1981). Schmitt recommends three tests. In a test of the homogeneity of the variance-covariance structures, a significant difference should be interpreted as (1) a change in the factor pattern (or concept redefinition), (2) a change in scale units (or scale recalibration), (3) a change in uniquenesses (or reliability), or (4) some combination of these possibilities. Schmitt argues that even if the test results are nonsignificant, the second test is needed to analyze the factor pattern.

The objectives in the second test are similar to those in the Transformation Method and the Coefficients of Congruence Method in that the pattern of the factor solutions is analyzed. The third test compares the observed variance-covariance matrices for time-1 and time-2 with reproduced variance-covariance matrices for time-1 and time-2 in which no concept redefinition has occurred. In all three tests a X^2 test of significance is computed. Unlike the Coefficients of Congruence Method, the X^2 test is an overall comparison of the matrices rather than a factor-by-factor comparison.

An Example. Schmitt, Pulakos, and Lieblein (1984) provide an example of the application of this procedure. Included in Table 3 are the results from the LISREL V analyses for experimental and control groups. The conclusions from the analyses were as follows: (1) for the similarity of the time-1 and time-2 covariance matrices, a significant X^2 was found for the experimental group but a nonsignificant X^2 was found for the control group; (2) for the factor pattern comparison, the X^2 was significant for the control group but nonsignificant for the experimental group; (3) for the comparison of the observed with the reproduced factor analytic matrices, a significant X^2 was found for the control group but a nonsignificant X^2 for the experimental. In short, Schmitt et al. concluded that concept redefinition had occurred in the control group but not in the experimental group (see Table 3).

Table 3. Results of the Analysis of Covariance Structures in Detecting Concept Redefinition

Model	df	Experimental Group			Control Group		
		X^2	GFI	RMR	X^2	GFI	RMR
1	136	212.09*	.622	.078	154.50	.576	.066
2	196	317.27*	.638	.078	273.11*	.741	.041
3	206	329.70*	.613	.094	333.04*	.703	.056
4	218	363.69*	.532	.122	355.95*	.634	.066
5	234	388.15*	.514	.125	369.72*	.629	.068

Difference	df	Cell Means	
		Experimental Group	Control Group
3-2 (Concept Redefinition)	10	12.43	59.93*
4-3 (Scale Recalibration)	12	33.99*	22.91*

*$p < .05$

Source: Schmitt, Pulakos, and Lieblein (1984). Comparison of three techniques to assess group-level beta and gamma change. *Applied Psychological Measurement, 8,* p. 258. (Copyright: *Applied Psychological Measurement, Inc.* Reprinted with permission.)

Assessment. The three statistical methods employed to detect concept redefinition were the Transformation Method used by Golembiewski et al. (1976), the Coefficients of Congruence Method used by Armenakis and Smith (1978) and Armenakis and Zmud (1979), and the covariance analysis used by Schmitt (1982) and Schmitt et al. (1984). All three methods use different mathematical computations yet are purported to detect concept redefinition. With common data sets, do they produce identical conclusions regarding concept redefinition?

One study published by Armenakis, Randolph, and Bedeian (1982) used a common data set and compared the conclusions drawn with the Transformation Method and the Coefficients of Congruence Method. A Comparison of the data in Tables 1 and 2 reveals that the results of the two methods differ—differences can be observed in the similarity of the factors. Apparently, the differences are due to the differences in mathematical computations, a predictable but disappointing result.

The statistics that accompany the Coefficients of Congruence Method, showed that Factor One had been redefined. Researchers and practitioners may find it useful to draw conclusions (based on inferential statistics) on a single factor instead of the overall matrix. Dealing with a single factor may be advantageous if an intervention is intended to redefine specific concepts whereas the measuring instrument taps numerous concepts. A researcher may find this useful in performing a manipulation check of the experimental intervention. In other words concept redefinition on one or two factors may be masked if the practitioner were to draw conclusions based on overall statistics. An example is the overall statistic of common variance. Golembiewski et al. (1976) have proposed a heuristic guideline, viz., if common variance (CV) is less than 50 percent the subjects have redefined the concepts. While a guideline may provide useful overall estimates, there are advantages in being able to make inferential statements regarding specific factors. For instance, if the 50 percent heuristic guideline were used, the overall conclusion would be that no concept redefinition had been detected. A factor-by-factor comparison using the Coefficients of Congruence Method would, however, permit the conclusion that the first factor had been redefined.

A similar study by Schmitt et al. (1984) compared the conclusions drawn from analyzing a common data set using an adaptation of the Coefficients of Congruence Method and covariance analysis. They concluded that the results of the covariance analysis were consistent with those of the Coefficients of Congruence Method.

As for detecting concept redefinition, what do these findings mean to researchers? Can one method be recommended over another? Is one method more accurate than the other? Do factor analysis and factor comparison methods actually detect concept redefinition, or have researchers inappropriately assumed that they do? The importance of these questions cannot be overemphasized. Obviously, the degree of convergent validity among the three methods is questionable. Future research in concept redefinition should investigate the different procedures more fully and recommend a *universal procedure*.

Design Approaches: Group Level of Analysis

Howard and his colleagues (cf. Howard & Dailey, 1979; Howard, Schmeck, & Bray, 1979; Howard, Dailey, & Gulanick, 1979; Bray & Howard, 1980; Howard et al., 1979) began experimenting with the retrospective procedure in an attempt to provide the *standard of measurement* described above. That is, if the responses change when they should not, is the change due to uncontrollable changes in the stimulus or concept redefinition or scale recalibration? Howard et al. reasoned that if respondents who had been exposed to an intervention could accurately reassess their earlier pretest states and if these reassessments were different than those original pretest assessments, then the respondents had changed their measurement scales. After numerous studies were published in educational and measurement journals (cf. Howard, Schmeck & Bray, 1979; Howard, Dailey, & Gulanick, 1979) Terborg joined with Howard to introduce the retrospective procedure to change researchers by isolating the types of change (Terborg, Howard, & Maxwell, 1980). Terborg, Howard, and Maxwell's research differed from that of most of the other researchers (cf. Armenakis and Zmud, 1979; Golembiewski et al., 1976; Porras and Singh, 1986; Randolph, 1982; and Schmitt et al., 1984): they were measuring self-competencies while other researchers were measuring the behavior of others.

Terborg et al. have proposed using the retrospective procedure to detect concept redefinition. This procedure requires respondents to recall earlier events, behaviors, or self-competencies and is used in conjunction with the traditional before-after designs. For example, at time-1 respondents are administered a pretest. At time-2, the same subjects are administered a posttest *and* are required to execute the retrospective procedure.

To complement their design, Terborg et al. proposed three methods for detecting concept redefinition. First, they recommend computing correlations between each pair of pre, post, and retrospective responses from each individual (profile shapes). If the post/retrospective correlations ($r_{post/retro}$) are greater than the pre/retrospective correlations ($r_{pre/retro}$) and the pre/post correlations ($r_{pre/post}$), Terborg et al. conclude that concept redefinition has been detected. Second, they recommend computing standard deviations for the pre, post, and retrospective responses (profile dispersions). If the standard deviations for post responses (σ_{post}) and retrospective responses (σ_{retro}) are not different but each is different from the standard deviation of the pre responses (σ_{pre}), the subjects have redefined the concepts. Third, they recommend analyzing the degree to which both shapes and dispersions have changed. Substantial differences in both should be interpreted as concept redefinition.

An Example.   Table 4, adapted from Schmitt et al. (1984), contains results of computations using the Terborg et al. procedure. Schmitt et al. concluded that some concept redefinition is indicated in the experimental group, a conclusion based on nonsignificant differences between the appropriate statistics for profile shapes for the experimental and control groups (see Table 4, Panel A). As regards the profile dispersions, the σ_{post} were larger than the σ_{pre} or σ_{retro} for the experimental and control groups; therefore, both groups experienced some concept redefinition (see Table 4, Panel B).

Assessment.   Schmitt et al. (1984) analyzed data using the Terborg et al. (1980) procedure and compared the conclusions drawn from that analysis to those drawn from LISREL V. The Terborg procedure, however, employed the retrospective procedure whereas the analysis using LISREL V did not use data derived from the retrospective procedure. Yet the comparison is interesting. The Schmitt et al. data are contained in Table 3 above.

Schmitt et al. indicate that LISREL V found concept redefinition in the control group but not in the experimental group. Based on profile shapes, the Terborg

Table 4.   Results of the Retrospective Procedure
in Detecting Concept Redefinition

A. Profile Shape

	$r_{pre/post} - r_{pre/then}$			$r_{post/then} - r_{pre/post}$			$r_{post/then} - r_{pre/then}$		
	$\bar{X}c$	$\bar{X}e$	Z	$\bar{X}c$	$\bar{X}e$	Z	$\bar{X}c$	$\bar{X}e$	Z
Inst	−.041	.005	−.61	.007	.008	−1.11	−.034	.093	−1.28
StIn	−.128	−.152	.04	.078	.134	−1.25	−.050	−.018	−.14
CD	−.032	−.019	−.84	−.004	.135	−1.35	−.036	.116	−.93
CO	.058	−.107	.53	.032	.263	−1.69	.089	.246	−1.11

B. Profile Dispersions

	$SD_{post} - SD_{then}$			$SD_{post} - SD_{pre}$			$SD_{pre} - SD_{then}$		
	$\bar{X}c$	$\bar{X}e$	Z	$\bar{X}c$	$\bar{X}e$	Z	$\bar{X}c$	$\bar{X}e$	Z
Inst	.36	.46	−1.35	.33	.31	.08	−.04	−.15	1.92
StIn	.39	.27	1.10	.34	.31	.37	−.06	.04	−.44
CD	.38	.42	−.64	.33	.39	−.73	−.06	−.04	−.51
CO	.06	−.04	1.55	−.01	−.01	−.37	−.07	.02	−1.24

Note: $\bar{X}c$ and $\bar{X}e$ refer to the means of the control and experimental groups, respectively. Z refers to the test of
significance of the difference of the ranks in the two groups. None of the Z's in this table are statistically
significant.

Source: Schmitt, Pulakos, and Lieblein (1984). Comparison of three techniques to assess group-level beta and
gamma change. *Applied Psychological Measurement, 8,* p. 254. (Copyright: *Applied Psychological Measurement, Inc.* Reprinted with permission.)

procedure found concept redefinition in the experimental group but not in the control group. In terms of profile dispersions, Schmitt et al. concluded that both groups experienced some small amount of concept redefinition. Therefore, there is little agreement across methods in detecting concept redefinition.

In addition to the differences between a statistical approach and a design approach, some research has been conducted on the use of the retrospective procedure. Although Terborg and his colleagues have used the procedure exclusively for evaluating self-competencies, available research on the retrospective procedure has not produced findings to support using this procedure to recall the behavior of *others* (cf. Green & Wright, 1979; Huber & Power, 1985; Rippey, Geller, & King, 1978). Armenakis, Buckley, and Bedeian (1986) conducted laboratory research on the retrospective procedure. Their investigation permitted random respondent assignment, exact stimuli replication, and systematic time interval variation. Five groups of subjects ($n=328$) were required to use the retrospective procedure in recalling supervisory behavior (over either a two- or three-week period). The findings from this study and others suggest that the retrospective procedure should not be used for evaluating organizational change interventions.

Design Approaches: Individual Level of Analysis

To date, only one design approach for the detection of concept redefinition at the individual level of analysis has been proposed—the procedure recommended by Terborg et al. (1980). That approach requires either one or both of the following computations: First, compute the correlation coefficient for the pairwise combinations of the pre, post, and retrospective responses to the questionnaire for each individual, that is, $r_{pre/post}$, $r_{pre/retro}$, and, $r_{post/retro}$. Terborg et al. conclude that concept redefinition has occurred when $r_{post/retro} > r_{pre/post}$ and $r_{post/retro} > r_{pre/retro}$. Second, compute the standard deviations (σ) for the respective administrations of the questionnaire. Terborg et al. conclude that concept redefinition has been detected when the following conditions exist: $\sigma_{post} = \sigma_{retro}$; $\sigma_{post} \neq \sigma_{pre}$; and, $\sigma_{pre} \neq \sigma_{retro}$.

Assessment. No studies exist that could be used to compare the results of the retrospective procedure with the results of another procedure to detect individual level concept redefinition. But the same arguments advanced against the retrospective procedure in the group level of analysis are valid for the individual level of analysis.

DETECTING SCALE RECALIBRATION

The research on identifying scale recalibration can be grouped into (1) statistical approaches and (2) design approaches.

Statistical Approaches: The Group Level of Analysis

The statistical approaches used for the detection of scale recalibration are the (1) Transformation Method (Golembiewski et al., 1976) and (2) Analysis of Covariance Structures (Schmitt, 1982; Schmitt et al., 1984).

Transformation Method. Golembiewski et al. defined scale recalibration as the extent to which respondents have recalibrated responses at time-2 relative to their responses at time-1. These researchers admitted that they could not specify the precise measurement procedure for detecting scale recalibration. However, they developed a heuristic guideline that the common variance (CV) of two factor analytic matrices should fall within the 50 percent to 75 percent range (Golembiewski, 1986).

An Example. The example in Table 1, taken from Armenakis, Randolph, and Bedeian (1982), indicates that CV for the two factor analytic solutions is 74 percent. Using Golembiewski's guideline then, a researcher would conclude that scale recalibration has been detected.

Analysis of Covariance Structures. As described above, Schmitt (1982) has proposed the use of LISREL V to isolate the types of change. He argued that the equality of the scaling units across time can be assessed by testing the equality of the factor loadings. "[S]ince the (factor loadings) are the maximum likelihood estimates of the regressions of observed scores on true scores . . . the constraint of equality across time tests the equality of the scaling units" (p. 350).

An Example. To test for scale recalibration, Schmitt proposes using LISREL V. If the models produced by LISREL V are compared sequentially, each possibility can be analyzed. Model 3 and Model 4 (included in Table 3) provide the necessary information for scale recalibration.

The LISREL V procedure tests the goodness of fit between observed and reproduced matrices. When scale recalibration occurs, a significant decrease is realized in the goodness of fit (GFI). Schmitt et al. (1984) state that "the significance of that loss of fit can be tested using the differences in X^2s that result when factor loadings are restricted as opposed to the case in which two sets of loadings are estimated" (p. 257). From the findings reported in Table 3, Schmitt et al. concluded that scale recalibration had been detected in both experimental and control groups.

Assessment. The two statistical approaches to scale recalibration have not been compared to determine if the conclusions drawn from each are consistent. The heuristic guideline developed by Golembiewski et al. (1976) and still supported by Golembiewski (1986) has face validity but no empirical support. Two questions seem relevant. First, can the heuristic guideline be supported empirically? Second, can scale recalibration on a specific dimension or construct be isolated?

The LISREL V procedure proposed by Schmitt has a strong mathematical foundation, but no one has compared the two approaches to establish convergent validity. Golembiewski has not demonstrated how a researcher can use the results of the Transformation Method to test for scale recalibration on individual constructs or dimensions. Schmitt et al. (1984) provide some general guidance on testing for scale recalibration on individual constructs or dimensions. Future research should be directed toward testing the convergent validity of the two approaches and demonstrating how to test for scale recalibration on individual dimensions.

Design Approaches: The Group Level of Analysis

The design approaches that have been proposed as procedures for isolating scale recalibration at the group level of analysis are (1) the Ideal Scale Approach (Zmud & Armenakis, 1978), (2) the Retrospective Procedure (Terborg, et al., 1980), and (3) the Criterion Approach (van de Vliert, Stok, & Huismans, 1985). In each approach, the researchers were striving to establish a *standard of measurement* that could verify that respondents had recalibrated the scale used to articulate perceptions.

Ideal Scale Approach. Virtually all of the research on evaluating change interventions has been conducted in field settings where researchers have little or no control over experimental conditions. Even so-called comparison groups in field settings are suspect because of the many influences that can affect outcome criteria. In other words, are changes in comparison group criteria due to a change in environmental conditions or to the subjects' changing their responses? Armenakis and Smith (1978), for example, administered a modification of the Survey of Organizations (SOO; Taylor & Bowers, 1972) to a military sample on two dates 10 weeks apart. There had been no obvious intervention and theoretically there should have been no change. The group could then have served as a comparison group in a natural field experiment. The criteria, however, evidenced a significant change (p < .05). Therefore, it was reasoned that one way to control for some influences might be to improvise a *standard of measurement* that if changed would signal that respondents were themselves calibrating change when in fact the stimulus (or stimuli) had not changed.

The logic for using the ideal scale was based on the need to identify a standard of measurement that could theoretically be used to determine whether respondents had recalibrated their scale or the stimulus had changed. The theory was developed and explained in Zmud and Armenakis (1978) independent of any empirical tests. Subsequently, Armenakis and Zmud (1979) empirically demonstrated that their theory passed the initial test. The theory set forth some basic questions incorporating actual, ideal and difference scores. Actual scores were respondents' perceptions of leader behavior as measured by the SOO (Taylor & Bowers, 1972). Ideal scores were their perceptions of ideal leader behavior, and difference scores were computed by subtracting the actual scores from the ideal scores. Contained in Table 5 are the questions and the hypothesized types of change detected.

An Example.   Armenakis and Zmud (1979) administered the SOO to a military sample of trainers at time-1 ($n = 222$) and time-2 ($n = 242$) with an intervening time interval of 10 weeks. First, they tested for concept redefinition by factor analyzing the responses and using the Coefficients of Congruence Method to determine the similarity of factor structures. Two factors were extracted and labeled Factor-One and Factor-Two. Findings revealed that the subjects had not redefined any of the concepts being measured ($p < .05$). Second, using t-tests to determine significance of differences, Armenakis and Zmud compared actual, ideal, and difference scores of Factor-One and Factor-Two. The results of these computations are provided in Table 6.

The results of the t-tests presented in Table 6 reveal that for Factor-One and Factor-Two the difference scores were nonsignificant but that the actual and ideal scores were significant ($p < .05$). Armenakis and Zmud concluded that the subjects had recalibrated their responses for both factors. Furthermore, they reasoned that had they relied only on the actual scores, they would have concluded that behavioral change had been detected. By using the ideal scale, however, they determined that the subjects had recalibrated the measurement scale.

Retrospective Procedure.   Howard and his colleagues' rationale for using the retrospective procedure was similar to Armenakis and Zmud's for the ideal scale: they were attempting to adapt a design that would permit a researcher to assess whether or not the standard of measurement had changed. One interesting point is that the logic supporting the use of the ideal scale and retrospective procedures was developed independently at about the same time. Also, Howard and his colleagues were publishing their work in educational journals while Armenakis and his colleagues were publishing their work in management journals.

An Example.   The procedure recommended by Terborg et al. (1980) for isolating the change typology involves an analysis of the pre, post, and retrospective responses for each individual. Table 7 below depicts how the responses must be organized in making the necessary computations for scale recalibration.

For each individual, an index number is computed which represents the absolute difference between the mean of the pre responses and the mean of the retrospective responses. A group mean (of these differences) for the experimental and control groups is computed and compared using either a t-test or

Table 5.   Hypothetical Cases Involving Scale Recalibration and Concept Redefinition

				Type of Change Observed	
Case Description	Does $D_1 = D_2$?	Does $A_1 = A_2$?	Does $l_1 = l_2$?	Behavioral Change	Scale Recalibration
i. Perceptions of actual behavior are the same. Perceptions of ideal behavior are the same. Difference scores are the same. It is not likely that change has occurred.	Yes	Yes	Yes	—	—
ii. Although change has occurred for both the actual and ideal, the difference between ideal and actual behavior has not changed for the two periods. No change in actual behavior has occurred. What has occurred is a change in the measurement scale—the subject has redefined the measurement scale, but really has not changed his/her perception of the concept. Scale recalibration, not behavioral change, has probably occurred.	Yes	No	No	—	X
iii. Although no change in actual behavior was detected, the finding of shifts in both ideal and "ideal-actual" indicates that a relative change did occur between ideal and actual behavior. Obviously, there has been a shift in the measurement scale. It is not possible, however, to rule out the possibility of a corresponding behavioral change, although no change in actual behavior was detected. Scale recalibration has probably occurred but little can be inferred about behavioral change.	No	Yes	No	?	X
iv. With changes detected in actual, ideal, and "ideal-actual" behavior, both a change in measurement scale and a change in subject attitude appear to have taken place. Both behavioral change and scale recalibration have probably occurred.	No	No	No	X	X
v. The change in the difference between ideal and actual over the two time periods can be explained solely by the absolute change which did occur. The stability of the ideal responses is taken to mean no measurement scale changes occur. Behavioral change has probably occurred.	No	No	Yes	X	—

Source: Zmud and Armenakis (1978). Understanding the measurement of change. *Academy of Management Review, 3,* p. 668. (Copyright: *Academy of Management Review.* Reprinted with permission of the *Academy of Management Review* and the authors.)

Table 6.   Procedural Questions, Mean Data for Each Variable
and Resulting Answers Leading to the Detection of
Scale Recalibration

Questions	Variables	Means T_1	Means T_2	Answers to Questions
FACTOR ONE				
1. Does $DIFF_1 = DIFF_2$	DIFF-ONE	.51	.71	Yes
2. Does $NOW_1 = NOW_2$	NOW-ONE	3.52	3.82	No*
3. Does $ID_1 = ID_2$	ID-ONE	4.27	4.56	No*
FACTOR TWO				
1. Does $DIFF_1 = DIFF_2$	DIFF-TWO	.81	.60	Yes*
2. Does $NOW_1 = NOW_2$	NOW-TWO	3.51	3.84	No*
3. Does $ID_1 = ID_2$	ID-TWO	4.32	4.54	No*

*Tests of significance computed between the means at T_1 and T_2 were found to be statistically
significant at $p < .05$. The column entries labeled Answers to Questions were obtained from the
results of the statistical tests on mean data at T_1 and T_2.
Source: Armenakis and Zmud (1979). Interpreting the measurement of change in organizational
research. *Personnel Psychology, 32,* p. 716. (Copyright: *Personnel Psychology.* Reprinted with permission.)

Table 7.   Computations Necessary for Detecting Concept
Redefinition, Scale Recalibration, and Behavioral Change
Using the Retrospective Procedure at the Individual Level
of Analysis

Unidimensional Items	Pretest Responses	Posttest Responses	Retrospective Responses
1	X	X	X
2	X	X	X
3	X	X	X
.	.	.	.
.	.	.	.
.	.	.	.
n	X	X	X

Computations:

Concept Redefinition:	r pre/post = ? S.D. pre = ?
	r pre/retro = ? S.D. post = ?
	r post/retro = ? S.D. retro = ?
Scale Recalibration:	Dependent *t*-value between $\bar{X}$ pre and $\bar{X}$ retro, with *n* based on number of items.
Behavioral Change:	Dependent *t*-value between $\bar{X}$ post and $\bar{X}$ retro, with *n* based on number of items.

ANOVA. A significant difference is interpreted as scale recalibration. From the findings reported in Table 8 it can be concluded that scale recalibration has been detected in the StIn dimension.

Criterion Approach. Van de Vliert, Huismans, and Stok (1985) have proposed what they label the Criterion Approach. It is similar to the Ideal Scale Approach and the Retrospective Procedure because detecting scale recalibration incorporates an analysis of a focal (F) variable (i.e., the target variable of the change program) and a criterion (C) variable (i.e., the variable that will signal a change in the measurement scale). The Criterion Approach differs from the Ideal Scale Approach and the Retrospective Procedure in its reliance on *dynamic correlations,* that is, correlations between ΔC and ΔF.

Van de Vliert et al. prescribed three steps. First, verify the validity of the focal variable, longitudinally. Second, select a criterion variable that can be used to assess the extent of scale recalibration. Van de Vliert et al. argue that something other than ideal scales can be used, preferably, "relatively central, personal opinions or values that are not identical with the focal variable and that theoretically may be considered capable of influencing the distribution of intervals of the focal variable" (p. 273). Third, compute dynamic correlations (R) between focal and criterion variables. In any instance where R is significant, scale recalibration has been detected. The extent of recalibration is measured by the square of the correlation (R^2).

An Example. Depicted in Table 9 are the results of an experiment conducted by van de Vliert et al. The questionnaire was a self-report measure developed by Gordon (1960). Two types of variables are measured, namely, interpersonal values and interpersonal behavior associated with Support, Conformity, Recog-

Table 8. Results of the Retrospective Procedure in Detecting Behavioral Change and Scale Recalibration

	Behavioral Change			*Scale Recalibration*		
	$\bar{X}c$	$\bar{X}e$	Z	$\bar{X}c$	$\bar{X}e$	Z
Inst	−2.09	−.179	.07	−1.39	−.189	.69
StIn	−.230	−.066	−2.13*	−.307	−.143	−2.00*
CD	−.078	.026	−1.26	−.074	−.026	−.62
CO	−1.93	.015	−2.43*	−.160	−.130	−.44

Note: $*p < .05$. $\bar{X}c$ and $\bar{X}e$ refer to the means of the control and experimental groups, respectively. Differences were calculated by subtracting retrospective scores from post and pre scores for behavioral change and scale recalibration, respectively. Z refers to the test of significance of the difference of ranks in the two groups.

Source: Schmitt, Pulakos, and Lieblein (1984). Comparison of three techniques to assess group-level beta and gamma change. *Applied Psychological Measurement, 8,* p. 255. (Copyright: *Applied Psychological Measurement, Inc.* Reprinted with permission.)

Table 9.   Shifts in Criterion and Behavior on
Gordon's Interpersonal Values

Value	Criterion Shift[a] (ΔC)	Behavior Shift[a] (ΔF)	Dynamic Correlation ($R_{\Delta C \Delta F}$)
1. Support	−.20	2.05	.01
2. Conformity	−1.63	−1.71	.62**
3. Recognition	−1.89	1.28	.15
4. Independence	2.15*	1.15	.03
5. Benevolence	−3.35**	−1.10	.24
6. Leadership	2.59	.39	−.05

[a]Student t value for the shift in means ($df = 13$).
*p < .05
**p < .01

Source: van de Vliert, Huismans, and Stok (1985). The criterion approach to
   unraveling beta and alpha change. *Academy of Management Review, 10,*
   p. 273. (Copyright: *Academy of Management Review.* Reprinted with
   permission of the *Academy of Management Review* and the authors.)

nition, Independence, Benevolence, and Leadership. Van de Vliert et al. argue
that Gordon's scale of interpersonal values meets the requirements of their criterion variable.

The column labeled "Criterion Shift" refers to the change in C from T_1 to T_2.
On the ideal scale, this criterion shift would be equivalent to ΔI. Because Independence, Benevolence, and Leadership are shown to have changed by a statistically significant amount, van de Vliert et al. pointed out that the ideal scale may
lead to the conclusion that scale recalibration has been detected. However, using
the dynamic correlation the conclusion would be otherwise. Furthermore, it
appears that Conformity has been recalibrated, equal to R^2 of 38 percent
(i.e., $.62^2$).

Assessment.   Schmitt et al. (1984) compare the results of the three procedures
used to identify scale recalibration, namely, LISREL V, the Ideal Scale Approach,
and the Retrospective Procedure. They concluded that the findings (regarding
scale recalibration) from the Retrospective Procedure and LISREL V were more
similar than the findings from the Ideal Scale Approach and LISREL V.

These results are interesting for two reasons. First, the Retrospective Procedure and LISREL V are two different types of approaches, that is, a design
approach and a statistical approach. Drawing similar conclusions from different
approaches implies between-method convergent validity. However, it is important to realize that the procedures did not use the same data: the LISREL V
procedure used the pre and post responses; the Retrospective Procedure incorporated the retrospective responses.

Second, the research conducted by Armenakis, Buckley, and Bedeian (1986) revealed that, in a laboratory setting (where the experimental conditions were controlled), the retrospective design was unsuited for evaluating the behavior of others. In that experiment, the recall period for four groups was three weeks and for one other group two weeks. Schmitt et al.'s research was conducted in a field setting and used comparison groups to assess the behavior of others (specifically, the behavior of professors was assessed by students enrolled in their classes). The students were required to recall the professor's behavior over approximately a three-week interval.

Therefore, for these two reasons, the Schmitt et al. findings should be interpreted with caution. Additional research seems warranted. For instance, laboratory methodology should be used in comparing the findings from the Ideal Scale Approach and LISREL V.

The ideal scale has been criticized by a number of researchers because of apparent ceiling effects (cf. Ito & Srinivas, 1981; Schmitt et al., 1984; Terborg, Howard, & Maxwell, 1980; Terborg, Maxwell, & Howard, 1982). This criticism has been based on a hypothesized result without the support of any empirical research. Buckley and Armenakis (1987) conducted a laboratory study using 270 subjects (in 9 groups) to investigate, among other questions, ceiling effects with the ideal scale. Their conclusion was that although range was restricted, there was insufficient evidence that ceiling effects rendered the ideal scale useless.

Buckley and Armenakis (1987) also found that in the experiments in which no scale recalibration occurred (i.e., the stimulus remained constant and the responses to the questionnaire did not change), the ideal scale did not mislead the researcher into concluding that scale recalibration had, in fact, occurred. Their study was designed to detect scale recalibration if it had occurred. One conclusion was that it had not. The performance of the ideal scale was such that the researcher would not incorrectly conclude scale recalibration had occurred.

Realizing the findings of Buckley and Armenakis (1987) provided part of the needed answers in testing the effectiveness of the ideal scale, Granier (1987) also used laboratory methodology first to determine whether scale recalibration could be simulated and, second, to test the effectiveness of the ideal scale. Her study expanded the experimentation on the standard of measurement concept by testing the effectiveness of the ideal scale as well as the typical scale (i.e., articulating the behavior of the "typical" manager). Her findings revealed that scale recalibration can be simulated using laboratory methodology. In addition, she tested the efficacy of the ideal scale and the typical scale with positively and negatively worded items. The typical scale was more effective than the ideal scale in detecting scale recalibration with both positively and negatively worded items but was ineffective in distinguishing *between* scale recalibration and behavioral change. The ideal scale was effective in detecting scale recalibration with positively worded items and in distinguishing between scale recalibration and behavioral change.

Another criticism of the ideal scale has been levelled by van de Vliert, Huismans, and Stok (1985). They have argued that the ideal scale cannot be used to detect scale recalibration because the ideal scale does not conform to the principles of psychometrics. It has not been empirically demonstrated that the ideal scale is independent of the actual scale and that the changes in the ideal scale are in fact related to changes in the actual scale. No study has compared the Criterion and the Ideal Scale Approaches.

A final criticism specific to the Criterion Approach in detecting scale recalibration (but relevant to all methods that employ a standard of measurement, namely, the Ideal Scale Approach, the Retrospective Procedure, and the Criterion Approach for detecting *behavioral change*, discussed below) is made by Johns (1981). On the basis of a literature review, Johns has argued that difference scores, whose components are provided by a single individual are potentially subject to unreliability, systematic correlation with their components, and spurious correlation with other variables. Instead of using difference scores computed from components, Johns recommended ascertaining difference scores directly from respondents. By contrast, Overall and Woodard (1975) have argued that difference scores do not present potential problems in survey research methodology. The source of this disagreement should be investigated further.

Design Approaches: Individual Level of Analysis

The design approaches that have been proposed as procedures for isolating scale recalibration at the individual level of analysis are the Retrospective Procedure and the Ideal Scale Approach. The originators of both approaches realized the value in being able to determine whether scale recalibration had occurred for all individuals. Not only would this be of interest for research purposes, but the practical implications would benefit evaluation efforts.

Ideal Scale Approach.   Bedeian, Armenakis, and Gibson (1980) have proposed a four-step procedure that employs linear regression modeling in the detection of scale recalibration and in the isolation of behavioral change. In Steps One and Two a linear regression equation is fitted to the data (i.e., $Y'_j = a + bX_j$, where Y'_j = time-2 ideal scores, a = intercept constant, b = regression coefficient, and X_j = time-1 ideal scores). From this procedure estimates of the a and b terms are computed. Step Three, an analytical step, requires the researcher to make one of five determinations. Whether scale recalibration has occurred must be determined first. If b is not significantly different from *1* and if a is not significantly different from *0*, then scale recalibration has not occurred. If either condition is not met, then scale recalibration has occurred. By additional analyses, scale recalibration can be categorized as scale displacement, scale interval stretching, or scale interval sliding. Step Four is a transformation of any recalibrated responses. In other words, the recalibrated responses are salvaged by "correcting" the responses to the *actual* scales using the regression equation developed from the ideal scales. No empirical demonstration of this procedure has been performed.

Retrospective Procedure. Terborg, Howard, and Maxwell (1980) have extended the concept of the retrospective procedure to detecting scale recalibration at the individual level of analysis. They propose that scale recalibration can be determined by comparing the mean scores (across all items of a unidimensional construct) on the pretest and retrospective responses. The comparison would be made using a dependent *t*-test with *n* based on the number of items. No empirical demonstration of this procedure has been performed.

Assessment. Terborg, Maxwell, and Howard (1982) have critiqued the ideal scale approach. They offered seven arguments against the procedure. Armenakis and Bedeian (1982) provided a rejoinder addressing each point, as well as arguments against the retrospective procedure. No empirical test of either approach has been conducted. Consequently, no comparison of the conclusions from the ideal scale approach and the retrospective procedure has been published. But the arguments advanced against the retrospective procedure at the group level of analysis (described above) would also hold for the retrospective procedure at the individual level of analysis.

DETECTING BEHAVIORAL CHANGE

Prior to the Golembiewski et al. (1976) research, investigators were primarily concerned with analyzing respondent's perceptions using some test of significance, for example, ANOVA. If a significant difference was found, the researcher discussed the findings in terms of the sources of internal and external invalidity (Campbell & Stanley, 1963) affecting the research design used to collect the data (cf. Golembiewski & Carrigan, 1970).

Behavioral change is so labeled because it is the actual change in behavior detected with a measurement scale for which concept redefinition and scale recalibration have been ruled out. The approaches to detecting behavioral change can also be classified as statistical and design approaches.

Statistical Approaches: The Group Level of Analysis

The statistical approach proposed by Golembiewski et al. is the Transformation Method (Ahmavaara, 1954).

Transformation Method. According to the heuristic guideline proposed by Golembiewski et al., if the common variance (CV) shared by the factor solutions approximates 100 percent, any change that is detected is considered behavioral change. The investigator is expected to conduct further analyses using tests of significance to determine on which dimensions or constructs change has been detected. In the example depicted in Table 1, CV was equal to 74 percent; thus, according to the heuristic guideline, no behavioral change has been detected. Following the logic of Golembiewski, then, no further analyses on the dimensions or constructs are needed. Rather, as presented above, scale recalibration—not behavioral change—was the type of change detected.

Design Approaches: The Group Level of Analysis

The design approaches for detecting behavioral change are (1) the Ideal Scale Approach, (2) the Retrospective Procedure, and (3) the Criterion Approach.

Ideal Scale Approach. Like the other three approaches, the Ideal Scale Approach is based on sequentially testing for all three types of change. First, a comparison of the factor solutions using the Coefficients of Congruence Method is performed. If the factor solutions are similar, the test for scale recalibration is performed as outlined in Table 5, cases ii, iii, and iv. It is important to note that scale recalibration is hypothesized to occur in each case where the ideal scale has changed. By using difference scores, that is, the difference between the ideal and the actual scale, Zmud and Armenakis hypothesized that behavioral change can be isolated from scale recalibration (case v) and that scale recalibration can be said to be confounded with behavioral change (case iv). In the studies by Armenakis and Zmud and Schmitt et al. that empirically tested the Ideal Scale Approach, no behavioral change was detected (cf. Table 6). Granier (1987) empirically tested the efficacy of the ideal scale to detect behavioral change using covariance analysis and concluded that the ideal scale could effectively discriminate between scale recalibration and behavioral change. The typical scale, however, could not discriminate between the two types of change.

Retrospective Procedure. Terborg et al. (1980) hypothesized that behavioral change can be detected from the following computations: (1) compute a *t*-value for each individual between post and retrospective responses for each item; (2) compute a mean *t*-value for each individual within the experimental and control groups, and (3) compute a Mann-Whitney U-statistic between the individual *t*-values in the experimental and control groups. Table 8 contains the results of these computations. Another way of identifying behavioral change is to compute difference scores between retrospective and post responses. That is, for each individual compute (1) a difference score for each item; (2) obtain a mean difference score for all items; (3) compute a group mean for experimental and control groups for all difference scores; and (4) compare the mean difference scores using an F-test. Table 10 provides the results of such a test.

Table 10. Analysis of Variance of Student Evaluations
and Cell Means

Factor	df	F-values			
		Inst	*StIn*	*CD*	*CO*
Group	1	.760	.229	.600	.153
Subject × Group	108	(.720)	(.910)	(.576)	(.123)
Measure	2	11.398*	11.653*	.532	3.309*
Group × Measure	2	.420	.420	1.811	1.837
Subject × Measure	216	(.105)	(.134)	(.143)	(.189)

	Cell Means			
	Inst	*StIn*	*CD*	*CO*
Control Group				
Pre	2.74	2.60	2.73	2.51
Post	2.67	2.68	2.73	2.48
Retro	2.88	2.91	2.81	2.67
Experimental Group				
Pre	2.78	2.61	2.80	2.51
Post	2.79	2.68	2.85	2.65
Retro	2.97	2.75	2.82	2.64

Note: $*p < .05$. Numbers in parentheses are mean square errors associated with the F-values immediately above them in the table.
Source: Schmitt, Pulakos, and Lieblein (1984). Comparison of three techniques to assess group-level beta and gamma change. *Applied Psychological Measurement, 8*, p. 256. (Copyright: *Applied Psychological Measurement, Inc.* Reprinted with permission.)

Criterion Approach. As described above, van de Vliert et al. computed dynamic correlations (R) between the change in the focal variable (ΔF) and the change in the criterion variable (ΔC). The amount of scale recalibration was equal to R^2. Van de Vliert et al. contended that the amount of behavioral change (including error) was $1-R^2$. The amount of error was related to the reliabilities of the respective measurements (see van de Vliert et al., 1985).

Referring to Table 9, detected scale recalibration amounted to R^2 or 38 percent ($.62^2$) for the dimension, Conformity. Behavioral change (including error), then, is 62 percent. For the remaining constructs, the computations are performed similarly. For example, behavioral change (including error) was found to be 97.75 percent of the change on the dimension, Recognition.

Assessment. In order to isolate behavioral change, the Ideal Scale Approach and the Retrospective Procedure utilize difference scores. The arguments by Johns (1981) and by Overall and Woodard (1975) are therefore relevant for all three design approaches. While difference scores must be considered an important obstacle to overcome, their use is nevertheless worthy of future research efforts. Experimentation is needed to investigate this issue. If difference scores do present problems in detecting behavioral change, investigations should be directed at the possibility of modifying the procedures or identifying other statistical methods that can accomplish the same objectives without using difference scores.

A specific issue, related to the Criterion Approach, is concerned with establishing a norm for researchers to use in drawing conclusions regarding behavioral change. For instance, if scale recalibration amounts to 40 percent, behavioral change 40 percent, and error 20 percent, has the intervention been effective? At what point can researchers make definitive statements about the components of detected change?

DISCUSSION

The purpose of this chapter was to review the research that has been produced on the change typology since its introduction by Golembiewski et al. in 1976. The research issues discussed resulted from the necessity of using soft criteria in the diagnosis for and evaluation of organizational change. The research on the concept of organizational effectiveness (cf. Georgopoulos & Tannenbaum, 1957; Likert, 1967) established an important link between soft and hard criteria. Although a review of the research on the change typology reveals that the field has progressed significantly, more research is needed.

As pointed out above, the change typology has only been related to survey research methods. Other methods, like observation and the interview have not been researched with this in mind. Two questions can be posed: are these other methods subject to the same influences? If not, why not? The first is an empirical question. Researchers should not overlook the possibility of contamination in other methods. The issues that are relevant for survey research should be addressed for the other methods. The second question is intended to broaden the search for explanations. If the other methods are not subject to the change typology issues, does the training of observers and interviewers eliminate scale recalibration and concept redefinition? A rather radical implication is that respondents may need some orientation before being administered questionnaires (cf. Armenakis, 1979).

Based on the existing information in the literature, resolving the problems of scale recalibration and concept redefinition can range from not using survey research methods and relying only on hard criteria (cf. Nicholas & Katz, 1985) to using other methods, for example, structured observation (cf. Martinko & Gardner, 1985). But is enough known about the *causes* of unintended scale recalibration and concept redefinition (cf. Armenakis & Zmud, 1979)? Armenakis, Bedeian, and Pond (1983) have suggested that researchers should relate the unintended influences of scale recalibration to the time order error (TOE) research in psychophysics (cf. Hellstrom, 1985). TOE occurs in temporal research when stimuli are presented for comparative purposes and the second of a pair is judged to be different than would be expected. The sources of TOE are: (1) general level of stimuli, (2) range of stimuli, (3) time interval between stimuli, (4) observer experience, (5) background stimuli, and, (6) other incidental conditions. Taken from Guilford (1954), Armenakis et al. (1983) provide examples of conditions affecting TOE in survey research. For example, a time interval of 12 weeks between administrations of a questionnaire may be associated with more TOE than an interval of three weeks.

Relating the change typology to the organizational life cycle concept of Kimberly (1980), Armenakis et al. (1979) suggested that organizations may experience variations in external and internal conditions which will influence managerial actions and behavior. External conditions include changes in competition or legislation that may necessitate adaptations in strategy and other concomitant internal changes (e.g., changes in structure, policies, procedures). These *may* be obvious since they may be expected to occur relatively infrequently, yet may be related to a cyclical phenomenon. Internal conditions that may change with some degree of regularity would be the changes in managerial action and behavior of reaching monthly sales or production objectives or year-end closing for accounting purposes. These events may be overlooked because they are a normal reoccurring set of circumstances. Yet, these external and internal events may influence behavioral patterns sufficiently that respondent perceptions (as articulated via a survey research instrument) will reveal change. Without realizing it a researcher may be measuring *organizational maturation* and hence incorrectly draw conclusions about change programs. Therefore, the issue of measurement span (i.e., the duration of time over which measurements are taken) and measurement frequency (i.e., the number of observations) becomes critical in evaluating organizational change (cf. Armenakis, Bedeian, & Pond, 1983).

The need to control experimental conditions (i.e., TOE and variational patterns) has led to the use of videotape technology in investigating the change typology. Locke (1986) edited a collection of papers on the use of laboratory methodology and has concluded that findings from lab studies can, in fact, be generalizable to the field. Several laboratory investigations have been conducted (cf. Armenakis, Buckley & Bedeian, 1986; Buckley & Armenakis, 1987; Granier, 1987) testing some of the methods proposed to detect scale recalibration and related advantages and disadvantages.

The use of multiple methods in social science measurement has been preferred for some time (cf. Campbell & Fiske, 1959). Jick (1979) has demonstrated the concept of triangulation (Webb et al., 1966) as applied to social science research by combining survey questionnaires, semi-structured probing interviews, nonparticipant observation, and archival materials. The benefits from using multiple methods in field research are quite significant. For one, the errors resulting from unintended scale recalibration and concept redefinition (when using survey research methodology) may be minimized. Therefore, the impact of change programs can be more accurately assessed. For another, measurement approaches tested under laboratory conditions can be further tested in the field. For instance, observation and interview methodology could be combined with survey research methodology to determine whether a detected scale recalibration can be verified.

As shown, change researchers have adapted concepts, methods, and techniques that were developed for other purposes to detect concept redefinition, scale recalibration, and behavioral change as well. For example, the statistical approaches—the Transformation Method and the Coefficients of Congruence Method—were designed to test the similarity of factor structures across time. Change researchers have proposed that concept redefinition could then be tested by comparing the similarity of factor structures. The techniques were available, but Golembiewski et al. (1976) first applied them to redefinition.

Likewise, the design approaches used concepts, techniques, and methods that had been around for some time but had been used for different purposes. Nevertheless, they were adapted for detecting the change typology. For example, using the ideal scale originated from work on ideal self by Horney (1945) and Havinghurst and MacDonald (1955). These early applications were aimed at better understanding the developments that individuals go through during counseling. The ideal scale is identified with the work of Likert (1967) and in the development of the Survey of Organizations (Taylor & Bowers, 1972). These latter applications were intended to be used for management and developmental purposes, most likely for diagnostic and evaluation purposes, but certainly not for the detection of scale recalibration, as proposed by Armenakis and his colleagues. As pointed out above, Granier tested a *typical* scale (i.e., the respondents articulate their concept of the typical instead of the ideal manager) which shows promise but is in need of additional research and development. Similarly, the use of the Retrospective Procedure can be traced to applications by Colgrave (1898). Howard and his colleagues adapted the retrospective logic somewhat and proposed using the procedure in the detection of the change typology. The Criterion Approach, of van de Vliert et al. (1985) has its foundations in validation research (cf. Toops, 1944).

Obviously, there are advantages to applying existing theories and technologies to evaluating organizational change. But the lack of between-method and within-method convergent validity may be due as much to the application of these various theories and technologies to the change typology, as to the differences in the mathematical procedures of the statistical approaches. Before significant advancements can be made, some degree of convergent validity (not only within-method but also between-method validity) must be achieved. Whether the field progresses any further may depend on the introduction of new technology from related but separate fields. What may be needed is something similar to mathematical proofs to establish a *universal* procedure for detecting the change typology.

A point that may be implicitly overlooked is whether the issues of concept redefinition and scale recalibration are relevant for static designs. Some researchers apparently think these issues are relevant to temporal but not static research. Those who share this opinion should ask, "If time-2 responses are different from time-1 responses, and if the difference was not intended but can be related to concept redefinition and scale recalibration, which of the responses is 'correct'?" Only by comparing two measures can the researcher know that the responses are different. Static design researchers (e.g., correlational studies) should ponder whether their self-report data are indeed free from the sources that contribute to the unintended concept redefinition and scale recalibration.

Tennis (1986) has argued that an invisible college exists in the research on the change typology. If this is true, it is an unintended result. Change typology researchers have attempted to invite others to enter the field as evidenced from the symposia conducted at the 1983, 1984, and 1985 National Meetings of the Academy of Management. That invisible college is not "closed"; admission is open to anyone interested in contributing. Perhaps Tennis' argument will encourage more researchers to enter this field and thereby advance the change typology.

REFERENCES

Ahmavaara, Y. (1954). Transformation analysis of factor data. *Annals of the Academy of Science Fennicae, Series B., 881*(2) 54–59.

Armenakis, A. (1979). Evaluation of organization development. In A. D. McIntosh and K. Schaeffer (Eds.), *Managing change: Keeping it going.* Madison, WI: ASTD Publications.

Armenakis, A. & Bedeian, A. (1982). On the measurement and control of beta change: Reply to Terborg, Maxwell, and Howard. *Academy of Management Review, 7,* 296–299.

Armenakis, A., Bedeian, A., & Pond, S., III. (1983). Research issues in OD evaluation: Past, present, and future. *Academy of Management Review, 8,* 320–328.

Armenakis, A., Buckley, M., & Bedeian, A. (1986). Survey research measurement issues in evaluating change: A laboratory investigation. *Applied Psychological Measurement, 10,* 147–157.

Armenakis, A., Feild, H., & Wilmoth, J. (1977). An algorithm for assessing factor structure congruence. *Educational & Psychological Measurement, 37,* 213–214.

Armenakis, A. & Smith, L. (1978). A practical alternative to comparison group designs in OD evaluations: The abbreviated time series design. *Academy of Management Journal, 21,* 499–507.

Armenakis, A., Randolph, W., & Bedeian, A. (1982). A comparison of two methods for evaluating the similarity of factor analytic solutions. *Proceedings of the Southwest Academy of Management Meeting.* Dallas, TX, March 17–22, 138–142.

Armenakis, A. & Zmud, R. (1979). Interpreting the measurement of change in organizational research. *Personnel Psychology, 32,* 709–723.

Barge, S. & Marks, G. (1974). *OSIRIS III.* Ann Arbor: University of Michigan.

Bedeian, A., Armenakis, A., & Gibson, R. (1980). The measurement and control of beta change. *Academy of Management Review, 5,* 561–566.

Bennis, W. (1965). Theory and method in applying behavioral science to planned organization change. *Journal of Applied Behavioral Science, 1,* 337–360.

Blake, R., Mouton, J., Barnes, L., & Greiner, L. (1964). Breakthrough in organization development. *Harvard Business Review, 42*(6), 133–155.

Bray, J. & Howard, G. (1980). Methodological considerations in the evaluation of a teacher-training program. *Journal of Educational Psychology, 72,* 62–69.

Buckley, M. & Armenakis, A. (1987). Detecting scale recalibration in survey research: A laboratory investigation. *Group & Organization Studies, 12,* 464–481.

Burt, C. (1948). Factor analysis and canonical correlations. *British Journal of Psychology,* Statistical Section, *1,* 245–276.

Campbell, D. & Fiske, D. (1959). Convergent and discriminant validation by the multitrait-multimethod matrix. *Psychological Bulletin, 56,* 81–105.

Campbell, D. & Stanley, J. (1963). *Experimental and quasi-experimental designs for research.* Chicago: Rand-McNally.

Colgrave, F. (1898). Individual memories. *American Journal of Psychology, 10,* 228–255.

Georgopoulos, B. & Tannenbaum, A. (1957). A study of organizational effectiveness. *American Sociological Review. 22,* 534–540.

Golembiewski, R. (1986). Contours in social change: Elemental graphics and a surrogate variable for gamma change. *Academy of Management Review, 11,* 550–566.

Golembiewski, R., Billingsley, K., & Yeager, S. (1976). Measuring change and persistence in human affairs: Types of change generated by OD designs. *The Journal of Applied Behavioral Science, 12,* 133–157.

Golembiewski, R. & Carrigan, S. (1970). The persistence of laboratory induced changes in organization styles. *Administrative Science Quarterly, 15,* 330–340.

Gordon, L. (1960). *Manual for the survey of interpersonal values.* Chicago: Science Research Associates.

Gorsuch, R. (1974). *Factor analysis.* Philadelphia: Saunders.

Granier, M. (1987). *A laboratory investigation of ideal and typical scales in detecting simulated scale recalibration in survey research methodology.* Unpublished doctoral dissertation, Auburn University, Auburn, Alabama.

Green, G. & Wright, J. (1979). The retrospective approach to collecting baseline data. *Social Work Research & Abstracts, 15*(3), 25–30.

Guilford, J. (1954). *Psychometric methods.* (2nd ed.). New York: McGraw-Hill.

Harman, H. (1976). *Modern factor analysis.* Chicago: The University of Chicago Press.

Harrison, R. (1962). Impact of the laboratory on perceptions of others by the experimental group. In C. Argyris, *Interpersonal competence and organizational effectiveness.* (261–271). Homewood, IL: The Dorsey Press.

Havinghurst, R. & MacDonald, D.(1955). Development of the ideal self in New Zealand and American children. *Journal of Educational Research, 49,* 263–273.

Hellstrom, A. (1985). The time-order error and its relatives: Mirrors of cognitive processes in comparing. *Psychological Bulletin, 97,* 35–61.

Horney, K. (1945). *Our inner conflicts.* New York: Norton Press.

Howard, G., Ralph, K., Gulanick, N., Maxwell, S., Nance, D., & Gerber, S. (1979). Internal invalidity in pretest-posttest self-report evaluations and a re-evaluation of retrospective pretests. *Applied Psychological Measurement, 3,* 1–12.

Howard, G. & Dailey, P. (1979). Response-shift bias: A source of contamination of self-report measures. *Journal of Applied Psychology, 64,* 144–150.

Howard, G., Dailey, P., & Gulanick, N. (1979). The feasibility of informed pretests in attenuating response-shift bias. *Applied Psychological Measurement, 3,* 481–494.

Howard, G., Schmeck, R., & Bray, J. (1979). Internal invalidity in studies employing self-report instruments: A suggested remedy. *Journal of Educational Measurement, 16,* 129–135.

Huber, G. & Power, D. (1985). Retrospective reports of strategic-level managers: Guidelines for increasing their accuracy. *Strategic Management Journal, 6,* 171–180.

Ito, J. & Srinivas, K. (1981). The use of impact and self-impact correlations in causal analysis. *Academy of Management Review, 6,* 301–308.

Jick, T. (1979). Mixing qualitative and quantitative methods: Triangulation in action. *Administrative Science Quarterly, 24,* 602–611.

Johns, G. (1981). Difference score measures of organizational behavior variables: A critique. *Organizational Behavior and Human Performance, 27,* 443–463.

Jöreskog, K. & Sörbom, D. (1981). *LISREL V: Analysis of linear structural relationships by maximum likelihood and least squares methods.* Uppsala, Sweden: University of Uppsala, Department of Statistics.

Kimberly, J. (1980). The life cycle analogy and the study of organizations: Introduction. In J. Kimberly, R. Miles, & Associates, *The organizational life cycle.* (1–17). San Francisco: Jossey-Bass.

Korth, B. & Tucker, L. (1975). The distribution of chance congruence coefficients from simulated data. *Psychometrika, 40,* 361–372.

Likert, R. (1961). *New patterns of management.* New York: McGraw-Hill.

Likert, R. (1967). *The human organization.* New York: McGraw-Hill.

Locke, E. (Ed.) (1986). *Generalizing from laboratory to field settings: Research findings from industrial-organizational psychology, organizational behavior, and human resource management.* Lexington, MA: D. C. Heath and Company.

Martinko, M. & Gardner, W. (1985). Beyond structured observation: Methodological issues and new directions. *Academy of Management Review, 10,* 676–695.

Nicholas, J. & Katz, M. (1986). Research methods and reporting practices in organization development: A review and some guidelines. *Academy of Management Review, 10,* 737–749.

Overall, J. & Woodard, J. (1975). Unreliability of difference scores: A paradox for the measurement of change. *Psychological Bulletin, 82,* 85–96.

Porras, J. & Singh, J. (1986). Alpha, beta, and gamma change in modelling-based organization development. *Journal of Occupational Behaviour, 7,* 9–24.

Randolph, W. (1982). Planned organizational change and its measurement. *Personnel Psychology, 35,* 117–139.

Rippey, R., Geller, L., & King, D. (1978). Retrospective pretesting in the cognitive domain. *Evaluation Quarterly, 2,* 481–491.

Schmitt, N., Pulakos, E., & Lieblein, A. (1984). Comparison of three techniques to assess group-level beta and gamma change. *Applied Psychological Measurement, 8,* 249–260.

Schmitt, N. (1982). The use of analysis of covariance structures to assess beta and gamma change. *Multivariate Behavioral Research, 17,* 343–358.

Taylor, J. & Bowers, D. (1972). *Survey of organizations.* Ann Arbor: Center for Research on Utilization of Scientific Knowledge, Institute for Social Research, The University of Michigan.

Tennis, C. (1986, August). The alpha, beta, gamma change typology: The response of an invisible college. Paper presented at the 46th Academy of Management Meeting, Chicago, IL.

Terborg, J., Howard, G., & Maxwell, S. (1980). Evaluating planned organizational change: A method for assessing alpha, beta, and gamma change. *Academy of Management Review, 5,* 109–121.

Terborg, J., Maxwell, S., & Howard, G. (1982). On the measurement and control of beta change: Problems with the Bedeian, Armenakis, and Gibson technique. *Academy of Management Review, 7,* 292–295.

Toops, H. (1944). The criterion. *Educational & Psychological Measurement, 4,* 271–297.

Tucker, L. (1951). *A method for synthesis of factor analysis studies* (Personnel Research Section Report, No. 984). Washington, D.C.: Department of the Army.

van de Vliert, E., Huismans, S., & Stok, J. (1985). The criterion approach to unraveling beta and alpha change. *Academy of Management Review, 10,* 269–274.

Webb, E., Campbell, D., Schwartz, R., & Sechrest, L. (1966). *Unobtrusive measures: Nonreactive research in the social sciences.* Chicago: Rand-McNally.

Wrigley, C. & Neuhaus, J. (1955). *The matching of two sets of factors* (Contract report, No. A-32, Task A). Urbana, IL: University of Illinois.

Zmud, R. & Armenakis, A. (1978). Understanding the measurement of change. *Academy of Management Review, 3,* 661–669.

EXPERIENCE, ACTION, AND METAPHOR AS DIMENSIONS OF POST-POSITIVIST INQUIRY

Peter Reason

ABSTRACT

This essay explores the epistemology of a post-positivist approach to inquiry. The questions posed are: What are genuinely post-positivist criteria for valid knowing? and, What procedures or guidelines can we develop for applying these criteria in inquiry projects? It is argued that we need a way of experiencing, acting, and thinking which can respond to Bateson's (1972) challenge to learn to think in a new way. This new way is nondualist, in that it does not separate the knower from what is known; avoids making processes into things; and has a deep reverence for all forms of life. The nature of high-quality experience, the form of right action, and the use of metaphor are explored as aspects of sound inquiry, and some suggestions for the training of researchers are made.

Research in Organizational Change and Development, Vol. 2, pages 195–233.
Copyright © 1988 by JAI Press Inc.
ISBN: 0-89232-772-3

INTRODUCTION: THE TRANSITION TO POST-POSITIVISM

Henryk Skolimowski argues that the history of mind in Western civilization can be seen as a series of cosmologies or world views, each of which simplified and gave order and meaning to human experience for a period, and encouraged the flowering of the genius of that age. Each world-view also withered and slowly died, to be followed by a period of relative ontological and epistemological disorder until a new cosmology emerged. He describes how Mythos, the belief structure of early Greece based on the stories of gods and heros, was replaced by the Logos of classical Greece and Roman civilization. The flowering of this culture had a profound and lasting impact on Western civilization, but the culture itself crumbled around the fifth century A.D., to be replaced by the medieval Theos, a world-view "inspired by and guided by the mono-theistic Judeo-Christian God" (1985, p. 21). This cosomology in turn began to disintegrate during the fourteenth and fifteenth centuries, to be replaced in time by the culture of science and technology which arose in the seventeenth century, which Skolimowski terms Mechanos.

> The new world view which is created under the auspices of Mechanos is of course the mechanistic cosmology. It starts at first very tentatively; with Galileo and Descartes it gathers momentum; and finds its epitome in Newton's epochal work *Principia Mathematica Philosophia Naturalis* 1686. During the last three centuries we have been sitting at Newton's feet and licking his boots. For the rational people that we claim to be we have been completely swayed by one kind of dogma—that of Mechanos.
>
> We are all aware that the mechanistic cosmology, via science and technology, has brought about enormous material benefits. But we are also aware of the dark side of the mechanistic cosmology—ecological devastations, human and social fragmentation, spiritual impoverishment. (1985, p. 22)

Skolimowski argues that Western civilization is in crisis because mechanical metaphor is collapsing, and that many people are aware instinctively that the "official knowledge" is no longer adequate. Many other writers are making a similar thesis: for example, in a challenging pamphlet, the "Second of January Group" argue that we face a time when our capacity for clear knowing has disappeared, that we are in a period *after* the possibility of truth:

> Our story begins with crisis. Our most sacred values, our most certain judgements, our most solid truths have lost their value, their certainty, their truth. We can neither live with them nor without them. . . . (The Second of January Group, 1986)

The replacement cosmology for Mechanos has not yet crystalized, and so we live in confusing and anxious times. But new themes do seem to be emerging quite consistently as central aspects of a new world view. One of these is the notion of *wholeness*—while mechanos is "piecemeal, atomistic, fragmentory and fragmenting," the variety of new visions are holistic and unitary. And the second is the idea of *evolution*, that whole systems may spontaneously shift to higher levels of complexity. (Teilhard de Chardin, 1959; Jantsch, 1980; Prigogine & Stengers, 1984).

Skolimowski terms the world-view which is emerging to replace Mechanos the *Evolutionary Telos*, and argues that its methodology is one of participation, which we will explore in detail later. For the moment we should note that he is making the case for a radical shift in the form of our consciousness and of our inquiry: rather than know through separateness and detachment, which is the stance of the "objective" mind, he suggests that we know through participation, and following that through empathy and identification. Yet surely one of the strengths of the objective mind at its best has been this capacity of critical detachment. This presents us with an enormous challenge: How can we develop inquiry methods which embrace participation yet remain rigorous and self-critical?

This chapter is my personal exploration of these questions. It is based on my earlier work with the paradigm of cooperative and experiential inquiry (Reason & Rowan, 1981a; Reason & Heron, 1986; Reason, in preparation), and hopefully takes this work another step into a post-positivist era. The essay is written with the intent to be provocative, to sketch out some possibilities rather than agonize over details. Much of the passion in my argument comes from personal experiences of the limits of our current world-view, experiences in psychotherapy, in meditation and spiritual discipline, and in a variety of experiential workshops; and my experiences of using the cooperative inquiry paradigm. Colleagues who have read drafts of this writing have pointed out that it contains a curious mixture of bold assertion and careful argument. This reflects my character and, since part of my thesis is that we can no longer separate the personal from the epistemological, it seems both inevitable and appropriate. Writing this chapter has forced me to think hard and feel strongly about my epistemological position. I will be delighted if it provokes similar hard thinking and feeling on the part of readers.

ONTOLOGY

Any new world-view must include in its vision new understandings of the cosmos and of our place within it. In a positivist view of the world, reality is experienced as independent of the consciousness of the person who interacts with it:

> There is a single tangible reality "out there" fragmentable into independent variables and processes, any of which can be studied independently of the others; inquiry can converge onto that reality until, finally, it can be predicted and controlled. (Lincoln & Guba, 1985, p. 37)

This view of the world crumbles in the face of the revolutions occurring in disciplines as diverse as physics and theology (Schwartz & Ogilvy, 1980), so that we must realize that as we act in our world we co-create that world: as Skolimowski argues, "Evolution is a creative process and mind is a creative instrument in evolution" (1985, p. 2). For Lincoln and Guba

> There are multiple constructed realities that can be studied only holistically; inquiry into these multiple realities will inevitably diverge (each inquiry raises more questions than it answers) so that prediction and control are unlikely outcomes although some level of understanding (verstehen) can be achieved. (1985, p. 37)

At one level these multiple realities are social constructs. Thus in an organization, different organization members will "see" events in different ways, according to their perspective on events. Their perspective is influenced by a whole range of factors, including personality, needs, social class, and position within the organization.

But the argument for multiple realities goes beyond this: it cannot be reduced to a simple matter of differential perspectives on one "true" reality, although different perspectives undoubtably are significant.

> While receiving reality, or any aspect of it, the mind always processes it. In processing it, the mind actively transforms reality. Let us reflect for a moment on the meaning of the two expressions: "processing reality" and "transforming reality." Both are fundamentally inadequate. For they suggest that there is such a thing as an autonomous reality "out there," to which the mind applies itself and on which it works. Such a picture is fundamentally misconceived. There is no such thing as *reality as it is,* which the mind visits and on which it works. Reality is always given together with the mind which comprehends it in the act of comprehension, which is, at the same time, the act of transformation. We have no idea whatsoever what reality could be like *as it is,* because always, when we think of it, when we behold it (in whatever manner) *reality is invariably presented to us as it has been transformed by our cognitive faculties.* (Skolimowski, 1986, pp. 467–68; emphases in original)

Similarly, the "Second of January Group" argue that we are in a state "Beyond Truth" because we now know that our conceptualizing and framing is an irreducible element in our experience. There is no reality independent of experience, so truth cannot be regarded as a simple "correspondence" to reality and "There are many conceptual schemes, hence many realities and many truths" (1986, p. 14).

So the argument is that we must learn to accept that the world which we inhabit—material, psychological, social, spiritual—is but one form of the Universe, created in collaboration with our particular form of consciousness. If we choose to take the trouble to learn how to enter other forms or states of consciousness, we may find that we co-create a different Universe—and we know that this is within the range of human capabilities because of what we have seen of other cultures, of healing and non-Western approaches to medicine, of mystic and religious experiences, and altered states of consciousness.

As Skolimowski argues, the Mind and the Cosmos are co-creative: the world we know is the creation of the human mind, and has been made and re-made in many different cosmologies. It is as if the Cosmos is saying:

> "I am capable of assuming ever new astonishing forms if you come to me with insights powerful enough to elicit these forms from me. . . ."
>
> The cosmos invites the mind to ever new forms of dancing. The mind is the choreographer, the cosmos is the dancer. Yet this distinction is tenuous and breaks down immediately when we look at the matter deeper. We are the dancers with the cosmos. The dance cannot be separated from the dancers. And from the choreographer. In recognising the dance we are making it. In seeing the world as a particular form of the articulation of the cosmos, we are structuring the cosmos according to our patterns of articulation. This is the power of the human mind: it finds in the cosmos what it puts into it. This is the mystery of the cosmos: it reveals only what the mind ingeniously assumes about it. . . . (1985, pp. 7–8)

What is Real behind this dance of co-creation is a profound Mystery; this is, I believe, the fundamental re-visioning of our world we are now invited to accomplish. The cosmos in its origin, however we may conceive or image it, is "a pure primordial ontological datum," and if it remains in this realm, untouched by human understanding then "it is *nothing* for us, completely outside our world" (Skolimowski, 1985).

However, once we enter, or accept, or co-create a particular reality it becomes "realized" for us as a tautology: it becomes predicted by the sensory and sense-making processes we adopt. As Bateson points out, our epistemology is encoded in our sensory apparatus. This means that a shift in forms of consciousness, an opening of new sensitivities, will bring about a shift in epistemology and thus in our reality. But the Real beyond these separate realities is of a different order, a different logical type, and we must be aware of confusing statements about an ultimate unknowable Reality and the particular realities we inhabit.

There is a story that Gregory Bateson tells which illustrates this point. However much understanding we may have, it is an understanding of what he calls "the pattern which connects," which must remain ultimately almost totally mysterious.

> There's a well-known story of Bertrand Russell and Whitehead, which I think is related to . . . this tragic desire of man to think he understands things. Russell had been Whitehead's student and collaborator . . . and, when Whitehead had gone to Harvard, Russell came to give a lecture in one of the big auditoria, on a hot August night, and all the professors and the professors' wives turned out to hear the great man. The great man lectured on the quantum theory, which has never been an easy subject, and in its early stages was probably more difficult even than it is now. . . .
>
> Russell laboured to make the matter clear to the wives and the professors and finally sat down sweating. Then little Whitehead rose to his feet, with his falsetto voice, "to thank Professor Russell," he squeaked, "for his brilliant exposition and especially. . . for leaving unobscured. . . the vast darkness of the subject." (in M. C. Bateson 1972, p. 302)

Elsewhere Bateson (1978) points out that every textbook is devoted to the project of obscuring the vast darkness of the subject, of trying to persuade the reader that there is no darkness, that we really know something. We have got ourselves into a position, through the domination of mechanistic nineteenth-century science on our culture, in which at root we view our world through the eyes of a naive realism. And this despite the challenge of quantum physics, our understanding of perceptual processes, the apparent popularity of phenomeno-logical and interpretive approaches to inquiry, the influence of esoteric Western and Eastern spiritual traditions. It seems to me that this positivist world-view is an addiction we find hard to give up. But we do not know how the world fits together: Reality, as a thing-in-itself separate from our perception of it, is always an absolute mystery (Hunter, 1983).

The danger is that we think we know, when we don't. As Catherine Bateson (1972) argues, this appetite for certainty is in many ways our undoing. If we are to accept the implications of the emerging world-view, let alone save our world from its self-inflicted injuries, we need to find a way of being ontologically radically open-minded, to be able to accept the coexistence of all sorts of extraor-dinary realities. As the Second of January Group points out, there is no primi-tive, given, preconceptual layer which provides certainty and foundation for thought. This means adopting a position of radical relativism, which has never been a comfortable existential position.

> We are led to a position summarised by the well-known slogan, 'all truth is relative.' Everyone is led there but most want to go back. The place is far from comfortable. Many find even a short stay unbearable. The most obvious reason for this is that, once we are there, we can no longer draw any cognitive distinction between worlds. We cannot distinguish on 'rational grounds' between better or worse conceptual schemes, outlooks, traditions. It is no longer clear that science is 'more true' than magic, that one society is 'more just' than another, that liberalism is 'more acceptable' than racism. (Second of January Group, 1986, p. 17)

The authors continue to point out that this leads many to try to "dilute" their relativism, but that this is impossible. Once embraced, the relative position leads us into an inevitable regress in which we must question the basis of every position we take, including relativism itself. It is no longer possible to think rigorously and rationally, "all truth is relative."

Because of this I find myself very much at odds with what I understand of the "realist" philosophy of science as, for example, set out in Manicas and Secord's article (1983) entitled, "Implications for Psychology of the New Philosophy of Science," Briefly, they acknowledge that positivism is a dead duck. But when they peer into the Kuhnian alternative notion of normal science existing within paradigms of thought and practice (1962), they decide that this "account of science precipitously courted irrationalism" because it suggests that there is no independent reality against which findings and theories could be checked. Their alternative is the "*realist*" view of science:

> The crucial point is that it is possible for these criteria (of truth) to be rational precisely
> because, on realist terms, there is a world that exists independently of cognising experience.
> Since our theories are constitutive of the known world but *not* of the *world,* we may always be
> wrong, but *not* anything goes. One must be realist ontologically to be fallibilist epis-
> temologically. (p. 401, emphases in original)

In other words, we cannot have science as we know it unless there is some notion
that there is a reality out there that our knowing can approach.

I think this stance is simply damage limitation in the face of the challenge of
radical relativism; it seems to be a reactive position, intellectually and emotionally defensive, closing down against the disturbing opportunities and the
possible diversities of the worlds we might create.

Whatever knowing we can discover or create about ourselves and our world is
inevitably relative, and rests on our profound and inevitable unknowing. There is
a certain dangerous hubris about our claims to truth: science is in part one
expression of this hubris, and it is well argued that a very large part of the
scientific endeavor has been defensive (Maslow, 1966; Devereaux, 1967;
Griffin, 1984). Asking questions about truth can be just an intellectual game;
taken seriously they shake the soul to its very roots. In Don Juan's terms, our
knowing might be seen as the *tonal,* and the ground of our unknowing as the
nagual—that for which "there is no description, no words, no names, no feelings, no knowledge" (Castaneda, 1974, p. 126). We can, as Don Juan warns us,
"knock ourselves out trying to understand this," because it is Mystery. We
need, I believe, to rediscover our capacity for acknowledging Mystery, and for
approaching our world in wonder and astonishment.

DIALECTICAL ONTOLOGY

The world as we know it is co-created in the dialectical tension between this
unknowable, mysterious primary reality and the categories and forms of consciousness we bring to it (Hunter, 1983). So now our task in considering the
nature of valid knowing becomes both much more simple and much more
paradoxical.

> So we have to learn to think dialectically, to view reality as a process, always emerging
> through a self-contradictory development, always becoming; knowing this reality is neither
> subjective nor objective, it is both wholly independent of me and wholly dependent on me.
> This means that any notion of valid knowledge must concern itself with both the knower and
> what is known, and be a matter of relationship. (Reason & Rowan, 1981b)

We have to learn to live and to inquire within the flow and tension of this
dialectic:

> One extreme is the idea of an objective world, pursuing its regular course in space and time,
> independently of the observing subject; this has been the guiding image from modern science.

> At the other extreme is the idea of a subject, mystically experiencing the unity of the world
> and no longer confronted by an object or by any objective world; this has been the guiding
> image of Asian mysticism. Our thinking moves somewhere in the middle, between these two
> limiting conceptions; we should maintain the tension between these two opposites. (Heisen-
> berg quoted by Wolf, 1984)

In other words, we both create our reality, and reality has an independent process which can surprise us. While a traditional logic would create a dichotomy, and argue that reality is either fully independent of us or fully dependent on us, a dialectical ontology would embrace the paradox of both these positions. Dialectics involves a recognition of the inseparability of two apparent opposites; and an exploration of the interplay between these interdependent poles, because "what lies between the poles is more substantial than the poles themselves" (Watts, 1963). As Watts points out, this understanding of polarities is quite different from the splitting of opposites into a duality. In dialectical thinking and experience, we explore and seek to understand the interdependence, interpenetration, and in the end, the unity of the two poles. Then we can maybe understand the co-created realities within which we live as moments within this dialectic where we may exist for a while.

Lincoln and Guba (1985) provide a helpful framework when they set out four ontological positions that have been proposed by different philosophical traditions. The first two of these—Objective reality, or naive realism; and Perceived reality, or perspectivism—I have already referred to. The third is Constructed reality:

> Those who see reality as a construction in the minds of individuals assert that it is dubious
> whether there is a reality. If there is, we can never know it. Furthermore, no amount of
> inquiry can produce convergence on it. There is, in this ontological position, always an
> infinite number of constructions that might be made, and hence there are multiple real-
> ities. . . . (Lincoln & Guba, 1985, pp. 83–84)

And the fourth is Created Reality:

> (There) is no reality at all. Reality is best understood as a standing wave that is not *realised*
> (note the term) until some observer "pops the qwiff" (Wolf, 1981), "qwiff" being a
> quantum wave function. Until it is "popped," the quantum wave function (or *probable*
> reality) remains simply probabilistic. (Lincoln & Guba, 1985, p. 85, emphases in original)

Lincoln and Guba say they are drawn to adopting the position of created reality, but that this is an unnecessarily radical stance for their purposes, and so they adopt the position of contructed reality. My argument is that we must accept all these positions as moments within the dialectical process of co-creating our world. As the world-view of Mechanos continues to crumble, we will have to find the flexibility to exist in *all* these kinds of realities: the world is given *and* we invent it, all at the same time. Not only are there multiple co-existing realities, but multiple *kinds of realities*.

This is relatively clear in the field of social and interpersonal processes—we are familiar with the idea that social forms are constructed by their members, whether this is at the level of the family, the organization, or the whole culture. And we are familiar with that curious way in which these social forms appear to have a life of their own and in that sense to be ontological givens, apparently out of the control of the members, who nevertheless act to maintain them. So social forms are both given and created.

One area in which this dialectical ontology may be fruitfully used is in understanding the health of the body-mind. Reality is completely independent of me in that there are plagues in our world, there are wars, badly driven motor cars, and carcinogens; the germ theory of disease is not complete nonsense. And reality is completely dependent on me: people do seem to choose to get ill or well, to destroy and to heal their bodies, in ways that at times defy allopathic medical theories; some body-minds seem "wiser" than others, to use Dossey's term (1982). It is arguable that the quality of a person's health and illness is in some sense related to their character.

So in a world of holistic health-care, in which wellness is viewed as a quality of the body-mind-spirit, we must seek to understand the subtle interplay of this dialectic. Maybe we can "really" chose our reality, so that the healer creates a particular place in this moving dialectic, and the surgeon another, and the self-healing patient another. As the dialectic shifts and turns in these places of uncertainty it is most open to our influence, if only we know how to make that influence. It is arguable that a healing community would be able to exert considerable power to create a reality appropriate for healing, or in a hospice, for dying.

In this view, our body-mind is manifesting within this dialectic of the "material world" and the "creative mind," these are unconsciously interpenetrating, creating a synthesis in which we can live for a while. A transformation of consciousness and of the social world we choose to belong to can give us the power to chose an interpenetration with awareness—at least for a while.

The most curious (for materialist Westerners) area in which we may seek to understand this dialectic is in relation to the "material" world of things. There does seem to be a radical difference between the deterministic world of brute fact, and the world of imagination. In everyday life we experience these as quite separate, as in the well-known story of Dr. Johnson who, when Boswell observed that they had no means to refute Bishop Berkley's theory of the nonexistence of matter, "struck his foot against a large stone, till he rebounded from it, saying, 'I refute it thus!' " (Oxford Dictionary of Quotations). It is becoming a cliché, but remains curious, that it is on the frontiers of physics that questions about the independent existence of matter are becoming most challenging (Wolfe, 1984).

I am personally convinced, on the basis of both reading and direct experience, that the solid reality of the physical world is an illusion, or rather that is one moment, a creation 'realized' in the interaction of our consciousness and the mysterious cosmos.

As I have struggled with the experiences behind this writing, I have been impressed by two contradictory aspects of my experience. On the one hand, I inhabit a world which is radically there for me, such that I cannot get away from its concrete presence; and, on the other, I am aware how my experience of the world as fact is a lie. There seems to be a fundamental paradox between the world as given and the world as created.

The existentialists suggest we are "thrown" into the contingencies of the world and its mysteries and that in this world we are our choices.

> Dasein is "to be there" (da-sein), and "there" is the world: the concrete, literal, actual, daily world. To be human is to be immersed, implanted, rooted in the earth, in the quoditian matter and matter of factness of the world ("human" has in its *humus,* the Latin for earth). . . The world *is*—a fact which is, of course, the primal wonder and source of all ontological asking. (Steiner, 1978, p. 81)

It is this matter-of-factness which we co-create, and this must be a matter of wonder and astonishment. Maybe we can discover, with awe and wonder, that "truth which passeth all understanding"? And as we do this we may have to re-vision inquiry as a spiritual as well as a material quest.

CO-OPERATIVE INQUIRY AND CRITICAL SUBJECTIVITY

I have long been curious about how to establish sound approaches to inquiry within the kind of post-positivist world-view I have explored in the last section. My own first steps toward this arose from my realization that it is impossible to conduct intimate inquiry into human relationships as an outsider (Reason, 1976). Later, in collaboration with members of the New Paradigm Research Group, which met regularly in London for several years, we thought through the implications of our practice as humanistic psychologists, educators, and organizational consultants, and of our commitment to working with the self-directing capacities and potentials of human beings (Reason & Rowan, 1981a). John Heron pointed out how orthodox inquiry methods, while assuming without question that the researcher is a creative, self-directing human being, necessarily relegate the subjects of an inquiry to objects whose behavior is determined by the conditions to which they are subjected (Heron, 1971, 1981). We argued that orthodox methods

> are neither adequate nor appropriate for the study of *persons,* for persons are to some significant degree self-determining. Orthodox inquiry methods, as part of their rationale,

exclude the experimental human subjects from all the thinking and decision making that generates, designs, manages, and draws conclusions from the research. Such exclusion treats the subjects as less than self-determining persons, alienates them from the inquiry process and from the knowledge which is its outcome, and thus invalidates any claim the methods have to being a science of persons. (Reason & Heron, 1986)

As an alternative to orthodox inquiry we have developed and applied a cooperative and experiential paradigm for research. In this perspective on inquiry, research is not a neutral, value-free process, but is always supporting or questioning something, at times with passion. A fundamental principle is that research is not just the province of professional researchers, that the mutually exclusive roles of "researcher" and "subject" must give way to a more cooperative relationship. In such a cooperative inquiry relationship, all those involved in the inquiry endeavour contribute *both* to the creative ideas that go into the research—the initial ideas, the methods, the conclusions, and so on; and *also* participate in the activity which is being researched. Research in this sense is not just a systematic quest for understanding, but an action science (Torbert, 1981) which involves learning through risk taking in living. The slogan or motto for this "Human Inquiry" has been "research *with* people not *on* people."

This approach to inquiry can be described simply in terms of four cycles of action and reflection.

Phase 1

A group of co-researchers agree on an area for inquiry and identify some initial research propositions. They may choose to explore some aspect of their experience, or agree to try out in practice some particular actions or skills. They also agree to some set of procedures by which they will observe and record their own and each other's experience. . . .

Phase 2

The group then applies these ideas and procedures: they initiate the agreed actions, and observe and record the outcomes of their own and each other's behavior. At this stage they need to be particularly alert for the subtleties and nuances of experience, and to ways in which the original ideas do and do not accord with experience. . . .

Phase 3

The co-researchers will in all probability become fully immersed in this activity and experience. At times they will be excited and carried away by it; at times they will be bored and alienated by it; at times they will forget they are involved in an inquiry project. They may forget or otherwise fail to carry out and record the agreed procedures; or they may stumble on unexpected and unpredicted experiences, and develop creative new insights. This stage of full immersion is fundamental to the whole process: it is here that the co-researchers, fully engaged with their experience, may develop an openness to what is going on for them and their environment, which allows them to bracket off their prior beliefs and preconceptions and so see their experience in a new way. . . .

Phase 4

After an appropriate period engaged in stages two and three, the co-researchers return to consider their original research propositions and hypotheses in the light of experience—modifying, reformulating, and rejecting them, adopting new hypotheses, and so on. They may also amend and develop their research procedures more fully to record their experience. . . .

> This cycle of movement from reflection to action and back to reflection needs to be repeated
> several times so that ideas and discoveries tentatively reached in early cycles may be clarified,
> refined, deepened, and corrected. This "research cycling" clearly has an important bearing
> on the empirical validity of the whole inquiry process. . . . (Reason & Heron, 1986)

This practice of cooperative inquiry rests on an "extended" epistemology (Heron, 1981). Science as product has traditionally been concerned with propositional knowledge—knowledge expressed in statements, concepts, and theories about the world. However, the process of inquiry involves not only propositional knowledge, but also experiential and practical knowledge.

Experiential knowledge is acquired through direct encounter face-to-face with persons, places, or things. Practical knowledge concerns "how to" do something. In the co-operative inquiry cycle, while the work of phase one concerns propositional knowings, phase two is based on practical knowing and phase three on experiential knowing. Thus, in this kind of inquiry the propositional knowledge stated in the research conclusions is rooted in and derived from the experiential and practical knowledge of all those involved in the inquiry process. But more than this, the outcomes of this kind of inquiry are not only sets of propositions or theories about the subject matter, but are also the validating competences (practical knowledge) and experiences (experiential knowledge) of those participating. We shall return in more detail to this extended epistemology later in this chapter.

In working with this extended epistemology, and resting our inquiry firmly in experiential knowing, we are working with what we have termed "critical subjectivity." As Schwartz and Ogilvy point out (1980) there has historically been a tension between subjective/active and objective/passive modes of knowing. The process of inquiry can be seen as starting in a naive inquiry based on our subjective experience of the world. This kind of knowing, like the knowing of a small child, is very prone to distortions arising from our biases and prejudices, from anxieties, and from the pressures of the social world. But it also has a lot of good qualities because it is alive, involved, committed, it is a very important part of our humanity, and we lose a lot if we try to throw it out altogether.

The move from this subjective and active knowing to the objective knowing of orthodox inquiry does just this: in order to get away from the confusion and potential error of naive inquiry, we develop the objective consciousness of scientific method. This parallels the development of ego and of what Freudians call the secondary process based on the reality principle. Skolimowski calls this process a "yoga of objectivity":

> The Yoga of objectivity consists of a set of exercises specific to the scientific mind. These
> exercises are practiced over a number of years, sometimes as many as fifteen. . . The purpose
> of these exercises is to see nature and reality in a selective way. It takes many years of
> stringent training. . . before the mind *becomes* detached, objective, analytical, clinical,
> "pure." (1985, p. 12)

This objective approach to inquiry deals with many of the problems of naive inquiry, but because it is separated from our subjectivity we are left with essentially dead knowledge, alienated from its source. It has been argued that this epistemology is a root cause of the fundamental problems which appear to beset our civilization (Bateson, 1972; Griffin, 1984).

Within a post-positivist world-view in which we co-create our world, we must go beyond this split between subjective and objective consciousness toward what may be called critical subjectivity. This is a state of awareness in which we do not suppress our primary subjective experience; nor do we allow ourselves to be overwhelmed and swept along by it; rather we raise it to consciousness and use it as part of the inquiry process. Critical subjectivity is similar to the Schwartz and Ogilvy notion of "perspective" which borrows from both objective and subjective, "defining a personal view from some distance" (1980, p. 53), but I believe involves a greater shift in consciousness than they propose. John Rowan (1979) drawing on Hegelian thinking, has referred to this as a leap to the Realized level of consciousness:

> because we now see the world as *our* world, rather than *the* world, we can see clearly through our own eyes. Being rational. . . at this stage, is doing justice to the whole thing—to all that is out there in the world and all that is in here, inside ourselves (Rowan & Reason, 1981, p. 116; emphases in original).

Wilber (1980) has systematically mapped these potential areas of human consciousness which can be seen as "post-egoic" or "trans-personal."

What is important, in this transition to post-positivism, is that we keep hold of and develop this quality of critical knowing. We are not in the business of lapsing back into naive inquiry, nor of resting with objective consciousness with all its epistemological errors; rather we are seeking ways to move forward to a new form of integrated consciousness and critical awareness.

STEPS TOWARD VALIDITY

Clearly, notions of validity in post-positivist knowing are of supreme importance; but they are also rather confusing. If our reality is in some sense "constructed" or "created" as well as "discovered," a process in which we participate, how can we comprehend a notion of valid knowing? Interestingly, the term validity is not synonomous with truth, but refers to the quality of being "well-founded" (Oxford Shorter Dictionary) "well-grounded or justifiable" (Webster), and "applicable to the case or circumstances" (Oxford again). So valid knowing in a post-positivist sense is through critical subjectivity; it involves well-founded and self-aware experience, action, and understanding as we participate to co-create our world.

The challenge is to discover how to do this. For it seems to me profoundly difficult to establish criteria for post-positivist inquiry that do not rest in some sense fundamentally on positivist assumptions.

It may be as well here to refer to the work of Popper (1963) who has done so much to influence our understanding of the scientific process. Popper argued that all knowledge is tentative and conjectural; it is never final, always provisional and open to reformulation. It is reshaped by the process of relentless criticism which eliminates error and moves us' on toward a new and improved theory. Skolimowski (1986) points out that Popper offered a pluralistic epistemology and an open-ended rationality which was especially liberating.

For Popper the demarcation between science and nonscience is that scientific statements are *falsifiable*. If a statement is made which under no circumstances is testable through observation or experiment, if there is no means of establishing whether it is false, then while the statement may be a valuable and significant aspect of human culture, it is not scientific.

So while Popper acknowledges the active role of the mind in formulating knowledge, reality itself seems to be given: the idea of empirical refutability is central to his thinking

> You must have a firm and unequivocal nature "out there" (or call it reality) which will shout "no" to some of your conjectures. The *idea that reality is given* is reinforced by Popper's relentless defense of the classical (or the *correspondence*) *theory of truth*: truth consists of the correspondence between facts (or phenomena) and their description. (Skolimowski, 1986, p. 457; emphasis in original)

So Popper's philosophy is one of critical realism, and as such it does not fit well with a view that reality is not exclusively given by whatever is "out there," but is in some sense co-extensive with mind. Popper is an "epistemological realist of the traditional kind" (Skolimowski, 1986). Critical realism is not the same as critical subjectivity.

In working to develop validity within the co-operative inquiry paradigm, I have, with John Heron and other colleagues tried to find ways to develop capacities for critical subjectivity within an inquiry group, and to develop a set of procedures which may serve to counteract the threats of self-deception and consensus collusion (Reason & Rowan, 1981b; Heron, 1982; Reason & Heron, 1986).

John Heron defines empirical validity in co-operative inquiry as the extent to which the statements that express the findings of the inquiry are supported by the experiences and actions of the co-subjects. He points out that there are two aspects to this, accuracy and agreement.

> the accuracy of our findings is not a property that we can get at over and above our agreement. Accurate findings can only be findings that we chose to agree are accurate because they have withstood certain agreed tests. We can never depict the real-as-such apart from ourselves, but

only the reality-in-which-we-are-involved. The accuracy of our findings, the reality we claim to portray, is entirely relative to what we chose to agree are appropriate tests or procedures for distinguishing the apparent from the real, the illusory from the veridical. (1982, p. 2)

Heron continues in his paper to outline a set of such procedures, including research cycling, the balance of experience and inquiry, the management of unaware projections, authentic collaboration, and falsification (see also, Reason & Heron, 1986).

I have adopted this approach to validity in my work for several years. My concern about this perspective now is that words such as "empirical," "accurate," "veridical," "illusory," even if placed within a framework of relative rather than absolute truth, as we have done in our writing, because of their historical connections imply a realist perspective and a correspondence theory of truth. It is as if these words "carry" the ethos of Mechanos, so that in using them we are in danger of re-creating this world-view.

For example, I have always contended that "research cycling" is a crucial feature of cooperative inquiry:

there need to be multiple cycles, where the theory, concepts, and categories are progressively extended and refined, differentiated and integrated, reaching toward a theoretical saturation. This is a rigour of clarity, accuracy, and precision. (Reason & Rowan, 1981b, p. 249)

Research cycling involves looking carefully and repeatedly at the phenomena, not being content with testing an idea through experience and action once, but "taking an idea several times around the cycle of reflection and action" (Reason & Heron, 1986). We have argued that through convergent cycling we exhibit the careful side of science, and that cycling can involve "correction. . . the negative feedback cycle" (Heron, 1982). Are we not in danger here of implying once again that there is a firm reality onto which our inquiry can converge, and that we can come to some correct findings? What is the careful side of science, what is correction within a dialectical ontology?

Now, the counter-argument from a relativist perspective is that while we can never know reality as it is, but only the realities we co-create, we need to remain open to the way the cosmos may surprise us, otherwise our inquiry is totally circular and solipsistic. This is the essence of the dialectical ontology. And further, terms like truth and accuracy do not imply a naive realism, but can sit quite happily within a relativist framework, since they pose the question: Are we accurate given our way of framing our world?

Another validity procedure Heron and I have used and urged on others is falsification. We have argued that cooperative groups may band together in defense of their beliefs, and ignore experience or evidence to the contrary. To counteract this tendency we have developed procedures through which the fundamental assumptions of an inquiry group can be rigorously challenged:

The basic point of experiential research is that you and your colleagues take an idea to the test of your experience and action in order to eliminate error in the idea. . . This accords with Popper's view that knowledge is a conjecture that has so far passed the test of experience; and that what marks off a scientific from a non-scientific statement is that the former is framed in such a way that it is open to refutation by appeal to experience. (Heron, 1982, p. 13)

Clearly we need to have ways of exploring whether we are fooling ourselves. But I am not satisfied that by using terms such as falsification we are not falling onto the objectivist side of the dialectic. I believe we must find a way of better preserving the tension that "reality is wholly independent of me and wholly dependent on me." (For a discussion of validity in the light of this critique see Heron, in press)

Lincoln and Guba have made a most interesting contribution to the debate about validity in their work with the naturalistic inquiry paradigm. Their early contribution (1985) takes the criteria of the conventional inquiry paradigm, which they identify as internal validity (or truth value), external validity (or applicability), reliability (or consistency), and objectivity (or neutrality) and to develop what they call parallel criteria of trustworthiness. But they also suggest that other quite different criteria might be generated from different epistemological assumptions, and offer the valuable challenge:

Suppose one didn't have the "rigor" criteria from conventional scientific inquiry toward which one might work in some parallel fashion? Suppose one were charged simply (or not so simply, as the case may be) with developing criteria for trustworthiness and authenticity which were grounded solely in the naturalistic paradigm? Suppose that rather than being analogous to conventional criteria, the new trustworthiness criteria were "indigenous" to the new epistemology, were grounded in the assumptions, and arose solely from that particular system? (Lincoln, personal communication, 1986)

In my attempts to rise to this challenge I have tried to reach back behind the foundations of positivism, and thus behind the philosophy of Descartes and the subject-object split which he instituted.

GETTING BEHIND DESCARTES

I have already pointed out that, in the traditions of the West, knowing has been primarily associated with thinking and reflection, and thus with propositional knowing. I wish to extend the concept of knowing to include at least knowing through experience and knowing through action. Here I can take a lead from Macmurray who challenges the Cartesian starting point of the thinking self— *cogito ergo sum*—because this sees the Self primarily as subject rather than as agent. Macmurray starts his argument by substituting "I do" for "I think," since:

In thinking the mind alone is active. In acting the body is active, but also the mind. Action is not blind. When we turn from reflection to action we do not turn from consciousness to unconsciousness. When we act, sense, perception, and judgement are in continuous activity, along with physical movement. . . . Action, then, is a full concrete activity of the self in which all our capacities are employed; while thought is constituted by the exclusion of some of our powers and withdrawal into an activity which is less concrete and less complete (1957, p. 86).

It is amusing to see how this philosophy of *cogito* arose. The story is told (Russell, 1946) that Descartes was seeking places for quiet meditation. In Bavaria, in the winter of 1619–20, in very cold weather, he got into a stove in the morning (Yes, Russell assures us, *in* a stove) and stayed there all day meditating, his philosophy being half finished by the time he came out.

It seems to me to be unsurprising that, since the founder of modern philosophy was a quiet retiring man, even a bit of a recluse, who liked to meditate and who developed his philosophy sitting in the warmth of a stove, our world-view should be based on the passive self as subject. But the serious point is that all philosophies which start from the thinking self, which share the *cogito* as their starting point and center of reference, institute a formal dualism (rather than a polarity) of theory and practice and between mind and matter. In presupposing the primacy of the theoretical, they are faced with the dilemma: How can pure reason become practical? (Macmurray, 1957, p. 80) Hence the dualism of action and reflection:

"Cogito ergo sum" is self-contradictory because it asserts the primacy of the theoretical; while in truth, as Kant rightly concludes, it is the practical that is primary. The theoretical is secondary and derivative. (p. 81)

"The theoretical is secondary and derivative." It is worth pausing for a while to take this sentence in, to savor its challenge to the Western intellectual. The theoretical is *secondary* and *derivative*. This implies that in our attempts to build cognitive epistemologies, our attempts to know intellectually and theoretically, we are starting in the wrong place, and engaging in an inappropriate, self-defeating activity. We need to go back behind Descartes and replace *cogito* with action and experience as the starting points for valid knowing.

The Existentialists (Tillich, 1944), in asserting that existence proceeds essence, similarly have tried in their work to go back behind the assumptions of Descartes to the immediate experience of Being. Sartre asserts that we are our choices, and Heidegger describes how the world meets us in action. When we use a hammer, for example, we don't simply contemplate its use theoretically, rather:

The less we just stare at the hammer-Thing, and the more we seize hold of it and use it, the more primordial does our relationship with it become, and the more unveiledly it is encountered as that which it is—a tool. . . (quoted in Steiner, 1978, pp. 87–88)

So the Western epistemologies based on the *cogito* are epistemologies of cognition, of thinking (I think therefore I am) and are essentially and necessarily dualistic: in separating mind from the world and basing their inquiry method on viewing the world from a distance they create the problems of positivist knowing we have been struggling with. If we take Macmurray's argument seriously, it is starting from *cogito* which is the problem: we cannot arrive at criteria for valid knowing if knowing starts from thinking.

Ways of Knowing

From an existential perspective, being-in-the-world implies being-in-action; this implies experience of action, and we may then reflect on our experience and find ways to represent it if we wish to communicate to others. So as I pointed out above, in relation to cooperative inquiry, we can extend our epistemology to include at least practical, experiential, and propositional forms of knowing. (Propositional knowing is one way in which experience may be presented; it may be better to include it as one form of presentational knowing, which includes knowings expressed through visual art, poetry, dance, etc.)

My considerations lead me to suggest that knowing as action (practical knowing) is primary, and reflection and representation (propositional knowing) a necessary secondary—we must remember that action without awareness is blind, while awareness without action is important. But what *links* action and reflection together and integrates them, so that we may act with awareness rather than oscillate in an ungainly fashion between action and reflection, is the quality of our experience.

So when I consider the issue of valid knowing within a post-positivist paradigm, my questions concern the soundness of practical knowing, of experiential knowing and of propositional knowing: what are the qualities of sound action, sound experience, and sound articulation?

How do we act? Often we must act decisively when we cannot know the outcome. Nietzsche asked about a truth, "Can one live it?"; and in the Sufi tradition, truth arises in action. So *what is the form of valid action?*

What is the nature of experience we can trust? We have been taught for so long in Western civilization to doubt our experience, yet it is the fundamental basis of all our knowing. *So what is the quality of sound experience?*

How do we articulate our knowing, express it in words, ideas, and theories; in poetry, drama, and dance? If we accept that the map is not the territory, that the Tao that can be told is not the eternal Tao, we must recognize what Bateson bluntly points out, that "all knowledge is metaphorical." So what can we say about the *use and choice of metaphor?*

I turn now to examine each of these ways of knowing in turn, to get some kind of feel for their quality, and to begin to get an understanding of valid, sound use of each.

THE NATURE OF EXPERIENCE

In Western traditions we are invited to doubt our experience; this tradition of doubt has been central to the rise of science. Again, this started with Descartes, who used the method of radical doubt to reject the authority of the Church in matters of belief, and to create a completely new philosophical edifice. But Macmurray argues that he took it further than this, and that in systematizing doubt he "set it up as a canon for the proper employment of the intellect in the search for truth." This has been so thoroughly accepted by modern thought, and it is now so familiar to us that we fail to recognize how paradoxical it is. It really is most unlikely that systematic doubting would lead to any form of knowing at all, rather it is more likely that "our capacity for scepticism is as unlimited as our credulity, and increases, rather than decreases, with exercise" (Macmurray, 1957, p. 76).

Macmurray goes on to assert that belief and doubt are primarily practical, and that if in practice I believe something, it makes very little sense to pretend that I can doubt this as an act of will. So a body of propositions, however logical, cannot be seen as knowledge unless somebody believes them. Thus, doubt must be held in relation to belief, for these are experiential concepts, not propositions split away from experience.

> The point is simply that, if there is to be any life and movement at all, the attitude of faith must be basic—the final and fundamental attitude—and the attitude of doubt secondary and subordinate. (Watts, 1960, p. 38)

Another way of looking at this is that we can hold our belief and our doubt lightly. As we develop our capacity for critical subjectivity, we do not need to become stuck either in credulity or in compulsive doubt—to do so is again to fall into the trap of dualism, valuing one pole of a dialectic at the expense of the other. We can, in this state of mind, maybe seek a quality of experience we might trust without becoming over-committed to it, without treating the knowing of that experience as a certainty.

Such high-quality experience can be seen as having three interrelated qualities: it is emotionally competent; it is mindful; and it is participative and loving.

Emotional Competence

By emotional competence I refer to a quality of being which is not caught up in and overly attached to the drama of our life. It means that I "know where I am coming from," that I am neither captured by my own subjectivity, nor pursuing an alienated pretense of objectivity. Rather, I am finding ways to integrate these within a critical subjectivity. Elsewhere (Reason & Marshall, 1986) we have described three aspects of this life drama.

The first of these are the existential givens of our life situation which we bring to research: the background of our gender, class, age, race, employment status, and so on; with the need to deal with relationships that may be in various stages of development or decay; with our concerns about the state of the world and our own life within it. Often, for the graduate student in particular, the time spent in research at a university is a time for retreat, for taking stock and making sense of life and experience so far.

We work with these existential issues by recognizing that in a profound sense we *are* our choices, that we are into the research business for some purpose, that it is most unlikely that our research is simply a high-minded search for truth: more likely it is fueled by some passion, some personal or social commitment, some purpose in the world. My friend and colleague John Rowan has suggested that the purpose of inquiry is to "discover the rigidities in social relations, so that they may be transformed"; this is an example of such a commitment.

A second aspect of the drama of our life comes from a psychodynamic perspective: many of the limitations on being here-and-now have their roots in childhood experiences, as has been well described by writers from the human potential movement:

> The theory here is that people in our sort of society carry around a good deal of unresolved distress—grief, fear, anger—from past experience, especially from the very beginnings of life and from childhood; and that there is a tendency for this to be projected unawarely into all sorts of present situations, distorting preception of a situation and/or behaviour within it.
>
> Let's look a bit more closely at how this distortion process might work. If as a child I want to express my true real nature, my true self, and this urge is repeatedly interrupted and interfered with, I feel the distress of grief, fear, and anger. If I am also constrained to suppress these valid distress feelings, then I am conditioned to become false to my real self. . . and to erect a false and alienated self with which I identify. I then become addicted to projecting onto the world the anxiety of my denied distress, seeing the world as a negative, threatening place which therefore reinforces my addiction to my false and alienated self. I am stuck in a viscious circle (Heron, 1982).

The research experience has a particular ability to restimulate old patterns of distress, particularly if we are inquiring into something dear to our hearts (and why else bother to inquire?). We can work with this unresolved distress through the variety of forms of psychotherapy and psychological education. I believe that it is not possible to pursue an inquiry effectively unless one engages in some form of work sufficiently powerful to reach into unconscious processes and explore the disturbance triggered by the research experience.

A third aspect of the drama of our life is transpersonal and imaginal. Drawing on archetypal psychology (Hillman, 1975) we may see the inquiry process as an expression or enactment in our life of a myth or archetypal pattern, and as such an expression of the collective unconscious. We can explore the images that arise to awareness in the researcher, for example, in spontaneous free-association, dream, fantasy, and active imagination, and manifest them through the inquiry process. The importance of this imaginal perspective lies not in the "correctness" of its imagery, but in the challenge it throws out to the materialistic and rational world within which we live. It draws attention to the unconscious as an essential source of our creativity, and to the role of our imagination in co-creating our world.

Thus for inquiry, the notion of emotional competence directs the researcher to explore the life perspective they bring to their work, the emotional "baggage" from the personal past, and the archetypal patterns which are expressed through their lives. This is where we start from; in the American Indian tradition, these are our Beginning Gifts (Storm, 1972) from which perspective we approach our world. I do not argue that if we work in these areas we can establish some kind of objective consciousness. To think this is to miss the point. Our work rather is to clarify the perspective of our vision, to better know and be less compulsively attached to the existential ground from which we co-create our world.

Mindfulness

While developing emotional competence and clarifying the perspective we bring to inquiry are essential starting points, we can go much further in developing high-quality awareness if we borrow from the nondualistic teachings of the world—teachings within what may be generally termed the perennial philosophy (Huxley, 1958). The various disciplines associated with these teachings are aimed at furthering and developing Mindfulness, or Wakefulness, or Self-Remembering; their purpose is to break through the robot-like, mechanical, trance-like behavior which is characteristic of human beings for much of the time (Deikman, 1966; Masters, 1981). Torbert (e.g., 1983) has drawn attention to the significance of these teachings for inquiry.

Reb Anderson, a Zen Buddhist monk and meditation teacher, describes the Zen quality of awareness (1984). He talks about Buddhism as the art of the Middle Way between our limited, painful existence, on the one hand, and, on the other, some boundlessness.

He quotes a short Chinese poem which encapsulates the Awakened Way:

In my middle years I have become rather fond of the Way,
I've retired to the. . . foothills.
When the spirit moves me, I go off by myself
To see wonderful things that only I can see.
I follow the stream to the source and sit
And watch for the moment when the clouds crop up. . .

Anderson says that this is a story of the quest for what is life.

It's an image of the human being going back to the source, walking to the source of our life, and at that point sitting and watching for the moment when life crops up—to catch life as we create it. Life is not passed to us, we are not the victims of a creator outside ourselves. We are all powerful magicians, and are able to conjure up life moment by moment. We are also completely effective meditators, in the sense that we return to the source moment by moment, and then conjure up a new life again.

The point of meditation is to slow ourselves down and stabilize ourselves so we can see ourselves in this creative work:

If we don't catch ourselves as we create forms, as we create perceptions, as we create feelings, as we create emotions, then we feel like they are happening to us.

But if through meditation we can learn to experience the way we create our world, we will no longer be deceiving ourselves into experiencing our world as separate from us:

our practice of meditation is so that we can be there as whatever life is first begins to break forth from the womb. . . So the following the stream to the source is what we call stabilisation, or calming. Watching for the moment when the clouds crop up is what we call insight, or wisdom. And the wisdom is that we understand that forms are illusory. And the reason why we understand them is that we create them. A magician is not fooled by his tricks: he catches them at the beginning. But if you wait for five minutes, the magician can create quite a scene. If you don't catch your own pain at the moment you create it, then you can be pushed around by it, frightened by it. . .

Within the Buddhist perspective it is impossible to *know* what life is as an object, but we *can* be completely alive if we can learn to catch ourselves in these continual acts of creation. The Buddhist expression of stopping the mind means that you calm the mind so you can see it for what it is. So when we wake up in the morning we can ask ourselves, ''Are you awake?'' All day long we can ask, ''Are you awake?'' And we can with discipline and practice begin to be aware of the process by which we create our world and our place in it. This is a discipline of more developed consciousness than that which is taken as normal in our society. It can be a part of the research experience, as Comfort (1987) suggests, the emerging forms of inquiry are more like a neo-Buddhism than like positivism.

This Buddhist practice of attending to life as we create it has its parallels in other disciplines. If it is what Zen masters call stopping the mind, it is what shamans call stopping the world. Joan Halifax teaches a map of awareness which is derived from the American Indian tradition. The map contains five attentions. The first attention is that of the physical senses; it is conscious, immediate, and with no memory engagement. The second attention is abstract and conceptual; it has a superficial memory engagement, and deals with words and concepts. The third attention concerns psychodynamic memories, is unconscious and symbolic.

The fourth attention is transpersonal, is engaged with deep archetypal patterns of the collective unconscious, and is concerned with memories of other lives, with psi capacities, and spiritual possibilities. It is the fifth attention which most concerns us here: it can be seen as *unobstructed awareness,* and thus is non-relative and absolute. And again, access to this attention comes through the variety of meditative disciplines. Halifax refers to it as "Keeping your seat," not being thrown by the relativeness of the other attentions, and not rejecting them either, but being there.

It is with this quality of awareness that we can passionately and wholehearted-ly engage with the most intense and even remarkable experiences—fight with a loved one; experience bereavement; get caught up in a riot or civil disturbance; re-experience the traumas of childhood; enter nonordinary realities; and so on—and still be fully, simply, present. And this is not a mere return to childhood and the consciousness of naive realism, because it embraces fully the paradox of form and nothingness:

> Before a man studies Zen, for him the mountains are mountains and the waters are waters; when, thanks to the teaching of a good master, he has achieved some inner vision of the truth of Zen, for him the mountains are no longer mountains, and the waters are no longer waters; but later, when he has really arrived at the asylum of rest, once more the mountains are mountains and the waters are waters. (Benoit, 1959, p. 89)

A modern approach to mindfulness is the Enlightenment Intensive workshop designed by Charles Berner (Love, 1976). In this workshop we work with a series of questions, beginning with "Who am I?" and proceeding to "What is Life?" "What is the Truth?," and so on. The fundamental form of this work is in pairs: one person in a supporting and listening role asks the other their question, for example, "Tell me who you are." The seeker takes the question, and using a particular form of meditation contemplates it with the intent of reaching a *direct experience of the truth:* they then communicate their experi-ence, whatever it is, to their partner. This process continues rigorously, along with "working meditation," "eating meditation," and "sleeping meditation" for a minimum of three days of intensive work.

In working with this method the seeker typically goes through layers of being, through roles and attributes, through occupation and relationships, through char-acter structure and personality. This is at times an agonizing and alarming pro-cess, because what is discarded in the process are the forms of life to which we are attached. It seems then that the "direct experience" has qualities of knowing which are in some way nonegoic, or beyond ego. In Wilber's (1980) sense this is *trans*-personal, beyond the experience of the personal ego—and importantly contrasted with the pre-personal experience (i.e., naive subjectivism) of the earlier phase of human development. My own experience is that once this direct experience has been touched, it becomes more available to everyday life.

My colleague John Crook has described to me his experience of conducting "Western Zen Retreats" (Crook, in press) in the mountains of Wales which encorporate the Enlightenment Intensive workshop. His experience over the years has been that those seekers who experience this nonegoic knowing discover that it is also a profound experience of love and compassion for themselves and for their world. Thus it seems that the attitude of mindfulness encompasses both an awareness that all form is in some deep sense illusion, *and* feeling of deep compassion for the world and for all sentient beings. Thus Halifax works with the "Compassionate Warrior" way: intensely disciplined and completely loving.

I am sure that many readers will know better these experiences than I have been able to write them, and that others will have experience of other disciplines that have taken them in similar directions. There is nothing new in what I have written, and my attempts at description bear all the faults of writing about something which is fundamentally beyond words. But my argument is that this kind of trans-egoic experience—maybe we can see it as spiritual—is also an essential and central part of the research experience. If we seek a post-positivist inquiry, we must also seek an experience that takes us beyond the body-mind split which the West has pursued since Descartes, and thus behind the egoic character structure which (at least in part) derives from it (Ogilvy, 1977). We cannot claim valid inquiry unless we can be fully present with the persons and things with whom we inquire. So just as many research students currently learn complex forms of statistical analysis, I would also have them learn to meditate.

Participation and In-Dwelling

Susan Griffin (1983, 1984) tells us that Bacon, who is seen by many as the first empiricist, said that we must put Nature herself on the rack and wrest her secrets from her. Heidegger makes a similar reference, and argues that knowing is not a grasping or an acquisition, "not a process of returning with one's booty to the "cabinet" of consciousness" (quoted in Steiner, 1978). Knowing for Heidegger is rather a kind of being, a form of being-with, of concern, of "tarrying alongside."

More recently Skolimowski has argued for a form of knowing which is holistic and participatory:

> Wholeness means that all the parts belong together, and that means that they partake in each other. Thus from the central idea that all is connected, that each is part of the whole, comes the idea that each participate in the whole. *Thus participation is an implicit aspect of wholeness.* You cannot truly conceive the structure of wholeness unless you grant that the meaning of wholeness implies that all parts partake in it, or put otherwise—participate in it. (1985, p. 25; emphasis in original)

Just as wholeness implies participation, so participation means empathy, "an almost complete identification with the subject of our attention"; and empathy implies responsibility, since we "cannot truly participate in the whole unless we take responsibility for it."

Similarly, Martin Buber (1958 edition) writes of the "two primary words I-Thou and I-It." I speak the primary word I-Thou when, as a whole being, I am in relationship with the other, equally as whole being. The world of I-Thou is a world of no bounds, a world of relations. On the other hand, I speak the primary word I-It when I relate to my world in terms of bounded objects, thus fragmenting both myself and my world.

This notion of knowing through participation lies at the core of the co-operative inquiry paradigm: I have that quality of attention so that I may be with you, alongside you, empathizing with you; and yet not losing myself in confluence with you because the dialogue between us both bridges and preserves our differences. Discussed below are some of the ways we may develop this quality of experience so that we may integrate it within our research practice.

THE FORM OF ACTION

Macmurray's argument concerning the primacy of action has consequences for our understanding of validity. He points out that it is the distinction between "right" and "wrong" which applies to action, rather than that between "true" and "false," which applied to reflection. Valid action, then is right action.

The Buddhist sense of right action is derived from the precepts which the lay person undertakes, as set out in the Pali Canon:

> to refrain from destroying living creatures;
> to refrain from taking that which is not given;
> to refrain from sexual misconduct;
> to refrain from incorrect speech;
> to refrain from intoxicating liquors and drugs which lead to carelessness.

These are practical rules for reflection and meditation. My own meditation suggests the following:

- action which is mindful, conscious, fully present and awake in the moment;
- action which is Selfless, from an empty heart, not motivated by personal desires or aversions;
- action which responds simply to the appropriate needs of the moment;
- action which fully allows things to be as they are now, and is nonattached to particular results, but open to any outcomes;
- action of the Self, of the inner being rather than ego;
- action which is wise and compassionate (since these two are inseparable) coming from insight into the oneness of all things and a concern for the well-being of all sentient beings;

- action which is total, wholehearted, without resistance;
- action in the sight of God and glorifying God; action which is a sacrament, a form of worship of all creation;
- finally, right action is the action of right being: it is based on and nurtured by the kind of mindfulness practices I outlined above.

This is of course a rather tall order—simple, but by no means easy in practice. But we can see the validity of this perspective if we contrast it with the attitude of some modern science, where it does indeed sometimes seem that Nature is "put on the rack." The danger is, that since the objective mind is detached and nonemotional, the action that it initiates is likely to do violence.

Right action involves the kind of intention which we bring to our acts, as Bateson explores Gregory in an essay titled *"Conscious Purpose versus Nature"* (1972). He makes the point that all natural systems, while containing the potential for runaway, exponential growth of constituent populations, are kept in dynamic balance by various forms of complex feedback loops which conserve the stability of that system within some limits. In contast to this, human consciousness selects and attends solely to what is relevant to its purpose:

> Consciousness. . . is organised in terms of purpose. It is a short-cut device to enable you to get quickly to what you want; not to act with maximal wisdom in order to live, but to follow the shortest logical or causal route to get what you next want, which may be dinner; it may be a Beethoven sonata; it may be sex. Above all, it may be money and power. (pp. 433–34)

Bateson contrasts purpose with wisdom, that "knowledge of the larger interactive system—that system which, if disturbed, is likely to generate exponential curves of change" (p. 433). Wisdom here is knowledge of whole circuits of feedback, not just of arcs.

Since, "lack of systemic wisdom is always punished" (p. 434)—especially in this age when consciousness is allied to hugely powerful technologies—Bateson proposes as remedies humility, responsiveness, and attention to the unconscious processes revealed in dream and creative art. And these not as moral principles, but as items of scientific philosophy. These may be ways to temper the arrogance of purpose and attend to those shadowed or muted aspects of the situation which are hidden by our concern for purpose, yet are essential for ecological stability. In my terms, an extended consciousness and high-quality awareness may be able to encompass wider forms of action with wisdom.

I have learned a lot about the form of action from my T'ai Chi practice. Each movement in T'ai Chi is driven with a little push from one foot which is then connected through the legs and waist to the whole body. This active work of the legs is known as the yang cycle. You just need a little push at the right moment, and then you can let the body flow through the rest of the action, watching for when the next little push is needed. I learn from this that right action involves taking little steps rather than big ones, taking action and then waiting to see the consequences of the action. It means seeing our action as taking place within a system of variables, not abstracting one or two for our attention. You only need a little of the active yang principle, and then you can let the process flow; but if you keep pushing, using too much yang, you cannot see the consequences of your acting.

By this view, right action is action within an ecology we can dwell with, one in which we can see the consequences of our actions. It is action based on a reverence for the ecological systems that support our lives. In research terms this means working with relatively small cycles of action and reflection; it means being aware of the impact of those cycles on the systems involved, and taking these into account. This is vastly different from the intrusive action of orthodox research, which involves impersonal data gathering from a large population to a fixed schedule. Right action is an epistemological as well as a moral imperative.

USE OF METAPHOR

Among those writers who are reaching beyond a positivist view of the world toward a world of multiple realities, the notion that all knowledge is metaphorical is well established. Lakoff and Johnson (1980) see metaphor as "not merely a matter of language," but "a matter of conceptual structure" (p. 235), and Bateson muses, with apologies to Browning: A man's reach should exceed his grasp, Or what's a meta for?" (Brockman, 1977).

Mangham and Overington (1987) write of "metaphorical framing," that organizing of experience through frameworks of concepts so that we understand one thing in terms of another. They assert that metaphors are far from being mere embellishments of language, but are more importantly the organizing forms which serve as our perspectives on life. They illustrate their thesis with many delightful examples, and continue to assert their own choice of the dramaturgical metaphor to explore organizational life.

Cunningham (1984) points out how Western thinkers have tried to reduce metaphor into linear and analytical concepts, and argues that this is a grave error:

> metaphor and related analogical linguistic modes provide the balancing yin half of a yin-yang complementarity. . . . (B)y virtue of an over-commitment to linear, digital modes Western society has lost track of the symbolic, the mythical, the metaphorical; except that we harmlessly side-track such activity into the harmless arts well away from "meaningful activity" (like managing). (We) try to forget that the mythical symbolic life still does live (and that in earlier times we put the expression of such activity at the centre of our culture not at the periphery in art galleries and museums). (p. 7)

Mythical, symbolic life still *is* at the center of our lives and our sciences. Both Mangham and Overington and Cunningham illustrate their thesis with many examples of use of metaphor in managerial and organizational life, while Harre (1981) points out that scientific theories are judged in terms of the plausibility of the image of the hidden world they help to create. We create theories to explain that which we cannot directly see, and thus at root, all scientific explanation is metaphorical.

Metaphor is based on a comparison of form of two entities or processes, in that the same formal structure is seen to run through both: in this sense my left arm is a metaphor of my right, and indeed of a bison's leg. Thus metaphor concerns primarily the patterning of our world, what Bateson called "the pattern which connects" (1979). The most significant metaphors are those we can scarcely see at all *because* they create the structure of our world. In exploring different ways in which ideas are organized, Bateson (1978) points out that there are two kinds of syllogism. One is the syllogism of linear rational thought, which is that

> Men die
> Socrates is a Man
> Socrates will die.

The other kind of syllogism, which Bateson argues is how mental operations *really* work at a primary level, goes like this

> Men die
> Grass dies
> Men are grass.

Materialist scientists do not like this kind of syllogism and dismiss it as poetical. But the first kind of logical syllogism is always laid over the second: thus within the world-view of Newtonian Physics, the Universe *is* a machine; within the world of a playwright all the world *is* a stage; for a traditional Catholic the Bread *is* the Body and the Wine *is* the Blood. The point about metaphors (as opposed to similes) is that when we use them in the fullest sense they are not labeled as metaphors, so we enter fully into their world. Thus dream images and their relationships are entirely metaphorical, and confuse us because they appear so "real"; similarly, as Laing points out, persons with a schizophrenic disturbance confuse us because they speak in unusual metaphor without labeling it as such.

> Julie said she was a "tolled bell" (told belle), that she was 'tailored bread' (bred). . . . One saw Julie daily sitting passively while her mother combed her hair, put ribbons and hairpins in it, powdered her face, applied lipstick to her lips and mascara to her eyes, so that the final appearance resembled nothing so much as a beautiful, lifesize, lifeless doll which her mother has 'told' (tolled) (1971, pp. 99–100).

In recognizing the metaphorical nature of our understanding we recognize that "Truth is a form of fiction. . . . Truths are the stories through which we have

our worlds and ourselves'' (The Second of January Group, 1986). In recognizing
that a metaphor that is labeled as such is merely a simile, and thus loses much of
its power, we are confronted again with the ''vast darkness'' which is the
backdrop to our knowing.

So we can appreciate Castaneda's confusion when he asks Don Juan after his
experience with the ''devil's weed''

> ''Did I really fly don Juan?''
> ''That is what you told me. Didn't you?''
> ''I know, don Juan. I mean, did my body fly? Did I take off like a bird?''
> ''You always ask me questions I cannot answer. You flew. That is what the second portion of
> the devil's weed is for. As you take more, you will learn to fly perfectly. It is not a simple
> matter. A man *flies* with the help of the second portion of the devil's weed. That is all I can
> tell you. What you want to know makes no sense. Birds fly like birds and a man who has
> taken the devil's weed flies as such.''
> ''As birds do?''
> ''No, he flies as a man who has taken the weed.''
> ''Then I didn't really fly, don Juan. I flew in my imagination, in my mind alone. Where was
> my body?''

And the argument proceeds to the end of the chapter

> ''Let's put it another way, don Juan. What I mean to say is that if I tied myself to a rock with a
> heavy chain I would have flown just the same, because my body had nothing to do with my
> flying.''
> Don Juan looked at me incredulously. ''If you tie yourself to a rock,'' he said, ''I'm afraid
> you will have to fly holding the rock with its heavy chain'' (1976, pp. 128–29).

Let me take another example from T'ai Chi and sensory awareness exercises.
Stand up. Remember that the mass of the earth exerts a gravitational pull on your
body. Experience the pull of gravity which keeps you on the floor; experience the
weight of your body, and the tonus of the muscles which hold you up: see if there
are muscles which are more stressed than they need be and let them go. Now
realize that this all is metaphor. And let us now change the metaphor. Know that
the earth is yin and receptive, that the heavens are yang and creative; know also
that the lower part of your body is yang, and the upper part is yin. Experience the
yang quality of your lower body resting on and interacting with the yin of the
earth; and experience the yin of your upper body resting on the lower, and held
also by a thread that goes from the top of your head to the heavens. And notice
the change in your experience of your body. And know that this too is metaphor.

How then can we use this notion of metaphor? Well, of course, the first and
radical answer is that we can't, no more than we can know the meaning of
dream, if metaphor is accepted as the very structure of our world. But more
pragmatically, we *can* play with the metaphors of our inquiry.

1.   We can enter the dialectic of total acceptance and radical doubt of our metaphors. On the one hand, we can use them with certainty, wholeheartedly, entering fully into their spirit, yet still wearing them lightly, without compulsive attachment. On the other hand, we can remember that all frameworks contain the danger of clarity, and that we need to be able to test them in action and discard them once they have given us their insight. In this way we can live "as if" the metaphor is "real," while at the same time holding awareness of its fiction.

2.   When we adopt a metaphor we can ask whether our inquiry is accurate, given this way of framing the world. Mangham (1986) points out that there are four criteria which may be used to judge an interpretation: completeness, correctness, comprehensiveness, consistency. This leads us to consider whether our interpretation covers all we know of the situation (completeness); honors the accuracy of what is known (correctness); adequately illuminates all aspects of the situation (comprehensiveness); without undue straining of metaphor (consistency). But we can only apply these criteria once we have wholeheartedly entered that definition of the situation, once we have leapt into the hermeneutic circle through which any world-view defines itself.

3.   However, once we have adopted a metaphor we can use it, live with it either lazily or courageously. If we are lazy, then the metaphor becomes a cliché, losing its power to illuminate our experience and to guide our actions. But if we take the metaphor and live it with courage we inevitably test it, challenge its boundaries, and thus transform it. This is the process through which, in Kuhn's view of scientific revolution, paradigms become inadequate and replaced by new ones; it is also the process through which societies grow and decay (Capra, 1982), and by which men live through the "Seasons" of their lives (Levinson, 1978).

4.   As we live and work within a metaphor, we can ask: Is it fruitful? Is it illuminating and creative? Does it show the phenomena in new ways? Is it *interesting* in Davis' (1964) use of the term? In a world of multiple realities, fruitfulness will often be more important than accuracy. For example:

> In our view the field of organisational study stands now more in need of exemplars in thinking creatively than ever it does of another illustration of painstaking application of rigorous techniques of inquiry. . . (Mangham & Overington, 1987, p. 25).

In the final analysis, judgments about the fruitfulness of metaphors must be aesthetic: responsive to the "pattern which connects" with recognition and empathy (Bateson, 1979).

5.   Once we have chosen and established a metaphorical perspective on our world, lived with it and given it some life, we can begin to establish dialogue between our metaphor and those used by other people. From such a dialogue, new world-views may emerge. This use of metaphor leads us away from questions as to which theory or metaphor is true, and encourages us to live equally

with two or more world-views. Thus in the field of holistic medicine, allopathic medicine with its metaphor of the body as a mechanical-chemical machine can co-exist in creative and illuminating tension with acupuncture with its metaphors of meridians of *chi* energy.

6. Finally, we can borrow the perspective of Jungian psychology and look for the Shadow, look to see what the metaphor hides as well as what it illuminates, and the consequences of this hiding. As Jung points out,

> The shadow is a moral problem that challenges the whole ego-personality, for no one can become conscious of the shadow without considerable moral effort. To become conscious of it involves recognising the dark aspects of the personality as present and real. This act is the essential condition for any kind of self-knowledge, and it therefore, as a rule, meets with considerable resistance (Jung, CW 9ii, para 14).

We tend to become over-attached to our metaphor precisely because it hides the shadow, because it hides that which we do not wish to see. And this is as true with the shadows of our research metaphors as in our personalities. The shadow of Mechanos has been pointed out by Skolimowski. It would be instructive if each piece of inquiry were required to address the question, What have I been hiding, and hiding from in this work?

IMPLICATIONS FOR INQUIRY

The perspective I have explored in this chapter has considerable implications for the practice of inquiry, and while it is not at this stage possible to set these out as firm criteria for valid knowing—indeed it probably never will be—it is possible to suggest some approaches to both the training of researchers and research facilitators, and some ways in which a piece of inquiry might be reviewed and assessed, for example, in a Ph.D. examination or in a review of a possible journal article.

Training for Post-Positivist Inquiry

Since we have all been rather thoroughly trained in the Yoga of objectivity, so that our consciousness accepts without question the ordinary reality of our Western civilization, it is evident that would-be researchers in a post-positivist tradition must undertake some fairly rigorous training to open their body-mind-spirit to alternative possibilities, to uncover new vistas in what Jean Houston (1982) calls *unlensing* consciousness. We can explore this in terms of the extended epistemology and look at ways of developing high-quality awareness, right action, and use of metaphor.

Practice of High-Quality Awareness.   In our research group and inquiry conferences at the University of Bath, we have been exploring ways of developing high-quality awareness over the past seven years. I suggest that any person broadly competent within experiential disciplines such as humanistic and trans-personal psychology, and who is interested in a collaborative approach to educa-tion, can find their own way to practices and disciplines similar to ours; the key is to regard them as a part of the research experience. But since what we do appears to be rather peculiar, certainly in England, and in a university, I shall briefly mention some of the practices we have explored.

1.   Meeting as a circle. We meet informally as a circle of people. Sometimes we take time to "attune" with each other, holding hands, eyes closed, to experi-ence the energy of our circle. Sometimes we use circle dances (Wosien, 1974)—those ancient sacred dances from Old Europe and the Middle East to establish ourselves as a circle. In doing this we intentionally evoke the archetype of the circle, of human equality and presence. This is the "Circle of the People—a living, organic democracy stressing equal right to voice and vision" (Bleakley, 1984). Meeting this way means we don't have to "agree" in a limited, cognitive sense to be a whole community.

This may seem simple, but it produces an interesting sense of shock to start a research conference in a university setting by holding hands in a circle, attuning, and dancing the Greetings Dance, rather than with a keynote address!

2.   Being there as people. In a world dominated by impersonal and formal forms of relationship, we need to learn and re-learn to be together as human beings. We cannot say I-Thou to those with whom we inquire if we cannot learn to relate personally with our teachers and fellow students. So our research group, while being an intellectual seminar and experiential laboratory, is also a support group and an encounter group. We take time to attend to our interpersonal relationships and we struggle, not always successfully, to meet each other as whole persons.

3.   Confronting distress. For us, research is very much a personal process (Reason & Marshall, 1987), and we have discovered in practice how inquiry can stir up psychological defenses and restimulate old hurts and patterns. Many members of the group have used processes such as humanistic psychotherapy and co-counseling (Heron, 1973) to explore personal issues which have arisen during research.

We also borrow and adapt widely from the experiential psychotherapies. Using Gestalt methods we have set up two chairs, one for the research and one for the researcher, and invited the researcher to speak from each chair in turn, holding a conversation between the two, thus giving the research a voice of its own, and deepening the understanding of its place in the researcher's life. Simi-larly, one group member used methods adapted from psychosythesis (Ferrucci, 1982) to identify and work with the various subpersonalities who were arguing within her about the research project, and included an account of this within her dissertation (Mellor-Ribet, 1986). And another developed a process he calls phenomenological psychodrama (Hawkins, 1986; in press), which can be used to explore the researcher's relation to the topic.

4.   We are just beginning to extend our experiments into developing mindfulness through the disciplines of T'ai Chi and Buddhist meditation. This is a field in which there is much space for disciplined work—so far we have touched on it with a little sitting meditation together, by using some of the exercises suggested by Houston (1982) and the Mindfulness exercises developed by Masters (1981).

5.   We have explored the area of participative knowing primarily through using psychodrama. When we use psychodrama as a phenomenological method, we re-create, by psychodramatic sculpting, some aspect of the research situation we wish to explore. So if we are looking at the process of a family, we would invite the primary researcher to re-create that family within the room, using other members of the research group to play different members. For example, the primary researcher can, by taking the place of each family member in turn, or by speaking as the whole family, experience more directly the family process. (Hawkins, 1986; in press).

Finally we have used exercises introduced to us by Skolimowski—he calls them a yoga of participation—which are in the form of disciplines that will help develop a participative relation to the world. He invites you to approach various natural phenomena—a tree, a rock, water—and to meditate with it in three different ways. First, to explore *identification,* to sense what it would be to experience the world with that form of consciousness. Second, to approach with *reverence.* And third, to commune in *silence.* In our development of these methods, we invite people to identify a small area of the natural world and first of all to view this as a set of objects, as I-It, seeing how many "things" can be identified, named, counted, and classified. After a while in this activity, we invite people to switch into a participative, or I-Thou relation to the same area of ground, identifying with it, treating it as sacred, and being with it in silence. The difference in consciousness can be extraordinary.

Right Action.   We have paid less attention to the form of training for right action, but some directions seem clear. Partly this is a form of action which will evolve naturally from high-quality awareness, and can be developed through practices such as T'ai Chi, Karma Yoga, and sensitivity training. In T'ai Chi we learn to act from our center and without unnecessary effort; we learn to act and watch the action at the same time. In Karma Yoga, we take our awareness into the activities of our lives in the world, so that we, say, do the dishwashing, or clean the house as an exercise in right action. Similarly, sensitivity training is one way in which people may learn about the quality of action in interpersonal settings.

Use of Metaphor.   The positivist attitude of the world, with its reductionist assumptions and its operational definitions, is responsible for radically impoverishing our language. Bateson frequently points out how the metaphorical quality of the liturgy of the Protestant Churches was destroyed, when the sacrament of the bread *is* the Body and the wine *is* the Blood of Christ becomes the Bread *stands for* the Body and the wine *stands for* the Blood.

We can re-educate ourselves into using diverse, elegant, and illuminating metaphor in several ways. We might start by working with the world's great literature, reading Shakespeare as well as Glaser and Strauss in our research seminars. Several of us at Bath have found Steinbeck's *Log from the Sea of Cortez* (1958) takes us to new perspectives on the research process. Or we might take a lead from Hillman (1975) and explore the metaphor of mythology. And we might consider ancient archetypal systems such as astrology and alchemy as potent sources of metaphorical illumination.

What we need to do is to shock ourselves out of our taken-for-granted, literal metaphors; to break the habit of seeing the world as made of things linked in mechanical ways. Thus when Mangham (1986) suggests that much organization life can be seen as comedy rather than as melodrama, we are immediately challenged out of any view that business life is only serious, rational, and self-important. When Hillman (1975) opens his book with the assertion that the purpose of life is soul-making, we may be surprised into a new perspective on ourselves. When Bateson (1979) writes a book which asks if we know the meaning of terms as diverse as *entropy* and *sacrament* we are offered a feast of new metaphors for our world. This is the realm of what Houston (1982) calls imaginal thinking. Our propositional thinking is broadened and deepened when nurtured by intentional metaphor as in poetry.

Training for inquiry involves learning how to express ideas and how to play with metaphor. In our work with storytelling we have borrowed a range of techniques from creative writing and experiential learning to help people in this play (Hawkins, 1986; Reason & Hawkins, in press). We have also used creative dance and art therapy to explore our inquiries in different expressive modalities. There is much more that might be done in this area.

Assessment of Inquiry Projects

Most universities have a pro-forma which examiners are expected to use when reviewing a Ph.D. dissertation; similarly journals tend to have clearly established guidelines. This application of supposedly objective external criteria is singularly inappropriate for the kind of inquiry which will emerge in a post-positivist inquiry paradigm, and the research community needs urgently to develop new assessment processes.

I have with my colleagues at Bath been encouraging students to engage in a personal review of their work, and to make a self-assessment which can be the basis of discussion during a face-to-face examination.

I first encourage them to read and reflect widely on the issue of valid and sound inquiry; this is not difficult since this topic continually reoccurs during our research group discussions. Inevitably my students are influenced by my own and my colleagues writings, although we continually try to widen our epistemological range. The second part of the assessment starts early in the inquiry, and becomes more rigorously addressed as the work proceeds; it is addressing the question, What is sound knowing for me in this piece of work? Thus each student, informed by reading and discussion, and paying attention to their own unique inquiry style, begins to develop their own sense of soundness and criteria of validity. It is important at this stage to remind both myself and my student that perfection is the privilege of the gods: there is no way that a piece of work can meet all possible criteria, what is important is to choose what is appropriate for this piece of work, maybe limiting this choice to six areas.

Toward the end of the work, when the dissertation is nearly complete, I encourage students to make a rigorous self-assessment of their work on the basis of these criteria, and to either include it as part of the dissertation or send it with the dissertation to the examiners. We can then, examiners and student together, negotiate the criteria, and make some human judgment as to how adequately the writing and the experiences behind it lives up to them.

Gill Robertson (1984) undertook this process for her dissertation examination. She included her own validity assessment within the dissertation, and re-wrote the University of Bath criteria to conform with her own epistemology, so that:

> Does the candidate's work show that he has studied the subject of his thesis with adequate industry and application?

Became

> Does the candidate's work show she has studied the subject and participated as subject in the inquiry with the fullest use of her potential, and with insight and imagination as well as industry and application?

And

> Has the candidate shown that he is able to conduct original investigations. . . .

Became

> Has the candidate shown that she is able to conduct original investigations, to identify, clarify, and explore her own ideas as well as those of others, and has been able to facilitate the development of a new perspective with a firm basis in the lives and experiences of others? Has the candidate's own world view been exposed and disturbed?

Similarly, Hawkins (1986) bound within his dissertation an assessment of his work in relation to Heron's (1982) criteria, and included a critical discussion about the work between himself and his devil's advocate critic. We need to continue exploring ways of assessing inquiry within a post-positivist paradigm.

FINAL REMARKS

Inquiry, as explored in this chapter, is about reflective action in our world. The soundness of such action depends on the quality of the experience which informs it, and I have argued that for high-quality inquiry our consciousness must be both deepened and extended.

Heraclitus is believed to have remarked that "You can't put your foot in the same river twice"; he was followed by Cratylus, who corrected him by saying, "You can't put your foot in the same river (even) once" (Hainer, 1968). In this strange world of ours each of us is

> partly blown by the winds of reality and partly an artist creating a composite out of the inner and outer events. (Bateson, in Brockman, 1977, p. 245).

I suspect that this era after the possibility of truth will call for extreme courage and creativity from those artists who wish to pursue a sound and valid inquiry.

ACKNOWLEDGMENTS

Many of the ideas in this chapter were hatched in meetings of the Postgraduate Research Group at the University of Bath, and I very much appreciate the stimulating atmosphere of that group. Judi Marshall, Iain Mangham, John Heron, John Crook, Peter Tatham, Malcolm Parlett, and Peter Hawkins all read and commented on drafts at various stages. Nirodha offered the basis of the meditation on right action. I am particularly grateful to Judi Marshall, who read the whole thing twice, and offered some particularly important insights.

REFERENCES

Anderson, R. (1984). Dartington Conference Lecture. Dartington Trust, Dartington, England.
Bateson, G. (1972). *Steps to an ecology of mind*. San Francisco: Chandler.
Bateson, G. (1978). The pattern which connects. Informal Esalen Lectures, 1975–1980. Big Sur, CA: Dolphin Tapes.
Bateson, G. (1979). *Mind and nature: A necessary unity*. New York: E P Dutton.
Bateson, M. (1972). *Our own metaphor*. New York: Alfred Knopf.
Benoit, H. (1959). *The supreme doctrine*. New York: Viking.
Bleakley, A. (1984). *The fruits of the moon tree*. London: Gateway Books.
Brockman, J. (Ed.) (1977). *About Bateson*. New York: E P Dutton.
Buber, M. (1958). *I and thou*. New York: Charles Scribner.
Capra, F. (1982). *The turning point*. London: Wildwood House.
Castaneda, C. (1976). *Tales of power*. London: Penguin.

Comfort, A. (1987). What real world? *Guardian,* January 23.

Crook, J. (in press). A model of mind for Western Zen. To appear in *Meeting Points in East-West Psychology.*

Cunningham, I. (1984). *Teaching styles in learner centered management development programmes.* Ph.D. dissertation, Lancaster University.

Davis, M. (1971). That's interesting! Towards a phenomenology of sociology and a sociology of phenomenology. *J. Philosophy of the social sciences, 4,* 309–344.

Deikman, A. (1966). De-automatisation and the Mystic Experience. *Psychiatry, 29,* 324–338.

Devereaux, G. (1967). *From anxiety to method in the behavioural sciences.* The Hague: Mouton.

Dossey, L. (1982). *Space, time, and medicine.* Boulder, CO: Shambhala.

Ferrucci, P. (1982). *What we may be: The visions and techniques of psychosynthesis.* Wellingborough: Turnstone Press.

Glaser, B. & Strauss, A. (1967). *The discovery of grounded theory.* Chicago: Aldine.

Griffin, S. (1983). Schumacher Lecture. Bristol, England.

Griffin, S. (1984). *Woman and nature: The roaring inside her.* London: The Women's Press.

Hainer, R. (1968). Rationalism, pragmatism, and existentialism: Perceived but undiscovered multicultural problems. In E. Glatt and M. Shelly, *The research society.* New York: Gordon and Breach.

Halifax, J. (1979). *Shamanic voices: A survey of visionary narratives.* New York: E P Dutton.

Harre, R. (1981). The positivist-empiricism approach and its alternative. In P. Reason and J. Rowan (Eds.), *Human inquiry, a sourcebook of new paradigm research.* Chichester, England: Wiley.

Hawkins, P. (1986). *Living the learning: An exploration of learning processes in primary learning communities and the development of a learning perspective to inform team development.* Ph.D. dissertation, University of Bath.

Hawkins, P. (in press). Psychodramatic research. In P. Reason (Ed.), *Human inquiry in action.* London: Sage Publications.

Heron, J. (1971). *Experience and method.* Human Potential Research Project, University of Surrey.

Heron, J. (1973). *Re-evaluation counselling: A theoretical review.* Human Potential Research Project, University of Surrey.

Heron, J. (1981). Philosophical basis for a new paradigm. In P. Reason and J. Rowan (Eds.), *Human inquiry, a sourcebook of new paradigm research.* Chichester, England: Wiley.

Heron, J. (1982). *Empirical validity in experiential research.* Human Potential Research Project, University of Surrey.

Heron, J. (in press). Validity in Cooperative Inquiry. In Reason, P. (Ed.), *Human Inquiry in Action* London: Sage Publications.

Hillman, J. (1975). *Revisioning psychology.* New York: Harper Collophon.

Houston, J. (1982). *The possible human.* Los Angeles: J. P. Tarcher.

Hunter, J. (1983). Truth and effectiveness in revelatory stories. *Re-vision, 6,* 2, 3–15.

Huxley, J. (1958). *The perennial philosophy.* London: Fontana.

Jantsch, E. (1980). *The self-organising universe.* New York: Pergamon.

Jung, C. (1971). *Collected works,* Vol. 9, Part ii. R. F. C. Hull (Trans). London: Routledge and Kegan Paul.

Kuhn, T. (1962). *The structure of scientific revolutions.* Chicago: University of Chicago Press.

Laing, R. (1971). *Self and others.* London: Penguin.

Lakoff, G. & Johnson, M. (1980). *Metaphors we live by.* Chicago: University of Chicago Press.

Levinson, D. (1978). *The seasons of a man's life.* New York: Ballantine.

Lincoln, S. & Guba, E. (1985). *Naturalistic inquiry.* Beverly Hills: Sage Publications.

Love, J. (1976). *The quantum gods.* London: Compton Russell.

Macmurray, J. (1957). *Persons in relation.* London: Faber and Faber.

Mangham, I. (1986). The human comedy: Improvisation, ensemble playing and alienation in executive teams. Paper read at the International Workshop on Aspects of Organization, University of Lancaster.

Mangham, I. & Overington, M. (1987). *Organizations as theatre*. Chichester, England: John Wiley and Sons.

Manicas, P. & Secord, P. (1983). Implications for Psychology of the new philosophy of science. *American Psychologist, 38*, 399–413.

Maslow, A. (1966). *The Psychology of science*. New York: Harper and Row.

Masters, R. (1981). Introduction to Mindfulness in the Sacred Psychologies. *Dromenon, 3*, 3, 55–61.

Mellor-Ribet, E. (1986). *Revisioning group process: Towards a female perspective*. Ph.D. dissertation, University of Bath.

Ogilvy, J. (1977). *Many dimensional man: decentralizing self, society, and the sacred*. New York: Oxford University Press.

Popper, K. (1963). *Conjectures and refutations: The growth of scientific knowledge*. London: Routledge and Kegan Paul.

Prigogine, I. & Stengers, I. (1984). *Order out of chaos: Man's new dialogue with nature*. New York: Bantam.

Reason, P. (1976). *Explorations in the dialectics of two-person relations*. Ph.D. dissertation, Case Western Reserve University.

Reason, P. (in press). *Human inquiry in action*. London: Sage Publications.

Reason, P. & Hawkins, P. (in press). Inquiry through storytelling. In P. Reason, *Human inquiry in action*. London: Sage Publications.

Reason, P. & Heron, J. (1986). Research with people: The paradigm of co-operative experiential inquiry. *Person Centred Review, 1*, 4, 456–475.

Reason, P. & Marshall, J. (1987). Research as personal process. In D. Boud and V. Griffin (Eds.), *Appreciating Adults Learning: From the learner's perspective*. London: Kogan Page.

Reason, P. & Rowan, J. (1981a). *Human Inquiry, a sourcebook of new paradigm research*. Chichester, England: Wiley.

Reason, P. & Rowan, J.(1981b). Issues of validity in new paradigm research. In P. Reason and J. Rowan (Eds.), *Human inquiry, a sourcebook of new paradigm research*. Chichester, England: Wiley.

Robertson, G. (1984). *Experiences of learning*. Ph.D. dissertation, University of Bath.

Rowan, J. (1979). Hegel and self-actualization. *Self and Society, 1*, 5, 129–138.

Rowan, J. & Reason, P. (1981). On making sense. In P. Reason and J. Rowan (Eds.), *Human inquiry, a sourcebook of new paradigm research*. Chichester, England: Wiley.

Russell, B. (1946). *History of western philosophy*. London: George Allen and Unwin.

Schwartz, P. & Ogilvy, J. (1980). *The emergent paradigm: Changing patterns of thought and belief*. Analytical Report No 7, Values and Lifestyles Program, SRI International, Menlo Park, California.

Second of January Group. (1986). *After truth*. London: Inventions Press.

Skolimowski, H. (1985). *The co-creative mind as a partner of the creative evolution*. Paper read at the First International Conference on the Mind-Matter Interaction. Universidada Estadual De Campinas, Brazil.

Skolimowski, H. (1986, February). The interactive mind in the participatory universe. *The World and I*.

Steinbeck, J. (1958). *The log from the Sea of Cortez*. London: Heinmann.

Steiner, G. (1978). *Heidegger*. London: Fontana

Storm, H. (1972). *Seven arrows*. New York: Harper & Row.

Teilhard de Chardin, P. (1959). *The phenomenon of man*. London: Collins and Harper & Row.

Tillich, P. Existential philosophy. *J History of Ideas, 5*, 1, 44–70.

Torbert, W. (1981). Why educational research has been so uneducational: The case for a new model of social science based on collaborative inquiry. In P. Reason and J. Rowan (Eds.), *Human inquiry, a sourcebook of new paradigm research*. Chichester, England: Wiley.

Torbert, W. (1983). Initiating collaborative inquiry. In G. Morgan (Ed.), *Beyond method*. Beverly Hills: Sage Publications.

Watts, A. (1963). *The two hands of God: The myths of polarity*. New York: George Braziller.

Watts, A. (1978). *This is IT: And other essays on Zen and spiritual experience*. London: Rider and Co.

Wilber, K. (1980). *The Atman project: A transpersonal view of human development*. Wheaton, Illinois: Quest.

Wilber, K. (1981). *Up from Eden: a transpersonal view of human evolution*. Garden City, NY: Doubleday/Anchor.

Wolf, F. (1981). *Taking the quantum leap*. San Francisco: Harper and Row.

Wolf, F. (1984). *Mind and the new physics*. London: Heinemann.

Wosien, M. (1974). *Sacred dance: Encounter with the gods*. London: Thames and Hudson.

CREATING EXPECTATION EFFECTS IN OD:
APPLYING SELF-FULFILLING PROPHECY

Dov Eden

ABSTRACT

Interventions designed to raise performance expectations in order to create productive self-fulfilling prophecies (SFP), and prevent negative ones, are proposed.
These include creating the Pygmalion and Galatea effects, eradicating the Golem
effect, manager-expectation training, immunization of subordinates against negative SFP, fighting negative stereotypes, setting challenging goals, clearing the
personnel record of outdated information, piggybacking on naturally occurring
changes, and fostering high-expectation cultures through positive myth making.
Limiting conditions include how high expectations should be raised, how many
times it can be done effectively, and how the consultant should anticipate and
respond to potentially dysfunctional discrepancy effects. Higher order expectation
effects include the impact of consultant expectations on client performance and the

Research in Organizational Change and Development, Vol. 2, pages 235–267.
Copyright © 1988 by JAI Press Inc.
All rights of reproduction in any form reserved.
ISBN: 0-89232-772-3

impact of our expectations on OD's prospects for the future. The Messiah effect in consulting occurs when the very arrival of an expert of great reknown mobilizes clients' energy so that they redouble their efforts and fulfill their own positive expectations. The role of awareness in SFP interventions and the ethical and practical advantages and shortcomings of the various ways of applying expectation effects in OD are discussed.

INTRODUCTION

Expectations can have a significant impact on the course and outcomes of an OD effort. Many scholars and practitioners intuitively "know" that expectations are important in OD. Client expectations have been shown to make the crucial difference in the effectiveness of an intervention. The potential implications of expectation effects for OD theory and practice are profound. Despite this, there has been surprisingly little systematic discussion of how and why expectation effects operate, and how they can be profitably utilized. The treatment of expectations in the OD literature can best be described as uninformed neglect. According to Weick, the frequency with which expectation effects occur

> may be underestimated because of the inflated image implied by the phrase *self-fulfilling prophecy*. The image of a prophecy suggests. . . a major activity preceded by considerable fanfare and, consequently, rare. The more appropriate image would be that in everyday/anyday life people expect, anticipate, foresee, and make mundane predictions all the time. (1979, p. 164; italics in original)

Elsewhere I have described the ubiquity of these phenomena, explicated the role expectations play in OD, and provided a theoretical model of the process (Eden, 1986a). The purposes of the present chapter are to review the experimental data demonstrating the power of expectation effects in OD and to propose ways in which expectations can be utilized to improve the effectiveness of OD practice.

EXPECTATION EFFECTS IN ORGANIZATIONS

King (1971) was the first to produce an experimental Pygmalion effect in industry. His subjects were hard-core unemployed welder trainees. King replicated the design of Rosenthal and Jacobson's (1968) now classic Pygmalion-In-The-Classroom experiment in which they had shown that raising teacher expectations concerning pupil performance causes an increase in pupil performance. King similarly informed a welding instructor that several randomly designated trainees had high potential for success in the program. As in many previous and subsequent classroom experiments (see Dusek, Hall, & Meyer, 1985, and Rosenthal & Rubin, 1978 for reviews), the so-called "High Potential Personnel," or

"HAPs," learned faster and better than their control co-trainees as assessed by objective tests, scored higher in both peer and supervisor ratings, and had a lower drop-out rate. Replicating the Pygmalion effect among adult industrial trainees showed that performance in organizations was in part influenced by what Merton (1948) had called self-fulfilling prophecy (SFP). Subsequent field-experimental replications by my students and I have demonstrated SFP effects among soldiers in the Israel Defense Forces (IDF).

Pygmalion Goes to Boot Camp

The setting for the first IDF experiment (Eden & Shani, 1982) was a combat training base. The trainee sample included 105 soldiers, all men, in an intensive combat command course. Their instructors were four experienced training officers, each aided by an assistant instructor. Each pair instructed a group of about 30 trainees. Prior to the trainees' arrival at the base, we imparted differential expectations to the instructors and their assistants by informing them that, on the basis of information from a number of credible sources, some of their trainees had high command potential (CP). Each instructor was given a list of his trainees in which about a third were designated with an asterisk to indicate high CP, a third were unmarked to indicate regular CP, and a third were marked with a question mark indicating that they were unclassifiable due to insufficient information. Unbeknownst to the instructors, the assignment of trainees to the three CP conditions was random.

The above procedure replicated Rosenthal and Jacobson's classroom experiment as closely as was feasible in this military situation. Like them, we manipulated the instructors' expectations but abstained from intimating in any way how they should treat their trainees. Except for collecting data on attitudes and performance, we made no further interventions. Any subsequent differences in attitude, behavior, or performance, among either the instructors or the trainees, could have been caused only by the induced expectations.

The results confirmed the SFP hypothesis. Those designated as high in CP outperformed their classmates by significant and substantial amounts in each of four objectively graded subjects. The differences in performance evidenced a Pygmalion effect of substantial size—about 15 points on a conventional 100-point grade scale. Trainees in the high-expectancy condition also expressed more favorable attitudes towards the course as evidenced by significantly higher scores on an attitude scale.

We measured leadership as a potential mediator of expectation effects. Each trainee described his instructor's leadership behavior using items borrowed from the University of Michigan's Survey of Organizations (Taylor & Bowers, 1972). These items operationalize the four factors of leadership conceptualized by Bowers and Seashore (1966). The factors are Support, Interaction Facilitation, Goal Emphasis, and Work Facilitation. We used the 10-item version that Eden and Leviatan (1975) had translated into Hebrew and Eden and Daniely (1979) had adapted for use in the IDF. The trainees about whom we had imparted high expectations to the instructors rated their instructors' leadership significantly more positively. This pattern of leadership differences was replicated with a high degree of consistency for each of the four factors of leadership. These findings demythologize the Pygmalion effect. Supervisor expectations work their "magic" on subordinates by inducing supervisors to provide better leadership to subordinates expected to perform well. Other things being equal, better leadership promotes higher performance. Leadership is therefore a means by which supervisors fulfill their prophecies regarding their subordinates' performance.

Pygmalion and Galatea: The Adjutancy Experiment

The second IDF experiment (Eden & Ravid, 1982) was conducted in a seven-week adjutancy course. The purposes of the adjutancy experiment were to replicate the combat experiment and to test the Galatea hypothesis. (Galatea was the statue sculpted by the mythical Pygmalion; the Galatea effect refers to raising subordinates' self-expectations). We reasoned that the subordinate's level of self-expectations mediated the Pygmalion effect, and therefore a boost in performance could be achieved by bypassing the supervisor and directly raising the subordinate's self-expectations. The procedure used in the adjutancy experiment was similar to that of the combat course, except that only 25 percent of the trainees were described to the instructors as having high potential (Pygmalion condition) and 25 percent were designated regular (Pygmalion-control condition), while 50 percent were designated as having unknown potential due to incomplete information. This unclassified category was further split in two and assigned to two trainee-expectancy conditions, Galatea and Galatea-control, each comprising 25 percent of the trainees. All these assignments were random. The instructors' expectations regarding trainee performance were manipulated in the same manner as in the combat experiment. In addition, the adjutancy trainees received information about their potential according to the experimental conditions to which they had been assigned. Each Galatea trainee was given a five-minute interview by a military psychologist in which he was told he had high potential. As in the combat experiment, we analyzed achievement, but we also measured changes in self-expectations throughout the course.

Inspection of the statistically significant changes in mean self-expectations revealed a pattern of substantially rising expectations among trainees in both high-expectancy conditions in contrast to stable or slightly declining expectations among the controls. This confirmed the hypothesis that raising the supervisor's expectations of certain subordinates causes those subordinates to expect more of themselves. Analysis of performance scores revealed that raising instructor expectations and raising trainee self-expectations boosted performance significantly and substantially. When performance was averaged across all seven weeks, each high-expectancy group outscored its control group by 15 points, replicating the Pygmalion effect and confirming also the Galatea hypothesis. However, the two effects were not significantly different from each other, indicating that Pygmalion and Galatea are equally potent. For a more comprehensive review and critique of the experiments and several other relevant studies, and a theoretical model of how SFP operates in management, see Eden (1984).

THE POWER OF EXPECTATIONS IN OD

Organization-wide Expectation-Raising

King (1974) broke new ground by shifting his focus from the individual member to the entire organization as an object of SFP amenable to expectation effects. He hypothesized that managers' *expectations* regarding the outcomes of organizational innovations produce effects on those outcomes that are independent of the effects of the innovations themselves. He has reported the most compelling data to date demonstrating the impact of expectations on the success of interventions in organizations.

King conducted his experiment in four plants of a company that manufactured clothing patterns. The machine operators whose productivity was targeted in each plant were 10 six-man crews who had loading, operating, and take-off duties. King had the firm's director of manufacturing present to plant management the same changes differently in each plant. Job enrichment was the "organizational innovation" installed in two plants in the form of job enlargement and withheld from the two enrichment-control plants, which got job rotation as a sham innovation. The second independent variable was plant management's productivity expectations, which were manipulated to be high in one enlargement plant and in one rotation plant and, by design, unmanipulated and therefore at control levels in the two remaining plants. This resulted in four comparable plants getting different treatments: a high-expectation job enlargement plant, a high-expectation job rotation plant, a control-expectation enlargement plant, and a control-expectation rotation plant.

The results were that enrichment had no effect but expectations *did*. Over the 12-month follow-up period, both high-expectation plants increased their output by similar amounts irrespective of whether they had gotten enlargement or rotation, whereas output in both control-expectation plants remained unchanged. In other words, *if managers' expectations were raised, productivity improved regardless of which intervention was introduced.* If expectations were not raised, productivity remained unchanged regardless of which change was installed. King concluded that "managerial expectations concerning performance resulting from an innovation may serve as a self-fulfilling prophecy. When managers expected certain changes in jobs to result in greater productivity, those changes did result in greater output'' (p. 229).

Interpretations of King's Experiment

King's results can be interpreted in the context of OD. Job enlargement is not the intervention most OD researchers would choose to pit against expectation effects, and the study has yet to be replicated. Nevertheless, until more data are available, I choose to set aside my suspicions about the external validity of King's experiment, assume expectation effects operate in OD, and pursue the practical implications of this assumption.

King's manipulation of managers' expectations deserves detailed scrutiny. He purported to create two levels of expectations—high and unchanged. However, the explanations that the manufacturing director gave the managers in the two "unchanged" expectation plants may have actually *lowered* their expectations. In the control-expectation plants, he followed a brief description of the program with the statement that "Several limitations can be expected to arise.'' He then enumerated four specific limitations using such phrases as "workers may become less proficient in performance of elements making up job tasks'' and "workers may become less capable of eliminating wasted and ineffective motions'' (King, 1974, Table 1, p. 223). The presentation was concluded by telling the managers that, due to these factors, productivity should be the same.

The plant managers may have interpreted King's words as strongly implying that performance may slip. Enumerating four "limitations'' that will challenge managers having to cope with implementation of the innovation is not the best way to insure unchanged output expectations. Unfortunately, King did not measure managers' output expectations as a manipulation check. Therefore, it is quite possible that his "no-change'' manipulation actually depressed output expectations. Telling managers that they would have to contend with new problems and that productivity would remain unchanged might have hamstrung the very same interventions that appreciably raised productivity when introduced with high expectations in the other two plants. Thus, due to the things said to the no-change managers and the lack of a manipulation check, it is unclear whether King's treatment raised expectations in the high-expectation plants, depressed expectations in the no-change plants, or both.

Therefore, two different substantive interpretations of King's results are equally tenable. The first is that raising expectations boosted output. The second is that imparting expectations for unchanged productivity nullified the beneficial effects of the interventions. It is important to distinguish between positive and negative expectation effects. Positive expectation effects occur when improvements in productivity follow from raised expectations. Negative expectation effects, dubbed "Golem effects'' (Babad, Inbar, & Rosenthal, 1982), occur when low expectations produce poor performance. King may have unintentionally produced a Golem effect in his control plants.

Methodological vs. Practical Implications

Few have seized upon the practical implications of these findings, including King himself. Instead, he and most others who have commented upon his experiment have emphasized a *methodological* interpretation. King proposed that "a special effort" be made to control the potential confounding of studies of organizational innovations by expectancy effects, and called for "systematic use of procedures for assessing the effects of expectation" (p. 230). But he did not call for a special effort for systematic use of procedures for raising expectations in order to reap the productivity gains produced by expectation effects in his own experiment!

A slip-of-the-tongue reveals how overpowering the methodological focus can be. King wrote, "The method used in the present study illustrates one way of explicitly and systematically examining *experimenter* expectancy effects and serves to demonstrate the utility and desirability of employing expectancy control groups" (p. 222; italics added). The managers in King's experiment were not experimenters, and the productivity gains obtained were not an experimenter effect. Confusing management expectation effects with experimenter bias (Rosenthal, 1966, 1976) has obscured the practical implications of the former. Elsewhere, I have clarified this distinction (Eden, 1986b). Experimenter effects are a methodological nuisance which should be eliminated through sound research design and statistical analysis. But manager expectation effects are *not* spurious methodological flukes which are best handled by experimental control. Rather, they should be treated as a substantive part of a planned change effort. OD innovators should be designing ways of *maximizing* positive expectation effects and eliminating Golem effects in the practice of OD.

As a rule, authors have shown little awareness of the potential payoff of purposefully raising expectations. A rare exception is French and Bell (1978), who stated that, for the OD practitioner, expectation effects have "definite positive implications: tell the clients to expect positive gains from the program (any program) and 'expectation effects' will help positive gains to be realized" (p. 248; parentheses in original). However, French and Bell did not elaborate. Another exception is Woodman and Tolchinsky's (1985) recent discussion of expectation effects in OD. They invoked several psychological theories to explain how expectations influence the OD process and addressed discrepancy effects, that is, the impact of achievements that are appreciably higher or lower than the level initially expected.

A utilitarian approach to manager expectation effects has a medical parallel in the placebo effect. Control of the placebo effect has a proper place in research, particularly in evaluating the effectiveness of new treatments (Critelli & Neumann, 1984). However, we should judge harshly the clinical practitioner who abstains from using the placebo effect as an aid to treatment. If smiling, nodding reassuringly, and saying to a patient, "Take the medication that I've prescribed and I'm sure you will feel better" can augment the drug in promoting the healing process, then the physician should certainly add these interventions to his treatment repertoire. Not to do so for methodological reasons would be wrong both practically and ethically.

PASSIVE VS. ACTIVE APPROACHES TO SFP

Emphasizing the methodological significance of expectancy effects without contemplating their utilization treats them passively. Another passive approach is to comment on the unintended effects that expectations might have on a program's impact without following through with recommendations for strengthening these expectation effects in order to maximize their payoff. An example is the following quote from Turnage and Muchinsky's (1984) report on their examination of the validity of assessment center evaluations:

> Finally, it is conceivable that a primary function of an assessment center is to elevate individuals' expectations and self-esteem. That is, the candidates attribute their selection for assessment to their perceived worth to the company, and then they seek to perform both in assessment and later on the job at a level high enough to substantiate the lofty esteem in which they are perceived to be held. Thus selection into the assessment center may be the initiation of a subtle Pygmalion effect that generalizes beyond assessment. Therefore the assessment center itself could be a constant error affecting both assessment and subsequent job performance, a source of error that may bedevil the researcher but delight the practitioner (p. 602).

Turnage and Muchinsky's appreciation of expectancy effects is passive because they stopped short of recommending the deliberate exploitation of the selection of workers into assessment centers as an opportunity for raising their expectations. Relegating the assessment center to the status of "a source of constant error" is too harsh an indictment. The assessment center can be viewed more practically as a vehicle for raising expectations in order to trigger productive SFP.

As a final example of a passive approach to expectation effects, consider this quotation from a young professional's reaction to overseas training:

> Being sent to Europe for a two-week training program during your first few months with the firm impresses the hell out of you. It makes you think: "This is a class outfit." It also both frightens you and gives you confidence. You say, "Boy, they must think I'm good if they're prepared to spend all this money on me." But then you worry about whether you can live up to it: it's very motivating (Maister, 1985, p. 7).

It is apparent from this person's reaction that being treated as described resulted in elevated expectations. This may passively *explain* the training's effectiveness.

Making sure that training personnel know that expectation-raising is part of what they are expected to accomplish while conducting training programs would be treating expectation effects *actively*. Incredibly, but typically, neither Craig's revised (1987) *Training and Development Handbook,* nor Lambert's (1984) *The Complete Book of Supervisor Training,* mentions Pygmalion or expectation effects!

The active stance proposed here is that we grab the expectation bull by its horns and intentionally raise expectations in order to reap the benefits of positive SFP. The current practice of ignoring expectations and unwittingly raising and lowering them in interaction with clients should be replaced by consistent consultant behavior that serves to raise client performance expectations. OD affords abundant opportunities to imbue clients with high performance expectations and to help rid organizations and their managers of the crippling effects of low expectations. Some widely used interventions have raising expectations as a naturally built-in component, for example, management-by-objectives (MBO) and goal-setting. Interventions that chiefly target other variables can be augmented by expectation-raising add-on microinterventions.

Expectancy-raising is not feasible as a stand-alone program; merely telling managers to raise their expectations will not work. This chapter is not an endorsement of "The Power of Positive Thinking" as advocated by Norman Vincent Peale. Expectation-raising has to be embedded in a credible program that can serve as a basis for convincing clients that performance will improve. Recall that King did not have a "high-expectation only" condition. In his 2 × 2 design he piggybacked his high expectation manipulation onto job rotation as the "low innovation" condition. Expectation effects are powerful enough to boost output even when combined with so diluted an "innovation" as job rotation, which ordinarily is considered a very weak treatment even by proponents of job redesign, let alone OD professionals. But expectation-raising cannot stand alone. This add-on nature of expectation-raising does not signal any restriction of its applicability to the task of unleashing now-dormant human potential in organizations. On the contrary, it can conveniently supplement virtually any other intervention with little effort or cost. Such easy applicability should make it appealing to practitioners.

To illustrate, consider the above examples of assessment centers and management training. Proposing that posh assessment programs or training junkets be lavished upon young professionals merely in order to raise their expectations would be absurd. No one would embark on a costly program of assessment or training with the sole intention of tricking individuals in the program into raising their expectations. But every assessment or training center that does not have expectation-raising on its agenda is wasting golden opportunities for the organization to gain the additional benefits of expectation effects. The marginal cost of adding expectation-raising is negligible, and the payoff can be substantial.

CREATING PRODUCTIVE SFP

The following proposals are intended to provide OD professionals with practical suggestions for expectation-raising in their field work and to stimulate further thinking about expectation effects on the part of OD scholars. These proposals differ along several dimensions. Some are directed towards individual clients, some towards organizations; some aim at implanting positive expectations while others are geared towards the eradication of negative expectations; some entail deception and others do not; some have been tried and tested and some have not.

Create the Pygmalion Effect

In addition to the huge and growing data base demonstrating the Pygmalion effect in educational settings (Dusek, Hall, & Meyer, 1985; Rosenthal & Rubin, 1978), reinforced by seven meta-analyses (Rosenthal, 1985), there is evidence that Pygmalion effects occur among adult members of work organizations as well (Crawford, Thomas, & Fink, 1980; Eden & Ravid, 1982; Eden & Shani, 1982; King, 1971; Schrank, 1968). The practical implication of this research is that practitioners should create the Pygmalion effect by deliberately raising the expectations of their manager-clients towards their subordinates. In the course of myriad interactions with managers at different levels in the client organization during an OD project, the consultant who would convert his client into a more positive Pygmalion should repeatedly point out to the client untapped abilities among the client's subordinates, and in general get the client to expect more of his subordinates. If successful, raising the client's expectations towards his subordinates' performance will trigger a Pygmalion effect and improve those subordinates' performance beyond any gains that may result from the major OD intervention. Relevant information about subordinates' underutilized talents can be recovered from personnel files, conversations with people in the training department, and interviews with managers and with the employees themselves.

A bolder application of the Pygmalion effect would be to raise the expectations of managers regarding their subordinates *without* specific evidence of surplus subordinate potential. In the typical Pygmalion experiment, subjects are assigned to high- and control-expectation conditions at random; therefore, those whose performance is enhanced by the Pygmalion treatment comprise a mix of relatively high- and low-ability individuals. It follows that being treated as a high-potential subordinate is productive for subordinates of quite different ability levels. In training experiments, the Pygmalion effect has been found to explain from approximately one-third (Eden & Ravid, 1982) to almost three-quarters (Eden & Shani, 1982) of the variance in the performance of randomly assigned trainees. Eden and Ravid (1982) tested the interaction between manipulated expectations and trainee aptitude, and found that it was not significant. This means that trainees of all levels of aptitude benefited equivalently from having their supervisors' expectations towards them raised indiscriminantly. Therefore, the OD consultant can raise managers' expectations across the board knowing that no harm will come to any subordinate, and that many may gain.

Not every attempt to raise performance expectations will succeed. Particularly, when supervisors have prior personal knowledge of subordinate productivity, their expectations become resistant to change and require information that is especially convincing and credible. Sutton (1986) recently reported a bold attempt to produce a Pygmalion effect among retail sales personnel. The fact that she did not obtain confirmatory findings highlights some potential pitfalls in willfully producing expectation effects.

Sutton was introduced to the sales managers in two stores as being from corporate headquarters. She presented a personality test described as "similar to those used successfully by insurance companies to identify individuals with exceptional sales potential." She told them that "the test had been used by a limited number of retail stores, with a 93 percent success rate in identifying employees with high sales potential," and that headquarters "was attempting to validate the test for use in its retail chain" (p. 53–54). Though intended to raise managers' expectations toward randomly selected subordinates purportedly identified by the test as having exceptional potential, some of the details Sutton provided could have aroused doubts in the managers' minds regarding the usefulness of the information. Many laymen (as well as psychologists) are wary of personality tests. Sales managers might be skeptical about information derived from personality tests found useful by insurance companies but by only a "limited number" of retailers, especially when their own company implies doubt by saying that it is currently trying to validate the test. For the layman, if it needs validation, it might not be any good.

Sutton provided a hint that doubts did indeed arise in the managers' minds: "During the meeting with this researcher, a few sales managers expressed surprise at the names on their list of associates with exceptional potential, and a few asked for information about the test" (p. 54). This remark alludes to an additional pitfall. Apparently, the managers had gotten to know the sales associates before Sutton's attempt to manipulate their expectations. Sutton did not state precisely when she imparted the information concerning "exceptional potential." We know only that the relevant information was given to the sales managers "After the initial hiring was completed" (p. 53), but we do not know *how long* afterwards and how much of an opportunity was available for the managers to form their own initial expectations of their subordinates. There is evidence that performance expectations are formed on the basis of very limited acquaintance, can become resistant to change, and then require more than the classical test-result manipulation to change them (Brophy, 1983; Dusek, Hall, & Meyer, 1985; Eden, 1984; Eden & Shani, 1982; Jussim, 1986). Finally, Sutton delayed her manipulation check until the end of her experiment, and although the independent variable was expectations, none of the four items in the manipulation-check measure directly assessed expectations. For all these reasons, it is doubtful whether Sutton actually did raise her managers' expectations. If expectations were not raised, the Pygmalion hypothesis was not tested.

To summarize, conveying information based on personality, purportedly useful in a different industry and in need of validation, after managers have direct personal acquaintance with their subordinates, and using delayed, indirect measures of expectations, may each or in combination explain the failure to detect a Pygmalion effect among these sales personnel. One can only concur with Sutton's conclusion that, on the basis of her study, it would be premature to regard the Pygmalion effect as irrelevant for business organizations. Rather, her work is useful for mapping out some of the boundary conditions that must be respected in our attempts to create the effect. Hopefully, Sutton's call for additional research will soon be answered by others willing to accept the challenge of learning under which conditions expectation effects can—and cannot—be obtained. Dealing with expectations is a doubly risky enterprise when one must concern one's self, as a consultant, with the requisite conditions for producing the effect and, as a researcher, with the demands of rigorous scientific methodology. Practitioners applying the Pygmalion effect must beware "only" of the former.

Eradicate the Golem

Low expectations are the bane of multitudes of people who are not utilizing their potential. Many underachievers have grown accustomed to just getting by with minimally acceptable performance simply because nothing more is expected of them. Although experimental evidence for the Golem effect is scarce due to the obvious ethical restrictions self-imposed on researchers reluctant to create low expectations, the debilitating Golem effect is undoubtedly widespread and costly in terms of wasted human potential. Raising the currently low expectations harbored toward underachieving victims of the Golem effect should yield appreciable productivity gains because underachievers, by definition, have great potential for improvement before reaching the limits imposed on performance by their ability. If, as one might suspect, the number of underachieving members in organizations who are blighted by Golem effects is large, then eradicating these effects could potentially make many people much more productive.

A narrative example of the shrewd demise of a costly Golem effect will illustrate how easy it is to apply. A plant manager in Israel, who had heard a lecture about SFP and expectation effects, was having a problem with the low productivity of consecutive waves of new employees. Production workers in the plant, who assembled and packaged disposable sterile medical kits for use in blood dialysis and transfusions, were native or immigrant women from Eastern Europe. In this plant, "everyone knew" that, in comparison to immigrants, natives were poor workers, adjusted slower, were undisciplined, took longer to achieve standard levels of production, and had difficulty maintaining them. In particular, the head production supervisor, who for years had been responsible for putting new hires to work, "knew" that the native women would give her trouble and not reach standard production soon, if ever.

The plant manager believed that the native workers were every bit as capable as the immigrants. Suspecting the operation of a Golem effect, he summoned the head production supervisor and told her that (a) he had personally hand-picked the group of native new hires slated to come on board the following week and they were excellent people, (b) they should be expected to give her no problem and to attain standard production quickly, and (c) as usual she, the head supervisor, was to assume personal responsibility for their integration into the plant and to report any problems to him. This brief "manipulation" was followed by the smoothest intake of native new hires that anyone in the plant could remember. They achieved standard production in record time and soon appreciably exceeded it. The supervisor complimented the plant manager for having improved his hiring decisions. A subsequent visit to the plant by this author corroborated the story, although no research was conducted. Surely opportunities for such inexpensive, quick, and effective applications of SFP abound.

Create the Galatea Effect

Eden and Ravid (1982) distinguished the Pygmalion effect, in which we raise *supervisors' expectations* of their subordinates, from the Galatea effect, in which we bypass supervisors and directly raise subordinates' *self-expectations*. Since supervisor expectations influence subordinate performance by raising subordinate self-expectations and thereby enhancing subordinate motivation (Eden, 1984; Eden & Ravid, 1982), both ways of initiating a productive SFP ought to be practical. Eden and Ravid's (1982) results showed similar effect sizes for the Pygmalion and Galatea treatments in their field experiment. Therefore, an additional intervention, distinct from the Pygmalion treatment and applicable whether or not a Pygmalion treatment is contemplated, is to trigger the Galatea effect by directly conveying to personnel at different levels in the organization that they have high potential. The Galatea treatment can complement the Pygmalion treatment or be applied in lieu of Pygmalion, as when the manager's expectations appear to be intractable. OD consultants should take advantage of the numerous opportunities available during an extended intervention to convey positive expectations to a variety of persons in the organization, for example, formal and informal interviewing, training, feedback sessions, and widely circulated written reports.

Expectation Training

This is the intervention that comes closest to qualifying as a stand-alone expectation intervention, as it most literally grabs the expectation bull by its horns. Rather than seeking a variety of channels to convey high expectations to clients, expectation training educates clients about SFP, expectation effects, and Pygmalion, and teaches them how conscious utilization of this knowledge might improve motivation and boost productivity. It involves fully informing clients about the entire process in advance. This precludes any ethical problems arising from the use of deception.

Expectation training is best illustrated by the U.S. Navy's Pygmalion-at-Sea project. Crawford, Thomas, and Fink (1980) identified a number of chronically low performing sailors, who had come to be labeled "dirtbags," on a combatant ship. These men were targeted for remedial treatment in a program designed to improve their motivation and performance. Supervisory personnel in the command were given a one-and-a-half day motivation and leadership workshop intended to change their negative expectations toward the problem sailors. Second, 15 senior enlisted supervisors, selected to serve as shipboard role models and mentors for the low performers, were given a one-day workshop in counseling and guidance skills designed to train them to enhance the low performers' self-concept and expectations. Finally, 12 low performers participated in two separate three-day workshops. The first was devoted to personal growth and self-improvement. This was followed by three one-day workshop meetings a week apart, dealing with issues raised by the low performers themselves.

The low performers' training was introduced by the ship's CO who informed the men that although they "were indeed problem sailors, the command felt that they had the potential to improve their performance" (p. 491). Thus, the low performers were told outright at the outset that they were expected to improve. Also, the CRM McGraw-Hill training film titled *Productivity and the Self-fulfilling Prophecy: The Pygmalion Effect* was screened and discussed at length in the workshops with both the supervisors *and* the low performers. Although it is impossible to isolate the effects of each of the several independent variables manipulated by these workshops, it is clear that the communication and cultivation of high performance expectations—on the part of both the supervisors and the subordinates—were the hallmark of this intervention.

However, the high expectations had to be supported by other means. Crawford et al. reported that the supervisors' "initial reluctance gave way to guarded optimism and later to enthusiasm . . . due in part to the training segment that consisted of teaching the principles of behavior modification and then brainstorming actions that would constitute positive reinforcers in the eyes of the low performers. The supervisors were thus given some *specific tools to back up their newly acquired positive expectations*" (p. 489; italics added). This is probably as close as a program can get to being a stand-alone expectation-raising intervention. Without providing the tools it is doubtful that positive effects would emerge; providing tools *without* raising expectations is what many unsuccessful programs do.

The impact of the intervention was evaluated by comparing the low performers on the experimental ship to 34 of their shipmates and to 20 low performers on four other ships. The posttest included only the 8 of the original 12 experimental low performers who remained till criterion evaluation after three had completed their enlistment contracts and had left the Navy and one had been discharged for disciplinary reasons. These comparisons revealed improvements in the experimental low performers in both overall performance and discipline. In post-intervention interviews, the low performers attributed the program's success to the fact that "someone had taken an interest in and believed in them," and for some this "had been their first positive encouragement since joining the Navy" (p. 497). The CO "was extremely pleased with the outcome of the intervention." He "also stressed the importance of changing the negative expectations of the LPs" (low performers). The authors concluded that "the apparent success of the intervention centered on changes in the self-fulfilling prophecies engendered in the LPs and their supervisors" (p. 497).

Due to the initially low expectations towards these problem sailors, Pygmalion-at-Sea was an intervention undertaken to overcome a past Golem effect. It is no accident that the first serious attempt to apply expectation training was not designed to improve the motivation and productivity of average performers, but rather of poor performers with problematic records. It is this kind of remedial use of expectation effects that is most frequently contemplated in the education literature. Such a project is most responsive to clients' pressing needs. However, expectation training should not be limited to remediation. The subjects who benefited from expectation effects in the experiments of Eden and Ravid (1982), Eden and Shani (1982), and Schrank (1968), as well as in the cases described by Livingston (1969), were of average or above average aptitude. The data at hand do not preclude positive expectation effects for persons of *any* aptitude level.

Immunize Potential Victims against the Golem Effect

Individuals who perform far below their ability due to the negative influence of their superiors' low expectations on their own self-expectations may be unaware of the process, and therefore defenseless. Training could make them conscious of the process, immunize them against it, and thereby help prevent its recurrence. Immunization training should have two focuses. One focus should be on what potential victims can do, behaviorally, to raise the expectations of their superiors in order to prevent having their superiors treat them as Golems. The second focus should be on the considerable power that the potential victims have to disrupt the SPF process by not responding to low expectations in a manner that turns them into Golems. This would entail telling these trainees, "Now that you understand what SFP is and how it can influence both you and your supervisor, you can use this knowledge to protect yourself. You need not succumb to low expectations any longer. Even if you can't get your supervisor to treat you like a high-potential employee, and he persists in expecting little of you due to stereotypes, prejudice, your past record, or whatever, and treats you in a way that encourages you to be a low performer, you don't have to accommodate his expectations! If you know where those low expectations are coming from, maintain your own high expectations of yourself, and persist in trying to do the best job you can, you may break the vicious SFP cycle and succeed *despite* your supervisor's expectations. You can prevent yourself from becoming his Golem by being your own Pygmalion. If your supervisor deals you a bad hand by expecting you to fail, your own high self-expectations are your trump card that gives you immunity. In this way, you can master SFP and make the most of what you have.'' The population that stands to benefit most from immunization is that which is most at risk for Golem effects, including those already identified as low performers, those stigmatized by blemishes on their record, and persons readily stereotyped as likely to fail.

Fight Negative Stereotypes

Stereotypes produce SFP because they involve expectations toward individuals on the basis of perceptions of their belonging to some social group or class (Snyder, Tanke, & Berscheid, 1977). Negative stereotypes produce Golem effects. Two of the examples of SFP described by Merton (1948) in his classic treatise on SFP involve blacks and Jews who, as targets, come to behave in a manner that fulfills the expectations of those who hold the stereotypes. When individuals are expected to perform poorly merely because of their race, age, sex, or any other ascribed characteristic not related to actual performance potential, a Golem effect is likely. The locations in organizations where counterproductive stereotypes are most likely to be operating are those staffed by racial and ethnic minorities, women, very old and very young employees, and others about whom stereotypes abound. The case of the medical-kit assembly plant described earlier exemplifies a Golem effect deriving from a stereotype and how it can be profitably overcome. The use of epithets, such as ''dirtbag'' aboard the Pygmalion-at-Sea ships, signals the operation of a negative stereotype whose termination should be worth some investment of energy.

Not all stereotypes are negative. Positive stereotypes should not be discouraged. Belonging to a minority group that is stereotyped as industrious or intelligent can be a boon to individual members of that group and help make them more productive. There is no reason to deprive either individuals or organizations of this SFP-based blessing.

Set Challenging Goals

The goal-setting and the Management-by-Objectives (MBO) approaches converge in dealing more or less explicitly with performance expectations and in prescribing that performance goals and output objectives be high and difficult to achieve. "Objectives are statements of *expected output*" (Odiorne, 1969, p. 20; italics in original). Successful MBO may be SFP. Challenging objectives are explicit expressions of high expectations. When a manager and a subordinate agree upon challenging objectives, they are setting the stage for double expectation effects, that is, a Pygmalion effect on the part of the manager and a Galatea effect on the subordinate's part.

Similarly, goal-setting experimentation has shown that difficult goals result in greater output than do intermediate or easy goals (Locke, Sarri, Shaw, & Latham, 1981). Furthermore, Garland (1984) has revealed how expectations mediate the influence of goals on output. Setting difficult goals raises expectations, which in turn spurs improved performance. In other words, one evidently effective way to produce a Pygmalion effect is to set difficult goals, or, in MBO terminology, set high objectives. On the other hand, setting easy goals and/or low objectives produces a Golem effect in which subordinates realize that little is expected of them and adjust their efforts downward accordingly. Thus, MBO and goal setting are techniques for triggering SFP and owe their success to expectation effects. Both of these expectation-raising techniques share a limitation in that output must be specifiable, and preferably quantifiable, in order to set goals or objectives. This limitation is not shared by other approaches to expectation-raising.

Clear the Record

Individuals who get off to a bad start to school, in a job, or in life, are often locked in to their past by an unforgetting—and unforgiving—record. Worse perhaps even than the living memory of teachers, supervisors, and peers who have witnessed past failure, the written record remains as an indelible reminder that refreshes memories and contaminates—lowers—the expectations of persons who had no involvement in the original disgrace. Perusing a record rife with failures creates expectations for "more of the same." There are undoubtedly multitudes of individuals scattered throughout society whose potential is never realized because they are victimized by their past record.

Managers' access to the record thus contributes materially to low-performer recidivism through the operation of self-*sustaining* prophecy. Salomon (1981) introduced the latter concept to refer to the expectation effects that result from a teacher's low expectations of a pupil who has a poor record. Although the present teacher had no part in producing the record, his expectations for future achievements *are* influenced by it. The teacher is influenced by a record of failure to expect further poor performance and proceeds to treat the pupil accordingly as a poor performer, thereby *sustaining* the underachievement.

It is this self-sustaining Golem scenario that is most widespread "in nature." The experimental expectation effect constitutes a self-*fulfilling* prophecy that does not simulate real life with complete fidelity because, in true experiments, including field experiments, randomization assures preexperimental equivalence;

in a randomized experiment the high-expectation subjects as a group have a past that is equivalent to that of the control subjects. However, in natural settings, managers do not get subordinates with equivalent records. Instead, managers form expectations of their subordinates in part on the basis of a record that may validly reflect past performance. However, the record may grossly underestimate potential performance, and thereby distort expectations, particularly in the case of underachievers. In short, the typical manager does not originate positive or negative expectation effects; rather, he inherits them, sustains or even strengthens them, and passes them along to the next manager by adding his ratings and evaluative comments to the subordinate's record.

One important implication of the distinction between self-sustaining and self-fulfilling prophecy is that *present managers are not to be blamed for past SFP effects*. Ignoring self-sustaining prophecy and emphasizing only SFP imply that present managers are somehow at fault for underachieving subordinates' poor performance and naturally stiffens their resistance to corrective measures. Failure to distinguish between the two types of prophecy may partially explain the long history of vociferous criticism of expectation-effect experiments and staunch rejection of the entire notion of expectation effects by professionals who have apparently felt themselves implicitly but unjustly accused of malpractice. Some experimental social psychologists have vigorously resisted the notion of experimenter effects (see Rosenthal & Rubin, 1978, and the sequel titled "Open Peer Commentary" on pp. 386–415 in the same issue of *Behavioral and Brain Sciences*), and some educational psychologists have voiced severe—and exaggerated—criticism of the teacher expectation experiments (Rosenthal, 1985). In a field application, teachers participating in a workshop designed to train them in the use of positive Pygmalion behaviors in the classroom were reported to have "felt insulted by the implication that they may be doing something wrong in their classrooms and became quite defensive" (Banuazizi, 1981, p. 48). In a similar vein, Crawford et al. (1980) wrote that in their supervisor workshops they had to deal with

> considerable resistance on the part of some of the supervisors toward dealing with these issues . . . their reluctance to assume ownership of the problem was reflected by "blaming" any of several factors that can contribute to their personnel problem. The recruiting system, recruit training, parents, and society at large were named as influencing low performance—factors that were well beyond the control of the supervisors (p. 488).

It is therefore crucial for the success of manager expectation training that the consultant refrain from any accusatory words or tone. Empathy is called for here no less than in any other intervention intended to aid beleaguered managers to cope with tough problems. Particularly when it comes to raising the productivity of chronically low performers, the manager is being called upon to succeed where everyone else has failed.

A second implication of the self-sustaining prophecy is that we need ways of freeing individuals from the shackles of their records. This could be done by clearing the record of certain kinds of entries that are likely to arouse negative expectations in a new supervisor. Information retained in dossiers is often notoriously mistaken, ambiguous, irrelevant, outdated, and meaningless (Laudon, 1986). Stigmatizing labels, if they must be used at all, should be expunged at the end of a reasonable period of time. Like foodstuffs on the supermarket shelf and moving-violation points on the driving record, a diagnostic, disciplinary, or evaluative entry in an employee's record should include an expiration date. Furthermore, a company could withhold the record of a new hire or a new transfer from the supervisor for an initial period of, say, a month, during which time expectations would be formed on the basis of that month's experience rather than on the basis of the past preserved in the record. An obvious limitation to this kind of solution exists in companies in which it is easy for a manager to phone a new transfer's previous supervisor and obtain a quick evaluation. It is more applicable to newly hired employees from outside the organization.

Organizations need "worker protection programs," akin to the witness protection programs used by the FBI and Interpol to save the lives of criminals who turn State's evidence and then have to be obscured from the long arm of mob revenge. If a worker with a bad performance record could be relocated in the same company or elsewhere, be given a new employee identity, and get "another chance" at a job free from the persecution of his own work history and the inevitable Golem effect that it triggers each time anew, the recurrence of a destructive SFP would be blocked and his chances of utilizing his potential would be greater. Both the supervisor and the organization would enjoy the benefits of having a more productive employee.

I have often wondered if the upward mobility characteristic of immigrant societies might derive in part from the fact that newcomers find it relatively easy to leave a damning record behind and get a fresh start. Once the past has been obliterated, the only thing that really counts is what the individual does "from now on." We need to invent new ways of enabling more people with unproductive records to become "organizational immigrants" with clean expectation slates and a chance to begin anew.

Piggyback on Changes in Personnel and Organization

The interminable changes in organizational structure, personnel assignments, product lines, work methods, and operating procedures provide virtually limitless opportunities for raising expectations almost unobtrusively. This is not a mere restatement of the Lewinian conceptualization of the Unfreezing—Moving—Refreezing process that is so widely known and accepted in OD theory (Lewin, 1951). Rather, it is a call for the opportunistic utilization of the unfreezing of expectations wrought by organizational changes, whether "natural" or planned, for expectation-raising. Any nontrivial change unfreezes expectations, as members anticipate repercussions that might impact positively or negatively on their work and career. These vague moments of unclear expectations, when members are unsure what is in store for them, invite the alert, nimble manager or OD consultant to intervene with timely words of assurance, encouragement, confidence, and optimism, all varieties of positive expectations. When members are apprehensive due to their anticipation of an imminent turn for the worse in their situation, the optimistic words and deeds of a sanguine consultant can reduce the suspense and potentially avert a Golem effect as negative expectations are replaced by positive ones. The example of the medical-kit plant illustrates how a manager changed expectations concerning the impact of a naturally occurring change in personnel—the intake of a new group of workers—by piggybacking onto a change which was occurring anyway and opportunistically raising naturally low expectations, thereby successfully disrupting an entrenched, recurring Golem effect.

There are countless examples of changes whose success was augmented by positive expectations and changes that failed at least in part due to negative expectations. Elsewhere I have mustered documentation in support of the argument that even the classical Hawthorne experiments may have succeeded in boosting productivity by unwittingly raising expectations (Eden, 1986a). It is also possible that participative management, when it succeeds, owes part of its success to the raised expectations of individuals who have taken part in discussions in which the purported advantages of the changes contemplated were fully aired and they were given the opportunity to influence decision making in the directions they deemed appropriate. When participation is implemented properly, participants will have higher post-decision performance expectations than those who have not participated. Such expectation effects may contribute as much or more to the success of participation than the mediating variables commonly cited, for example, psychological "ownership" of the decision-making process, acceptance of the resulting decisions, and improved information flow (Sashkin, 1976). Thus, expectations probably mediate the effects of participation on performance. The practical implication is that those managing participation, as other management techniques, should piggyback and use these opportunities deliberately to raise participants' expectations.

Ruinous debilitating effects can be wrought on any change program by individuals who harbor negative expectations toward it. It is common OD knowledge that a strategically placed skeptic can doom a program by saying to peers and subordinates, "Those Wiz Kids up there have cooked up another one of their great inventions for us; personally, I don't think it has a chance." The added thrust of the piggyback proposal is that even changes undertaken for extraneous reasons and changes initiated by *force majeure* should be seized upon as opportunities for the deliberate creation of productive SFPs. Telling people that the new computer system, the redesigned office layout, the revised procedure, the improved routing, the replacement engineer, the changes in the sources of raw material, the new software, the new warehouse forms, the weekend retreat, the divisional reorganization, the new chief of accounting, or any other change should be expected to improve productivity may make these changes more productive than otherwise. The cost of piggybacking is nil, and the potential payoff is appreciable.

Foster High-Expectation Culture: Create Positive Myths and Uproot Negative Myths

Culture is intimately involved in organizational SFP because it is such a rich source of performance expectations. Schein (1985) has described how intimately organizational culture influences organizational effectiveness. In his words, "Productivity is a cultural phenomenon par excellence, both at the small-work-group level and at the level of the total organization" (pp. 43–44).

Myth making is a promising way of influencing organizational culture. Boje, Fedor, and Rowland (1982) have proposed ways of intervening in the myth-making process in the interests of organizational effectiveness. Their recommendations should be applied to building up the stock of myths that convey high performance expectations and to rooting out negative myths that imply organizational impotence or helplessness. Consider the positive SFP that might flow from the widespread belief that "we are a can-do organization" or that we are "lean and mean" compared to the collective Golem effect generated by myths such as "Nothing ever gets done right around here" or "We operate on Murphy's Law and the Peter Principle."

Mastery of myth making requires macro-level leverage over a pervasive, systemwide source of expectations. The impact of myths on expectations can be particularly insidious and persistant because, as part of the organization's culture, myths summarize complex, underlying beliefs and assumptions about the organization's capabilities and frailties, assumptions which have slipped out of awareness and become highly resistant to change: "Do not assume that culture can be manipulated like other matters under the control of managers. Culture controls the manager more than the manager controls culture. . . ." (Schein, 1985, p. 314). Indeed, if Schein was right when he wrote, "If we take the concept of culture seriously, we may have to face the possibility that cultural assumptions are virtually impossible to change. . . ." (p. 45), then much of the recent talk about culture change in organizations may be pie in the sky. What does seem clear is that, if anyone is able to change organizational culture and replace pernicious myths with positive ones, it must be the CEO or other top-ranking officers with very high visibility and credibility. Managing myths is a worthy task for those at the organization's pinnacle, for *"the unique and essential function of leadership is the manipulation of culture"* (Schein, p. 317; italics in original). The OD consultant's role is to enlighten top executives as to their unique leverage over organizational culture, and the performance expectations that the culture implies, through the medium of myth making.

Summary of SFP Interventions

The above interventions are not the only ones conceivable. Hopefully, as more scholars consider the possibilities, more SFP interventions will be invented and tested. It may be helpful to think of SFP interventions in terms of Lewin's (1951) field theoretical distinction between driving forces and restraining forces in changing any system and moving it toward a new equilibrium. Raising expectations, as in the Pygmalion and Galatea interventions, expectation training, setting challenging goals, and creating positive myths, parallels the addition of driving forces toward a desirable new end-state of higher productivity, whereas eliminating pockets of particularly low expectations, as in eradicating the Golem effect by raising low expectations toward individuals and toward stereotyped groups, clearing the record, and uprooting negative myths are a form of removing counterproductive restraining forces. OD consultants who prefer the removal of restraining forces to the addition of positive ones might prefer contributing their energy to the fight against the Golem effect.

Merton's (1948) analysis of the operation of the Federal Deposit Insurance Corporation (FDIC) exemplifies the direction our thinking can take to devise innovation means of disrupting negative SFP. Banks were failing at a horrendous rate during the Depression because depositors, who lost faith in their bank— even solvent banks—and expected the bank to fail, panicked and precipitously withdrew their deposits in order to get out in time with their savings intact. This action by these "prophets of banking doom" created the kind of pressure that no bank, no matter how solvent, could withstand, and the prophecy was fulfilled as bankruptcy rapidly ensued. The establishment of the FDIC has protected the banks and their depositors from this tragic SFP by eliminating depositor anticipation of personal financial loss in the event of bank failure. We need to enrich the existing stock of OD interventions with organizational inventions that will provide FDIC-like blocks to negative SFP.

LIMITATIONS

How Much Should We Expect?

Raising expectations has its limits. Unattainable goals can produce demotivating feelings of failure and frustration. High expectations improve performance when they motivate greater effort; too high expectations are liable to erode the credibility of the source of those expectations, will not raise productivity, and may trigger indifference and even scorn. What Locke and Latham (1984) wrote about unattainable goals applies as well to unrealistic expectations: "A goal could be perceived as so hard that an individual would not only give up trying to reach it, but would even give up trying to get close to it. Total apathy could result" (p. 23). In Livingston's (1969) words,

> Managerial expectations must pass the test of reality before they can be translated into performance. . . . Subordinates will not be motivated to maximize productivity unless they consider the boss's high expectations realistic and achievable. If they are encouraged to strive for unattainable goals, they eventually give up trying and settle for results that are lower than they are capable of achieving (pp. 84–85).

This would seem true of any form of expectation-raising. It is fruitful to expect people to perform at higher than current levels, for most people know that they can. Yankelovich and Immerwahr (1983) reported that only 27 percent of the workers they surveyed claimed that they were working to the best of their ability. It is reasonable to expect people to use their ability. A high level of expectation is legitimate, and even expected of managers by subordinates. However, it is *not* reasonable to expect people to perform at levels that far surpass their ability, or even to do their best all the time. Unattainable expectations do not arouse motivation and are communicated only at the risk of losing credibility. Thus, in the expectation-raising interventions proposed above, the level to which expectations should be raised is that level which is high, challenging, difficult to attain, but reasonably within reach of the targeted individuals or organizational units.

Discrepancy Effects

Woodman and Tolchinsky (1985) similarly concluded that it is preferable for the consultant "to establish high, but reasonably attainable, expectations among participants of a change program" (p. 485). They reached this conclusion after considering the potentially dysfunctional effects of achieving outcomes that are different from those expected. Suspecting that such "discrepancy effects" could be counterproductive, they invoked dissonance theory, contrast theory, and assimilation-contrast theory in weighing the implications of discrepancy effects of different orders of magnitude. Some of these theoretical implications concern participants' evaluations of, and satisfaction with, the OD intervention, rather than its productive outcomes. For example, Woodman and Tolchinsky reasoned that, according to contrast theory, initially understating the eventual outcomes of interventions might lead to greater satisfaction with those outcomes. Such reasoning might lead one to conclude that initial expectations ought to be kept low.

Granting that postintervention affective and attitudinal by-products are important in their own right, they would not appear as crucial to the OD enterprise as assuring success in the first place by establishing high initial expectations for success. However, discrepancy effects imply a contradiction inherent in expectation-raising inasmuch as setting high initial expectations might be incompatible with long-term success when intermediate progress is assessable. Initially arousing high expectations for success will produce more success than will lower initial expectations. However, Woodman and Tolchinsky's analysis indicates that when actual outcomes fall short of initial expectations, dissatisfaction and subsequent demotivation may result. Thus, the high expectations that are helpful at the beginning of a program may come back to haunt the consultant in later stages. This is the apparent dilemma posed by discrepancy effects. Fortunately, there is a way out.

The consultant has a crucial role to play in shaping client reactions at critical junctions in the developmental process when interim assessments of success or failure can be made. When progress falls short of expectations, emphasis should be placed on how great an accomplishment it is to have progressed so far from where we started and to have come so close to a difficult goal. Competent attribution management on the part of the OD consultant can facilitate making both interim success and failure motivating for the client. Skillful progress assessment and postintervention counseling entail helping clients make attributions that prevent the erosion of confidence and build motivation. The consultant should channel attributions of success in meeting initial expectations to internal causes such as client ability and effort, and attributions of failure to unstable factors such as lack of effort or bad luck (Weiner, 1980). Such attributions help set the stage for the next round of OD by energizing clients to sustain their efforts toward the goal of renewed success.

Opportunities for interim expectation-bolstering can be built into an OD program by using a strategy of "small wins" (Weick, 1984). That is, a big project can be defined in terms of a series of small stages. Then one can build momentum towards eventual overall success by encouraging participants to savor the rewards of successive small accomplishments that signal milestones along the way toward achieving more ambitious development goals. Reaching each milestone justifies high expectations. Failure in any particular stage need not be a devastating setback, since it can be interpreted as a surmountable delay in progress toward ultimate success, not total program failure. "The important tactic for dealing with the flops implicit in trying for small wins is to localize the disconfirmation of expectations" (Weick, 1984, p. 48). The small-wins strategy circumvents the threat of discrepancy effects by simultaneously defining relatively easy short-term goals and more challenging long-term goals. Expectations at different levels are established and fulfilled at different stages. Thus, although creating realistic high initial expectations can result in discrepancy effects, these effects can be handled in ways that either utilize them or render them harmless.

Protect the Successful Golem

One particularly disturbing form of discrepancy effect warrants special attention. Rosenthal and Jacobson (1968) reported in the original "Pygmalion in the

Classroom'' experiment that teachers developed negative attitudes towards high-achievement pupils in the control condition, concerning whom high expectations had not been imparted. This was especially true of those control-condition pupils who were in the school's slow track. Tracking is institutionalized expectation setting. Thus, discrepant high achievement on the part of individuals initially expected to do poorly may result in negative supervisor attitudes that are likely to impede further progress. Unanticipated high performance, which should come as a pleasant surprise and give cause to celebrate, can be greeted instead with hostility. We need to be alert to potentially dysfunctional reactions on the part of individuals who become frustrated when their prophecies are disconfirmed instead of fulfilled. This particular discrepancy effect must be better understood and prevented.

How Frequently Can Expectations Be Raised?

Besides limiting how high expectations should be raised, there is the question of how many times expectation-raising can be implemented before losing its productive impact. As I paraphrased Honest Abe regarding repeated creation of the classical Pygmalion effect with managers, ''you can fool many managers once or twice, but you won't be able to fool many of them more than that'' (Eden, 1984, p. 69). Consultants can probably raise expectations repeatedly, using different techniques each time, without the approach ''wearing out.'' Varying the technique appears necessary. For example, it is unlikely that the manager of the medical-kit plant described above could credibly tell his production manager that he had hand-picked every future cohort of new hires. Perhaps several successive successes would sufficiently weaken or terminate the stereotype which produced that Golem effect in the first place, and in that sense become a positive self-sustaining prophecy, obviating the need for repeated intervention. It is also possible that several visible successes in creating productive expectation effects meld into a positive SFP climate in the organization. We need more research on the cumulative effects of expectation-raising interventions.

HIGHER-ORDER EXPECTATION EFFECTS

SFP in Consulting: Consultant Expectation Effects

Wittingly or unwittingly, OD consultants also take the role of the prophet in SFP. High expectations on the part of a consultant who believes in the potential of the client to improve influence the consultant to treat the client as a high-performance client thereby triggering a positive SFP. This may be dubbed a second-order Pygmalion effect. This is the naturally occurring field variant of King's high-expectation condition with the OD consultant replacing the experimenter as prophet. In parallel fashion, if a consultant harbors negative expectations about the client's capacity for improvement and does a poor job of conceal-ing these low expectations, a negative SFP, or second-order Golem effect is likely to result. Thus, OD consultants can unwittingly trigger expectation effects among their clients that are similar in kind to manager expectation effects.

Therefore, the same caveats apply to OD consultants as to managers. A consultant who believes in the client's ability to improve will act towards the client in a manner similar to what physicians do to their patients when they produce a placebo effect. Treating the client as one who will most certainly improve conveys high consultant expectations that raise client self-expectations, initiating SFP as an auxiliary force that helps the organization achieve the im-provements sought by the OD program. Consultants who do not believe in a client's capacity to improve should disqualify themselves from working with that client, lest they produce an unintended Golem effect. In short, OD consultants consult better for clients from whom they expect more.

The Messiah Effect

The phenomenal success of some leading OD consultants and consulting firms may be in part an unwitting consequence of their ability to inspire high self-expectations and self-confidence in their clients. Some consultants may be fully aware of what they are doing and use expectation-raising deliberately as a "se-cret weapon" whose power they know would be diluted by disclosure. In the case of famous consultants of high repute, their very arrival on the scene is sufficient to raise the expectations of some key individuals in the organization that "things will certainly improve now." The resulting optimism causes these clients to redouble their efforts in getting on with what has to be done to revitalize the organization. It is this mobilization of client energy and subsequent SFP brought about by the very arrival of a reknowned OD consultant that I call the "Messiah effect." The "Messiah's" power to relieve the client's woes is derived from the client's own positive expectations, sparked by the would-be redeemer's coming, and fueled by the client's eagerness to cooperate in fulfilling his own expectations. Any organizational change of transformational proportions requires effective tapping of existing sources of human energy and the creation of new ones (Ackerman, 1984; Bradley, 1986). The arrival of a Messiah expands the amount of energy available in an organization due to the high expectations that it arouses. Deeper understanding of the underlying expectation processes at work in these phenomena will further demystify SFP and turn it into a practical tool to be used by more managers and OD consultants.

Third-Order Expectation Effects:
The Impact of Our Expectations of OD as an Enterprise

There are many "prophets" who voice expectations with regard to OD. Prophets of doom who expect OD to sink and be relegated to the stagnant backwaters of organizational science will undoubtedly contribute to precisely that outcome. On the other hand, high expectations regarding the future contributions of OD to management and organization science will improve its chances of ultimately succeeding. In this sense we are all prophets. OD specialists have no *prima facie* claim to immunity from expectation effects.

A development that I find particularly troubling in this context is a recent trend which, if misinterpreted, might legitimize failure in OD and weaken its effectiveness. Mirvis and Berg (1977) have done us a great service by publishing *Failures in Organization Development and Change* to redress the imbalance inherent in a publication process that favors successful accounts and deprives us of the potential learning from failure. However, treating failure too positively has its dangers. For example, Michael and Mirvis (1977) wrote, *"There is no need to expect that with the application of knowledge and skill things should always turn out right"* (p. 317; italics in original). They encouraged practitioners "to free themselves and their clients of expectations that knowledge and skill guarantee successful change results" (p. 322). These authors coined the oxymoron "successful failure." In describing the benefits to be reaped by practitioners and clients as an organization increases its capacity for "embracing its errors" they use the phrases "expect problems," "expect errors," and "lower their expectations."

Embracing failure so wholeheartedly is liable to produce unintended Golem effects. Learning from failure is fine—up to a point. When we embrace failure too intimately and begin celebrating it, then it has gone too far. *Successful success* must remain the OD prize we seek. "Successful failure" is a booby prize. We should beware of the dangers of negative SFP as we dredge OD failures for their golden nuggets of learning. Those who expect failure are more likely to fail, and failure further reduces expectations (Weiner, 1980). Hopefully, those who read *Failures* learn and therefore strengthen their expectations of success. However, given what we know about how individuals respond to failure, even vicarious failure (Bandura, 1986), negative SFP is an outcome of delving into failure that should not be ignored.

THE DILEMMA OF AWARENESS

Expectations-Only Interventions

The interventions proposed in this chapter differ considerably in the role of client awareness in expectation-raising and in the type of expectations manipulated. In King's experiment the managers were not aware that their expectations were being raised, and whatever changes were brought about in managerial behavior were indirect consequences, rather than direct objects, of the experimental manipulation. The direct object of the manager expectations that were manipulated was the potential of the *innovation,* not of the manager, to effect productivity gains. No manager *self*-expectations were targeted for change. This is also true of King's earlier Pygmalion experiment with disadvantaged trainees, of Schrank's labeling study, and of our IDF experiments, as well as of other expectation-raising interventions proposed above, such as creating the Pygmalion effect. They can be called "expectations-only" interventions. These interventions prescribe no role for the manager. This expectations-only approach gets the manager to play the role of Pygmalion unwittingly.

Expectations-cum-Skills Interventions

In contrast, in the Pygmalion-at-Sea project the supervisors were made aware of the hypothesized SFP effects by being prebriefed about the entire process, and they were given workshop training designed to change their supervisory behavior. Therefore, both their expectations *and* their behavior were openly targeted for change. This can be dubbed an "expectations-cum-skills" intervention, and it entails full client awareness of SFP. Furthermore, in addition to raising supervisors' expectations regarding their subordinates' potential to be high performers, the supervisors' *self*-expectations were also targeted for change. The supervisors were trained to expect that their subordinates could improve and to expect that they, the supervisors, could lead their subordinates to higher performance. If successful, expectation training changes *two* supervisor expectations, as they come to expect more of their subordinates *and* more of themselves.

Thus, although both the King and the Crawford et al. experiments produced positive expectancy effects, they tested two very different manipulations. King convinced managers to expect productivity gains or not to expect such gains in a *five-minute* manipulation that was randomly determined. It was a five-minute expectations-only intervention with no awareness of SFP. In contrast, Crawford et al. enlightened supervisors and subordinates about SFP and related issues by investing a total of *eight and a half days* of expectations-cum-skills training with awareness of SFP. Crawford et al. thereby presumably raised supervisors' expectations concerning both their subordinates' potential to improve and their own potential to get their subordinates to improve their performance. Unfortunately, expectations were not measured in either experiment, and the performance measures are not readily comparable. King's five-minute expectations-only manipulation, coupled with enrichment/enlargement, increased actual daily output by about 1500 units, or between 7 percent and 8 percent plantwide in two plants, whereas at best the Navy's eight-and-a-half days of expectations-cum-skills training raised supervisors' subjective assessments of eight subordinates' performance by a statistically significant amount. King's experiment seems to have had a much greater impact on productivity at a fraction of the cost of the Navy program.

What makes expectations-only so much more cost-effective? Since behavior must mediate the effects of expectations on performance, raising expectations must lead to effective changes in supervisory behavior, which in turn cause improvements in subordinates' productivity. In the expectations-only approach, supervisory behavior changes—improves—even though it is not directly targeted by the intervention, no consulting or training resources are invested in it, and the manager is unaware that it is occurring (Eden & Shani, 1982). In expectations-only, the manager is told that something about the subordinates or the OD intervention program is the key to higher productivity, whereas in expectations-cum-skills he is told that *he* is the key. The expectations-only intervention bypasses the supervisors' awareness. The success of expectations-only means that managers already *possess* the requisite supervisory skills for getting subordinates to increase their productivity; raising their expectations gets them to *use* these skills more than they do when their expectations are lower. Training is useful for getting skills "into" managers; raising their expectations is an effective way of getting the skills "out" of them. Hence, some of the costly investment in skill training can be saved by the inexpensive energizing of underutilized managerial talent that appears to result from raising managers' expectations.

While the enormous investment required in conducting an expectations-cum-skills intervention may not be cost effective in the short term, it may still be the expectancy intervention of choice for many OD consultants. For one thing, whereas there are uncertainties about fade-out and repeatability with the 5-minute expectation-only manipulation, the behavioral and attitudinal changes presumably produced by the more tedious expectations-cum-skills approach are likely to lend this approach greater resistance to fade-out. Furthermore, it is repeatable and it deals with managers in a nondeceptive manner. In expectations-cum-skills, there is no attempt to convince the managers that there is allegedly something special inherent in *particular* subordinates, such as untapped potential or special talents, that can serve as a pretext for supervisors' accepting higher expectations. It does not involve assigning positive labels such as "High Aptitude Personnel" or "High Command Potential" to some subordinates. Rather than being led to believe anything about the characteristics of (some of) their subordinates, managers are given reason to believe that all or most subordinates can become more productive through their own leadership efforts. In short, the expectations-cum-skills approach is geared towards directly changing managers' behavior towards *all* their subordinates. It teaches managers to use the effective supervisory behaviors that have been found to characterize managers' treatment of high-expectation subordinates so that they can knowingly play the part of Pygmalion, the high-expectation supervisor, and effectively treat their subordinates as Galateas. There are undoubtedly managers who do this "naturally," without training. If identified, they can serve as helpful models in training other managers.

An assumption underlying expectations-cum-skills is that managers who are made aware of SFP effects can be trained to create such effects at will by treating all subordinates as they treat high-expectation subordinates. In this context, the SFP research serves as a didactic tool for teaching managers what the effective managerial behaviors are and convincing them that mastery and use of these behaviors on their part would be worthwhile. The expectations-cum-skills approach appears very promising but, like the other SFP interventions, needs further testing.

In schoolroom settings the expectations-cum-skills approach is being tested in Project STILE (Student-Teacher Interactive Learning Environment) (Banuazizi, 1981; Greenfield, Banuazizi, & Ganon, 1979; Terry, 1985) in which teachers are being trained in the use of those behaviors found to mediate the effects of high expectations. The assumption is that if teachers increase the use of these behaviors, pupil learning will improve. The STILE program was derived from the Pygmalion concept and based on teacher expectation research and is thus similar to Pygmalion-at-Sea. After the teachers are made fully cognizant of the teacher-expectation phenomenon, the STILE program invests a lot of time in hands-on workshop skill training. Unlike the uses to which expectation training is likely to be put in organizations other than schools, where productivity is a central concern, the main declared objective of the STILE program is to achieve equality of opportunity in the classroom, although improving pupil learning is also a goal.

An earlier teacher skill-training program in Los Angeles, titled "Equal Opportunity in the Classroom," trained teachers in the use of classroom behaviors used frequently with high achievers but seldom with low achievers, and encouraged more frequent use of these behaviors with the latter pupils. Workshops focused on why some of the effective teaching techniques are not practiced as often with the "lows" as with the "highs." Kerman (1979) has reported that this project achieved academic gains and reductions in absenteeism and discipline referrals. Hopefully, OD consultants will soon be testing similar programs with managers. The fields of management and education have much to learn from one another.

To conclude, the dilemma posed by comparing these different kinds of SFP interventions is that what appears to be most practical, at least in the short run, is not what seems to be most ethical. Furthermore, it is not yet clear whether or not awareness is an impediment to positive expectation effects. Should we circumvent managers awareness, as in expectations-only, in the interests of (at least short-term) cost-effectiveness? Or should we fully inform managers, as in expectations-cum-skills, in the interests of ethical concerns, knowing that full disclosure and the requisite skill-training will increase costs, in some cases prohibitively, and may reduce effectiveness? Will long-term benefits accrue from fostering OD's bedrock values of openness and trust that will compensate for the short-term sacrifices? Finally, once an OD consultant knows about, and believes in, SFP and expectation effects of any variety, is there not an ethical imperative to apply this knowledge rather than to abstain from doing so on (other) ethical grounds?

REFERENCES

Ackerman, L. (1984). The flow state: A new view of organizing and managing. In J. Adams (Ed.), *Transforming work*. Alexandria, Virginia: Miles River Press.

Babad, E., Inbar, J., & Rosenthal, R. (1982). Pygmalion, Galatea, and the Golem: Investigations of biased and unbiased teachers. *Journal of Educational Psychology, 74,* 459–474.

Bandura, A. (1986). *Social foundations of thought and action: A social-cognitive view*. Englewood Cliffs, NJ: Prentice-Hall.

Banuazizi, A. (1981). An evaluation of the first year's activities of the National Demonstration Title II Project (Basic Skills Improvement Program) in selected elementary grades of Cambridge public schools. Unpublished manuscript, Department of Psychology, Boston College, Chestnut Hill, MA 02167.

Boje, D., Fedor, D., & Rowland, K. (1982). Myth making: A qualitative step in OD interventions. *Journal of Applied Behavioral Science, 18,* 17–28.

Bowers, D. & Seashore, S. (1966). Predicting organizational effectiveness with a four-factor theory of leadership. *Administrative Science Quarterly, 11,* 238–263.

Bradley, R. (1986). *Transforming order: A study of charisma, power, and communion*. New York: Paragon House.

Craig, R. (Ed.) (1987). *Training and development handbook: A guide to human resources development* (3d ed.). New York: McGraw-Hill.

Crawford, K. S., Thomas, E. D., & Fink, J. J. (1980). Pygmalion at sea: Improving the work of effectiveness of low performers. *Journal of Applied Behavioral Science, 16,* 482–505.

Critelli, J. W. & Newmann, K. F. (1984). The placebo: Conceptual analysis of a construct in transition. *American Psychologist, 39,* 32–39.

Dusek, J. B., Hall, V. C., & Meyer, W. J. (Eds.). (1985). *Teacher expectations*. Hillsdale, NJ: Lawrence Erlbaum.

Eden, D. (1984). Self-fulfilling prophecy as a management tool: Harnessing Pygmalion. *Academy of Management Review, 9,* 64–73.

Eden, D. (1986a). OD and self-fulfilling prophecy: Boosting productivity by raising expectations. *Journal of Applied Behavioral Science, 22,* 1–13.

Eden, D. (1986b). Team development: Quasi-experimental confirmation among combat companies. *Group & Organization Studies, 11,* 133–146.

Eden, D. (in press). *Pygmalion in management: Productivity as a self-fulfilling prophecy*. Lexington, MA: Lexington Books.

Eden, D. & Daniely, S. (1979, September). *Survey-based OD in the Israel Defense Forces: A field experiment*. Paper presented at the meeting of the American Psychological Association, New York, NY.

Eden, D. & Leviatan, U. (1975). Implicit leadership theory as a determinant of the factor structure underlying supervisory behavior scales. *Journal of Applied Psychology, 60,* 736–741.

Eden, D. & Ravid, G. (1982). Pygmalion vs. self-expectancy: Effects of instructor- and self-expectancy on trainee performance. *Organizational Behavior and Human Performance, 30,* 351–364.

Eden, D. & Shani, A. B. (1982). Pygmalion goes to boot camp: Expectancy, leadership, and trainee performance. *Journal of Applied Psychology, 67,* 194–199.

French, W. & Bell, C., Jr. (1978). *Organizational development: Behavioral science interventions for organization improvement* (2nd ed.). Englewood Cliffs, NJ: Prentice-Hall.

Garland, H. (1984). Relation of effort-performance expectancy to performance in goal-setting experiments. *Journal of Applied Psychology, 69,* 79–84.

Greenfield, D., Banuazizi, A., & Ganon, J. (1979). Project STILE: An evaluation of the second year. Unpublished manuscript, Department of Psychology, Boston College, Chestnut Hill, MA 02167.

Jones, R. (1977). *Self-fulfilling prophecies: Social, psychological, and physiological effects of expectancies*. Hillsdale, NJ: Lawrence Erlbaum.

Jussim, L. (1986). Self-fulfilling prophecies: A theoretical and integrative review. *Psychological Review, 93*, 429–445.

King, A. (1971). Self-fulfilling prophecies in training the hard-core: Supervisors' expectations and the underpriviledged workers' performance. *Social Science Quarterly, 52*, 369–378.

King, A. (1974). Expectation effects in organizational change. *Administrative Science Quarterly, 19*, 221–230.

Lambert, C. (1984). *The complete book of supervisory training*. New York: Wiley.

Laudon, K. (1986). *Dossier society: Value choices in the design of national information systems*. New York: Columbia University Press.

Lewin, K. (1951). *Field theory in social science*. New York: Harper & Row.

Livingston, J. (1969). Pygmalion in management. *Harvard Business Review, 47*(4), 81–89.

Locke, E. & Latham, G. (1984). *Goal setting: A motivational technique that works!* Englewood Cliffs, NJ: Prentice-Hall.

Locke, E., Saari, L., Shaw, K., & Latham, G. (1981). Goal setting and task performance: 1969–1980. *Psychological Bulletin, 90*, 125–152.

Maister, D. (1985). The one-firm firm: What makes it successful. *Sloan Management Review*, Fall, 3–13.

Merton, R. (1948). The self-fulfilling prophecy. *Antioch Review, 8*, 193–210.

Michael, D. & Mirvis, P. (1977). Changing, erring and learning. In P. Mirvis & D. Berg (Eds.), *Failures in organization development and change: Cases and essays for learning*. New York: Wiley.

Mirvis, P. & Berg, D. (Eds.) (1977). *Failures in organization development and change: Cases and essays for learning*. New York: Wiley.

Odiorne, G. (1969). *Management decision by objectives*. Englewood Cliffs, NJ: Prentice-Hall.

Rosenthal, R. (1966). *Experimenter effects in behavioral research*. New York: Appleton-Century-Crofts.

Rosenthal, R. (1976). *Experimenter effects in behavioral research: Enlarged edition*. New York: Irvington Publishers, Halstead Division of Wiley.

Rosenthal, R. & Jacobson, L. (1968). *Pygmalion in the classroom: Teacher expectation and pupils' intellectual development*. New York: Holt, Rinehart & Winston.

Rosenthal, R. & Rubin, D. (1978). Interpersonal expectancy effects: The first 345 studies. *Behavioral and Brain Sciences, 3*, 377–386.

Salomon, G. (1981). Self-fulfilling and self-sustaining prophecies and the behaviors that realize them. *American Psychologist, 36*, 1452–1453.

Sashkin, M. (1976). Changing toward participative management approaches: A model and methods. *Academy of Management Review, 1*, 75–86.

Schein, E. (1985). *Leadership and organizational culture*. San Francisco: Jossey-Bass.

Schrank, W. (1968). The labeling effect of ability grouping. *Journal of Educational Research. 62*, 51–52.

Snyder, M., Tanke, E., & Berscheid, E. (1977). Social perception and interpersonal behavior: On the self-fulfilling nature of social stereotypes. *Journal of Personality and Social Psychology, 35*, 656–666.

Sutton, C. (1986). Pygmalion goes to work: The effects of supervisor expectations in a retail setting. Unpublished doctoral dissertation, Texas A & M University.

Taylor, J. & Bowers, D. (1972). *The survey of organizations: A machine scored standardized questionnaire instrument*. Ann Arbor, MI: Institute for Social Research.

Terry, J. (1985, February). Student performance and school related attitudes as a function of teacher expectations and behavior. Unpublished manuscript, Cambridge: Massachusetts Institute of Technology, Program for Science, Technology and Society.

Turnage, J. & Muchinsky, P. (1984). A comparison of the predictive validity of assessment center evaluations versus traditional measures in forecasting supervisory job performance: Interpretive implications of criterion distortion for the assessment paradigm. *Journal of Applied Psychology, 69,* 595–602.

Weick, K. (1979). *The social psychology of organizing* (2nd ed.). Reading, MA: Addison-Wesley.

Weick, K. (1984). Small wins: Redefining the scale of social problems. *American Psychologist, 39,* 40–49.

Weiner, B. (1980). *Human motivation.* New York: Holt, Rinehart & Winston.

Woodman, R. & Tolchinsky, P. (1985). Expectation effects: Implications for organization development interventions. In D. Warrick (Ed.), *Contemporary organization development: Current thinking and applications.* Glenview, IL: Scott, Foresman, 477–487.

Yankelovich, D. & Immerwahr, J. (1983). *Putting the work ethic to work.* New York: Public Agenda Foundation.

THE RACE RELATIONS ADVISORY GROUP:

AN INTERGROUP INTERVENTION

Clayton P. Alderfer, Robert C. Tucker,

Charleen J. Alderfer, and Leota M. Tucker

ABSTRACT

A race relations advisory group is a structural innovation within a formal organization to assist with the objectives of eliminating racism and improving race relations among black and white managers. The group consists of approximately equal numbers of black and white organization members, balances membership by gender within race, and reflects a representative cross section of hierarchical levels and functional departments. The group meets on a regular basis, receives assistance from a race- and gender-balanced consulting team, and participates in all major decisions and programs that affect race relations among members of an organization. Such a group is created when an organization makes a major commitment to

Research in Organizational Change and Development, Vol. 2, pages 269–321.

diagnose and change working relationships between black and white managers. This chapter presents the theoretical basis for such a group, describes the seven-year developmental history of one group, and reports systematic data on the behavior and attitudes of members.

INTRODUCTION

Any organization in the United States that attempts to work seriously on race relations between black and white members cannot do so effectively without taking account of the historical forces that have shaped racial dynamics in this country. During the period between June and December 1986, for example, there were numerous reports of blatant racism on college and university campuses throughout the country (McDonald, 1987; Yardley, 1987). Less than 20 years ago, when the National Advisory Commission on Civil Disorders made its report to the nation, they recognized an often denied psychological reality—the racial attitude and behavior of white Americans toward black Americans.

> Race prejudice has shaped our history decisively in the past; it now threatens to do so again. White racism is essentially responsible for the explosive mixture which has been accumulating. . . since the end of World War II. At the base of this mixture are. . . the most bitter fruits of white racial attitudes: . . . The first is surely the continuing exclusion of. . . [blacks] from the benefits of economic progress through discrimination in employment and education and their enforced confinement in segregated housing and schools. (Kerner & Lindsay, 1968, p. 203)

Black Americans are unique among racial and ethnic groups who have immigrated to the United States because most arrived as slaves (Bennett, 1962; Holt, 1980). The United States has always been—and to this day remains—enormously conflicted about this "American dilemma" (Myrdal, 1944). How does a country established on the tenets of freedom and opportunity nevertheless base a significant proportion of its original economy on slavery? The consequences of those earliest conditions remain with us today. Laws, occupational practices, and educational institutions continue to be modified in order to bring the behavior and attitudes of Americans into greater accord with the country's stated ideals; yet those changes are also regularly resisted. Social scientists have contributed toward the efforts to effect change through research and intervention, and they have also fortified the forces that impede change (Clark, 1973; Sarason, 1981).

Although research on race relations by social scientists is nearly a hundred years old, the study of racial dynamics within the context of organizations is more recent. In *Management and the Worker* Roethlisberger and Dickson (1939, p. 460–61) reported data indicative of racial tension in the Bank Wiring Room study, but they did not analyze or interpret their findings. The extensive research on *The American Soldier* conducted during World War II included an entire chapter devoted to "Negro Soldiers" (Star, Williams, & Stouffer, 1949). Also during this period, Clark and Clark (1939) conducted the research assessing the self-concepts of black elementary school children from northern and southern schools, which eventually was to influence the 1954 *Brown versus Board of Education* decision to desegregate public schools. Even though these early studies varied in the relative degree of attention they paid to racial and organizational factors, all were conducted with the cooperation of organizations. With the benefit of an historical perspective, we see them as establishing a pattern in which business, the military, and schools became classes of organizations in which race relations research was possible.

Between these early studies and present day activities, the Civil Rights Movement stimulated another period of change in the laws and legal institutions of this country. Efforts to desegregate public schools followed from the *Brown* decision and the movement for social change that followed. The concept of affirmative action was developed in the mid-1960s to bring about greater equity for blacks and other disenfranchised groups in organizations dominated primarily by white men. After a stimulus had been provided to improve race relations in organizations, social scientists again found themselves participating as investigators. In schools, in the military, and in business efforts to understand these attempts to bring about change were again undertaken (Hochschild, 1984; Binkin et al., 1982; Alderfer et al., 1980).

In the period following World War II, the contributions of social scientists expanded to include planned intervention as well as research. Laboratory education in the United States was developed in response to a request from the Connecticut Interracial Commission (Bradford, 1967). More than 20 years later, Aronson (1978) and his colleagues developed a program of research on the "jigsaw" classroom as a means of promoting cooperative interdependence among black and white students in public school classrooms. Landis, Hope, and Day (1984) reported on an extensive training program for desegregation in the military during the Vietnam period. When data have been collected on these programs, they usually suggest that some favorable consequences follow from the activities, but there is also a recurring problem identified by a variety of authors. Educational interventions by themselves tend to be inward looking and, as a consequence, tend to be highly vulnerable to disturbing forces that promote racial inequality from the wider environment in which the educational programs are embedded (Aronson, 1984; Cohen, 1984).

We undertook the present intervention as a means to work with the wider environment in which a race relations improvement program was set. In this situation, our activities were closely tied to intergroup theory (Alderfer, 1986). The design and conduct of the Race Relations Advisory Group was directly derived from the theory. The chapter, therefore, begins with a statement of the major elements of the theory, moves to a description of the seven-year developmental history of the group, and then reports systematic data on the behavior and attitudes of members.

AN INTERGROUP THEORY FOR CHANGING RACE RELATIONS IN ORGANIZATIONS

The theory takes race relations as a special case of the more general problem of intergroup relations. Concepts and propositions pertain to human units from individuals to organizations in scope. The group is the focal entity of the framework. Within this psychological set, individuals appear mainly as group representatives; small groups show the forces of subgroups within them; organizations consist of interdependent groups with relations among them reflecting the characteristics of intergroup dynamics; and interorganizational relations are negotiations among groups of groups (Rice, 1969; Alderfer & Smith, 1982). In accord with the principles stated above, the theory has specific concepts to deal with end-states and other terms for change processes.

Material about end-states consists of a definition of groups-in-organizations, propositions about intergroup dynamics in organizations, explanation of embeddedness, a definition of human organization, and an explication of race relations in organizations through the terms of the theory. Change processes involve the concepts of racism, dialectical conflict, resistance-denial, and parallel processes. Changing race relations in organizations means altering end-states of racial groups through the change processes identified by the theory.

Groups in Organizations

The definition of groups-in-organizations used in this work deals with both internal and external properties. In addition, it takes account of the multi-level nature of group life and differentiates the external environment of groups specifically to take account of relations with other groups (i.e., intergroup relations). The definition states:

> A human group is a collection of individuals (1) who have significantly interdependent relations with each other; (2) who perceive themselves as a group by reliably distinguishing members from non-members; (3) whose group identity is recognized by non-members; (4) who have differentiated roles in the group as a function of expectations from themselves, other group members, and non-group members; and (5) who, as group members acting alone or in concert, have significantly interdependent relations with other groups (Alderfer, 1977).

Our concept of the group takes account of individual, interpersonal, and intergroup levels of analysis. According to this view, any phenomenon pertaining to a person is multiply determined by the internal dynamics of the person, the interpersonal dynamics of her or his group, and the intergroup dynamics of other groups in interaction with her or his own group. In turn, the intergroup relations among the interdependent elements of complex multi-group systems are a function of the internal dynamics of individuals, the interpersonal dynamics within groups, and characteristics of the environment within which the system is embedded.

Propositions About Intergroup Dynamics in Organizations

To understand group behavior in organizations it is useful to distinguish between *identity groups* and *organization groups*. Members of identity groups share common biological characteristics, participate in equivalent historical experiences, and as a result tend to develop similar world-views. The most commonly recognized identity groups are those based on race or ethnicity, gender, age, and family. Members of organizational groups are assigned similar primary tasks, participate in comparable work experiences, and as a result, tend to develop common organizational views. The most commonly recognized organization groups are those based on task or function and on hierarchy. From this perspective "organization structure" can be viewed as the reification of the intergroup dynamics that accompany enactment of the principles of hierarchy of authority and division of labor. People carry identity group memberships and their consequences from organization to organization, while their organization memberships depend on individual's relationships to particular organizations.

Every person is simultaneously a member of all her or his identity and organization groups. However, the group he or she represents at a given moment depends on the intergroup context in which events occur. The intergroup context is determined by other individuals who are present representing other groups, and by the state of group boundaries, power differences, affective patterns, cognitive formations, and leadership behavior of one's own and other groups.

Group Boundaries

Both physical and psychological group boundaries determine group membership. Transactions among groups are regulated by variations in the permeability of the boundaries. Excessive permeability produces the pathologies of an underbounded system, and insufficient permeability results in the hazards of an overbounded system (Alderfer, 1976, 1980).

Power Differences

The types of resources that can be obtained and used differ among groups. The variety of dimensions on which there are power differences and the degree of discrepancy among groups influence the degree of boundary permeability among groups.

Affective Patterns

The permeability of group boundaries varies with the polarization of feeling among the groups, that is, it varies with the degree that group members associate mainly positive feelings with their own group and mainly negative feelings with other groups.

Cognitive Formations, including "Distortions"

As a function of group boundaries, power differences, and affective patterns, groups tend to develop their own language (or elements of language, including social categories), condition their members' perceptions of objective and subjective phenomena, and transmit sets of propositions—including theories and ideologies—to explain the nature of experiences encountered by members and to influence relations with other groups.

Leadership Behavior

The behavior of group leaders and representatives reflects boundary permeability, power differences, affective patterns, and cognitive formations of their group in relation to other groups. The behavior of group representatives, including formally designated leaders, is both cause and effect of the total pattern of intergroup relations in a particular situation (Alderfer et al., 1983).

Embeddedness

Embeddedness of intergroup relations refers to interpretation of group level effects across different units of analysis; it concerns how system and subsystem dynamics are affected by supra system dynamics and vice versa (Alderfer & Smith, 1982; Alderfer, 1986). One may observe embeddedness from the perspective of individuals in relations to one another, of subgroups within groups, of whole groups in relation to one another, of intergroup relations within organizations, etc. Regardless of which unit is the focus of attention, the phenomenon of interpenetration across levels will be operating. Individuals carry images of their own and other groups as they serve in representational roles. Subgroup splits within face-to-face groups reflect differing degrees of identification and involvement with the group itself. These splits, in turn, reflect the group's relations to other groups in the system and to the larger system as a whole. The concept of embedded intergroup relations applies to both identity and to organization groups (Alderfer & Smith, 1982; Alderfer, 1986).

Definition of Organization

A human organization is a set of interdependent groups who consciously accept a collection mission, who subordinate their group interests as necessary to the organization's mission, and who publicly receive support from the large social order to pursue their organization's mission.

This concept of organization takes account of the unit from inside and outside, recognizes the subordination of group interests to the authority of the organization, and connects the organization to the society on which it depends for legitimacy. Empirically, this means that some kind of mission statement is necessary to assert that a system has met the internal conditions necessary to be called an organization, and that some record of legitimate transactions with society's representatives are necessary to meet the external conditions. The definition is consistent with the principle of embeddedness and makes the organization subject to intergroup dynamics internally and externally.

Race Relations in Organizations

Racial groups are identity groups in organizations. Black and white groups, in particular, differ in the degree to which they generally are consciously aware of the full range of group forces acting upon them. In predominantly white organizations, for example, the "success" or "failure" of a black person is often seen by black and white members as reflecting upon the entire racial group, while the performance of a white person is seen as more of an individual matter (Alderfer et al., 1980). White people are less likely to see themselves as a group than are black people. Both the ideology of individualism and ethnic differences among whites tend to be perceived by whites as reasons why they do not experience themselves as a group. Nevertheless, when white managers meet together and attempt to describe "the white group" in their corporation, a high degree of convergence among the attributes can be observed. Empirical studies show that membership in the white group alone and white group membership in interaction with specific kinds of individual experiences predict how the white group is perceived by blacks and whites (Alderfer et al., 1983). There is little doubt that white people perceive blacks as a group or that blacks perceive whites as a group (Griffin, 1960; Carmichael & Hamilton, 1967; Silberman, 1964; Campbell, 1971; Schuman & Hatchett, 1974). Empirically, as well as conceptually, black and white individuals are members of racial groups. We state this obvious conclusion because of repeated evidence that many white people, including those who study race relations, do not approach the subject with an awareness that their racial group membership is a variable of significance.

In predominantly white organizations, the group boundaries, power differences, affective patterns, cognitive formations, and leadership behavior of blacks and whites differ. These differences follow, in part, from how whites and blacks tend to be distributed among organization groups. Blacks tend to find membership in lower ranking hierarchical groups and in less central staff groups. One result is that blacks tend to have less power and leadership potential than whites. This pattern follows from the historical pattern of white society that kept blacks largely outside predominantly white organizations until the last two decades and from beliefs among white people that blacks are inherently inferior and therefore "deserve" to be kept in less central, less influential positions (Bennett, 1962; Alvarez, Lutterman & Associates, 1979; Davis & Watson, 1982).

The boundaries of black and white groups differ in permeability within predominantly white organizations. Even though black people rarely appear in the most senior management positions, whites typically do not see this as a consequence of their group boundaries being closed to blacks. Nevertheless, descriptively speaking, the top management groups of most corporations are white groups. Faced with relatively small numbers, less access to influential positions, and a sense of isolation from the mainstream of corporate activities, black members may establish formal and informal support systems. Reactions of senior white officials to these activities by blacks vary in important ways. In some instances, the response is highly punitive and prohibitive (Davis & Watson, 1982). In other cases, the white reaction is more supportive (Alderfer et al., 1980).

The manner in which black employees are embedded in predominantly white corporate organizations is therefore complex. When there are black officials in senior positions, when there is committed public recognition that race is a significant dimension of organizational life, when there are officially sanctioned support systems for black employees, and when the organization relates to its environment in a manner supportive to blacks, then a predominantly white organization is taking necessary first steps to deal with its racial dynamics. If these conditions do not exist, the outlook for constructive change in race relations is far less favorable.

Changing Race Relations

Concept of Racism

A concept of racism is essential in a theory of changing race relations. Racism is the problem that progressive change aims to solve and the condition that regressive change re-establishes. In the context of this theory, racism applies to researchers as well as to respondents. Making the concept explicit and central guards against blindspots that white investigators have often shown in their research on race. The concept makes the value position of the theory clear and avoids the illusion that one can study race relations in this society from a neutral or value free position.

The term itself, however, is subject to misunderstanding. Rarely is the word used without evoking strong feelings. Understanding these emotions is a crucial element in learning about race relations. Eliminating the term does not eliminate the feelings. Using the term accepts the feelings and increases the chances that learning can occur. For some people the term means only blatant aggressive destruction of one racial group by another. Here the meaning includes multiple dimensions.

The idea of racism begins with the power relations between racial groups in conflict. For racism to be an appropriate term, the racial groups must be of unequal power; and the dominant group must use its superior power to damage or to destroy the individual and collective well-being of the subordinate group. Racism is, therefore, not equivalent to ethnocentrism, which may occur among groups of approximately equal power. White racism is the more common form in this culture because blacks rarely have enough power to be racist.

Racism occurs at several units of social groups (Jones, 1972). Prejudiced individuals represent just one version of racism. Unless these individuals occupy positions of substantial authority, this form of racism may be the least potentially damaging. Collective forms of racism affect groups, organizations, and the culture as a whole. One is alerted to collective forms of racism when destructive effects continue to occur in members of a low power group regardless of who the members of either racial group are.

Racism also varies in how consciously people support racist practices. When organizations such as the Klu Klux Klan openly advocate assaults on black people, there is relatively little doubt that one is witnessing collective racism. But racism can also be practiced covertly. If a situation involves conflict between members of racial groups with unequal power, and if members of the dominant group deny that race is a factor in influencing what happened, then signs of unconscious racism are present. To deny that race is relevant when it might be is to show an insensitivity that is demeaning to potentially aggrieved parties. The power of unconscious racial feelings is strong enough that one can be more certain that the race is getting appropriate attention if people examine whether race is relevant in a conflict rather than if they energetically deny that racial forces could be operating. The fact that black and white people may both voice denial is not evidence against the influence of racial factors. As the less powerful group, blacks may deny the presence of racial feelings as a means of survival.

Finally, racism varies by degree of virulence. The most destructive form involves killing and injuring members of the less dominant group by members of the more dominant group. A less virulent form may involve members of the more dominant group telling racial jokes at the expense of members of the less dominant group.

Dialectical Conflict

Not all disagreements, differences of opinion, or variations in perception about racial matters are evidence of racism. Black and white people generally have different life experiences on matters of race, and, as a result, bring different affective patterns and cognitive formations to any serious work on race (cf. Baldwin & Mead, 1970). Dialectical conflict is the process of respecting these natural differences and using them to eliminate racism and improve race relations.

The methods of dialectical conflict draw upon several ideas already presented. People are viewed as both individuals and racial group members. Among the individuals from each racial group, we assume that there are different opinions and different perspectives. When racial matters are under consideration, we assume that a person's race is *always* relevant. Thus the questions, What is the black perspective? and What is the white perspective?, are readily acceptable modes of dialogue. Similarly an individual may say, "Speaking as a black person. . ." or "Speaking as a white person. . ." The concept of dialectical conflict does not assume that blacks and whites always disagree on matters of race, that all disagreements follow racial groups, or that blacks always have the more progressive views and whites always have the more conservative perspectives. When racial matters can be thoroughly and openly examined, people find that blacks and whites often can agree, that important disagreements occur within both racial groups, that whites sometimes advocate more progressive views than blacks, and that the more progressive stance may not always lead to the more effective outcome.

Structurally, the implementation of dialectical conflict calls for enough blacks and whites so that each racial group can experience its own group forces, that each person can be differentiated from her or his racial group, and that intergroup racial dialogue can occur. Resolving differences of opinion, when possible and desirable, is both an intragroup and an intergroup matter. Problem-solving approaches search for outcomes that respect the interests and satisfy the needs of both racial groups. The most favorable outcome of dialectical conflict consists of solutions that are synergistic. Often these kinds of solutions can occur. But "win-win" solutions are not always possible. When issues pertain to scarce resources, the dialectical process should produce outcomes that reflect the compromise of roughly equal partners. Neither exclusively white domination, nor unilateral imposition of black preferences is desirable. White domination maintains the status quo, or more likely, results in regressive change. Unilateral imposition of black preferences generates white resistance that cannot be worked through and eventually produces white backlash. To achieve an effective dialectic requires complementary structures when normal conditions do not naturally lead to dialogue among equal parties.

Resistance and Denial

Change processes go hand and hand with stability forces. Without a standard against which movement can be measured, any concept of change is meaningless. Unless one's objective is total destruction of a system, some degree of continuity is essential for any significant change. Systems of all kinds regularly demonstrate conservative impulses in the face of the most dramatic changes

(Marris, 1974). To a person or group committed to progressive change, conservative forces may seem like they are inimical to change. In fact, resistance is so natural as to cause concern if it is not observed. Accepting resistance and working with it is a recurrent theme implicit in the concepts of racism, dialectical conflict, and parallel processes.

Denial is a special form of resistance. It is helpful insofar as it signals that resistance is present. In clear form, denial blocks inquiry. Denial negates questions about racial matters, transforms statements in a manner that weakens their impact, or inverts assertions so that confusion about their meaning occurs. Examples are many. A white employee says, "We have no racial problems because there are no black people in our work group." A white man shoots a group of four black youths who were trying to rob him, and a white political official says, "The episode has no racial meaning because the young men were thugs." Denial is an especially powerful and frequently used defense because racism represents a major contradiction to the espoused value system of the United States.

Parallel Processes and Microcosm Groups

The term parallel processes refers to the occasions when related units change in a manner that one takes on similar affect, cognitions, and behavior as the other. A sense evolves that one unit is injecting its condition into the other and that the other is receiving that condition. In time, the two units seem to follow similar paths although they start in different places.

Parallel processes usually begin without conscious awareness of either party. With adequate attention, parallel processes can be raised to consciousness and utilized in the service of constructive change. Without competent attention, parallel processes maintain the status quo through the operation of unconscious resistance-denial or through the outbreak of destructive irrational processes (Alderfer, 1986).

Parallel processes may occur between units of the same order. An interpersonal relationship between two individuals, for example, may have the effect of infecting one person with the feelings, ideas, and behaviors of another (Searles, 1955). Members of a group, as another example, may take on the roles and behaviors of another group with whom they have had intensive interaction (Alderfer, 1976, 1977, 1986).

Parallel processes may also occur between units at different levels of analysis. Systems, regardless of the unit, may reflect parallel processes in their suprasystem or from their subsystems. The condition of race relations in the society in which the business is located will affect relations between blacks and whites in the organization—an example of the suprasystem influencing the system by parallel processes. The state of race relations in a work group will affect how that group relates to other groups in the organization—a situation in which subsystems affect a system through the mechanism of parallel processes.

Parallel processes involve absorptive and projective movements, and may have constructive or destructive effects (Alderfer, 1986). Absorbing effects may be useful for diagnostic purposes, if a unit can permit itself consciously to take on the properties of another system for the purposes of empathic understanding. On the other hand, merely taking on the condition of another system unconsciously, robs the absorbing system of its own unique identity. Projective effects may be useful for change purposes, if the unit projecting is in significantly better condition than the receiving units, if the process is undertaken with sufficient consciousness by both parties, and if the receiving unit chooses actively to receive the projection. But unexamined projective processes may simply cause a subordinate unit to take on the character of an oppressor (Bettelheim, 1960).

Parallel processes may be observed naturally, or conditions may be created to heighten their visibility. Taking a passive or active stand toward parallel processes depends on whether one has an hypothesis about the relevant dimensions in a particular setting and whether one has the resources to establish social structures that heighten their accessibility. The more precise the hypothesis and the more available the resources, then the more feasible it is to establish an active relationship toward parallel processes.

The chief means to heighten the visibility and accessibility of parallel processes is to create a microcosm group that reflects the dimensions of whatever intergroup relationship is central to one's hypothesis. In the case of race relations, for example, the microcosm group should include sufficient numbers of black and white members so that no major within-group or between-group differences are suppressed or obscured (Alderfer & Smith, 1982). Under the best conditions there are equal numbers of black and white members, and they are also balanced by gender. Total size of the groups is also an important consideration. The group should be large enough to pick up the most significant variations within and between groups and yet not so large that members are unable to develop a sense of themselves as a group. We have worked fruitfully with groups ranging between four and twenty members.

Microcosm groups may be created outside and inside organizations (Alderfer, 1977; Alderfer et al., 1980). Outside the group takes the form of a research or consulting team. Inside the groups is an advisory group assisting with the project. The most desirable situation includes both inside and outside groups. On matters of race, regardless of whether one or two microcosm groups are used, strong representation from both black and white groups is essential to establish and maintain dialectical conflict. Members of the outside team need their own knowledge of race relations rooted in their own well-developed sense of racial identity. As a group, they need to have the individual commitment and collective capacity to operate effectively as a team. Members of the inside group should represent a cross section of organization groups by hierarchy and function, include a range of views about race relations in both racial groups, and exhibit a willingness to learn more about race relations. When groups can be created outside and inside the organization, parallel processes and dialectical conflict occur within the outside group, within the inside group, between the inside and outside groups, and between the inside group and the organization. These intergroup and inter-racial relationships carry the seeds and force for changing race relations in organizations.

The basic contention in presenting the intergroup theory of changing race relations in organizations is that more than "hard data" is needed to effect change in the structures and processes that maintain racism in the organizations of our society. A strong theory is also required. We have presented such a theory. No one experienced with changing race relations can expect an easy time, regardless of which conceptual position is utilized. Nevertheless, a strong framework offers promise of improving upon the efforts that have gone before.

DEVELOPMENTAL PHASES OF A RACE RELATIONS ADVISORY GROUP

The Race Relations Advisory Group was established to assist with implementing recommendations that evolved from a thorough diagnosis of race relations in management. A twelve-person microcosm group balanced by race and gender and representative of corporate organization groups had assisted a four-person race- and gender-balanced consulting team with the diagnosis. During the diagnosis, meetings of the advisory group were chaired by the chief consultant who was a white male (Alderfer et al., 1980). When the project moved from diagnosis to change, the size of the group was expanded to 20 members, and the chairperson became the corporate director of human resource management, who was a white male and had corporate responsibility for the change program. All members of the original group who wished to remain members were encouraged to do so. New members were recruited with explicit consciousness that the new group was a key element in the change program. Thus, members were selected because they were viewed as influential and represented major department and hierarchical levels in the corporation.

Three members of the consulting team remained with the project after the work moved from diagnosis to implementation. The black female member, however, left the team and was replaced by a black female from the corporate organization development staff. The purpose of her leaving was to begin developing internal professional resources for the program. However, when the internal consultant was killed in an automobile accident approximately a year after the change began, then the original black female member rejoined the consulting team. The consulting team worked with the chairperson between meetings to design the sessions and served as facilitator during the actual events. In the sessions, when the group was working in subgroups, the chairperson and consulting team met as a staff subgroup.

Membership in the group was voluntary and by invitation from the chairperson, who conferred informally with the consulting team and members of the group to identify potential members. The group as a whole also participated in the discussion of what type of member in terms of level, department, age, and racial orientation would be desirable whenever an opening on the group became available.

Attendance at meetings was carefully monitored, and when a pattern of missing meetings was observed, the person was asked to consider whether he or she wished to continue. Members also stepped forward to resign when their commitments changed to prohibit adequate attention to advisory group business. In this manner, membership on the group changed gradually over the course of the project. After eight years, nine of the twenty members of the advisory group were people who had been members of the original twelve person diagnostic group.

Advisory group meetings occurred approximately bi-monthly over the course of the project. Each meeting was uniquely designed. In the early phases the group's work was almost exclusively done during day long meetings with consultants present. In the later phases, project task forces were established to carry out specific assignments between total group meetings without consultants present, and the group reduced its meetings to half days. Project task groups were virtually always balanced by race and gender. Eventually this manner of working became an unquestioned norm in the operation of the advisory group.

From the outset the group viewed itself as a learning group as well as a work unit. As we shall see, the group renegotiated its mission statement several times throughout its history, but at no time was there any question about omitting learning from the group's charter. This is a most important element in the overall orientation to the change program. They would also be less likely to improve on other conditions that they themselves had not experienced and found to be of value. When the group projected its parallel processes into the organization, the effects were shaped in important ways by what the group itself and the individual members had learned.

At various times throughout the course of the project, the question arose as to whether restricting the group's attention to matters of race was somehow an error. Whenever these issues arose the group retained its original focus. The basic reasoning had two parts. First, having a race relations advisory group did not prohibit other groups from forming to pursue their interests. Indeed, the presence of an effective race relations advisory group might be helpful to others. Second, if the group began to deal with other issues, there was a real danger that members' energies would become easily dissipated without being effective on any efforts. People were aware that one tactic employed by those who wished to interfere with efforts to improve race relations was to require people interested in race to take on all "human relations" problems. The result of retaining the group's central focus on race did stimulate other groups to form during this period (e.g., an Hispanic managers group) and did prevent other problems from impeding this group's efforts.

White people had important positions of authority in this project throughout the undertaking. The person who started the project from within the corporation was a white male, who in turn contacted a white male external consultant. The external consultant formed the four person cross race and gender team. Chairpersons of the advisory group were all white. Three were men and one was a woman. In a predominantly white corporation, the presence of white people in important roles gave the symbolic message that the program was race relations for black and white people, not "a social program" just for blacks. At the same time, the centrality of whites in the program ran the real risk that the net effect would be white domination. The crucial question was how to structure a balanced program that neither set up blacks to be rejected by the more powerful white majority, nor used the program as yet another vehicle to retain exclusively white dominance. The basic process used throughout the project was to be sure that black and white people in approximately equal numbers were present when key program decisions were being made and to be certain that different perspectives, if present, were respected.

From the outset, the race relations advisory group kept a documentary history of its activities. In the life of the group, the document was called the meeting minutes, although in practice the recording was far more extensive than one usually finds in most organization records. Depending on the length and intensity of the meetings, the minutes might range from 20 to 25 pages of double-spaced type, not including appendices. The white male consultant was willing and interested in taking minutes. One person's doing so provided for continuity of scope and style. This method of working was talked through thoroughly among members of the consulting team and between the team and the advisory group for it, too, could have another relationship of potential white dominance. After each meeting the minutes were written and distributed to all group members for review. At the start of each subsequent session time was provided for group members to criticize and amend the minutes of the preceding meeting. During the review period, the scribe's behavior was simply to clarify and record the comments of group members, which in turn appeared in the subsequent meeting's minutes.

Whenever the group was discussing a topic in detail, the minutes became as close to a transcription of the events as the scribe could achieve. All people were identified by race and gender group except for the chairperson and consultants, who were identified by name. Sample dialogue appears below:

> Charleen (consultant): Our feedback suggests that white people may not feel safe in the workshops.
> BM (black male): Why don't whites feel safe anywhere—even in their own groups?
> WM (white male): I remember that blacks have fun in the workshop, and whites do not. . .

WF (white female): Individual whites may not have thought much about race.

BF (black female): Blacks tend to have more positive things on their lists than whites. Whites relate competitively to the subject of race.

WM: There was more camaraderie in the black group. I wanted to be in that group.

BF: It doesn't surprise me that blacks have an easier time.

WF: There may be no way for whites to get there sooner.

Clay (consultant): Yes, the consultants have been criticized for the suffering of the whites.

WM_1: Yes, I criticized the consultants.

WM_2: I remember I went through a denial syndrome. There was no other way.

BF: Blacks enjoy getting together. Whites are already together.

Jimmy (consultant): One does not learn if one is trying to protect oneself. For blacks, the workshop is personal and political. For whites, it is political. There is also the perception that the workshop is "for blacks."

The minutes served a variety of functions in addition to providing a rough written history of advisory group activities. With six to eight weeks between meetings, the minutes provided a means for group members to refresh their memories between events. The detail of the minutes helped to remind members of the diversity of views in the group and thereby, to keep the process of dialectical conflict alive. People who spoke openly in meetings had the reassurance that their contributions would be preserved without the personal hazard of their being held "individually" responsible for stating controversial opinions. Because the consultants managed the minutes and invited feedback every session, this mechanism provided a means for consistently giving attention to the relationship between the consulting team and the advisory group. Overall, the minutes provided a most important element in the overall conduct and understanding of the race relations advisory group.

The identification of notable phases in the life of the group over a seven year period was made possible through a detailed review of the minutes. Identification of phases turns on the complex interdependencies among the internal dynamics of the group, the products the group was creating, and the relationship of the group to the corporation as a whole (Gersick, 1983). More familiar developmental theories of groups are concerned only with the internal dynamics of the group and were based mainly on all white male composition (Bennis & Shepard, 1956).

The internal dynamics of the group refer to the processes and structures the group used to work together. Included are defining the mission of the group; establishing the roles of chairperson, members and consultants; and developing a shared understanding of how black and white members of the group work together.

Throughout its life, the group produced or sponsored the creation of innovations for managing race relations in the corporation. In some instances, they were alterations in organization structures and processes for dealing with racial matters. In other cases, the group produced a variety of written products.

As a microcosm group of the management of the organization, the advisory group had to be concerned with (1) how members represented their identity (race and gender) and organization (function and hierarchy) groups in the advisory group; and (2) how members represented the advisory group to their identity and organization groups.

We describe the phases of the group's life in terms of these three classes of variables: internal dynamics, products, and external relations. Both the relative weight and the qualitative content of these issues varies from phase to phase. Moreover, the notion of phases includes both the modes of sharp demarcation and of gradual transition. Sometimes changes in the group were marked by dramatic events signaling the presence of great tension. Other times the work was marked simply by gradual and persistent movement. Table 1 provides a summary of four phases in the life of the group.

Phase 1: Start Up

The operation of the Race Relations Advisory Group for implementation of the change program began after the organization accepted the validity of the race relations diagnosis and committed itself to the recommendations that grew out of the diagnosis (Alderfer et al., 1980).

During the start-up phase, the advisory group expanded its membership, established a chairperson from the organization, and developed its norms of working together. All of these changes increased the boundary permeability of the group and ushered in a period of affective turmoil. The work of this period was to establish sound group boundaries, to formulate a clear mission for the group itself and in relation to the large organization, and to set the stage for the group to relate effectively to key elements in its wider organizational environment. Events of this period consisted of twelve day-long meetings from May 1980 to May 1981.

Looking inward, the first step in this process was to formulate a succinct mission statement for the group and to reach agreement about the duties of members, the chairperson, and the consultants. The process was begun by the chairperson bringing a draft mission statement along with position description for members, consultants, and chairperson to the first meeting. The chairperson's role initially consisted of managing advisory group meetings and receiving input from the group. The member's role originally involved representing oneself, acting as advisor, and implementing program designs. The group proposed modifying the chairperson's role to include reporting back to the group regarding the consequences of their recommendations and enlarging the member's role to include bringing information from the organization to the group and from the group to the organization. Group members also expanded their own and the chairperson's role definitions to enlarge the nature of learning all would undertake.

In addition, the consultants interviewed members by race-gender groups to identify their hopes and fears about the project. Results of those interviews

Table 1. Phases in the Life of the Race Relations Advisory Group

Phase	Dates	Internal Dynamics	Products and Processes	External Relations
1. Start Up	May 1980 to May 1981	Roles & Responsibilities Black-white tension in committee Committee-chairperson negotiations Committee-consultant differences	Mission Statement Diagnosis Summary Concept of Race Relations Competence Upward Mobility Program Design	Size of group expands; members commit and recommit White and black PR writers work with group BMA writes to group Delegation to Board of Directors Committee
2. Major Intervention	September 1981 to December 1982	Group criticizes workshop Members leave Meetings canceled Review accomplishments	Workshop Designed and Implemented Upward Mobility Program Undertaken	Black male consultant joins management New members join Reactions to Workshop and Upward Mobility Program are prominent
3. Crisis and Realignment	January 1983 to December 1983	Examine benefits and costs of membership Chairperson changes Task force model of work considered	Reports on Workshop and Upward Mobility History of Group Reviewed Internal Complaint Review	Change in Personnel Department leadership Consultant team changes membership Inquiry to antiblack group Corporate mission changes
4. Stabilization	March 1984 to December 1986	Chairperson changes again Task force structure implemented Meetings shortened Black-white dialectic on group purpose Formal objective setting by group	Corporate Policy Formulated Information Program Planned Composition of Personnel Committees Change Research Evaluation Completed	Presentation to top management Corporate Communications staff assistance QWL cooperation Consultants reduce number Board has Race Relations Workshop CEO Speaks to Urban League

categorized by race-gender subgroup were presented to the advisory group as a whole. These data recognized the similarities and differences about improving race relations that black and white members brought to the advisory group. Both racial groups hoped for better understanding of the races and wanted the group to be a positive for active change. White members, however, represented concerns from white managers. From white men, there was the question of "double standards" for the promotion of blacks. From white women, there was concern over why the Black Managers Association was allowed to exist. Blacks were forceful in wondering whether channels for upward mobility for blacks would become more open. Whites expressed uncertainty about whether group meetings would be too comfortable or too uncomfortable and whether the group's work would turn out just to be an "academic exercise."

In short, both organization group and identity group issues were alive for advisory group members from the outset. The effects of advisory group members negotiating with the chairpersons was for all to become more committed to learning at an individual level and for everyone to become more conscious of the two-way relationship between the group and the organization in which it was embedded. Examining expectations about the group by race-gender groups gave legitimacy to the major subgroups, identified areas of agreement, and pointed to likely sources of conflict between black and white members. This process shows how the methods of dialectical conflict were used from the outset of the group.

In the early sessions, black-white tension in the advisory group turned on the relative weight to be given to "power versus education" in effecting change in race relations. The simplified version of the conflict had blacks favoring power methods and whites preferring education. However, at a deeper level, both racial groups knew that either orientation alone would be less effective—perhaps even counter-productive—than the two in combination. At an intellectual level, the question was what mix of power and education would bring about the desired results. However, at an emotional level, the question was what kind of relationship would emerge between black and white members of the group. Indeed, there was an unstated concern about whether the group would stay together as a force for changing race relations.

Two important products emerged from the start-up phase of the advisory group. The first was a non-technical summary of the race relations diagnosis, written by members of the corporate communications department in consultation with the race relations advisory group. The second was a statement on race relations competence as an element of overall managerial effectiveness, prepared by the advisory group with the assistance of the consulting team. Both of these documents reflected a commitment by blacks and whites to work together in order to improve race relations. Both, too, were designed to provide explicit recognition of black and white differences in how to pursue this goal and what indicators of progress would be. The diagnosis summary looked backward toward the diagnosis undertaken by a team of outsiders and brought that analysis into the organization in a language and mode suitable to its members. The competence statement looked forward by establishing a set of concrete indicators of race relations competence as defined by current members of the corporation.

Preparing the diagnosis summary was a strenuous and difficult undertaking. The communications department writer was a white male who believed that he understood race relations and who faced a group that treasured their newly discovered racial group autonomy. Frequently, the writer's efforts were criticized and returned for modification by the advisory group. Eventually the white writer accepted the idea that his assignment would become easier if he had a black partner. He enlisted the aid of a black male from his department, and together the two finished the work to the satisfaction of the advisory group. Even though the final product was viewed most favorably by all involved, the emotional costs of his exchanges with the advisory group were carried for years afterward by the white writer. Four years after the diagnosis document was completed, he was cautioning colleagues to be wary of the difficulties involved in working with the advisory group.

A special feature of the diagnosis summary was that it presented the same "facts" simultaneously from both black and white perspectives. Thus, not only the words conveyed the idea that blacks and whites had different perceptions about race relations in the corporation, but the presentation also demonstrated that these differences had unique meanings for the separate racial groups. Table 2 shows excerpts from the report. The struggles in the production of the diagnosis summary reflect the operation of a variety of forces including an early stage in the life of the group and the strain inside the group on racial matters. During this phase, white men in particular were subject to special scrutiny by other subgroups in the advisory group. These processes touched the consulting team, the white men in the advisory group, and the communications department writer. At stake was the question of what kind of power and authority blacks would have in implementing the race relations improvement program. Would whites, directly or subtly, act as if they alone were in charge? Would blacks be able to exercise significant and sustained influence in the change program? During this period whites had the task of learning about their own blindness on these matters, and blacks had to determine whether they could help to fashion structures that solidly reflected joint influence processes. Shaping the diagnosis summary indicated that both racial groups could be acceptably represented, although not without strain and tension.

Writing the race relations competence document was truly a group undertaking. In doing this task, the group showed it could be creative because all material in the paper came from group members. The process was tedious and stressful. Starting in race-gender-alike subgroups, the members produced statements they thought were characteristic of managers who were "high performers" on matters of race. The conflict between education and power strategies was dealt with in a variety of ways: by acknowledging it in the preface of the document, by defining

Table 2. Excerpts from the Diagnosis Summary

Status of Race Relations

Black Perspective	White Perspective
According to black managers, numbers are not enough. Meeting affirmative action goals doesn't ensure that blacks will have the chance to compete equally with whites. Black managers believe that getting a good job, or winning a promotion by working twice as hard and waiting twice as long, doesn't guarantee success. . . . 99 percent of black managers agree that race relations at the company could be improved, and only half would characterize race relations as "good."	It is sometimes hard for whites to understand what all the fuss is about. A high percentage of whites believe that race relations in the corporation are good, and that the company has been responsive to black needs while just over 80 percent agree that there is room for improvement, as many think there has been improvement since they joined the company . . .

Informal Black/White Relations

Black Perspective	White Perspective
Black managers believe that blacks and whites tend to stay with their own kind and think that good one-to-one relationships are rare in the corporation. For black managers, that distance doesn't result just in a lack of friendship, it means that crucial information, usually shared informally, is not available. In addition, about 75 percent believe that white managers are uncomfortable with competent blacks . . .	Most whites (about 75 percent) believe that good white-black relations are common at the company, and about half report having had serious conversations about race relations with blacks. However, white managers agree that whites and blacks tend to socialize with members of their own race, but only 10 percent agree with the statement that white managers are uncomfortable with competent blacks . . .

competence in terms of both understanding (i.e., education) and behavior (i.e., power), and by providing extensive lists of "understandings" and "behaviors" that were to be expected of corporate managers, who aspired to race relations competence. Throughout the period of document creation the consulting team performed a variety of roles. Between meetings they edited and organized the group products. Within sessions they devised a series of work activities—sometimes in race-gender-alike subgroups and sometimes in cross-race groups—to preserve the clarity of the separate racial perspectives and to forge a holistic document. During this period the consultants also prepared a series of lectures, which offered a conceptual orientation to how the members were working and what they were producing. Ultimately, it turned out that this period of experimentation and learning was setting the stage for the Race Relations Workshop. Many of the activities invented to help the group work through the formulation of the competence document became elements of the structure eventually used to provide learning about race relations competence.

In final form, the race relations competence document consisted of seventeen pages of double spaced type. There were four major sections defined by classes of supervisory relationships: blacks supervising whites, whites supervising blacks, whites supervising whites, and blacks supervising blacks. Each section included a series of ''understandings'' and a series of ''behaviors'' applicable to the class of supervisory relationship. Table 3 contains excerpts from the race relations competence document.

Approximately half way through the start-up phase, at the beginning of the fifth meeting, the advisory group offered its first strenuous criticism of the

Table 3.   Excerpts from the Race Relations Competence Document

---

Blacks Supervising Whites

I.   Understandings

A.1.   In order to survive and advance in the business, blacks must understand the norms of the white setting in which they work. Blacks should anticipate that they will be compared to white role models, and must anticipate the difficulty they will have when their behavior does not conform with white expectations . . .

B.1.   White subordinates may be devalued by others or feel resentment themselves because they have a black supervisor. Thus, black managers may feel embarrassment and a loss of self-esteem, which may tempt them to react inappropriately . . .

D.2.   Black managers must clearly understand and accept their own black identity in order to appreciate and appropriately deal with how whites respond to them.

II.   Behaviors

A.4.   Black managers should also extend themselves to understand the feelings of white subordinates and to assure them that their legitimate concerns are considered . . .

B.5.   Black managers should establish alliances inside and outside the immediate work group with whites as well as blacks. These alliances can counter negative characterizations which dissatisfied or prejudiced whites may attempt to spread and can help to develop the support to advance both white and black subordinates.

Whites Supervising Whites

I.   Understandings

A.1.   Many white managers and their subordinates may be disinterested or opposed to efforts to improve race relations . . .

A.4.   When a white manager acts as an advocate for black managers, or takes positive action to improve race relations, other whites may accuse her or him of being too liberal.

II.   Behaviors

A.2.   White managers should not condone behavior by whites that undermines effective race relations. They must actively discourage racial joking, racist remarks, and other actions that generate non-productive racial tensions . . .

A.4.   White managers should initiate open discussion of race relations rather than ignore issues and permit them to smolder underground.

minutes as prepared by the white male consultant. The content of the criticism covered a variety of dimensions: that the minutes had inaccurately reported the words of a white male and a black female who had disagreed about the nature of racism; that a significant interpretation pertaining to the power versus education dispute had been left out; that a commitment by the consultants to circulate a document in advance of the next meeting had neither been kept nor recorded accurately; and that reports of certain aspects of the group's work where the consultant had been present were more detailed than elements where he has to rely on the reports of others. In this session, the members also revisited their statement of roles and responsibilities. This time the role of the consultants was renegotiated in a manner that directly paralleled changes that had been made in the chairperson's role during an earlier meeting. The confrontations signaled that the members were addressing their issues of authority with the outside experts as well as with their internal chain of command. Feelings that might otherwise have interfered with the tasks of the group became available for work. The competence document presents the cognitive formations of a group that had looked directly at its own racial issues and was coming to terms with ambiguity of its own authority in the corporation.

While this cognitive work was taking place inside the advisory group, plans were also underway to establish a new upward mobility program for the corporation. The objective of the program was to alter the barriers in the corporation that interfered with qualified black employees being promoted to middle and upper levels of the corporation. The upward mobility program represented a very major intervention into the corporation. Many groups in the system in addition to the advisory group had vested interests in how promotion decisions were made. These included the top officers of the corporation, the personnel committee of the board of directors, the existing management personnel committee system, and the Black Managers Association. The burden of negotiating with these groups fell to the chairman of the advisory group. Each of these groups had its own perspective on the proposed program, and, in some instances, it was literally impossible to meet the concerns of one group without frustrating those of another group. Take two questions: Should there be a special program at all? Should it be a cross-racial program (i.e., for whites and blacks) or for blacks only? The existing personnel committee system viewed the idea of a special program as a sign that they were not doing their work, and asked for an opportunity to improve on their past record of promoting few blacks. In a letter distributed to the group, the Black Managers Association was a strong advocate for a black-only program with defined percentages of promotions. The question of the racial composition of the program was a source of debate in most groups consulted about the program. The advisory group ultimately recommended in favor of a black-only program. The consulting team, on the other hand, favored a mixed racial design, as did the chair. Virtually all corporate groups who were consulted on the question expressed concern about the whites who would not be chosen, if there was a mixed racial program. Thus some white managers outside the advisory group strongly favored a black-only program. In the end, the decision to have a mixed program was made by senior management. Those who favored a cross-racial program had a variety of reasons for their views. A black-only program had the flavor of a social program for blacks, not an intervention for the entire corporation. Such a program would then be vulnerable to charges of reverse discrimination and subject to being labeled a second-class venture. Moreover, the whole corporation needed to improve its corps of managerial talent—including identification, selection, and development. Building racial consciousness into a management development program for the entire corporation served the interests of the several groups (not just blacks) and addressed a number of problems faced by the corporation (not just race relations).

The corporate picture was additionally complicated by the fact that the corporation had determined that it had an excess of managers and was in the process of reducing its management force. How do you institute a special program designed to insure more rapid promotion of some people, while others were being invited to retire early?

The last element in phase 1 of the advisory group work was making a presentation to the personnel committee of the board of directors. A team led by the chairperson and consisting of two group members (a black female and a black male) and the white female member of the consulting team made an extended report to the board committee. Covered in this meeting were the diagnostic study results by the white female consultant, the background and operations of the advisory group by the black female group member, the development and use of the race relations competence document by the black male group member, and the upward mobility program by the chairperson. The team asked the committee to approve a policy making race relations competence an element of management competence for the corporation.

When they returned to the advisory group, the team reported that the board committee had greeted them warmly and enthusiastically. The board, however, had not been willing to approve the concept of race relations competence as policy. Instead they "endorsed" and "encouraged" the group's efforts. Advisory group members were troubled by what they perceived as equivocal support for the concept of race relations competence. But perhaps more importantly, they were disturbed by the fact that the team—and especially the chairperson—had proposed a mixed-race upward mobility program, after the advisory group made it very clear that it favored a black-only program. Considerable time at the advisory group meeting after the board presentation was spent discussing the group's reactions to the team's work with the board. On balance, people viewed the event as decidedly mixed. They appreciated the interest and enthusiasm of the board committee, and they recognized that they had not received the clear and definite support they had sought.

Phase 2: Major Intervention

The next period in the life of the advisory group consisted of five meetings between September 1981 and December 1982 and was marked by a notable change in the nature of the group's work. During the period between May and September 1981, the consultants were asked to prepare a design for a three-day workshop to provide corporate managers with an opportunity to learn race relations competence. The activities of phase 2 were focused on the advisory group's providing assistance with the design and implementation of the two major interventions—the upward mobility program and the race relations competence workshop. This second period in the life of the group, therefore, was marked by the group's reacting to initiatives whose origin was outside themselves. Instead of providing a means to harness the perspectives and energy of group members as they literally wrote the competence document, this period called for their critical skills. As work moved outside of the group and into the organization itself, members had an opportunity to experience the direct effects of attempting to bring about change.

The two major interventions directly paralleled the power and education emphases called for by the competence document. The upward mobility program was aimed directly to influence promotion policy and practice, a subject at the center of corporate power. The workshop, on the other hand, was first and foremost an educational intervention designed to provide learning opportunities. But, of course, each program had elements of both education and power. The upward mobility was in part a method for teaching the organization how to improve the fairness of its promotional system, and the workshop was populated by the most senior managers and others who served on the corporation's personnel committees.

The primary innovation of the upward mobility program was to select people with the aid of an eight person task force balanced by race and gender that worked independently of and in cooperation with the existing personnel committee system. This task force initially accepted information from the existing personnel system to determine who should be considered for the program. Later their data were supplemented by information collected by a set of outside interviewers also balanced by race and gender, who spoke with a candidate, a candidate's boss, a referral person named by the candidate, and a referral person named by the supervisor. Interviewers coded their data according to a preexisting numerical system and returned the information to the corporate task force. This group made an initial determination about who should be selected, who should be rejected, and who might be selected based upon further deliberations. Final selections were then made by the departmental personnel committees. There was also provision for an appeals committee consisting of four senior managers who were willing to hear the requests of individuals who believed their personnel records justified their being considered for the program. This basic design was rooted in the method of dialectical conflict and parallel processes. Unlike the normal personnel committees, the special task force was balanced by race and gender. It offered the normal system a selection process that was not so heavily weighted by white male perspectives. Some members of the task force were also members of the advisory group, so in the case of those individuals there was a direct transfer of advisory group learning and processes into the task force. The task force, in turn was in a dialectical relationship to the department personnel committees.

In the case of the upward mobility program, the advisory group's role was to give their views of the detailed design. This process was shaped in part by the fact that some advisory group members were also candidates for the program. The process of review involved two steps. The first consisted of the group as a whole raising questions about the overall design, and the second involved breaking the group into race alike subgroups so that both black and white perspectives on the program could be identified clearly. Members of the advisory group raised no questions about the basic design of the program, although they had many questions about specific details. For example: from the total group came the question of how the special task force members would be selected. From the white group came a request to be sure that feedback was sensitively delivered to people who were not selected. From the black group came the observation that the special task force should not be used as a justification for the corporation's failing to increase the number of black managers on the normal personnel committees.

The race relations competence workshop was designed to help managers learn the knowledge and behavior defined by the competence document that had been written by the advisory group. Preparing the competence document, of course, set the parameters for the content of the workshop. It also turned out that several of the lectures and exercises that had been developed to help the advisory group work together effectively in its early stage also found their way into the workshop design. Finally, a large proportion of advisory group members were participants in the first workshop. In the case of the workshop, the consultants did not tell the group about the design in advance of their attending. This was because no regular participants who came to the workshop would know the design in advance. Advisory group members were invited to attend, and the next meeting was devoted to reporting their experience and criticism to the consulting team.

Lasting three days and organized to accommodate approximately 42 people, the workshop had several modes of learning. Four lectures provided conceptual material on racism, thinking-feeling, role-playing, and change processes in organizations. With a black-white participant ratio of approximately 1:2, workshop members carried out semi-structured and unstructured activities in race-alike and cross-race discussion groups. Generally the race-alike activities took place during the first half of the workshop, and the cross-race work in the second half. The final stream of learning was built on a series of role playing exercises that derived directly from the race-alike and cross-race sections of the competence document.

The advisory group generally had a favorable reaction to the workshop's first run, and they also had some pointed and strongly felt comments. Questions about the balance of race-alike and cross-race time were raised by both black and white participants, but their emphases were somewhat different. Whites wanted more time in mixed race groups, and there was talk of the desirability of more "T-group time," so people would leave the workshop feeling better than they apparently did. Some whites expressed concern over the number of whites who left the workshop feeling depressed. Blacks, on the other hand, expressed a desire for more race-alike time in order to have more time to talk together about how to deal with whites. There were also a variety of critical comments directed toward the consulting team. People observed that the two male consultants seemed notably more active than the females, and that the male consultants seemed competitive with one another. People noted that the consultants were not as fully coordinated as they might ideally be, and they did not provide participants with adequate opportunity to give feedback during the workshop. All of these comments and others like them reflect natural problems in the development of a new and complex undertaking. In subsequent editions of the workshop, the consultants were able to adjust the design in ways that met many of the advisory group criticisms. This was especially true on matters pertaining to how the consultants carried out their roles and relationships. It was less possible to make changes that satisfied white and black requests for more race alike time and more cross-race time. The most notable aspect of the advisory group's reaction to the first edition of the workshop was the thoroughness and frankness with which they offered their comments. The people were committed and involved enough to look for and find problematic features of the program, and they felt strongly enough and free enough, for the most part, to speak their views directly to the consulting team.

Another episode pertaining to the relationship of the workshop and the organization arose during this period. A black male manager, known to have a promising future in the corporation, found a memorandum declaring "open season on porch monkeys" on his desk. Obviously well-written, the document said that the prey were also known as "jigoboos, saucerlips, jungle bunnies, spooks, and spear chuckers" and could be spotted by looking for "bright colors, Cadillacs, empty wine bottles, and hookers." Readers were encouraged to hunt and kill the identified species. The receiver of the memorandum brought it to the black male consultant, who in turn discussed it with the entire consulting team. The group decided to bring it to the advisory group. In extensive and sometimes heated discussion, the group entertained two options: (1) Ask that the president of the corporation write a letter to all managers condemning the paper. (2) Make the document an item of discussion in the race relations workshop. Differences in views on this matter were sharp and did *not* split along racial lines. In the end, the consultants decided to make it part of the lecture on racism. The article would be handed out as a specimen and collected after participants had an opportunity to read and discuss it. Asking the president to write about the incident would give it widespread notoriety and no opportunity for people to discuss and reflect upon their reactions in a supervised setting. In the context of the workshop the document provided an example of virulent racism from the corporation itself. Eventually we learned that the material had been entered into the corporation's computer, and ultimately, was available only to people privy to the appropriate code word. These facts indicated that the paper was not the product of a single "sick mind" as some people initially thought but rather the product of collective efforts.

Other indications during this phase of the group's life, however, were also suggestive of impending difficulties. For the first time, advisory group meetings were canceled by the chairperson without thorough explanation. Manifestly, the reasons had to do with excessive workload. A lot was going on outside meetings in connection with the upward mobility program and the workshops. Some advisory group members were active in both programs. Inwardly, however, there were other suggestions of trouble. Members expressed a need to review the group's "accomplishments to date," and to develop systematic ways of having old members leave and new members join the group. These feelings of impending change, too, were quite natural for a group who had worked strenuously for nearly 18 months on a controversial intervention program. At the time, there was a sense of euphoria about the group; real change seemed about to occur. Events that, in retrospect, were harbingers of more serious problems in the future were not interpreted as such at the time. Schooled in the theory of progressive and regressive cycles in changing race relations, the consultants among themselves were heard to ask, "Where is the resistance? This is too good to be true. What are we missing?" Of course, the signs were there. We, however, needed the perspective of time to interpret them completely.

A final important element during this phase was that the black male consultant joined the organization as a member of upper management in the personnel department. This was a difficult choice for both the individual and for the team, because, as a general rule, we hold to the principle that outside consultants do not become members of organizations after they have been consultants to them. But, in this instance, we agreed to violate the principle because the change seemed to be good for the individual and for the program. After the decision was made, the advisory group received the news and was offered an opportunity to discuss it. They responded with friendly banter, and, uncharacteristically, did not take the opportunity to explore or comment on the matter in depth. Our interpretation of this event was that the members did not wish to raise questions about a difficult personal decision for a person they had come to know and to respect.

Phase 3: Crisis and Realignment

The third period in the life of the advisory group consisted of five meetings between January 1983 and December 1983. During the time between May 1982 and August 1983, the interviewing program to select people for the upward mobility program had been undertaken, and the special task force to choose candidates had been put into place. By the end of the calendar year 1982, the organization—and especially the chairperson of the advisory group—was feeling the effects of the organization's resistance to the upward mobility program. At the close of the *last* advisory group meeting of 1982, which occurred in *March,* the chairperson had asked members to indicate whether they wished to continue with the group. Six members (30 percent) of the group indicated a desire to leave. The race and gender distribution of the departing subgroup was one white female, two black females, two black men, and one white man. When meetings of the advisory group from April to December 1982 were canceled, the chairperson asked again in September 1982 for the people to indicate whether they wished to stay or leave the group. This time only five members indicated a desire to leave. So when the advisory group met again in January 1983, after a hiatus of more than nine months, the group had a contingent of five new members: one white female, two black females, one black male, and one white male. The cancellation of meetings and the turnover of members turned out, in retrospect, to be a signal that the entire race relations program was entering a period of stress and turmoil.

The first meeting of this phase was devoted to assessment and appraisal of the program to date. Bringing five new people into the group became an occasion for members to examine the benefits and costs of membership. The design called for this to be done in race-gender-alike groups. Each subgroup met by itself and made lists of benefits and costs. As it turned out, a simple count of the items on these lists showed that the white men alone had a longer list of costs than of benefits, the other three subgroups showed more benefits than costs. Nevertheless, the overall pattern was one of marked ambivalence for all subgroups. No such group, except possibly the white women, showed a clear preponderance of benefits over costs. Table 4 provides a tabulation of benefits and costs for each subgroup. All of the subgroups independently identified several common themes. Among the benefits were increased self-awareness and learning and an opportunity to contribute actively to programs that seemed as if they were going to work. Among the costs were frustration and emotional tension and a sense that every small bit of change took too long to achieve. The white male chairperson of the group independently made his own list, which consisted of five benefits and five costs. His list alone contained the notion that he felt estranged from both black and white groups.

In the discussion that followed posting of the lists, an item on the white males

Table 4.   Tabulation of Benefits
and Costs of Advisory Group
Membership by Race
Gender Subgroups
January 1983

	Benefits	*Costs*
Black Men	9	6
Black Women	12	10
White Men	8	10
White Women	11	5

list turned out to be of concern for all four subgroups. The white men had written, ''Concern whether the primary goal is improved race relations versus grants or published books and articles.'' This statement referred to the consultants and reflected the fact that the consultants had recently received a contract from ONR to assess the results of the program. Members revealed that they had a variety of perceptions and reactions. A white woman said, ''From my point of view, fine popularize it. Get more grants.'' A white man commented, ''When we put that on the board, I think it represents frustrations. Grants have been given, but race relations have not advanced. The upward mobility program is an accomplishment.'' Expressing these concerns openly in the advisory group allowed the members to proceed fruitfully to other dimensions of assessing the overall race relations program. But concerns about the motives of the consultants were not to go away for some time. In retrospect, the challenge to the consultants and the struggles of the white male members of the advisory group were elements of a larger pattern. The race relations improvement program was beginning to provide a real stimulus for change to the organization—principally through the workshop and the upward mobility program—and people associated with the change were beginning to feel the organization push back by the time it took to get things done. The resistance that our theory had long predicted, and which we had seen only in moderate doses, was now in full bloom.

The remainder of the meeting was given to reports and discussion of other program features. A report on the upward mobility program indicated that an initial cohort of 32 people had been selected for the program, that special training for these people had already begun, that 6 had already been promoted, and that the data for selecting the second cohort were already being analyzed. The process of selecting the second cohort, which was to be much larger than the first, was turning out to be more complex than originally expected. Another report indicated that the corporation's program for labor management cooperation was being changed to include more black participants and to address racial issues in the non-management workforce. A report on the race relations workshop described the design changes made in response to the advisory group's feedback, identified the different reactions to the workshop from blacks and whites, and explained the strong effects on the workshop from the stance taken by senior corporate officials. When senior managers related to the workshop in a receptive manner, others followed their lead. When the high ranking people showed resistance, that also was associated with similar reactions from lower ranking participants. The report also noted that the white male consultant was the least popular among the team, that blacks liked the race-alike portions of the workshop, and that whites disliked race-alike activities and preferred to operate in cross-race exercises. Other reports touched on remaining aspects of the intervention program, including the corporate information program, the changes of race-gender composition of personnel committees, the status of the appraisal system review, and consequences of revising the corporation's discrimination complaint system.

A final aspect of this first meeting to the transitional phase was a beginning of change in the operating structure of the advisory group. Until this point the group had largely done its work during the day- or half-day-long meetings when all the members gathered together. Now, at the initiative of the chairperson, the group began to consider a new structure. From the reports about ongoing elements of the race relations program, members identified tasks that needed group attention. Volunteers from the group formed race- and gender-balanced task forces and agreed to do work between regular sessions of the advisory group. This change brought the possibility for more initiative back to members of the group, kept the group as a whole as a setting for monitoring and discussing, and ultimately, reduced the time required for the total group meetings. But, as we shall see, the new structure did not "take" instantly. Adjustments in the overall pattern of authority for the chairperson were necessary before the new structure of the group began to work effectively.

By the next meeting in this phase of the program, the full force of corporate changes was to be felt by the race relations advisory group. Amidst the extensive changes being sought through the race relations improvement program, the corporation itself was undergoing two most significant alterations. Senior leadership was changing. During this period, the president and all of the senior vice-presidents were to leave. Following a plan that had been in place for some time, an entire cohort of managers moved normally into retirement, and their successors took on new jobs. Also associated with the change in leadership in the corporation was the development of a new corporate mission. The organization was to open up entirely new lines of business in highly competitive markets. One effect on the race program was a new level of cost consciousness, as the organization aimed to control and reduce all unnecessary expenses.

By the next advisory group meeting, the effects of these changes on the group's work began to be experienced directly. A new corporate vice-president of personnel was named; the chairperson of the advisory group was reassigned to a position of planning for the new ventures; and the new personnel vice-president was also named chairperson of the advisory group. Thus, the group got a new person as chair whose corporate rank was higher than his predecessor. Along with the change in the group's leadership came turnover in the consulting team. The black members of the team left the roles of consultants—the black female to separate from the implementation phase of the project entirely and the black male to take a new higher ranking position in the organization, which made him project manager rather than consultant. These adjustments called for replacing the black members of the consulting team and set off a search process that was to take approximately six months to complete.

Needless to say, all of these changes heightened the uncertainty of an advisory group that was already nervous from the resistance it was carrying as a result of its own interventions. The question naturally arose: was this period of corporate transition to be a time for ending the race relations program? Outside the group meetings, conversations among the consultants and the new personnel leadership addressed the questions that had been raised about the consultants' motivation and commitments. At one point, a talk between the white male consultant and the corporation's chief executive examined the questions that had arisen and reaffirmed their separate commitments to the work. At a subsequent advisory committee meeting an additional report on the research program was made, and group members seemed satisfied that their concerns had been adequately addressed.

During this period of turmoil, evidence also came forward to suggest the operation in the corporation of a group of white people specifically dedicated to preventing the promotion of black men and women. The group had an acronym, a departmental location, and a hypothetical list of members. Initially, members of the advisory group attempted to determine the membership and activities of this group through informal conversations with people in the department where it was located. These efforts produced no unequivocal data, and after discussions among senior managers in the operating department and the personnel department, the task was turned over to the corporate security group. They obtained evidence that resulted in disciplinary action being taken in relation to the white man who was at the head of the white supremacist group.

Meanwhile the advisory group continued to review its mode of operation and the various project elements. The new corporate vice-president and chairperson, who had been one of the five new members of the group, acknowledged his need to learn more about race, encouraged members to stay with the group and keep the project moving, and pledged his own commitment and support. Outside of the group meetings, the new chairperson worked strenuously to keep the upward mobility program from being derailed. Inside the group, he asked the group to continue to review carefully the various program elements and the progress or lack thereof that had been made on each one. During this period the consultants prepared a brief historical outline of the advisory group activities over the three years of its life, completed an analysis of quantitative data that had been taken from the group, and presented this material to the group in order to assist with the self-review and to help in the process of teaching new members (including the chairman) about the group's efforts and accomplishments. Initially, group members were skeptical about these efforts, and their feelings were heightened when the new vice-president unexpectedly had to miss an advisory group meeting in order to take part in corporate-level labor negotiations. Eventually, however, members accepted the soundness of the new leadership.

Another issue that arose during this period was the role of race relations in the new corporate ventures. Group members observed that planning for these new corporate ventures had included no black managers, that few blacks were employed in the new enterprises, and that virtually all blacks who were operating in the new departments were doing so at comparatively low levels in the hierarchy. The response to these observations by those in charge of the new ventures was that the pressures of start up prohibited careful attention to race relations; the omission of blacks from significant roles in the new ventures was an oversight, not intentional. The fact that this omission occurred and was so visible, first to the advisory group and then to senior managers, served as a powerful signal to all. Unless conscious efforts were made to include race relations considerations in transition planning, the natural forces of a white-dominated system would simply reproduce themselves and result in the exclusion of blacks.

While the advisory group was grappling with its own transition and leadership succession, the task force structure was put into place and began to work, albeit with some fits and starts. Cross-race and gender subgroups met between sessions of the total group, carried out assignments, and reported to the total group. The task forces discussed the race relations workshop, the effects of the upward mobility program on people not selected for inclusion, and the statement of the corporation's equal employment opportunity policy. On the latter issue, the group had noticed that the corporation had a policy of disciplinary action against employees who practiced sexual harassment, but there was no comparable sanction for racial harassment. A task force rewrote the appropriate section of the corporate personnel handbook to correct this inconsistency.

When the new chairperson missed what would have been his second meeting of the group, members used the occasion of his absence to formulate the questions they had about his own and the corporation's commitment to the race program. They asked that he respond to the reports that had been made by the task forces in his absence and that he tell the group "where he was coming from" on matters pertaining to the race program. At the next advisory group meeting, the man did exactly that. He affirmed the corporation's commitment to improved race relations, explained that some "one-time only" adjustments related to the corporate mission had pulled energy away from the program, and stated that after labor relations the largest portion of his energy was devoted toward making the upward mobility program work effectively. At this time, the group again discussed the situation with regard to white men. The chairman confirmed the need to add two white men to the group. Within the group, people observed that the group pressures toward uniformity of views about race relations may have stifled some white men's willingness to speak up and offer opinions that differed from the majority of the group. The new chairman indicated that he hoped people would increase their risk taking and trust in the group.

The group also, once again, revised its core mission statement to include the facts that it now reported to the vice-president for personnel; that questions of harassment of employees came within the domain of the group; and that the group was expected to take initiatives to improve race relations, not merely respond to requests for advice.

As the group's mission and mandate seemed to become stable once more, energy became available for other facets of the race relations improvement program. The group performed a review of the internal complaint procedure. They also returned to a subject that had previously been treated most ambivalently in the past: a corporate-wide information program about race relations improvement in the corporation. Previous efforts to undertake such a program had stalled. The group had angered staff members from corporate communications when they worked on the diagnosis summary. The task force on the information program had had great difficulty in establishing meeting times. And whenever the subject of whether to have such a program arose in the group, the members seemed to speak in many voices. Now, however, the group seemed to have reached a point in its own development where the subject could again be examined thoroughly.

The method for conducting this inquiry in the advisory group consisted of asking the two race-alike groups to meet independently; to give their views on the advantages, disadvantages, and objectives of such a program; and to report this material to the total group. The reports showed that the black group identified many more advantages than disadvantages (eight to four), while the whites identified the same number of advantages as disadvantages. In the total advisory group discussion, the members agreed that a corporate-wide information program should be undertaken. Four key directions were identified as the central core of this effort: (1) to recognize that racism exists; (2) to understand that it will not be tolerated; (3) to create a desire to change it; and (4) to eliminate racism wherever it exists within the corporation. This new resolve seemed to indicate an end to the period of crisis and transition in the advisory group. The fact remained, however, that the new vice-president turned out to be in his position on an interim basis. At their next meeting, the advisory group was to have a new chairperson.

Phase 4: Stabilization

The fourth period in the life of the advisory group begins in March 1984 and continues to the present time. The key events signaling stabilization were the selection of a new (and permanent) vice-president for personnel and the decision by the former chairperson to stay with the group as a member. The permanent chairperson was a white woman who had been a member from the outset, knew the full history of the group, and was familiar with its way of working. Together with her predecessor, the two vice-presidents provided the group with a new degree of active organizational authority. During this period the group continued to review key elements of the change program, developed two new projects for itself, and solidified the pattern of operating between meetings with race-gender-balanced task forces.

At the start of this phase, the consulting team was reconstructed after the search for two new black members was completed. The search had been most difficult in terms of finding a black female who had the necessary qualifications and was available in the nearby geographic area. Members of the original team planned to stay together to complete writing about the project and thus planned to maintain their relationships with one another. Both the new consultants and the organization were alerted to the fact that the time frame for external consultants retaining a major role was limited. In late 1983 when the new consultants were being employed, all parties talked about a two- to three-year time span until the consultants left the project. Setting "an end" to consultant involvement with the project was a development that consciously originated with the consulting team and evolved from two basic considerations. First, there was a sense that some of the unconscious resistance that emerged during the third phase was rooted in a fear by senior managers that the consultants did not have a sense of when the relationship should end and therefore had to be driven out. Since these messages, which were never stated explicitly, came from senior white men who had been consistently supportive of the work, they had to be taken seriously. Second, there was a sense from the consultants that their work should end within a finite period. Full-fledged systemic resistance to the work had emerged. It had been worked on thoroughly by the advisory group and the larger organization. The project emerged in a strengthened condition. Establishing a period for ending also told the organization that in the foreseeable future they would have full responsibility for the program. In the meantime, the task would be to establish the structures and processes for the organization to carry on effectively without external consultants.

Reports on the status of the upward mobility program and the race relations workshop continued to occupy the attention of the advisory group. At the beginning of this phase, a representative from the personnel department provided a statistical account of the progress of the first cohort and indicated that a second cohort—more than twice the number of the first—had been selected for the second phase of the program. This development represented the results of great efforts by senior black and white members of the personnel department and signaled a resolution of the most strenuous resistance that had emerged in phase 3. Crucial elements in this resolution included enhanced influence by department personnel committees, increased overall size of the program, and addition of several white managers to the second cohort. The advent of new members of the consulting team also became the occasion for reviewing and revising the design of the race relations workshop. From the outset, white participants had objected to the amount of time they had to spend in race-alike groups. Initially, the original consulting team had responded to these comments by increasing the amount of time for cross-race discussions at the *end* of the workshop. Now the new team also found a method for slightly increasing the time available for cross-race discussions during the first day of the workshop. Both kinds of changes implemented during this period—the alterations in the upward mobility program achieved by organization members and the workshop design adjustments brought about by the consultants—represented movements in response to criticisms voiced by white people. They reflected the operation of dialectical conflict and were negotiated with strong participation by black and white people.

During this period, participation by non-management people in race relations competence workshops was also increased. In one episode, 10 members of the union leadership participated with managers in the ongoing design. As a result, workshop materials were substantially rewritten to provide role play experiences that were more in line with the work life of union members. This workshop was populated by more than 30 union members and three managers, all of whom were active in the corporation's quality of worklife program, and represented an important diffusion of the race relations improvement program beyond the management organization where it had originally begun.

The advent of a new chairperson of the advisory group also became the occasion for re-examining the group's agenda of project activities. Consultants were asked to review the group's minutes and bring to the group a list of incomplete tasks. The review process also served to help the new consultants to become familiar with the group's history. After the list was brought forward, the group as a whole worked to extend and modify the items that had been identified by the consultants. After this process was complete, the group split into race-alike groups to determine a priority ordering for the full list. When the two racial groups had completed their work, a surprising result emerged: the white group had taken the task as it had been given and returned to the total advisory group with a detailed list covering all the items. The black group, on the other hand, had determined that one issue had priority over all others, and until that problem was solved, other kinds of activities made little sense. The black group proposed that the group needed to develop a corporate policy on race relations and seek approval for it from senior management and the board of directors. After brief discussion, both black and white groups agreed that the policy statement should take first priority among all the group's activities.

In subsequent meetings, therefore, the group devoted a major portion of its attention to preparing such a document and to planning the steps to achieve its approval. As a first step in this process, the consulting team prepared a draft of a policy statement. Then during the next advisory group meeting, black and white groups proposed revisions. A key step in this process was asking the advisory group as a whole to examine the forces in the top management group that would aid and impede their receptivity to a strong race relations policy. This process was assisted greatly by the fact that two members of the advisory group were also members of top management. Deliberations about the policy document emphasized four major elements. The corporation: (1) supports racial diversity in the workplace; (2) recognizes that racism exists in society and organizations; (3) employs and promotes people to reflect racial diversity in all units and levels in the organization; and (4) gives responsibility for acting in accord with the policy to employees and supervisors. A task force for bringing this policy to the top management group was established and achieved enthusiastic approval after they set the race relations policy into a broad framework on the corporation's personnel philosophy. This step in the race relations program finished a process that had remained unfulfilled since the first phase of the advisory group's life. The work of bringing the policy statement to top management, preparing the supplementary material requested by that group, and reporting back to the advisory group was carried out by a race-gender-balanced task force, thereby further stabilizing that mode of carrying out advisory group work.

In fact, during this period, a variety of structural changes were made. The task force method of working was established firmly. Due to the pressures of other corporate activities, the group decided to change its meeting pattern to half days. A new constellation for planning advisory group meetings was also put into place. The senior black male, the chairperson of the group who was a white female, and the white male consultant became the planning group for advisory group meetings. The full consulting team shifted its attention exclusively to race relations competence workshops. When the black female member of the consulting team decided to leave the project, she was replaced by a black female member of the corporate organization development group, thereby setting the stage for moving conduct of the race relations workshop to internal staff.

Efforts to carry out a corporate information program about race relations, which had been begun again during the crisis, were continued in an energetic fashion. A race-gender-balanced task force from the advisory group, assisted by a staff person from the corporate communications department, produced a detailed 32-page plan for enlisting a variety of corporate communication vehicles to assist with the race relations program. The report from this group received an enthusiastic reception from the advisory group. This response was in sharp contrast to the strain that had marked the effort several years earlier for a communication's department staff person to prepare a summary of the diagnostic report. In general, the group was showing increasing signs of being able to work together effectively among its own members and to relate productively to the large corporate organization.

The years of 1985 and 1986 were noteworthy in the group's further evolution in relationship to the wider corporate community. This period was noted *both* for new orders of difficulty *and* new achievements. As is so often the case in this kind of work, the problems go hand-in-hand with the advances.

This period reflected the effects of a new leadership constellation taking charge of the organization and of the corporation adapting to significantly new business conditions. The new leadership constellation reflected a full generational change. By the time that the transition had been completed, the chief executive officer and an entirely new set of executives occupied the most senior positions. Of the top seven people, four had played key parts in the race relations improvement program at some point in their careers. Two were members of the Race Relations Advisory Group during this period.

The corporation maintained a formal management-by-objectives program. Included among the objectives of senior managers were specific goals for increasing the diversity of the management workforce. Traditionally, these objectives were stated at both the corporate and departmental levels. During the transition period, however, the corporate level objectives remained without their being translated into specific departmental level goals. Members of the advisory group were aware of this change and commented on it with some concern when knowledge of the change became known. But, at first, it did not become a major item of debate among group members. Instead, the analogous issue took the form of an internal discussion among advisory group members regarding the proper role of the group within the corporation.

A contributing factor to this debate was entry of new members into the group. New members bring with them their experience of the corporation. New members help to prevent the group as a whole from becoming isolated and separated from the organization. To the extent that the group is a progressive force for changing race relations, new members—perhaps especially new white members—help to keep group members in touch with conservative forces in the system. In this case, the dialectic took the form of differences between black and white members regarding how active a force the group should be in attempting to influence corporate goals about race relations.

White members tended to emphasize the term "advisory" in the group's name and to argue that doing more than advising would be inappropriately intervening into management. The strongest form of this argument stated that the personnel department and line managers had responsibility for the people side of the business, and the group needed to be careful lest it provoke a backlash from these two groups. Black members, in contrast, tended to remind the group that these subgroups always had had their respective duties, and the need for a race relations program was testimony to the fact that these groups needed some help. Black members of the group were line managers and some served in the personnel department. They had no interest in undermining people in these roles, but they certainly wished to exert influence on them.

While this debate was unfolding in the advisory group, members agreed that the group should receive periodic reports about hiring and promotions and about the composition of corporate personnel committees. These data served to add concrete points of reference to the black-white differences about the proper role for the group as a whole. After about a year, the effects of not having corporate objectives set at the departmental level became clear.

But in the meantime, another set of events were occurring in the relationship between the project and the external environment. The consulting staff, consisting of a black inside member and a white outside member, was asked to design a short form of the Race Relations Workshop for the corporate board. Because the board had only one black member and the design called for a ratio of one black member for each two white members, additional black members of the workshop were recruited from the most senior black managers from the advisory group. Lasting only a half day (in contrast to three days for the regular workshop), the directors' workshop turned out to be a rich and eye-opening experience for board members. Their reactions were overwhelmingly favorable, and at their next meeting, they passed a resolution praising the corporation's work on race relations and affirmative action. An article describing the directors' experience with the workshop and their subsequent resolution was then printed in the corporate newsletter.

Some months later, the chief executive officer was the featured speaker at an anniversary dinner of a local chapter of the National Urban League. He used the occasion to express his appreciation for the League's history and accomplishments and to welcome their efforts to exert influence on behalf of progressive race relations in the community and specifically in business organizations. He also briefly mentioned the corporate race relations improvement program and his own personal learning from the experience. This speech was printed and circulated to members of the corporation.

The article about the board's participation in a race relations workshop and the CEO's speech about race relations were concrete indicators that the corporate information program about race relations was bearing fruit.

Meanwhile, inside the advisory group, evidence was mounting that the pace of hiring and promoting black managers was decelerating. For a portion of this time, the corporation introduced a hiring and promotion freeze as part of a cost containment program introduced to cope with market pressures. Despite the freeze, special permission was obtained to promote more than 60 people from the bargaining unit into management. Not one of these people was black!

Sometime later, a major restructuring of the corporation was announced—again to cope with changing market conditions. When the organization changes were planned, the most senior black managers were not included in the process. When the results of the changes were announced, no black managers had received major promotions. One relatively senior black manager received a new assignment that was widely perceived as a setback for him personally and for race relations in general.

The year of 1984 was a period of very significant change in the composition of corporate personnel committees. In that year the proportion of black managers in these groups moved from a previous high of 5 percent to 12 percent. This proportion remained constant in 1985 and then dropped to 9 percent in 1986.

A further development during this period came about as a result of a strike that the corporation endured. While bargaining unit people were away from their jobs, managers took on their assignments. In this time of general turmoil, black managers who filled hourly positions experienced notable and significant racial harassment. These events occurred between June and December of 1986—the same time when outbreaks of racial tension were occurring throughout the United States.

For the duration of the strike, which lasted several months, advisory group meetings were canceled. When the group reconvened, however, they had quite an agenda. Feelings were powerfully engaged. The differences that had previously seemed to divide black and white members were far less noticeable, although blacks seemed to be more touched emotionally by what had occurred than whites. The two groups did not differ on whether the group had information of great importance before it. The statistics on the promotions from the bargaining unit to management, the absence of black promotions in the reorganization, the decrease in black representation on personnel committees, and the outbreaks of blatant racism during the strike established a pattern whose meaning no member of the group denied.

At the same meeting, however, members also received a report summarizing the research that had been conducted to evaluate the race relations improvement program since its beginning. With data that had been collected six months before the strike began, the report confirmed black members' experience of increased racial tension at the boundary between management and bargaining unit. But otherwise, the research report presented a rather favorable picture of the changes that had occurred over the life of the program from 1976 to 1984. The group was faced with a complex pattern of data indicating a serious short-term problem coupled with a long-term pattern of significant improvement.

The meeting in which this complex pattern of data came together was probably one of the most difficult in the history of the group. Black and white members openly questioned whether their efforts had been in vain. For some people who had been with the group since its beginning, the anguish was especially powerful. Black members talked openly of leaving the committee in order to pursue a more confrontational approach to change. The senior white members of the group who had participated in the mobility decisions that so disturbed the group experienced a special form of stress. Despite the strength of emotions, however, people did stay together. Strong words were spoken, and people listened. As strongly held views were expressed, members were also able to express their respect for each other's willingness to listen. In the end, the group stayed together, differences between black and white members over how active the "advisory" group should be vanished, and in subsequent meetings the group worked with members of the personnel department in forming an objective setting process that eventually will produce concrete numerical targets for recruitment, promotions, and personnel committee membership for all departments in the corporation.

QUANTITATIVE ANALYSES OF ADVISORY GROUP BEHAVIOR AND ATTITUDES

Throughout the life of the advisory group we kept careful records of attendance and periodically administered a short form of the diagnostic questionnaire to the members. The attendance information was kept in the advisory group minutes, where members could see the data and correct any errors they observed. The questionnaire consisted of a series of items designed to measure perceptions of racism in the organization and a number of open-ended questions to give members an opportunity to respond to the change processes in their own terms.

Table 5 shows the proportion of members in each race group and in each race-gender subgroup who attended advisory group meetings during the seven years from 1980 through 1986. For six of seven years, blacks had a higher proportion of their members present than whites. However, the difference in proportions was only especially notable in 1982, when the proportion of blacks was 0.90 and whites was 0.65. In 1985, the pattern reversed with a slightly higher proportion of whites than blacks attending. The largest mean subgroup difference, which was nearly 20 points, was between black women and white women, and in each of the seven years a higher proportion of black women than white women attended advisory group meetings. This translates to having approximately one more black woman than white woman present at each advisory group meeting. There is also a drop in overall attendance after the first two years from a

Table 5. Race Relations Advisory Group Attendance Patterns: Proportion of Members Present by Year and Race Gender Subgroup

Year	Number of Meetings	Black Men	Black Women	Black	White Men	White Women	White	Annual Mean
1980	7	.83	.94	.88	.89	.86	.87	.88
1981	8	.94	.91	.92	.94	.74	.84	.88
1982	2	.80	1.00	.90	.60	.70	.65	.78
1983	5	.76	.80	.78	.64	.64	.64	.71
1984	5	.68	.92	.80	.74	.68	.71	.76
1985	8	.52	.75	.64	.75	.72	.74	.68
1986	5	.72	.76	.74	.86	.52	.69	.72
Means	5.7	.75	.87	.81	.77	.69	.73	.77

proportion of 0.88 of all members to 0.74 in the next two years to an average of 0.72 in subsequent years.

Table 6 present the intercorrelations among the seven items that comprise the perception of racism scale. The median inter-item correlation is 0.44, and the Spearman-Brown reliability estimate is .85. All items correlate at .50 or higher with the total scale. There is solid evidence that the scale is highly reliable.

Table 7 shows the means of each race-gender subgroup as a function the meeting date when the measurement was taken. The black subgroups are higher than their white counterparts in every comparison (p < .0001, sign test). To test for the effects of administration date, we performed a race by date analysis of variance with repeated measures on the race-gender subgroups, shown in Table 8. The results indicate that the change in perceptions of racism by the group as a whole was significant ($F_{6,12} = 5.55$, p < .025). In addition, the Newman Keuls procedure shown in Table 9 performed on the time series data indicated that the mean of May 1983 was lower than that of March 1982, thus suggesting a significant reduction of perceived racism during the period of crisis and realignment. Although the statistical tests are not powerful enough to substantiate the trend, the pattern of subgroup changes shown in Figure 1 clearly suggests that the overall increase in perceived racism stems from changes by the white subgroup—perhaps especially among the white women. At every comparison the white women perceived more racism than white men (p < .0001, sign test).

Table 6. Perception of Racism Scale:
Single Items and Total Scale Correlations
(n = 111)

	Item 1	Item 2	Item 3	Item 4	Item 5	Item 6	Item 7
1. Most managers at XYZ are biased against blacks.	1.0						
2. Blacks expect too much. (reverse scored)	−.14	1.0					
3. Whites are given greater promotional opportunities that blacks.	.31	−.43	1.0				
4. Whites cannot deal with competent blacks.	.31	−.43	.49	1.0			
5. XYZ has already done too much on black-white issues. (reverse scored)	−.43	.31	−.45	−.44	1.0		
6. Race relations within XYZ are good. (reverse scored)	−.26	.23	−.44	−.44	.28	1.0	
7. Blacks are almost never evaluated fairly by white supervisors.	.36	−.49	.70	.66	−.52	−.48	1.0
TOTAL SCALE	−.50	.61	−.78	−.79	.65	.64	−.87

Table 7. Race Relations Advisory Group Perceptions of Racism: Race-Gender Subgroup Means, Standard Deviations, and Sample Size by Date of Questionnaire Administration

Date	Black Men	Black Women	White Men	White Women	Meeting Means
1. May 1980	$\bar{X}$ = 5.0 S = .37 n = 5	$\bar{X}$ = 5.0 S = .82 n = 3	$\bar{X}$ = 3.5 S = .65 n = 5	$\bar{X}$ = 3.9 S = .87 n = 5	4.3
2. July 1980	$\bar{X}$ = 5.1 S = .54 n = 4	$\bar{X}$ = 4.9 S = .65 n = 5	$\bar{X}$ = 3.7 S = .64 n = 5	$\bar{X}$ = 4.0 S = .69 n = 4	4.4
3. November 1980	$\bar{X}$ = 5.1 S = .46 n = 5	$\bar{X}$ = 5.0 S = .48 n = 5	$\bar{X}$ = 4.0 S = .71 n = 5	$\bar{X}$ = 4.2 S = .49 n = 5	4.6
4. February 1981	$\bar{X}$ = 5.3 S = .33 n = 4	$\bar{X}$ = 5.0 S = .50 n = 3	$\bar{X}$ = 4.1 S = .91 n = 2	$\bar{X}$ = 4.4 S = .38 n = 4	4.7
5. May 1981	$\bar{X}$ = 5.1 S = .44 n = 4	$\bar{X}$ = 5.2 S = .14 n = 4	$\bar{X}$ = 4.0 S = 1.03 n = 4	$\bar{X}$ = 4.8 S = .49 n = 4	4.8
6. March 1982	$\bar{X}$ = 5.2 S = .36 n = 4	$\bar{X}$ = 5.3 S = .53 n = 4	$\bar{X}$ = 4.6 S = 1.06 n = 4	$\bar{X}$ = 4.9 S = .91 n = 2	5.0
7. May 1983	$\bar{X}$ = 4.9 S = .30 n = 3	$\bar{X}$ = 5.1 S = .62 n = 3	$\bar{X}$ = 3.4 S = 0 n = 1	$\bar{X}$ = 4.5 S = .30 n = 2	4.5
Subgroup Means	5.1	5.1	3.9	4.4	4.6 GRAND MEAN

Black Mean 5.1
White Mean 4.1

Male Mean 4.5
Female Mean 4.7

311

Table 8. Two-Way Analysis of Variance
with Repeated Measures of Perceived Racism
by Race-Gender Subgroups

	df	MS	F	p
Between subgroups				
Race	1	6.22	14.80	$<.10$
Subgroups within groups	2	.42		
Within subgroups				
Date	6	.20	5.55	$<.025$
Race $\times$ Date	6	.07	1.94	n.s.
Date $\times$ Subgroups within groups	12	.036		

The open-ended section of the advisory group questionnaire consisted of three questions:

1. Based on what you now understand about race relations in corporate management, what issues have the most personal impact on your work life?
2. In your opinion, what would be the *most effective* thing that corporate management could do to improve race relations in management?
3. In your opinion, what would be the *worst* thing that corporate management could do to improve race relations in management?

Content coding systems were developed for question 1 and for questions 2 and 3.

Table 9. Tests on Meeting Date Means of Perceived Racism
Using Newman Keuls Procedure

Dates	May 1980 t_1	July 1980 t_2	May 1983 t_7	Nov. 1980 t_3	Feb. 1981 t_4	May 1981 t_5	March 1982 t_6
Ordered means	4.3	4.4	4.5	4.6	4.7	4.8	5.0
t_1	—	.1*	.2*	.3*	.4*	.5*	.7*
t_2		—	.2*	.2*	.3*	.4*	.6*
t_7			—	.1(ns)	.2*	.3*	.5*
t_4				—	.1(ns)	.2*	.4*
t_5					—	.1(ns)	.3*
t_6						—	.2*
r		2	3	4	5	6	7
$q_{.95}(r,12)$		3.09	3.27	4.20	4.51	4.75	4.95
$S_{\overline{date}}[q_{.95}(r,12)]$		.07	.09	.10	.11	.11	.12

*p $<$ .05

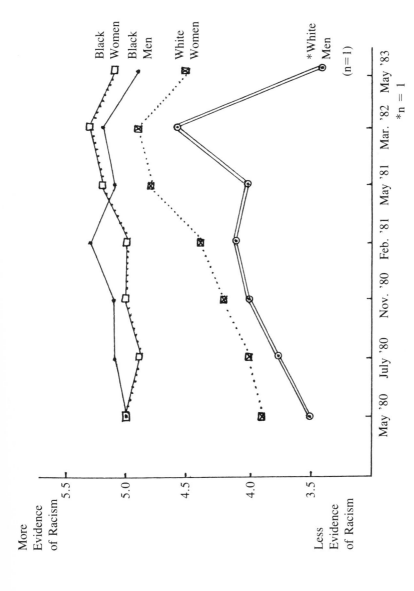

Figure 1. Race Relations Advisory Group Perceptions of Racism: Race-Gender Subgroups Means by Date of Questionnaire Administration.

Table 10.   Distribution of Responses by Unit
of Attention for Issues that Have Most
Personal Impact on Work Life

	Blacks	Whites
Self as individual	6	12
Own racial group	5	4
Self and own racial group	4	1
Other racial group	14	7
Relationship of racial groups	6	1
Corporate organization groups	8	5
None of the above	11	21

Responses to question 1 were scored according to three levels of analysis: (1) level of attention, (2) direction of movement, and (3) subject of learning. The reliability of coding responses to question 1, measured by Tau B as recommended by Dollard and Auld (1956), was .51 ($p < .02$), .52 ($p < .002$), and .38 ($p < .05$), respectively, based on black and white coders working independently.

Table 10 shows the distributions of responses by level of attention from black and white members of the advisory group across the seven administrations of the questionnaire. The distributions of responses among the categories are significantly different for blacks and whites ($X^2 = 13.64$, df $= 6$, $p < .05$). White members reported more learning about themselves as individuals, while black members give more responses about themselves and their own racial group. Blacks more than whites also indicated that their understanding increased with respect to the white group and with respect to various corporate groups, most of whom have white dominance. Table 11 shows the distributions of responses by direction of movement. For this category there are no differences between black and white response distributions; both groups report their greatest learning on the

Table 11.   Distribution of Responses
by Direction of Movement for Issues
that have Most Personal Impact on
Work Life

	Blacks	Whites
Resistance to change	28	22
Progressive movement	9	10
Dialectic movement	5	8
No sense of change	12	11

Table 12.   Distribution of Responses by Subject of
Learning for Issues that Have Most Personal Impact
on Work Life

	Blacks	*Whites*
Evaluations and promotions	26	11
Organization norms and culture	9	2
Knowledge and skill in race relations	10	14
Racism	3	8
Other	6	16

matter of resistance to change. Table 12 shows the distributions of responses by subject of learning. This category has different distributions of responses for blacks and whites ($X^2 = 17.91$, df = 4, p < .001). Blacks report learning more about promotions and evaluations and about the effects of organization norms and culture, while whites say they learn more about racism and about knowledge and skill in race relations.

Responses to questions 2 and 3 were scored according to inductively derived categories. The reliability of these categories, measured by Tau B, was .56 (p < .001), based upon black and white coders working independently. (Note: To convert Tau B into a scale comparable to the product moment correlation, take the square root.) Table 13 shows the distribution of responses to question 2 in terms of the most frequently used categories. There are no statistically significant differences between the racial groups. Table 14 shows the distribution of responses to question 3 in terms of the most frequently used categories. Blacks show a clear tendency to believe more than whites that the worst thing the corporation might do to improve race relations would be to do nothing or to take superficial actions ($\chi^2 = 11.59$, df = 1, p<.001).

Finally, Table 15 shows how members of the advisory group were distributed

Table 13.   Distribution of Responses to Most Effective
Corporate Action to Improve Race Relations

	Blacks	*Whites*
Place blacks in all departments and levels	12	5
Start new programs on race relations	10	12
Discipline managers who commit racist actions	5	2
Mandate improved race relations	7	6
Continue current programs to improve race relations	7	5
Speed-up current efforts to improve race relations	5	2
Other	11	17

Table 14.   Distribution of Responses to Worst
Corporate Actions to Improve Race Relations

	Blacks	*Whites*
Do nothing or carry out superficial efforts	40	19
Other	18	33

throughout the corporate hierarchy during each year of the project. White members representing each level are present each year. Black members represent levels I to IV from 1980 to 1983 and, in 1984, add a person to level V. To provide a rough estimate of the hierarchical position of blacks and whites in the group, we compute the average level for both racial groups for each year. Both groups show slight increases over the duration of the project. Among group members, one black man, three black women, one white man, and three white women were promoted while they served on the group. Other changes in the distribution occur because levels differed between people who left the group and others who replaced them.

Table 15.   Advisory Group Membership by Hierarchical
Level as a Function of Time

	1980	*1981*	*1982*	*1983*	*1984*
Black Level I	4	4	4	5	2
II	3	3	2	1	3
III	2	1	3	1	2
IV	1	1	2	3	3
V	0	0	0	0	1
VI	0	0	0	0	0
Mean Black Level	2.0	1.9	2.2	2.2	2.4
White Level I	3	3	2	2	1
II	2	2	2	3	3
III	2	2	1	1	2
IV	1	1	2	2	2
V	1*	1*	1*	1*	1
VI	2	2	2	2	2*
Mean White Level	3.1	3.1	3.4	3.3	3.4
Mean Total Level	2.6	2.6	2.8	2.9	2.9

*Chairperson

OVERVIEW OF DEVELOPMENTAL PROCESSES

As a microcosm of corporate management designed to change race relations, the advisory group demonstrated dialectical conflict and parallel processes throughout its history. Splitting the group into race- and gender-alike subgroups was a structural mechanism that permitted different perceptions and preferences to emerge as these were useful for the tasks of the group. Changes of behavior within the group reflected changes in the larger organization, and, in turn, changes in the group could bring about changes in the organization.

The attitude measures taken periodically through the life of the group indicated that black members consistently saw more racism in the organization than white members. Evidence for change during the first two phases of the group's history indicated that white women and men showed an increase in the degree of racism they perceived. Taking the data at face value, one might conclude that this change indicated an improvement in race relations in the organization. Yet, a fuller examination of events at the time gives a more complex interpretation. At the time in question, members of the advisory group were raising questions about the future of the project, the person to be chair of the group was in doubt, leadership of the personnel department was changing, the upward mobility program was facing severe resistance from the organization, and members of the advisory group were learning about the presence of a white supremacist group in the organization. These conditions indicated that major forces for change through the upward mobility program and the race relations competence workshop were facing significant resistance. Thus, the decrease in racism noted for all four subgroups is more accurately interpreted as a balance of favorable change combined with significant resistance. Pressures from the organization were pushing race relations more toward the predominantly white as well as toward a dialectical view during the third phase of the group's life; parallel processes were flowing strongly from the organization to the advisory group as well as from the group to the organization. This manner of interpretation makes use of the full range of information available to the researcher, not just the questionnaire data.

From the historical material, there was evidence of a complex relationship among the internal dynamics of the advisory group, the tasks the group was carrying out, and the external relations of the group. In its first phase, the group had a clear mandate from the organization to advise about the corporation's race relations improvement program. To become an effective group, the members had to establish their own agreements about the meaning of improved race relations. During this period, there was considerable strain among black and white members; consultants and group; and chairperson and group. A similar pattern was observed when staff from corporate communications worked with the group. By the end of this period, however, the group had established its way of working, and after helping create three important products (the race relations competence document, the race relations workshop, and the upward mobility program) it was poised to observe the effects of these efforts. During this period, the advisory group initially absorbed the racial conditions of the organization, transformed them through their own internal work, and then attempted to project them outward into the corporation.

In the middle phases, the group dealt with the organization's response to the interventions. During the second phase the group provided feedback to the chairperson, the consultants, the Black Managers Association, and the board of directors about how the various projects were unfolding. As their products moved outward into the organization, the role of the group became more passive and inevitably less creative. Attendance dropped; meetings were canceled; some members left the group; and attention turned to the joint tasks of self-assessment and project review. The third phase found the organization's processes once again affecting the group and the intervention program as corporate changes in mission and leadership intersected with resistance to the intervention program to produce a major crisis. In this period, the group served as a major stabilizing force by serving as a living source of program history. The questions that members raised with the new leadership provided a major corrective stimulus and helped to improve conditions under which the intervention continued. While the efforts of several key individuals were most important during this phase, the group provided another order of support without which it seems unlikely the program would have survived. The third phase was a time of the group's parallel processes projecting outward in a relatively narrow and precise manner to the new leadership of the personnel department. The working through of authority issues that had initially been done inside the group among members, chairperson, and consultants was carried outside the project to include several senior members of corporate management.

In the fourth phase, with the group again confident of its place in the corporation, new programmatic initiatives were observed. The mode of working in cross-race cross-gender task forces was well established. Projects to establish a strong corporate policy on race relations and to undertake a communications program about race relations were successfully pursued. Movements to place more responsibility for the program with organization members and less with consultants were begun. The group was repeatedly in a position of projecting its style of race relations outward to the whole organization, while relating receptively to the differences in perspective and preference represented by the larger system.

The years of 1985 and 1986 marked another period of both strain and opportunity for the race relations improvement program. During these two years, a number of different indicators showed either reduced rates of progress or decided signs of regression. This pattern may be explained by a combination of two kinds of powerful forces. First, as the corporation continued to adjust to its new business environment, the energy of senior executives who were supportive of changing race relations was inevitably drawn to other matters—at least temporarily. The chief measure of this was the inattention to departmental objectives for mobility at all levels of the organization. A member of the advisory group said at the time, "When everyone is responsible, no one is responsible." Second, the notable changes that had occurred by the end of 1984 set off a new round of resistance. The form of this opposition was the belief that the corporation had made clear progress and could afford to be less attentive to matters of race relations. For many kinds of problems that large organizations face, this kind of framework is sound. But not for race relations in the United States. On this issue, the historical pattern is cyclical. Because an organization inevitably reflects its external environment, the regressive changes taking place in the country as a whole were bound to appear inside the corporation. By the end of 1986, members of the advisory group had more fully incorporated the concept of cyclical change into their understanding of what it takes to change race relations. Utilizing this concept to them meant setting objectives in a manner that includes a five-year historical perspective and therefore identifies and responds to regressive phases promptly.

In sum, the seven-year history of the Race Relations Advisory Group documents developmental phases in the life of the body. Observations about the group pertain to internal dynamics, tasks, and external relations (Gersick, 1983). Key transition events involve negotiations with authorities who have a relationship with the group—the chairperson, the consultants, leadership of the personnel department, top management, and the board of directors. Each of these transactions, when it proceeded fruitfully, marked progressive movement in the group's effect on race relations in the corporation. Setbacks in successive stages also were evident and substantiated the concept of change as a cyclical, dialectical process. We now have evidence for adding a temporal dimension to the intergroup theory of changing race relations in organizations and for relating phases in the change processes to how groups are embedded in suprasystems.

ACKNOWLEDGMENTS

We thank Jack Gillette, Ed Mayhew, David Thomas, and the editors of this volume for their helpful comments on earlier versions of this chapter. This research was made possible by the office of Naval Research, Contract N00014-82-K-0715, for which we express our appreciation.

REFERENCES

Alderfer, C. (1976). Change processes in organizations. In M. D. Dunnette (Ed.), *Handbook of industrial and organizational psychology*. Chicago: Rand-McNally, 1591–1638.
Alderfer, C. (1977). Improving organization communication through long-term intergroup intervention. *Journal of Applied Behavioral Science, 13,* 193–210.

Alderfer, C. (1986). An intergroup perspective on group dynamics. In J. Lorsch (Ed.), *Handbook of organizational behavior*. Englewood Cliffs, NJ: Prentice-Hall, 190–222.

Alderfer, C., Alderfer, C., Tucker, L., & Tucker, R. (1980). Diagnosing race relations in management. *Journal of Applied Behavioral Science, 16,* 135–166.

Alderfer, C. & Smith, K. (1982). Studying intergroup relations embedded in organizations. *Administrative Science Quarterly, 27,* 35–65.

Alderfer, C., Tucker, R., Morgan, D., & Drasgow, F. (1983). Black and white cognitions of changing race relations in management. *Journal of Occupational Behavior, 4,* 105–136.

Alvarez, R., Lutterman, K. & Associates (1979). *Discrimination in organizations*. San Francisco, CA: Jossey-Bass.

Aronson, E. (1978). *The jigsaw classroom*. Beverly Hills, CA: Sage.

Aronson, E. (1984). A missionary for social psychology. *Psychology Today, 18,* 40–45.

Baldwin, J. & Mead, M. (1970). *A rap on race*. New York: Dell.

Bennett, L., Jr. (1962). *Before the Mayflower*. Baltimore, MD: Penguin.

Bennis, W. & Shepard, H. (1956). A theory of group development. *Human Relations, 9,* 415–438.

Bettelheim, B. (1960). *The informed heart*. New York: Free Press.

Binkin, M., Eitelberg, M., Schexnider, A., & Smith, M. (1982). *Blacks and the military*. Washington, D.C.: Brookings Institution.

Bradford, L. (1967). Biography of an institution. *Journal of Applied Behavioral Science, 3,* 127–143.

Campbell, A. (1971). *White attitudes toward black people*. Ann Arbor, MI: Institute for Social Research.

Carmichael, S. & Hamilton, C. (1967). *Black power*. New York: Vintage.

Clark, C. (1973). The role of the white researcher in black society. *Journal of Social Issues, 29,* 1–11; 109–118.

Clark, K. & Clark, M. (1939). Racial identification and preference in Negro children. In E. E. Macoby, T. M. Newcomb, and E. L. Hartley (Eds.), *Readings in social psychology*, (3rd Ed.). New York: Holt, Rinehart and Winston, 602–611.

Cohen, E. (1984). Design and redesign of the desegregated school: problems of status, power, and conflict. In W. Stephan and J. Feagin (Eds.), *School desegregation*. New York: Plenum, 251–280.

Davis, G. & Watson, G. (1982). *Black life in corporate America*. New York: Doubleday.

Dollard, J. & Auld, F. (1956). *Scoring human motives*. New Haven, CT: Yale.

Gersick, C. (1983). Life cycles of ad hoc groups. Technical Report No. 4. New Haven, CT: Yale School of Organization and Management.

Griffin, J. (1960). *Black like me*. New York: Signet.

Hochschild, J. (1984). *The new American dilemma: Liberal democracy and school desegregation*. New Haven, CT: Yale.

Holt, T. (1980). Afro-Americans. In S. Thernstrom (Ed.), *Harvard encyclopedia of American ethnic groups*. Cambridge, MA: Harvard, 5–23.

Jones, J. (1972). *Prejudice and racism*. Reading, MA: Addison-Wesley.

Kerner, O. & Lindsay, J. (1968). *Report on the National Advisory Commission on Civil Disorders*. New York: E. P. Dutton.

Landis, D., Hope, R., & Day, H. (1984). Training for desegregation in the military. In N. Miller and M. Brewer (Eds.), *Groups in contact*. New York: Academic, 257–278.

Marris, P. (1974). *Loss and change*. New York: Pantheon.

McDonald, M. (1987). Rights fight: only the faces change. *USA Today*, March 25, 2A.

Myrdal, G. (1944). *An American dilemma*. New York: Pantheon.

Rice, A. (1969). Individual, group, and intergroup processes. *Human Relations, 22,* 565–584.

Roethlisberger, F., & Dickson, W. (1939). *Management and the worker*. New York: Wiley.

Sarason, S. (1981). *Psychology misdirected*. New York: Free Press.

Schuman, H. & Hatchett, S. (1974). *Black racial attitudes: Trends and complexities*. Ann Arbor: Survey Research Center.

Searles, H. (1955). The informational value of the supervisor's emotional experiences. *Psychiatry, 18,* 135–146.

Silberman, C. (1964). *Crisis in black and white*. New York: Vintage.

Star, S. A., Williams, R. M., and Stouffer, S. A. (1949). Negro soldiers. In S. A. Stouffer, E. A. Suchman, L. C. DeVinney, S. A. Star, and R. M. Williams, *The American Soldier: Adjustment During Army Life*. New York: Wiley, 486–599.

Yardley, J. (1987). Ignorance feeds racial hostilities on campus. *New Haven Register,* March 27, 15.

abandon it after a short trial. These situations certainly exist, I personally could point to a number that are not reported in the literature.

There are some important exceptions to the general point about poor research that are worth mentioning. Schuster (1984a) has done a longitudinal study of the Scanlon Plan, and White (1979) has analyzed the experience of 22 companies with the Scanlon Plan. Goodman and Moore (1976) have also done a longitudinal study of the Scanlon Plan. Bullock and Bullock (1982) have provided longitudinal data on two custom-designed plans. Importantly, the better studies tend to report the same results as do the less well designed ones. Because there are a large number of studies that report gainsharing plans are successful, there are some high-quality research studies that document successful plans, and some gainsharing plans have been operating for over 30 years, it seems reasonable to conclude that gainsharing plans can and do work. Of course, it is important to have better evidence, but given its absence the most appropriate conclusion is that gainsharing can work.

Bullock and Lawler (1984) in their review provide some further data on how plans are structured and installed. They report, for example, that the typical plan pays out monthly, focuses on labor costs, shares over 50 percent of the gain with the employees and is implemented by a consultant with the involvement of the employees. A more recent study by O'Dell (1987) reports similar findings as well as data which suggest the typical plan pays bonuses that range from 5 to 10 percent of base pay, covers most employees in the organizational unit where they are installed, and are in organizational units with less than 5,000 employees. Unfortunately, no study has related features of the plan and its implementation to plan success. Thus, although we know something about how plans are structured and implemented little data exist on how these are related to success.

Quite a bit has been written about how to structure gainsharing plans. There are several books and articles that describe in some detail how to put together formulas, how to introduce plans, and how to manage the process side of gainsharing plans (see, for example, Moore & Ross, 1978). "How-to-do-it" knowledge is particularly available with respect to the Scanlon Plan. Indeed, a careful reading of the literature on the Scanlon Plan should make it possible for the skilled practitioner to develop and install a plan without the help of a consultant.

Some writings exist that deal with the situational factors that favor gainsharing plans. Table 3 describes 20 situational factors that are hypothesized to favor the plan (Lawler, 1981). White (1979) found that participation and managerial attitudes are critical to the success of gainsharing plans. Overall, little research has been done on just how many of the conditions in Table 3 need to be present in order to have a successful gainsharing plan. In fact, gainsharing plans have been successful even though many of these conditions are not present (e.g., Bullock & Bullock, 1982). When gainsharing is used in a lead sense, the objective often is to bring the organization toward such conditions as openness, participative management, and good, competent management. It is obvious, however, that some conditions are necessary for establishing a gainsharing plan. For example, it is virtually impossible to have a gainsharing plan without good performance measures, and in organized settings, union approval is needed. Thus, it seems reasonable to conclude that gainsharing cannot be put into some situations.

It also seems reasonable to hypothesize that the more the conditions listed in Table 3 are present the more likely it is that gainsharing will work. There may be an interesting twist to the issue of what conditions need to be present for a gainsharing plan to work. If all the conditions in Table 3 are present it may be that there is little need for a gainsharing plan and thus although the probability of success is high when they are present the amount of gain possible is small. This certainly fits my own experience with installing gainsharing plans. When most of

Table 3. Conditions Favoring Gainsharing Plans

Organizational Characteristic	Favorable Condition
Size	Small unit, usually less than 500 employees
Age	Old enough so that learning curve has flattened and standards can be set based on performance history
Financial measures	Simple, with a good history
Market for output	Good, can absorb additional production
Product costs	Controllable by employees
Organizational climate	Open, high level of trust
Style of management	Participative
Union status	No union, or one that is favorable to a cooperative effort
Overtime history	Limited or no use of overtime
Seasonal nature of business	Relatively stable across time
Work floor interdependence	High to moderate interdependence
Capital investment plans	Little investment planned
Product stability	Few product changes
Comptroller/Chief financial officer	Trusted, able to explain financial measures
Communication policy	Open, willing to share financial results
Plant manager	Trusted, committed to plan able to articulate goals and ideals of plan
Management	Technically competent, supportive of participative management style, good communication skills, able to deal with suggestions and new ideas
Corporate position (if part of larger organization)	Favorable to plan
Work force	Technically knowledgeable, interested in participation and higher pay, financially knowledgeable and/or interested
Plant support services	Maintenance and engineering groups competent, willing, and able to respond to increased demands

Table 4. Frequent Problems With Gainsharing Plans

1. *Formula structure.* The formula needs to accurately measure what is going on in the organization. Rigid formulas that do not reflect employee behavior are developed and lead to failure because employees see no relationship between performance and reward.

2. *Formula change.* The formula needs to change as the products, technology, and activities of organizations change. Rigid plans that do not put in place a process to allow for change often fail when change is called for.

3. *Payout level.* It is important that some bonuses be paid, particularly at the beginning. Sometimes this does not happen because the performance level that must be achieved before a bonus is paid is set too high.

4. *Management attitudes.* Unless managers are favorable to the idea of participation, the plan will not fit the management style of the organization. In some organizations, the plan has been tried simply as a pay incentive plan without regard to the management style, and it has failed because of a poor fit.

5. *Plan focus.* Many plans focus only on labor savings. This presents problems in organizations where other costs are great and are under the control of the employees. It can lead to the other costs being ignored or even increased in order to reduce labor costs.

6. *Communication.* For the plan to work, employees must understand and trust it enough to believe that their pay will increase if they perform better. For this belief to occur, a great deal of open communication and education is needed. Often this is ignored and, as a result, plans fail.

7. *Union cooperation.* The local union must be supportive. In most of the places where it has been tried, the local union has supported it. However, some failures have occurred in situations where unions have not supported it sufficiently.

8. *Threat to supervisor.* The plan changes the roles of supervisors. They are forced to deal with many suggestions, and their competence is tested and questioned in new ways. Unless supervisors are prepared for and accept these changes, the plan can fail. This point goes along with the general point that management must be prepared to manage in a different way.

9. *Participative structure.* This requires congruent participative structures. Sometimes these are not put in place or they are poorly managed and as a result the plan fails because as an incentive plan gainsharing is a relatively weak intervention.

the conditions listed in Table 3 are present the plans have worked but the gains have been smaller than those cited in the GAO study. On the other hand, when they haven't been present and the gainsharing plans have been used in a lead sense, they haven't always worked, but when they have, the gains have been large (see, for example, Bullock & Bullock, 1982).

Finally, as is shown in Table 4, quite a bit has been written about why some gainsharing plans don't work and which obstacles they have to overcome in order to succeed in many situations (Bullock & Lawler, 1984; Lawler, 1981; White, 1979). As can be seen, they often are resisted by managers who see their authority and competence challenged. They also put people in new roles that they may not be comfortable with.

In summary, there is considerable information available concerning the effectiveness and suitability of gainsharing plans. Much of what is known indicates that they can improve organizational effectiveness. It is precisely because of this that it is important to learn more about them.

NEED TO KNOW: THEORY AND RESEARCH

There are a number of interesting theoretical and research questions that remain unanswered about the workings of gainsharing plans. The following questions, in particular, need to be answered if gainsharing plans are to be improved and if more is to be known from a theoretical point of view about why and how they affect organizations.

Why Do They Work?

Relatively little is known about why gainsharing plans work. Their proponents cite numerous reasons, including the fact that they operate as effective pay incentive plans, they stimulate problem solving, they cause people to work smarter, they cause social pressures that encourage people to be good performers, they cause other organizational changes which contribute to organizational effectiveness, and they create organizational goals that lead to teamwork and cooperation. These may all be reasons why gainsharing plans work, but at this point, little research has been done which documents this and identifies the relative importance of the different reasons why gainsharing works. In fact, it is quite possible that they work for different reasons in different situations. Such factors as technology and organizational size may well influence why and how a plan will work. In addition, little has been done to determine if there are other reasons why gainsharing plans might have a positive or negative impact on organizational effectiveness.

Particularly interesting are questions having to do with what a bonus formula contributes to participative management and vice versa. The congruence argument, which is largely untested, suggests that either alone has little impact but that together they are quite powerful (Lawler, 1986). If this is true, it offers important support for the argument that organization change efforts should affect multiple systems. Partial support for this argument is provided by the data on the institutionalization of gainsharing plans. Most studies that have reviewed gainsharing plans have noted that some survive for many years (e.g., GAO, 1981; O'Dell, 1987). This is in contrast to the relatively short-term effectiveness of participative management programs such as quality circles (Lawler, 1986) and many pay incentive systems (Lawler, 1981).

What is needed are research data that look at gainsharing plans longitudinally and track the kinds of organizational, individual motivational, and normative or cultural changes which they bring about. Particular attention needs to be paid to the sequence of these changes and how important they are in influencing organizational effectiveness.

What Works Best: Formula

Theory and research are almost completely lacking on how an organization should go about choosing a formula and which formula is likely to work best. Proponents of different formulas (e.g., Scanlon, Rucker) and different approaches to formula construction often claim that their approaches are best. Still others sometimes claim the formula makes little difference. This point ties back to the issue of why and how gainsharing works. Formula development ought to focus on building in features that support the reasons plans work. It probably is true that the best formula for one situation is not the best for another, but no guidelines and little relevant theory and research exist to aid the choice.

Particularly interesting are some of the issues raised by the development of custom formulas. A case can be made that the most effective approach is to develop a custom formula for each situation so that it fits the conditions existing there, the organization can learn how to develop a formula, and commitment to the chosen one is created. However, it takes longer to develop a custom formula than it does to buy an off-the-shelf approach like the Improshare formula. At the extreme, I have seen off-the-shelf formulas installed in a day and I have seen custom plans take years. Thus an argument for a custom formula must deal with the issue of the extra development costs it involves.

The development of complex custom formulas raises some interesting questions about training and culture building. Little is known about just how complex a formula can be and still be understood and accepted. The key probably is that the formula be seen as fair and that awareness be developed of what individuals can do to influence the bonus payment. Unfortunately, little is known about why and how formulas come to be seen as fair and influencable despite the fact that this seems to be a key to their being successful. Studying this in an organization could represent a way to learn about gainsharing and a way to learn about how organizational cultures incorporate major organizational changes.

The need for research on formulas is particularly acute in the case of service organizations. They may require very different formulas because of the importance of customer service. It is quite possible that the wrong formula could lead to a short-term reduction in costs but to long-term reductions in business because of a reduction in customer service. It is possible that service quality can be measured and included in the formula in order to prevent this problem but little is known about the effectiveness of this approach. At the very least work is needed on the validity of different measures of service quality and on how to include measures of it in a gainsharing formula.

What Works Best: Process

Little is known about the key process issues that are involved in the installation and maintenance of a gainsharing plan. The variance in how different plans are installed in considerable. The Scanlon plan typically calls for a vote by all employees while custom plans often are developed by representative task forces. The Improshare plan, on the other hand, is typically developed by consultants and presented to the organization for acceptance or rejection.

It is sometimes hypothesized that particular processes are best for designing and installing a gainsharing plan, but research simply has not focused on this. For example, a theoretical case can be made for the importance of a participative design process. Among other things it is congruent with the participative philosophy of the plan, and it should help the organization if it needs to redesign the plan at a later time.

If it turns out that a participative design process is important, it would be nice to know how and why it is important. Is it because it leads to better understanding of gainsharing plans? Is it because it leads to an extra commitment to making it work? Or, is it simply because when participation takes place better information is developed, and a better plan results?

Congruence Issues

A great deal has been written about the importance of combining gainsharing with participative management. As was noted earlier, gainsharing plans such as the Scanlon Plan in fact prescribe a particular approach to participative management. As might be expected, research does show that most gainsharing formulas are installed in conjunction with an approach to participative management (O'Dell, 1987). However, little is known from both theory and research about the best forms of participative management for use in conjunction with gainsharing plans. There is virtually no research to guide in choosing the right form of participation to fit with gainsharing. The Scanlon Plan, for example, prescribes written suggestions and problem-solving groups, but is this in fact the most effective form of participation? It may well be in the case of simple labor-only plans, like the Improshare plan, but it may not be in the case of more complex plans like many of the complex multicost plans which exist. Overall, there are a whole set of issues concerning management style and its fit with gainsharing plans that need to be sorted out both conceptually and empirically.

Relatively little also is known about the fit between gainsharing and other parts of the total compensation package in an organization. It has been speculated that it is likely to fit particularly well with such practices as skill-based pay, flexible benefits, and employee ownership (Lawler, 1986). What is needed here is research and theory which help illuminate the congruence issues that are involved in creating a total reward system.

Lag–Lead

As was mentioned earlier, gainsharing can either lag or lead other changes that are designed to increase organizational effectiveness. Relatively little is known about what is most effective in terms of the installation of gainsharing. Should it lag? Should it lead? Or better yet, when and what should it lag or lead? Particularly interesting here are questions concerned with employee involvement and organization culture. One argument is that until trust is established and employees have a chance to input their ideas, having a gainsharing plan makes little sense because employees won't believe it is for real nor will they be able to increase organizational performance. On the other hand, it can be argued that the successful development and installation of a gainsharing plan can build trust and that a suggestion system or other form of employee involvement can be installed at the same time the financial formula is installed. Until these questions are answered and some theory is developed that can help decide the proper sequence for installing gainsharing, a large gap will continue to exist in our knowledge about the dynamics involved.

Research Needs: Conclusion

A great deal more needs to be learned about gainsharing if our understanding of it is to develop further. Research which addresses issues such as why gainsharing plans work, what is the best fit with other management practices, and what process should be used in designing gainsharing plans is critical. However, it is one thing to state that more needs to be known; it is quite another to specify what type of research studies are needed. It is very difficult to do research on complex organizational changes like gainsharing. Still, a great deal more is known about how to do research on organizational change than has been applied by the research on gainsharing.

There clearly is a need for better case studies of successful and unsuccessful gainsharing plans. For case studies to be useful at this point in time they need to be long-term studies. We do not need more after-the-fact reports on ''successful plans.'' We do need studies that track plans over time and studies which collect data from a wide variety of measures. Many of the key questions about gainsharing involve how and when variables impact each other. We can only answer these questions by studying how plans are implemented and by tracking financial, attitudinal, and practice measures over time (Lawler, Nadler, & Cammann, 1980). Of particular interest at this time would be multiple case studies using similar measures but focusing on gainsharing plans in different kinds of organizations and using different formulas.

There also is a need for systematic survey data on the experiences of organizations with gainsharing. This is the only way to get some sense of the frequency with which different approaches work and what organizational conditions are associated with success. This type of research typically is good at answering questions concerned with what works and where it works. None of the existing research provides definitive answers to these types of questions. Since it is based on convenience samples and/or published reports it runs the danger of seriously misrepresenting the popularity and effectiveness of gainsharing plans.

THEORY AND PREDICTIONS

Existing theory and research can be combined to make some testable predictions about the impact of gainsharing. The congruence argument when combined with expectancy theory suggests some specific predictions about when and how gainsharing will work. Congruence theory assumes that an organization's effectiveness is related to the degree that it consistently operates with a particular approach to decision making and power (Nightingale, 1982). This calls for a congruence among the way information, power, knowledge, and rewards are distributed in the organization (Lawler, 1986). The expectancy theory approach to motivation emphasizes the perceived relationship among effort, performance, and rewards. It argues that for a pay system to be effective as a motivator individuals must believe that their effort will lead to valued rewards (Vroom, 1964; Porter & Lawler, 1968).

Gainsharing plans move rewards for organizational performance downwards so that everyone's rewards depend on it. The implicit assumption is that this will change employee behavior in ways that will increase organizational performance. The only way it can change behavior is by affecting motivation since it does little to develop new skills. It follows from what is known about motivation that gainsharing plans will increase organizational performance to the degree that they do the following:

1. Establish the belief that rewards are based on organizational performance.
2. Provide communications about organizational performance to all employees.
3. Establish ways for employees to influence organizational performance as it is measured by the reward system.
4. Create opportunities for employees to learn how to contribute to organizational performance and how to interpret measures of performance.

These four conditions can best be viewed as combining multiplicatively and varying from zero to one. Viewing them as combining in this way is critical because it means that if any of them is completely absent organizational performance will not improve as a result of installing a gainsharing-type bonus. As is frequently noted, gainsharing works only when individuals are motivated to perform differently. If one or more of these is missing, the possibility of a bonus will not affect motivation because no link or line of sight and influence will exist between the bonus reward and the inputs (i.e., effort, ideas) that most people in an organization can control.

Working harder can improve individual performance but it may have a relatively small impact on organizational performance unless the organization already has good work methods and systems. Often improvements in organizational performance require major system and method improvements; without them, increased effort may be wasted and employees frustrated. It is also important to note that gainsharing may not have a major impact on effort. Particularly in large organizations, it does little to increase the relationship between effort and rewards; thus, its impact on motivation may be small or nonexistent.

As has been shown by research, gainsharing typically is more effective when combined with participative management. This follows because in the absence of a participative management approach that gives employees a chance to increase organizational performance through other than working harder, it is difficult to see how they can influence organizational performance in many situations.

Participative management can put into place two key elements: the ability to influence organizational performance through other than putting more effort into immediate job performance, and an understanding and trust of the relationship between improved organizational performance and the gainsharing bonus. In the absence of these, it is unlikely that a perceived connection between improved individual performance and the gainsharing bonus will exist. The one exception to this may be the case of small, relatively simple organizations. There a relationship between individual effort and organizational performance may exist in the absence of a participative management style. In this case a gainsharing-type bonus plan might work as an incentive much like group pay incentive plans have worked for decades.

Turning to the specifics of particular gainsharing plans, the congruence argument suggests that the participative approach used needs to be matched to the type of gainsharing formula used. Most plans advocate suggestion programs of some type. Although suggestion approaches give employees some additional power, they are very limited in the amount of power, knowledge, and information they move downward in the organization. They are, in essence, a parallel structure that does little to change the core operating style of the organization (Lawler, 1986). In this respect they differ appreciably from such approaches as work teams or semi-autonomous groups which push a considerable amount of power and knowledge to the lowest levels of the organization (Hackman & Oldham, 1980). Teams can give employees a chance to influence a number of the decisions that directly influence organizational performance.

The combined congruence-expectancy theory argument leads to some interesting predictions about which approach to participative management is needed to support the different gainsharing formulas. The Improshare formula is the simplest formula since it looks only at hours of work relative to units produced.

Because it is so simple and straightforward it is not difficult to establish a line of sight; employees know if they produce more product by either working smarter or harder they will earn more. Little extra communication and education are needed. Further, individuals do not need to influence many of the decisions which are made in organizations in order to reduce the amount of labor that goes into a product; they can simply work harder or smarter. In short, the Improshare plan has a chance of working as an incentive plan in the absence of a great deal of participation if there is a reasonable level of trust, the organization is relatively small, and the production process relatively simple. Therefore, the use of quality circles or some other suggestion type program is quite appropriate with the Improshare formula since suggestion programs can provide a reasonable vehicle for reducing labor hours through better work methods.

The situation is quite different for gainsharing formulas that look at multiple costs and involve complex computations (e.g., Rucker, multicost custom plans). These formulas cover a number of costs and, the bonuses they produce are influenced by a wide range of factors often including such things as purchasing and pricing decisions. If the employees are to influence the bonuses in this situation, a level of participation that goes far beyond quality circles and written suggestion is needed. They require at least the kind of participation that is present in teams and new design plants (Lawler, 1986).

Other congruence issues come into play with respect to formula choice. The formula needs to fit the type of work the organization does. A labor only formula, for example, fits only those operations where labor costs are dominant and need improvement. Situations where other costs are important need more complex formulas which reflect all the key operating costs. In the absence of a more complex formula there is the real danger that employees will only focus on reducing the measured costs and that the unmeasured costs will increase.

In summary, the congruence approach doesn't argue for a particular formula. Instead it suggests that the formula must measure and reward those things that employees influence, understand, and receive communications about. The prediction is that gainsharing will work best when the formula matches the participative management approach used. Simple formulas will work with suggestion programs while more complex formulas require more participative approaches to management such as teams. This point seems consistent with the finding that gainsharing plans generally have more impact than profit sharing plans (Lawler, 1981; O'Dell, 1987). The latter are typically based on difficult-to-influence measures and often are not combined with an appropriate level of participative management. This point may also help explain the success of the Scanlon Plan and the Improshare Plan. They tend to combine a limited kind of participation with a formula that typically measures only one or a few directly controllable costs.

The arguments so far suggest that an organization's decision to adopt a particular approach to gainsharing needs to be based on a contingency model. It seems clear that the type of plan which is adopted needs to fit the kind of technology and effectiveness issues which the organization faces. For example, organizations which use relatively simple manufacturing technologies and need to get their labor costs down probably can accomplish a great deal by adopting a plan like the Improshare plan. On the other hand, a complex-knowledge work organization that needs to focus on customer satisfaction and on a number of costs is in a different situation. It may need a custom multicost formula and a participative management approach that combines teams, open information, and task forces to study major business issues.

The congruence argument also suggests some predictions about the installation process. The effectiveness of the plan should increase if an organization uses a process which is congruent with the way the organization should operate after the plan is installed. This means that it should be a participative process with open communication and an emphasis on education. This type of process should help the plan be effective for a number of the reasons mentioned earlier. In addition, it should help the organization learn how to be a participatively managed one. The development of the gainsharing plan in effect becomes a learning experience about how to manage participatively. Participation in the design process probably is not as important in the case of the Improshare Plan as it is for more complex formulas. With the Rucker Plan and the complex cost approaches, participation in the design would seem to be necessary in order to develop both understanding and trust.

The congruence approach doesn't necessarily argue for either a lag or lead approach to installing gainsharing. It does argue, however, for installing both a gainsharing bonus plan and participative management since they complement each other. There is some suggestion in the research evidence that there is less tolerance for delaying participation after the formula has been installed than vice versa. A possible reason for this is that without participation there are few gains, so employees quickly become frustrated. On the other hand, the absence of a bonus plan often becomes an issue only after gains are realized and no rewards go to those who produced the gains. In my work on new high involvement plants, I have typically found that pay for organizational performance doesn't become an issue until two to four years after start up (Lawler, 1986; Perkins, Nieva, & Lawler, 1983).

One interesting prediction that was suggested earlier follows from this discussion. As compared to putting gainsharing in a participatively managed organization, if gainsharing is put into a traditionally managed organization the potential for gain is greater, but the chance of success is smaller. This prediction follows from the point that participation and a gainsharing formula are congruent and that the greatest gain results when they are combined. On the other hand, it is difficult to install both at the same time and thus when this is done failure is more likely than when a formula is put into an organization which already has a participative management system. In the later case, however, the potential for gain is smaller because some of the gains that are possible from introducing the combination of a formula and participation may have been realized already as a result of the earlier installation of the participative management system.

Finally, skill-based pay and job security guarantees would appear to be particularly important reward system features to combine with gainsharing. Skill-based pay rewards individuals for learning the kind of skills that are needed to understand and influence organizational performance (Lawler, 1981). Job security is a critical issue because people are asked to participate in reducing costs (i.e., suggestions, working faster) in ways that may eliminate jobs. In the absence of some security guarantee this type of participation is hard to obtain.

A Phases Model

The discussion so far suggests a possible sequential model of gainsharing plan, development, installation, and survival. Like most organizational change efforts, gainsharing has a number of phases, each with its own critical issues and activities.

During the first phase, often called investigation, success depends on the organization getting good information about gainsharing and doing a good diagnosis of the situation, so that proper decision can be made about whether or not to design a plan. This investigatory stage is very important because the information gathered forms the basis for the actual design. Little cultural change is expected during this period, although if the investigation is done in a participative manner, it can signal to the organization that gainsharing is a participative activity.

The next phase is the design process itself. During this period, literally hundreds of small decisions need to be made including formula design, participative system design, planning for training and education, and the specifics of how the payouts will be handled, as well as who is eligible, when the payouts will be made and so forth. Critical here are good decision making and widespread involvement in the design process. At this point, communications with people who are not directly involved in the design process can be quite useful because it makes it easier to win organizational acceptance for the plan. This phase can last for many months if a complex custom plan is being designed. It is the period during which the culture should begin to change.

The third phase is installation. At this point, the plan is presented to the organization for acceptance. Typically, this involves a vote or some demonstrative act on the part of the workforce indicating that it is willing to try the plan. It is critical that this be a strong endorsement because when broad-scale acceptance is lacking it is extremely difficult to get enough organizational change to generate a bonus. Education and training are also critical during this period since this is the first time the organization has actually had a developed plan to present to the workforce. At the end of this period, plan success depends on a large percent of the organization believing the plan can work.

The start up phase is the first time the employees can check their perceptions of the plan against the reality of how the plan operates. Thus, it is particularly critical that during this time period the participative management activities, information sharing, and the other support activities that are committed to actually take place. Failure to match the promises that are part of the plan can lead to an early failure. Also critical here is whether a bonus is paid. The situation with the first few bonus payments is much like the socialization of a new employee. Views are quickly developed about fairness and trust, which are difficult to change because they must be unlearned and new ones learned. Some arguments suggest that at this point, if no bonuses are paid, the plan will fail. This probably is true if individuals feel that performance is improving and no bonus is paid. However, if there is a recognition that performance is not improving, particularly if it is for reasons beyond the control of the people in the organization, then a bonus need not be paid in order for the plan to succeed. Indeed, I have seen plans continue for over two years without ever paying a bonus. Everyone recognized that the organization was in a difficult business situation, and that it would be foolish to pay a bonus.

Finally, most plans enter an institutionalization and maintenance phase. It is during this phase that an oversight or a steering committee needs to consistently monitor the effectiveness of the plan and improve it as indicated. Maintenance is particularly crucial if environmental change occurs and other changes occur that outdate the old formula or the old participative management processes. It is often helpful during this period to do surveys to check on the credibility and development of the plan, and to continue to do economic analysis to see if the formula is producing as it should. The critical issue here is the credibility of the monitoring process and the individuals doing it. If the employees are to believe in the plan, then it is very important that the maintenance and evaluation of the plan be done in a trusted manner.

In some respects, gainsharing plans go through a life cycle much like an organization does. Like an organization, they do not have to die if good maintenance is done along the way. There are plans which have existed for 30–40 years but they have changed so dramatically during that time period that they bear little resemblance to the original plan. The development process is not something that ends with the initial development of a formula. It needs to be a continuing activity of the organization.

Conclusions

Based upon the research and theory discussed so far we can reach some interesting conclusions about what is likely to lead to a successful gainsharing plan in addition to the conditions listed in Table 3. Success should be related to the degree to which the plans:

1. Are installed in an open participative manner.

2. Give employees a chance to understand and influence the measures of organizational performance that are used to compute the bonus.

3. Are combined with skill-based pay and job security.

4. Are managed in a way that is sensitive to the issues which arise at different phases in the development and installation of a plan.

5. Are based upon comprehensive measures that fit the characteristics of the business.

The discussion also suggests some interesting conclusions about what needs to happen for organizational change to be successful. Perhaps the most important conclusion concerns the importance of changing multiple systems in an organization. Very much related to this is the point that the effectiveness of a reward system is related to a number of situational factors including, but not limited to, organizational practices concerned with training, problem solving, and information.

The work on gainsharing also leads to some interesting points about motivation. Much of the research on motivation has been concerned with how organizations can motivate individuals to perform their jobs better. Research has typically concluded that it is important to relate individual rewards to individual performance (Lawler, 1973). The work on gainsharing clearly shows that individuals can be motivated by rewards based on organizational performance. This is an important point because in some situations it may be better to have individuals focus on maximizing organizational performance rather than their job performance. The work on gainsharing not only suggests this can be done, it suggests one way to do it.

NEED TO KNOW—PRACTICE RELEVANT

There are a number of practices that need to be better developed if gainsharing is to be more widely applied. Greater theoretical understanding can help, but in addition, some technological innovation is needed so that new approaches, structures, and designs will be available. Badly needed are innovations that will allow gainsharing to be effective in situations that do not fit the traditional gainsharing plans. Previous analyses have suggested that there are some organizational characteristics and some environmental characteristics which make traditional gainsharing plans inappropriate (see Table 3). Size, age, type of technology, product stability, and management style are among the key organizational characteristics that influence the appropriateness of gainsharing (Lawler, 1981). Key environmental conditions include business cycle and product/technology life cycle.

The evidence is mixed on the effects of size (e.g., White, 1979) but there is little question that gainsharing usually has been installed in organizations with less than 1000 employees and almost always in organizations with less than 5000. This finding is consistent with the argument that a line of sight or expectancy is needed for gainsharing to be effective. One major corporation, Motorola, has attacked the line of sight problem by installing multiple gainsharing plans in their large locations (O'Toole, 1986). This approach raises many interesting theoretical and empirical questions about the effects of this type of differentiation in an organization. For example, it could lead to unfavorable competitiveness, social comparison, and subunit optimization because of the strong emphasis it places on unit performance. So far these issues are largely unresearched.

The organization's age is another constraint that needs to be overcome. Traditionally, gainsharing has only been applied to older organizations. In new organizations, using a historical base doesn't make sense because learning curve gains are likely to occur without any gainsharing plan impacts. Some plans have been installed which use an annually set target as the standard. This is counter to the historical standard principle but theoretically it could work if the level set is credible and well accepted.

So far gainsharing has been applied largely to manufacturing organizations (Graham-Moore & Ross, 1983). This fits the emphasis on labor costs and a direct line of sight between input and output. However, most organizations in the United States today are not manufacturing based. The service sector is the fastest growing area, and relatively little is known about how to install gainsharing in service and information processing organizations. There has been some experimentation in restaurants, hotels, and hospitals, but at this point a great deal of additional work needs to be done on the installation of gainsharing in service and information-based organizations (Graham-Moore & Ross, 1983). As was noted earlier, there is little question that if gainsharing is to be applied to these types of organizations different measures and formulas need to be developed. It is also quite possible that new, more participative design and installation processes will be needed.

If gainsharing is to be applied to many nonmanufacturing situations, then measures need to be used which go beyond labor costs. In service situations, for example, quality as well as most costs should be covered. This leads to an interesting prediction: gainsharing will work best in service situations when multiple factors are measured and where participative approaches are used which allow individuals to influence key organizational processes and decisions.

There also has been relatively little installation of gainsharing in high-technology organizations. They have particular problems because they tend to have unstable performance histories and their product mix changes rapidly. Particularly interesting here are organizations which are project-oriented and which do not have traditional manufacturing cycles. Experimentation is beginning with plans that last only for the life of a project. In one plan I helped design, the bid price was used as the comparison standard. This appears to be a promising approach but a great deal more needs to be learned about how to design, install, and maintain this approach to gainsharing. Among other things it raises new cost effectiveness issues because the start up costs have to be recouped over a relatively short period of time.

Another example of an important constraint that must be overcome has to do with the business cycle. It seems to be best to start a gainsharing plan when there is strong demand for an organization's product or service. Typically, gainsharing is effective in producing savings because it leads to a reduction in labor for each product or service. This is relatively easy to do when there is demand for additional volume, but not easy to do when there is a decreasing demand for volume. In the latter case, the best way to save is to lay off individuals. This runs completely counter to the concept of employment stability, an important part of many gainsharing plans and participative management programs.

As already noted, if gainsharing is used in settings that do not have the kind of stability and maturity that is typical of those where it has usually been successful, something must be substituted for the sacred historical base. This one feature seems to rule it out of more situations than any other. It is used because unlike engineered standards it eliminates arguments over what performance should be, establishes trust, and gives performance measurement a sense of non-manipulable permanency. It also typically represents a performance level that employees feel they can improve upon, an important consideration where an attempt is being made to motivate performance.

Theoretically, the historical base approach could be abandoned if a trusted basis for establishing a standard could be developed or if a trusted process could be used to establish it. It seems unlikely in most cases that a new objective standard can be developed, thus the solution probably lies in using a process which is credible and leads to the perception that performance and rewards will be fairly related over the long term. Given what has been said so far about gainsharing, it seems that a participative process must be used to set the base if the historical standard is to be abandoned. Any other approach would be incongruent. If an organization-wide task force or some other representative group set the base then it is possible that the workforce would trust the result and that a viable gainsharing plan could be operated.

In conclusion, there are a number of practice and social technology issues that need further research and development. The widespread adoption of gainsharing in the workplace can only occur if innovations in practice take place. In some cases, new formulas may be needed, while in others, new installation and new communication processes may be required. Overall the thrust of the arguments made here is that if gainsharing is to be more widely applied it may need to be more frequently combined with such participative processes as teams and diagonal-slice task forces. It seems possible that with these more advanced forms of participation, gainsharing can work even when complex measures and a standard not based on history are used.

CONCLUSIONS

The promise of gainsharing is high. It has an impressive track record of producing positive results and has enjoyed relatively widespread application in the American economy. However, relatively little is known about it theoretically and empirically. So far, practice has led theory and research. Social innovators have structured gainsharing plans and installed them, leaving it to researchers and theorists to try to understand what has gone on and to document the results of their efforts. Much more can be done from a theory and research perspective. Research on the installation of gainsharing can contribute greatly to our understanding of how gainsharing works, and perhaps more importantly, how organizations work. From the viewpoint of theory development, work needs to be done which tests predictions that are based on the expectancy-congruence approach. This approach appears capable of helping explain when and why gainsharing works and supporting new developments in the practice of gainsharing.

REFERENCES

Bullock, R., & Lawler, E. (1984). Gainsharing: A few questions and fewer answers. *Human Resource Management, 5,* 197–212.

Bullock, R., & Bullock, P. (1982). Gainsharing and Rubik's Cube: Solving system problems. *National Productivity Review, 2* (1), 396–407.

Frost, C., Wakeley, J., & Ruh, R. (1974). *The Scanlon Plan for organization development: Identity, participation, and equity.* East Lansing: Michigan State University Press.

General Accounting Office. (1981). *Productivity sharing programs: Can they contribute to productivity improvement?* Washington, D.C.: U.S. General Accounting Office.

Goodman, P. & Moore, B. (1976). Factors affecting acquisition of beliefs about a new reward system. *Human Relations,* 571–588.

Graham-Moore, B. & Ross, T. (1983). *Productivity gainsharing.* Englewood Cliff, N.J.: Prentice-Hall.

Hackman, J. & Oldham, G. (1980). *Work redesign.* Reading, Mass.: Addison-Wesley.

Lawler, E. (1986). *High involvement management.* San Francisco: Jossey-Bass.

Lawler, E. (1971). *Pay and organizational effectiveness: A psychological view.* New York: McGraw-Hill.

Lawler, E. (1981). *Pay and organization development.* Reading, Mass.: Addison-Wesley.

Lawler, E., Nadler, D. & Cammann, C. (1980). *Organizational assessment.* New York: Wiley.

Moore, B., & Ross, T. (1978). *The Scanlon way to improved productivity.* New York: Wiley.

Nadler, D., & Tushman, M. (1977). Diagnostic model for organizational behavior. In R. Hackman, E. Lawler & L. Porter, *Perspective on Behavior in Organizations.* New York: McGraw-Hill, 85–97.

Nightingale, D. (1982). *Workplace democracy: An inquiry into employee participation in canadian work organizations.* Toronto: Univ. of Toronto Press.

O'Dell, C. (1981). *Gainsharing: Involvement, incentive, and productivity.* New York: American Management Association.

O'Dell, C. (1987). *People, performance, and pay.* Houston: American Productivity Center.

O'Toole, J. (1985). *Vanguard management.* Garden City, NY: Doubleday.

Perkins, D., Nieva, R., & Lawler, E. (1983). *Managing creation.* New York: Wiley.

Porter, L. & Lawler, E. (1968). *Managerial attitudes and performance*. Homewood, Ill: Irwin-Dorsey.

Schuster, M. (1983). Forty years of Scanlon Plan research. In C. Crouch & F. Heller (Eds.), *International yearbook of organizational democracy, Vol. 1, Organizational democracy and political processes*. Chichester, England: Wiley, 53–72.

Schuster, M. (1984a). The Scanlon Plan: A longitudinal analysis. *Journal of Applied Behavioral Science, 20*, 23–38(a).

Schuster, M. (1984b). *Union-Management cooperation*. Kalamazoo, Michigan: W. E. Upjohn Institute.

Vroom, V. H. (1964). Work and motivation. New York: Wiley.

White, J. (1979). The Scanlon Plan: Causes and correlates of success. *Academy of Management Journal, 22*, 292–312.

BIOGRAPHICAL SKETCHES OF THE CONTRIBUTORS

Charleen Alderfer is in the private practice of individual and family therapy. An accredited supervisor by the American Association of Marriage and Family Therapy, she serves as Adjunct Faculty for Southern Connecticut State University and the Bristol, Connecticut Hospital. Author of a variety of articles on family therapy, she writes a regular column on supervision of family therapy for the *Journal of Strategic and Systemic Therapies,* and consults to public and private organizations on race relations and on family dynamics.

Clayton P. Alderfer is Professor and Director of Graduate Studies in Organizational Behavior at the Yale School of Organization and Management and the Yale Graduate School of Arts and Sciences. Author of many articles and several books, editor of a two volume series on experiential methods, he consults to public, private, and nonprofit organizations on race relations, board-management dynamics, and organizational diagnosis and change.

Achilles A. Armenakis is Associate Dean for External Affairs and Professor of Management in the College of Business at Auburn University. He received his D.B.A. from Mississippi State University.

He is past-president of the Southern Management Association and is the 1987 Program Chair of the Managerial Consultation Division of the Academy of Management. His research interests include the diagnostic and evaluation phases of organizational consultation.

Jean M. Bartunek received a Ph.D. in social and organizational psychology from the University of Illinois at Chicago in 1976. She was a visiting assistant professor in organizational behavior at the University of Illinois at Urbana-Champaign from 1976 to 1977, and since then has been a faculty member at Boston College, where she is now an associate professor of Organizational Studies.

Jean's writing has focused on participative decision making, conflict management, and, primarily, organizational change. She has studied the effects of OD and QWL interventions as well as of planned and unplanned second order changes in a variety of organizational settings. Much of her current work aims at developing deeper understandings of the dynamics of second order organizational change and restructuring processes that typically accompany it.

Jean is a member of the editorial boards of *Administrative Science Quarterly,* the *Academy of Management Journal,* and the *Journal of Applied Behavioral Science* and is on the executive committee of the Organization Development division of the Academy of Management.

Dov Eden is an associate professor of management at Tel Aviv University's Graduate School of Business Administration, where he has served as chairman of the organizational behavior program and as academic director of the Top Executive Course. He received his Ph.D. in organizational psychology at The University of Michigan, Ann Arbor. A consultant to several of Israel's leading public and private organizations, he has received research grants from the National Institute of Mental Health, the U.S. Department of Labor, the National Institute for Occupational Safety and Health, the Ford Foundation, the Israel Institute for Business Research, and the Institute for Social and Labor Research. His areas of research include the Pygmalion effect and other self-fulfilling prophecies in organizations, team development, acute and chronic job stress and vacation relief, personnel training, work motivation, and leadership. His preferred research method is field experimentation. He is a member of the Editorial Review Board of *Group & Organization Studies,* and is currently completing a book titled "Pygmalion in Management: Productivity as a Self-fulfilling Prophecy" to be published by Lexington Books in its Issues in Organization and Management Series.

Mariann Jelinek is Lewis-Progressive Associate Professor of Management Policy in the Weatherhead School of Management, Case Western Reserve University. Her teaching there includes courses in policy, advanced manufacturing technology and corporate strategy, and organization theory. These topics are also the focus of her research and consultation. She is author or editor of six books, and is presently concluding a manuscript on the management of innovation in high technology firms. She holds the Ph.D. from the University of California at Berkeley, and the D.B.A. from Harvard University's Graduate School of Business.

Edward E. Lawler III is a Professor of Management and Organization in the Business School at the University of Southern California. He joined USC in 1978 and during 1979, founded and became the director of the University's Center for Effective Organizations. In 1982 Dr. Lawler was named Research Professor at USC.

After receiving degrees from Brown University (B.A. 1960), and the University of California at Berkeley (Ph.D. 1964), Dr. Lawler joined the faculty of Yale University. He moved to the University of Michigan in 1972 as Professor of Psychology and Program Director in the Survey Research Center at the Institute for Social Research.

Dr. Lawler is a member of many professional organizations in his field and is on the Editorial Board of five major journals. He has consulted with over one hundred organizations on Employee Involvement, Organizational Change and Compensation and is the author and co-author of over 150 articles and fifteen books.

His most recent books include *Pay and Organization Development,* published by Addison Wesley in 1981, *Managing Creation,* published by Wiley Interscience in 1983, and *High Involvement Management* published by Jossey-Bass in 1986. His works have been translated into 10 languages and he has been honored a top contributor to the fields of Organization Development, Organizational Behavior and Compensation.

Joseph A. Litterer is Professor of Management and Chair of the Management Department at the School of Business at the University of Massachusetts, Amherst. He has been responsible for graduate courses in organization theory, organization behavior and organization development there since 1969. He is author of seven books and numerous articles, and has over 25 years of university and executive teaching and consultation in public and private organizations, both in this country and abroad. His present research and consultation activities center on strategic processes. He holds the Ph.D. from the University of Illinois.

Meryl Reis Louis is an associate professor in the School of Management and a research associate at the Center for Applied Social Science at Boston University. She received her Ph.D. in organizational sciences from UCLA in 1978. She has served on the faculties of the University of Illinois at Urbana Champaign, the Naval Postgraduate School, and as a visitor at MIT's Sloan School of Management.

Meryl's writings have focused on career transitions, sense-making in organizational settings, workplace cultures, and epistomological issues in organizational research. She has been conducting a panel study of MBA graduates that is now in its tenth year. Most recently, she has been examining the use of automated information systems to support strategic human resource planning. Meryl is a member of the editorial review boards of *Administrative Science Quarterly,* the *Academy of Management Review,* the *Organizational Behavior Teaching Review* and *Organization Dynamics.*

Philip H. Mirvis is Associate Professor, School of Management and Center for Applied Social Science, Boston University. He has co-edited, with David Berg, *Failures in Organization Development and Change* and, with Stanley Seashore, Edward Lawler, and Cortland Camann, *Assessing Organizational Change.* He has a bent toward historical analysis and has published a "map" and guidebook to *Work in the 20th Century.*

Mirvis is currently active with research and interventions in organizational mergers and acquisitions and in the introduction of computer technology into organizations. He continues to undertake survey assessments of quality of work life and is moving into organization development in the Third World.

Peter Reason read Economics at Cambridge and, after a spell in industry in which he became deeply involved in Organization Development work, moved to the USA to study in the Department of Organizational Behavior at Case Western Reserve University. He completed his PhD in 1976, and returned to England to join the Centre for the Study of Organizational Change and Development at the University of Bath. His major academic work has been to develop and argue for a co-operative and experiential paradigm for research, and in pursuing this has built with colleagues a research group developing this tradition at the University of Bath. He is also deeply involved in humanistic and transpersonal psychotherapy and is part of the management of a growth centre in Bath.

Leota M. Tucker is Regional Human Resources Coordinator for the Connecticut Department of Mental Health. Formerly Associate Professor at New Hampshire College, New Haven Campus and Director of the New Haven Welfare Department, she is also a contributing editor for *Essence* magazine. She consults to a variety of private and public organizations on race relations, male-female dynamics, and group behavior.

Robert C. Tucker is Assistant Vice President of Organization and Management at Southern New England Telecommunications. Formerly Associate Professor of Psychiatry and Founder-Director of the Yale University Drug Dependence Institute, he is a contributing editor to *Essence* magazine. Author of a variety of articles on social and cultural change, he consults to private and nonprofit organizations on race relations, male-female dynamics, and organizational behavior.

Marvin R. Weisbord is a partner in Block Petrella Weisbord, a consulting firm specializing in organizational improvement, reorganizations and work redesign.

He has consulted with many corporations in banking, steel, chemicals, printing, software, textiles, and health care products in the United States and abroad. He became involved in this work as executive vice president of a family firm in the 1960's, where he experimented with self-managing work teams. Weisbord is a member of NTL Institute, Certified Consultants International, the Organization Development Network and the European Institute for Trans-National Studies in Group and Organizational Development (EIT). He also serves as a resource board member of the International Institute for the Study of Systems Renewal.

He was for six years an editor of the *Journal of Applied Behavioral Science* and has written widely on the theory and practice of organizational change. His new work, *Productive Communities: Managing and Consulting for Dignity and Meaning in the Workplace,* was published by Jossey-Bass in 1987. In spring 1987 he was a visiting professor at the Norwegian Institute of Technology, Trondheim. He is working on a video tape series based on his book.

Research in Organizational Change and Development

Edited by
Richard W. Woodman
Texas A&M University and
William A. Pasmore
Case Western Reserve University

Volume 1, 1987, 328 pp. Institutions:$58.50
ISBN 0-89232-749-9 Individuals:$29.25

CONTENTS: Editorial Statement. Preface, *Richard W. Woodman, Texas A&M University and William A. Pasmore, Case Western Reserve University.* **Organization Development Theory: A Typology and Evaluation,** *Jerry I. Porras and Peter Robinson, Stanford University.* **Development Organizations and Organizational Development: Toward an Expanded Paradigm for Organization Development,** *L. David Brown, Institute for Development Research and Boston University and Jane Gibson Covey, Institute for Development Research.* **Reasoning, Action Strategies and Defense Routines: The Case of OD Practitioners,** *Chris Argyris, Harvard University.* **Appreciative Inquiry in Organizational Life,** *David L. Cooperrider and Suresh Srivastva, Case Western Reserve University.* **The Case Meta-Analysis Method of OD,** *R.J. Bullock, University of Houson and Mark E. Tubbs, University of Missouri, St. Louis.* **Development at the Top: A Review and a Prospect,** *Robert E. Kaplan, Joan R. Kofodimos and Wilfred H. Drath, Center for Creative Leadership.* **Self Designing Organizations: Towards Implimenting Quality-of-Work-Life Innovations,** *Thomas G. Cummings and Susan A. Mohrman, University of Southern California.* **Biographical Sketches of Contributing Authors for Volume l.**

JAI PRESS, Inc.
55 Old Post Road - No. 2
Greenwich, Connecticut 06836-1678
or call: (203) 661-7602

ADVANCES IN MAN-MACHINE SYSTEMS RESEARCH

Edited by **WILLIAM B. ROUSE**
Center for Man-Machine Systems Research,
Georgia Institute of Technology

The purpose of this annual series is to report on advances in theory and applications within man-machine systems research. While contributions in all areas of man-machine systems will be considered for publication, topics of particular interest include human decision makming and problem solving, human-computer interaction, human monitoring and control of dynamic processes, and human error. All contributions should clearly explain the applicability of the contribution to analysis, design, and/or evaluation of man-machine systems.

Volume 1

CONTENTS: List of Contributors. Introduction, *William B. Rouse.* **A Control Theoretic Approach to Modeling Human Supervisory Control of Dynamic Systems,** *Sheldon Baron, Bolt Beranek and Newman, Inc.* **Supervisory Control of Remote Manipulators, Vehicles, and Dynamic Processes: Experiments in Command and Display Aiding,** *Thomas B. Sheridan, Massachusetts Institute of Technology.* **Strategies of State Identification and Diagnosis in Supervisory Control Tasks, and Design of Computer Based Support Systems,** *Jens Rasmussen, Riso National Laboratories.* **Human Problem Solving in Fault Diagnosis Tasks,** *William B. Rouse, Georgia Institute of Technology and Ruston M. Hunt, Search Technology, Inc.* **Knowledge Representation and Man-Machine Dialogue,** *Andrew P. Sage and Adolfo Lagomasino, University of Virginia.* **Human Decision Processes in Military Command and Control,** *Joseph G. Whol, Elliot E. Entin, David L. Kleinman, and Krishna Pattipatti, ALPHATECH, Inc.* **Index.**

ISBN 0-89232-404-X / cloth / 319 pp. / 1984
Institutions: $59.50 / Individuals: $29.75

Volume 2

CONTENTS: List of Contributors. Introduction, *William B. Rouse.* **The Dynamics of Resource Allocation,** *Christopher D. Wickens, Pamela Tsang, and Byron Pierce, University of Illinois.* **Evaluation of the Sensitivity and Intrusion of Mental Workload Estimation Techniques,** *Walter W. Wierwille, John G. Casali, Sidney A. Connor, and Mansour Rahimi, Virginia Polytechnic and State University.* **A Model-Based Theory For Analyzing Human Control Behavior,** *Ronald A. Hess, University of California at Davis.* **A Systems Approach to Modeling Discrete Control Performance,** *Richard A. Miller, Ohio State University.* **Adaptive User Models: Methodology and Applications in Man-Computer Systems,** *Amos Freedy, Azad Madni, and Michael Samet, Perceptronics Inc., Woodland Hills, Ca.* **Index.**

ISBN 0-89232-466-X / cloth / 320 pp. / 1985
Institutions: $59.50 / Individuals: $29.75

Research Annuals and Monographs in Series and Treatises in
MANAGEMENT SCIENCE

Research Annuals

Advances in Applied Business Strategy
Edited by Robert B. Lamb, *New York University*

Advances in Group Processes
Edited by Edward J. Lawler, *University of Iowa*

Advances in Health Economics and Health Services Research
Edited by Richard M. Scheffler, *University of California, Berkeley* and Louis F. Rossiter, *Virginia Commonwealth University*

Advances in Industrial and Labor Relations
Edited by David B. Lipsky, *New York State School of Industrial and Labor Relations, Cornell University*

Advances in Information Processing in Organizations
Edited by Lee S. Sproull and Patrick D. Larkey, *Carnegie Mellon University*

Advances in International Cooperative Management
Edited by Richard N. Farmer, *Indiana University*

Advances in Mathematical Programming and Financial Planning
Edited by Kenneth D. Lawrence, *Rutgers University*, John B. Gueard, Jr., *Lehigh University* and Gary R. Reeves, *University of South Carolina*

Advances in School Management
Edited by Samuel B. Bacharach, *New York State School of Industrial and Labor Relations, Cornell University*, and Sharon Conley, *College of Education, University of Arizona*

Advances in Strategic Management
Edited by Robert B. Lamb and Paul Shrivastava, *New York University*

Advances in the Economic Analysis of Participatory and Labor Managed Firms
Edited by Derek C. Jones, *Hamilton College* and Jan Svejnar, *University of Pittsburgh*

Advances in the Study of Entrepreneurship, Innovation and Economic Growth
Edited by Gary Libecap, *University of Arizona*

Applications of Management Science
Edited by Randall L. Schultz, *The University of Texas at Dallas*

Research in Corporate Social Performance and Policy
Edited by Lee E. Preston, *University of Maryland*

Research in Human Capital and Development
Edited by Ismail Sirageldin, *The Johns Hopkins University*

Research in Labor Economics
Edited by Ronald G. Ehrenberg, *New York State of Industrial and Labor Relations, Cornell University*

Research in Organizational Behavior
Edited by Barry M. Staw, *University of California, Berkeley* and L.L. Cummings, Northwestern University

Research in Organizational Change and Development
Edited by Richard W. Woodman, *Texas A&M University and* William A. Pasmore, *Case Western Reserve University*

Research in Personnel and Human Resources Management
Edited by Kendrith M. Rowland, *University of Illinois* and Gerald R. Ferris, *Texas A&M University*

Research in Population Economics
Edited by T. Paul Schultz, *Yale University*

Research in Public Analysis and Management
Edited by Stuart S. Nagel, *University of Illinois*

Research in Social Stratification and Mobility
Edited by Robert V. Robinson, Indiana University

Research in the Sociology of Organizations
Edited by Samuel B. Bacharach, New York State School of Industrial and Labor Relations, Cornell University

Research in the Sociology of Work
Edited by Ida Harper Simpson, *Duke University* and Richard L. Simpson, *University of North Carolina, Chapel Hill*

Research on Negotiations in Organizations
Edited by Roy J. Lewicki, *Ohio State University,* Blair H. Sheppard, *Duke University* and Max H. Bazerman, *Northwestern University*

Research on Technological Innovation, Management and Policy
Edited by Richard S. Rosenbloom, *Harvard University*

Monographs in Series and Treatises

Contemporary Studies in Applied Behavioral Science
Edited by Louis A. Zurcher, *University of Texas at Austin*

Contemporary Studies in Economic and Financial Analysis
An International Series of Monographs
Edited by Edward I. Altman and Ingo Walter, *New York University*

Decision Research: A Series of Monographs
Edited by Howard Thomas, *University of Illinois*

Handbook of Behavioral Economics

Edited by Stanley Kaish and Benjamin Gilad, *Rutgers University*

Monographs in Organizational Behavior and Industrial Relations
Edited by Samuel B. Bacharach, *New York State School of Industrial and Labor Relations, Cornell University*

Organizational Leadership of Human Resources: The Knowledge and the skills
by John M. Brion

Public Policy Studies: A Multi-Volume Treatise
Edited by Stuart S. Nagel, *University of Illinois*

Strategic Management, Policy and Planning
A Multi-Volume Treatise
Edited by Howard Thomas, *University of Illinois*

Please inquire for detailed subject catalog

JAI PRESS INC., 55 Old Post Road No. 2, P.O. Box 1678
Greenwich, Connecticut 06836
Telephone: 203-661-7602   Cable Address: JAIPUBL